TAT TV

The Universal Message

in the

Bhagavadgītā

TAT TVAM ASI

The Universal Message in the Bhagavadgītā

PATHIKONDA VISWAMBARA NATH

Volume I
(Chapters 1-10)

MOTILAL BANARSIDASS PUBLISHERS
PRIVATE LIMITED • DELHI

First Edition: Delhi, 1998
Reprint: Delhi, 2002

ISBN: 81-208-1584-x (Cloth)
ISBN: 81-208-1585-8 (Paper)

Also available at:
MOTILAL BANARSIDASS
41 U.A. Bungalow Road, Jawahar Nagar, Delhi 110 007
8 Mahalaxmi Chamber, 22 Bhulabhai Desai Road, Mumbai 400 026
120 Royapettah High Road, Mylapore, Chennai 600 004
236, 9th Main III Block, Jayanagar, Bangalore 560 011
Sanas Plaza, 1302 Baji Rao Road, Pune 411 002
8 Camac Street, Kolkata 700 017
Ashok Rajpath, Patna 800 004
Chowk, Varanasi 221 001

Printed in India
BY JAINENDRA PRAKASH JAIN AT SHRI JAINENDRA PRESS,
A-45 NARAINA, PHASE-I, NEW DELHI 110 028
AND PUBLISHED BY NARENDRA PRAKASH JAIN FOR
MOTILAL BANARSIDASS PUBLISHERS PRIVATE LIMITED,
BUNGALOW ROAD, DELHI 110 007

श्रीकृष्णाय नमः

ॐ पूर्णमदः पूर्णमिदं पूर्णात्पूर्णमुदच्यते।
पूर्णस्य पूर्णमादाय पूर्णमेवावशिष्यते॥
ॐ शान्तिः शान्तिः शान्तिः॥

Oṁ pūrṇam adaḥ pūrṇam idaṁ pūrṇāt pūrṇam udacyate
pūrṇasya pūrṇam ādāya purṇam evāvaśiṣyate
Oṁ śāntiḥ śāntiḥ śāntiḥ !

मूकं करोति वाचालं पङ्गु लंघयते गिरिम्।
यत्कृपा तमहं वन्दे परमानन्दमाधवम्॥

mūkaṁ karoti vācālam paṅguṁ laṅghayate girim
yatkṛpā tam ahaṁ vande paramānanandamādhavam

O Lord Kṛṣṇa,

Please make me blind for the pleasures of this world
from this mortal body,

Open my eye of wisdom

to Realise your immortal divine nature;

Let my bodily organs express your divinty

Light the lamp of antarātmā,

Be a guide and sārathī in my path

to attain salvation.

Please bless me to understand this

adhyātma vidyā.

To

All the Arjunas of the world

MRS. BETTY JAMES
Councillor Derwentiside District Council
3 Shafto Terrace
STANLEY Co. Durham, UK
28th June, 1999

Dear Dr. Nath,

Sorry I have taken so long to respond to the reading of the two volumes of your book *Tat Tvam Asi.* I wanted to attempt some understanding of your faith and how it can affect our attitude to life and dealing with people.

The universality of the message of the Gita is highlighted by your interpretation of the poem. Although it is difficult to fully understand the essential spiritual truths with little knowledge of the Hindu religion, I feel that the issues addressed affect us all. You give everyday examples which help to explain more complicated ideas. It becomes easier to recognise the link with Christianity and other religions.

Perhaps the issue of re-incarnation is more difficult, but there are obvious links with the idea of life after death and the belief of others of the soul moving to different planes. Also the caste system, (or social classes) seems inevitable but you explain that a person can move within the system by changing his/her life style.

What is made clear is the courage needed to face life's problems, the over concentration on self and the over attachment to worldly goods. You have reflected the meaning of the Gita text from life's experiences and I am quiet certain, as you acknowledge, that your wife Satya's contribution added to your thinking.

Thank you for your two volumes. As Hari Shukla says your analysis is thought provoking and the style is clear and lucid. It has inspired me to think again about the way we could and should live our lives in this materialistic society.

I am impressed by your dedication to such a huge task.

Yours Sincerely,

Sd/-

(Betty James)

CONTENTS

FOREWORD

Religion has been at all times a great social force. To masses religion defines their identity and their aspirations and in this sense religion has been contributing strongly to the cohesiveness and stability of the society. However, in recent years there has been a gradual erosion of the spiritual values of religion.

This book Tat Tvam Asi is being published at a time when people are searching for the right direction in a materialistic society. It will inspire its readers because it is thought-provoking and written in a clear and lucid style. It will impart peace and bliss to many students of the Gita. A careful study of the book will enable them to realise and appreciate the real value of the Gita and will inspire them to reap the full benefit from it. I am sure that this book will prove to be instructive and inspiring to all its readers.

Dr. Nath, the author, for the last twenty-five years has been engaged in labours wholly beneficial to society. Through speech and writing he has been propagating the Gita's message.

Dr. Nath is a confirmed optimist by nature. To him life is real and earnest not an empty dream. In his own life he embodies a trio of tenets. The first is to 'speak the truth' as the Gita advocates. This, he believes, leads to success. The second tenet is 'unwavering devotion to duty, acting his part well and trust in self and God.' The third he believes in is that 'Man is his own master and success smiles on those who help themselves.'

He believes that music, dance and drama are part of creative education which integrates man with himself, his environment, society and ultimately with God. He observes strict moral principles in his private as well as public life. He is an embodiment of clean living and objective thinking. He is the epitome of an honest man.

His knowledge of the Gita has contributed enormously to interfaith understanding in the North-East of England.

We sincerely congratulate him on his achievement and wish him every success.

Hari Shukla M.B.E.
Retired Director Tyne & Wear Racial Equality Council
Newcastle-Upon-Tyne, U.K.

MESSAGE FROM SWAMI HARI HAR JI

I am pleased to know that Dr. P. Viswambara Nath has written a detailed commentary on Śrimad Bhagavad Gītā as per my advice given to him while I was on a Gītā mission in London in the year 1994. The title of the book is TAT TVAM ASI.

The Bhagavad Gītā, the 18-chapter poem by seer Vedavyāsa expounds Vedānta philosophy in the dynamic setting of a battle-field where Lord Kṛṣṇa reveals the teaching of Vedānta to the warrior prince Arjuna. The quintessence of Vedānta is contained in *mahāvākyas*, great aphoristic declarations of the Supreme Truth. They are direct revelations of Brahma. The best known *mahāvākyas* are taken one each from the four Vedas. *Tat tvam asi* (That thou art) is the *mahāvākya* taken from Chāndogya Upanishad, Sāma Veda. The Lord exhorts us to experience that we are all 'TAT' (THAT), i.e., the spark of Brahma. The book successfully brings out the various facets of the *advaita* philosophy while it incorporates the *dvaita* as well as the *vishirtadvaita* philosophies in the light of the Universal Divine Message enshrined in the Bhagavad Gītā.

I congratulate Dr. Nath for including a comprehensive commentary on the holy scripture though he has been a general medical practioner only. I am confident that this publication, TAT TVAM ASI will be helpful to spiritual seekers in achieving their goal. May Lord Śrī Kṛṣṇa shower His divine blessings on Dr. P. Viswambara Nath and his family.

Bangkok
June 22, 1997.

NOTE AND ACKNOWLEDGEMENTS FROM THE AUTHOR

At the outset, I would like to say that the commentary in this book is what I learnt from reading various books on the *Gītā*. I found answers for various problems I faced in my life from the *Gītā* and it increased my faith in it.

I felt that there was a need to explain the *Gītā* in a manner that would suit the new generation of people. I have tried to give the commentary on that line.

My salutations to my parents and to my wife's parents.

My salutations to late Śrī TAPASWIJI MAHARAJ and Late Śrī MALLIGI MAHARAJ, two Swāmījīs who frequently visited our house and whose blessings have given me the strength to take up such a major task.

My salutations to Śrī HARI HARJI MAHARAJ who prevailed upon me to write the commentary and gave me his blessings.

My salutations to Śrī VIDYA PRAKASHANANDA SWAMY of Sukha Brahma Ashrama at Kalahasti, A.P., India and the Late Śrī SWAMI CHINMAYANANDA.

My Salutations to Śrī PRANAVANANDA SWAMY of Omkara Ashram who has given me a lot of insight into the *Gītā* in his discussions with me.

Prof. NANJUNDA SASTRY (retired Professor of English) corrected my entire manuscript. His Knowledge of the *śāstras* is immense. He corrected all my errors both in grammar and in the scriptural content. My salutations to him.

There are a number of people who have helped me in the preparation and publication of this book. It is difficult to mention them all by their names. My sincere thanks to all of them.

I must give names of a few who have helped me.

My thanks to my dear wife Satya who gave me her unswerving support in the task. She went through the commentary of each verse and has given her own views. It will not be an exaggeration to say that she is the co-author of this book.

During this task, my two daughters gave me all their love and encouragement. I thank them.

My sister-in-law, Mrs Majula Chellur (Principal District and Sessions Judge, Mysore) took all the trouble in organising various tasks towards publishing the book. I sincerely thank her. My work as a general practitioner in U.K. prevented me from going to India to arrange the publishing of the book and her help is sincerely appreciated.

I will be failing in my duty if I do not thank Mr. N. P. Jain of Motilal Banarsidass Publishers for agreeing to publish my commentary on the *Gītā*.

My wife had a guide dog called Lindsay which needs a special mention. Lindsay in her old age was disturbing us every night by waking up at 4 a.m. and asking us to take her to the toilet. I used to get angry with her for disturbing my sleep. When HARI HARJI MAHARAJ asked me to write the book, I used the opportunity to rise at 4 a.m. daily to take Lindsay to the toilet. It is such a wonderful, peaceful time of the day to read and write. Believe it or not, after about four weeks of my staring to write and getting used to waking up at 4 a.m., Lindsay stopped disturbing me and slept till I finished writing for that day. I sincerely belive that it was a divine act that made Lindsay disturb me. May Lord Kṛṣṇa bless her.

INTRODUCTION

The *Bhagavadgītā* is the most highly valued treasure-house for all Hindus. *Gītā* means song; the celestial song by Lord Kṛṣṇa is *Bhagavadgītā*.

Sage and Poet Vedavyāsa dictated the entire *Mahābhārata* to Lord Gaṇeśa. *Bhagavadgītā* is part of the *Mahābhārata* dictated by the poet. What is it? What is it all about? It is:

1. *Upaniṣad,*
2. *Brahmavidyā,*
3. *Yogaśāstra.*

WHAT IS UPANIṢAD?

To know *Upaniṣad* one must know the *Veda*s. Hindus believe that there were very great seers (*ṛṣi*s, sages) in the past. They are considered to be great scholars. Without any of the modern gadgets, they enquired into two things, viz.:

(1) What is the origin of existence?

(2) Where can one get happiness?

They found out that life existed because of energy. Without that energy, the physical body is considered to be a dead body. The dead body of all the creatures, great and small, is made up of the five elements called the *pañcabhūta*s. They are: (1) fire, (2) space, (3) air, (4) earth, and (5) water.

They came to the conclusion that this energy or vital force was the same in all beings. When the energy energises the elements, the physical body becomes alive. Then that body goes to an individual and is given a name. This is *nāma* and *rūpa*. They explored the theory further and gave a hypothesis.

Nobody can really, physically trace us back to the period of the beginning of existence of earth. Just like present-day scientists, they also gave us an explanation. This cannot be proved but it stands to reasoning. What are their observations? They were:

(1) That energy pervades the whole Universe.

(2) That energy is inside each one of us.

(3) That energy was the same yesterday, is the same today and will be the same tomorrow.

(4) That energy is not partial to anybody. It gives results in proportion to the amount of effort one puts in, e.g., if we sow seeds, they germinate into plants. The conditions are:

  (i) the seeds have to be of good quality;
  (ii) the soil has to be of good quality;
  (iii) the condition, i.e., the environment, has to be good, and
  (iv) the seeds need to be looked after like watering, protecting them from adverse weather conditions, clearing the weeds and manuring.

  If these are fulfilled, it does not matter who sows the seeds (it could be a king or a murderer), they will sprout.

(5) The energy sustains life. The energy in the soil, water, space is necessary for sustaining life. The energy is not seen by anybody (it is unmanifest). Its manifestation in the form of steam, electricity can be seen. The energy is all powerful. The energy is beyond comprehension at individual, mental and physical levels.

The *ṛṣis* realised that if the energy had all these (and other qualities not mentioned herein), it must be respected. Just as we respect our parents who brought us into this world, we must respect that energy that brought forth life in this world.

This primordial energy they called OṀ. OṀ is *akṣara. Akṣara* is a word. It also means that which does not perish. The first words one learns in younger days are imperishable. They are the basis of our communication with society for the rest of our lives.

The all-comprehending OṀ is considered as the *praṇava akṣara* and the *ṛṣis* uttered it first. Instead of describing the energy in detail, they declared that the word OṀ implies all the attributes of energy. When we say tomato, we mean the tomato we know of. But for somebody who does not know tomato, we need to describe all the qualities of tomato. OṀ represents the primordial energy. If one says OṀ it implies all the qualities enumerated above.

Our *ṛṣi*s then said that this energy symbolised by OṀ decided to create life. It went and energised the five elements. Brahmā the Creator (*Saguṇa Brahman*) came forth fast. The energy originally was *Nirguṇa Brahman* i.e., the Formless. Initially, out of his mind, he created some life. The people that were born were known as *mānasa putra*s. Later on, with the physical union between members of the opposite sex, the universe expanded and is still expanding. This is the theory of the formation of life.

The *ṛṣi*s then analysed the human behaviour. They found that whatever was created had to die as well. Life brought happiness and attachment to various objects in the Universe. But life also brought sorrow due to illness, injury, death etc. to the individuals or their beloved ones etc. Man with all his powers could achieve great things in the Universe. But there was no happiness which lasted permanently.

Our *ṛṣis* questioned this. Then, they found out that each of us has actually two elements in each body.

(1) The energy,
(2) The subtle body and the physical body.

(The subtle body is the mind and the intellect.)

The energy in every individual is a part of the Universal Energy, and is actually the real person. This is because, after death, the physical body decays, but the energy will remain. They called this energy the life-principle in each of us or the self. The Self developed contact with the world through the body and started enjoying the world and in the process, it forgot its real nature.

The real Self (*ātman*) forgetting its true nature, then becomes the ego (*ahaṁkāra*) or 'I'-ness. The ego assumes and individual identity. Instead of the Universal Energy, it becomes an isolated, individual person. (The children born to a mother initially associate with her. But soon develop their separate identity).

The ego (the false self) is the one who suffers the pairs of opposites of happiness and sorrow, due to his false identity. If one can realise this, then he will find peace in himself. Death, disease, ill-fame, injury all affect the 'ego'. The Real Self (*ātman*) witnesses all these and is not affected.

Knowing one's true nature, knowing one's true origin and knowing one's true destiny would bring happiness that does not end in sorrow.

This stage of merging of the ego with the *ātman* and merging of the *ātman* with the Universal Self is called liberation. This liberation from the worldly attachments to the five elements is *mokṣa*.

The *ṛṣi*s said that *OṀ* is:

(1) Truth, Truth of existence—*sat*
(2) The Knowledge, The real knowledge of life—*cit*
(3) The Happiness, The real happiness— *ānanda*.

Superimposed on this is name and form called *nāma* and *rūpa* to the physical body which has a life-force in it. We are all therefore physically *sat*, *cit* and *ānanda* but with *nāma* and *rūpa*.

Our *ṛṣi*s, enquiring into all this knowledge, did not say that they found it out themselves. They did not accept authorship of their hypothesis. They said some divine force at some divine inspirational moment, made them come out with statements in the form of hymns. The hymns have been grouped together into four Vedas— *Ṛgveda*, *Yajurveda*, *Sāmaveda*, and *Atharvaveda*.

WHAT IS BRAHMAVIDYĀ?

The primordial energy is *Nirguṇa Brahman* with all the unmanifest powers and properties. *Saguṇa Brahman* is manifest energy. *Saguṇa Brahman* and *Nirguṇa Brahman*—the knowledge of these two is *Brahmavidyā*. *OṀ* includes *Brahman* and the Universe created by *Brahman*.

- The knowledge of *OṀ* is *Brahmavidyā*.
- The knowledge of individual and universal existence is *Brahmavidyā*.

- The knowledge of the welfare of the individual and the Universe is *Brahmavidyā*.
- The knowledge which teaches that the individual is not a single entity but only a part of the Universe is *Brahmajñāna*. This non-duality is *advaita* and knowledge of *advaita* and *OṀ* is *Brahmajñāna*.

If all the members of the Universe acted with this knowledge, the Universe would be a happy place to live in. Our *ṛṣi*s, wishing the welfare of all (*sarve janāḥ sukhinobhavantu*) gave us this knowledge. Śrī Kṛṣṇa has simplified and explained the same knowledge in such a way in the *Gītā* that it is easier for understanding and also to follow.

WHAT IS YOGA-ŚĀSTRA?

Śāstras are scriptures. Scriptures are written for the moral and spiritual welfare of all. *Yoga* means union. Union of the ego, its merging into *ātman* is *yoga*. Union of this *ātman* with the Supreme Lord is also *yoga* (We will discuss this in the course in our study of the *Gītā*). Any method that deals with the union is *yoga*. The person who practises *yoga* is a *yogī*. The *yoga* that brings union, which results in *ānanda* (happiness, or bliss which does not end in sorrow) is *Yoga-śāstra*.

The *Bhagavadgītā* is therefore,

—*Upaniṣad*
—*Brahmavidyā* and
—*Yoga-śāstra*.

What do we have to learn from this *Gītā*? We have to learn that "WE ARE THAT" What are we? We are the *ātman* and not the 'ego'. What is "THAT"?—THAT is the *paramātman* or primordial energy. As the *ātman* (life in us) is part of the primordial energy, we are "THAT".

Thus,

TAT	-	THAT
TVAM	-	THOU
ASI	-	ART

i.e., YOU ARE THAT.

The *Gītā* declares, "O, you mortals, realise that you are *paramātman*. You are That, i.e., '*tat tvam asi*' ". Of course, if at this moment we say, we are *paramātman* we are no longer *paramātman* because we brought the 'I'-ness in us. By saying 'I' (I am 'so & so'), we have brought ego in it. Ego is not the real Self. By expressing divine actions, by not bringing 'I'-ness into our action, we can perform God's work in this world. If all of us do God's work, without selfishness, we will have a prosperous world (*rāmarājya*), i.e., a kingdom like that of Rāma which was happy and prosperous.

The *Gītā* tells us, *tat, tvam, asi.* It tells us *aham brahmāsmi.* It tells us we are all one and not two. It teaches us *advaita.*

The *Gītā* consists of 700 beautiful verses divided into 18 chapters. Each one of the verses is a gem which is full of meaning.

The philosophers agree that the first six chapters of the *Gītā* describe *'tvam'*, the second six chapters describe *'tat'* and the last six chapters describe *'asi'*. *Tat tvam asi* is called *a mahāvākya* (a great sentence). The *Gītā* therefore consists of three units of six chapters each. The *Gītā* can therefore be divided into three books which deal with one aspect each of the *mahāvākya.*

We should briefly look at the background of the *Gītā*. All of us, or at least the majority of us, know it already. But for the sake of ready comprehension, I have added a brief note about its background.

Approximtely 5000 years ago (3000 B.C.) there lived in a kingdom called Hastināpura, (land of the dynasty of Kurus) which is to the north-east of Delhi, a king called Dhṛtarāṣṭra. He was blind and was acting as a caretaker king when his brother King Pāṇḍu went to the forest for a short spell. Dhṛtarāṣṭra had one hundred sons, the eldest of them being Duryodhana. King Pāṇḍu had five sons known as Pāṇḍavas. Śrī Kṛṣṇa was a close friend, well-wisher and relative of the Pāṇḍavas.

While in the forest, unfortunately, king Pāṇḍu died. Technically speaking, the Pāṇḍavas should have been given the kingdom by their uncle Dhṛtarāṣṭra.

Duryodhana, their cousin did not think that Pāṇḍavas should be given the kingdom. Dhṛtarāṣṭra was elder to Pāṇḍu and should have been by right made the real king. But, he was blind. Pāṇḍu was crowned king because the *śāstras* prohibit the ascension of a physically disabled person as king.

When the Pāṇḍavas came back from the forest, a lot of political manoeuvring took place. The land was divided and Pāṇḍavas were given a small part. They expanded it by righteous means. Duryodhana tricked cousin Yudhiṣṭhira (the eldest of the Pāṇḍavas) in the game of dice. Yudhiṣṭhira lost his kingdom and was made to go to the forest for thirteen years. On his return, from the forest, Duryodhana did not allow his father to give the kingdom back to his cousins. Śrī Kṛṣṇa tried his best to mediate on behalf of the Pāṇḍavas but failed. The cousins decided to fight it out. The war which ensued is called the Great Kurukṣetra War. Arjuna, the third of the Pāṇḍavas was a close friend of Śrī Kṛṣṇa and himself a great warrior. He requested his friend to be his charioteer (*sārathī*) who would control and lead his chariot in the battlefield. Before the war started, Arjuna requested Śrī Kṛṣṇa to take his chariot to the middle of the battlefield. He wished to see the army of both sides and also pay his respects to his elders, teachers and friends in the opposite camp. Unfortunately (fortunately for mankind) Arjuna lost his nerve. He did not want to fight. He felt his relatives, friends and other soldiers would die unnecessarily. He decided that it would be better to be a *saṁnyāsī* and go to the forest and let his cousin Duryodhana rule the Kingdom. It is then, that Lord Kṛṣṇa teaches Arjuna who Arjuna really was, and who really Kṛṣṇa was, who all the soldiers really were. He tells Arjuna what is *dharma* and what is *adharma.* At the end, he asks Arjuna to do what he feels right. All of this is the *Gītā.*

Of course, if we put ourselves in Arjuna's place and consider our own life as a battlefield then the *Gītā* will have abundant meaning and significance in our life.

Sage Vyāsa asked Dhṛtarāṣṭra, if he wished to see the war. If he wanted to, he would give him special powers to actually witness what would happen in the far off place. In fact Dhṛtarāṣṭra declines this offer. He asks that his *sārathī* Sañjaya be given the power to "see" the war. Sañjaya, therefore, got the special power to see the events in the battlefield and he reported to his king all that happened on the battlefield. He thus became the War-Reporter. The *Gītā* is in the form of a narration by Sañjaya to his King Dhṛtarāṣṭra. The narration consists of Arjuna's despondency and Śrī Kṛṣṇa's remedy to that. Really speaking, Śrī Kṛṣṇa, the lord incarnate, is making Vyāsa speak through Sañjaya to millions of us who are blind to the *śāstra*s.

ĪŚĀVĀSYA UPANIṢAD

Many scholars believe that the *Gītā* is a description of the first *mantra* of *Īśāvāsya Upaniṣad*. We should, therefore, look into this in some detail.

Īśāvāsya Upaniṣad has eighteen *mantra*s and is known as *Mantropaniṣad*. Kaṇva and Mādhyandina are the two *ṛṣi*s who have been given the honour of being its authors.

> *oṁ īśāvāsyaṁ idaṁ sarvaṁ yat kiñca jagatyām jagat* ।
> *tena tyaktena bhuñjithā mā gṛdhaḥ kasya svid dhanam* ॥

(1) *iśāvāsyaṁ idaṁ*—indwelling or clothing of the Lord,
(2) *yat kiñca jagatyām jagat*—whatever in the Universe, moving world,
(3) *tena tyaktena bhuñjithā*—therefore, by Him, by abandonment (by that which is left) may enjoy,
(4) *mā gṛdhaḥ kasya svid dhanam*—do not covet anybody's wealth.

All things whatsoever move in this Universe and the Universe itself, is pervaded or clothed by the Lord. Thou should enjoy by abandonment, covet not anybody's wealth.

Idaṁ sarvaṁ (all this) *vāsyam* (clothing, enveloping, pervading). What is 'all this'? It is the *loka* we perceive. What impulses our five sense-organs bring in, what interpretation is given by our mind, what advice is given to our mind by the intellect—all this together constitute our world, i.e., the *loka*. The accepted opinion of the majority in this world, of the world perceived, constitutes the Universe. All 'THIS' is inside the Lord.

All 'THIS' is possible only in the presence of the life-force inside each encasement of matter (i.e., body). Without the spark of life inside us, our sense-organs, mind and intellect cannot function. So, the Lord is the master of the individual beings and also the master of the Universe. As He is inside us, as our senses receive impulses from outside, we are ignorant of the Lord. As he is enveloping us all, our senses cannot perceive Him as well. Just as we cannot directly see our own eyes (sense-organs), likewise we cannot see Him. Our mind cannot register His presence. We need special knowledge to see Him. This knowledge is given in *Vedas* and is simplified by Lord Kṛṣṇa in the *Gītā*. The *mantra* says "this, which is enveloped". It also says 'THIS' which is moving in this Universe, including the Universe. Whatever (*yat kiñca*) is in the Universe, i.e., all names and forms and not just man, have the spark of the Lord in them and are enveloped by Him.

Beneath the perception at all levels is a firm foundation who is the Lord. The L ord's light of consciousness illumines it. How can we recognise Him? The third quarter of the *mantra* gives us the answer. "May enjoy" by abandonment, Him, is its meaning. What is this we have to enjoy? It is *Īśvara*, "Our Lord", we have to enjoy. How to enjoy Him. We have to enjoy Him by realising Him.

By abandonment? By abandonment of what? Not surely by running away from this world. But it is abandoning the perceptions of happiness from the outer world brought in by sense-organs. It means by *niṣkāma karma*. Not *saṁnyāsa*. It is *saṁnyāsa* of pleasures but not *saṁnyāsa* of objects. The happiness obtained from the outer world is transitory. But the happiness of association with the Lord is permanent. To realise this 'happiness' from within is to realise the real truth. To realise the all-pervasiveness of Lord (while living in this world), is the theme of *Īśāvāsya Upaniṣad*. This theme is elaborated by Lord Kṛṣṇa in the *Gītā*.

Mādhavācārya has given a beautiful interpretation of the words *tena tyaktena*—"Whatever given away to you by the Lord", "enjoy what is given to you by the Lord", it means. What is given by the Lord, offer it to Him and then partake of it as his *prasādam*. (*Gītā,* III.12). It means that in this Universe where there is the Lord in all, whatever you get for your work, offer it back to the Universe and enjoy what is left. We have to understand it better.

We work everyday. We work to fulfil some role in the community we live in. The community gives us the due reward (pay) at the end of the month. Instead of using all the money one gets as his pay for personal pleasures, one should offer it to the Universe. How? Why?

The Universe is made up of able and disabled people. There are handicapped people, old people, children, and the unemployed who also need to survive. Everyone of us must share his wealth with the needy. We enjoy what is left after this and that is Lord's *prasāda*. Again this theme is elaborated by Śrī Kṛṣṇa. He says, one who eats without giving it to the Lord is a thief.

The last quarter says, "Do not covet anybody's wealth", which means earning what you can by righteous means.

Our sense-organs bring in impulses and our mind interprets them as likes and dislikes. If it is "likes" (desires) it would send the organs of action to get more and more of it. This leads one into immoral ways for achieving objects beyond one's means. Again Śrī Kṛṣṇa advises in detail on this aspect through *jñāna* and *karma yogas*. *Niṣkāma karma* and *karmaphala-tyāga* and attaining the knowledge of Truth is the meaning which is the theme of the entire *Gītā* Universal oneness, brought out in this is enunciated by Lord Kṛṣṇa as *advaita* philosophy.

"Renounce the fleeting world and the fleeting objects, renounce the pleasures you get from them, recognise that the Lord is "ALL THIS". See the Self in you and in all and you will get the *ānanda*. This is the summary of this and that of the entire *Gītā*.

THE PATH

In our battle of life, we should all be looking for realising the Truth (the truth of our existence). The Hindu philosophers by close analysis realised that what we needed was the "end-result". The end-result is and will be for each of us to exhibit our divinity. This means we must show love and respect to the divinity, from whom we have all come into this world. This is devotion which means total identification with the loved one.

One must develop all divine virtues (Chapter 16, verses 1, 2 & 3). We must show that in our actions. This achieves two end-results. They are:

1. We, individually, will attain the *paramātmā*, which means becoming one with *paramātmā*.
2. We, doing God's work as his servant, will be working towards a better, safer Universe for the present and future generations.

This can be achieved by dropping the sense of ego and trying to see God in us and in all. We have to continue living like this till our death.

Our ancestors, the *ṛṣis*, said there are four paths to realise the Lord. They are:

1. The path of *karma,* i.e., action, performing of obligatory duties to one's self, one's family and one's community;
2. The path of *jñāna*, i.e., knowledge by the study of scriptures, by learning from the scholars; by inward contemplation of what has been learnt one can understand the Truth;
3. The path of *bhakti*—which is devotion to God and accepting Him as someone above us all and asking Him for shelter and protection.
4. The path of *dhyāna,* i.e., meditation. By diverting the mind from contemplation of the pleasures of the world, and turning it to think and live in God.

These four paths all lead to one's common end-goal, i.e., self-perfection, i.e., *mokṣa* or liberation. This is liberation from pains and pleasures of the objective world.

This *Sanātana Dharma* of the Hindu Philosophy is symbolised as *Svastika*.

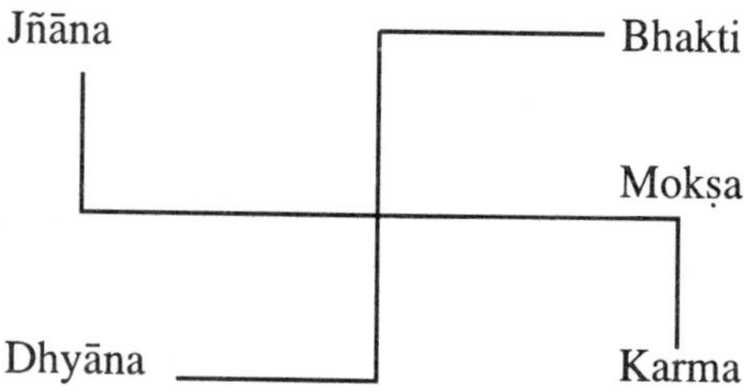

Unfortunately, the four paths advocated by Lord Kṛṣṇa have brought about division in our religion. People started advocating the path they liked best and they started ridiculing people who followed the other paths.

Śrī Kṛṣṇa through the *Gītā* says that what one wants to achieve is *yoga* or union of the ego with *ātman*, and Union of the *ātman* with the *paramātman*. All paths lead to the same end-result. We should realise that:

(1) All paths intermingle with each other;
(2) Real *karma* gives one *jñāna*;
(3) Real *jñāna* makes one perform proper *karma*;
(4) The real *bhakta* performs all actions and attains *jñāna;*
(5) By real *dhyāna*, one attains knowledge and performs *karma*s.

The Lord gives a 18-chaptered discourse. Each discourse is a *yoga*. If studied earnestly and followed properly, it leads to *mokṣa*.

I would now like to explain the meaning of some of the common words that we come across in the discourse.

MOKṢA AND SAṀSĀRA

Mokṣa is a state of mind wherein there is happiness which does not end in any sorrow and this comes from a true understanding of the knowledge given by the *Veda*s.

In our life, we should be able to face the innumerable problems we come across daily. Death, disease, injury etc., to oneself or to one's family or friend does bring distress. The law of nature is that death will come to us sooner or later. We all have to undergo changes in our existence in various stages of our development like babyhood, childhood, teenage, adulthood, middle age and old age. Death and disease can affect us at any time.

Modern science has helped us to avoid certain diseases and also cure certain other diseases. But we still suffer illness. During the time of illness and stress, we have to do our duty to our body which is suffering the illness and do our duty to our loved ones during their illness, by making use of all available treatments. Despite our efforts we come across situations where modern medicine cannot help us, and, during such times, we need courage from some sources to give us solace and comfort.

The scriptures give us such courage to face our problems. By following the code of practice, as prescribed by the *Gītā* one can develop spiritual strength. We, humans need physical and spiritual strength. Spiritual strength will help to lift us from the problems faced by the physical body.

Mokṣa does not mean going to heaven. It is not going to a far off place. It is a state of mind which can only be experienced and it is possible to do so even in this present life.

Saṁsāra is the cycle of births and deaths we undergo during our journey in life. *Saṁsāra* is contact of each individual with his surroundings and the attachment to those surroundings. *Saṁsāra* gives us the pleasures of our life but also gives us problems in relation to our attachment.

Till we attain total purity of mind, we cannot attain the state of *mokṣa* which is what everyone is aiming to achieve (those on the spiritual path). This is better understood by knowing about *vāsanā*s and *guṇa*s.

VĀSANĀS

*Vāsanā*s are thought-imprints. Our mind, through the medium of the sense-organs, has a constant exposure to various objects in the outer world. Every thought leaves an imprint on our mind. When the thought is translated into action, the imprint will get wiped out. Some thoughts come in more frequently in respect of an object that gives a feeling of satisfaction. They are then called desires. Desires leave a strong imprint. Every action we perform to fulfil those desires will bring in more thoughts and more desires.

The process of *vāsanā*-imprints becomes a vicious circle. At any one time, we have innumerable *vāsanā*s in our mind. Our mind, from its store of impulses received in the past, has a capacity to delve into this store house whenever it wants. Without the help of our sense-organs our mind can delve into the past memories. Thoughts during such moments also leave imprints. They are also *vāsanā*s.

Total destruction of *vāsanā*s give a pure mind and this is called *vāsanā-kṣaya*.

GUṆAS

Guṇa means rope. The *guṇa*s are quality of thoughts entertained and actions performed by us. They bind us like a rope. They can be classified readily into:

(*a*) pure thoughts and actions, i.e., *sattva-guṇa,*
(*b*) passionate thoughts and actions, i.e., *rajo-guṇa*, and
(*c*) lazy thoughts and actions, i.e., *tamo-guṇa*

We have a combination of all of the three *guṇa*s in us. But we express different *guṇa*s at different times and also have one dominant *guṇa* that characterises our personality.

(*a*) Preponderance of *sāttvika guṇa* is the quality of a brāhmaṇa;
(*b*) Preponderance of *rājasika guṇa* is the quality of a kṣatriya;
(*c*) Combination of *rājasika* and *tāmasika guṇa* is a vaiśya;
(*d*) Preponderance of *tāmasika guṇa* is the quality of a śūdra.

These are dealt with in detail in Chapter 14.

*Vāsanā*s are responsible for our *guṇa*s.

DEATH

At the time of death of the physical body, the subtle body, (the mind and the intellect) departs with its bag of *guṇa*s. Depending on the type of *guṇa*, the subtle body with the blessings of the Lord, will find a suitable medium (composed of the five gross elements) and forms a new life. Thus, the Lord gives a chance for all of us to fulfil our desires.

When we start looking for the truth, when we start following the percepts of the *Gītā* and the advice of the teachers and when we start performing *niṣkāma-karma* and *karmaphala-tyāga* (Chapters 3 and 5), we start burning all existing *vāsanā*s. The moment we burn all the *vāsanā*s and do not create any more new *vāsanā*s we achieve total purity of our mind. This is the state of a *jīvanmukta*.

A *jīvanmukta* continues to work for universal welfare and spreads the message of the *Veda*s by teaching. He also spreads it by actions which will be followed by others as an example. As his actions show pure divinity, he is said to be God in human form. He has transcended the level of the three *guṇa*s. He has overcome *tāmasika* and *rajo-guṇa*s. He has given up the thought of attaining *mokṣa* and gone above the plane of even *sattva-guṇa*. It is very rarely that we come across such *jīvanmukta*s.

Swami Vivekananda, Mahatma Gandhi, Mother Teresa can be considered as examples of *jīvanmuktas*.

GUṆĀTĪTA

The person who has by practice, lifted himself from *tamo-guṇa* to *rajo-guṇa*, from *rajo-guṇa* to *sattva-guṇa* and lifted himself even above that to the state of a *jīvanmukta*, is a *guṇātīta*. He has transcended the plane of the three *guṇa*s. He experiences absolute bliss in himself (*ānanda*). This state has to be experienced and cannot be explained.

SOUL

This is also known as *ātman*, as Self and the "Life within" the body. The energy which is inside all of us, which gives us the life-force is our *ātman*.

BODY

The body is composed of five gross elements. They are space, air, water, fire and earth. All of us, whether great or small, and all forms of life in this Universe, are composed of these five gross elements. The *ātman* gives it life. In the absence of the *ātman*, the body is considered to be dead.

EGO

This is also known as *jīva* or *ahaṁkāra*. The Self within is absolute, pure energy. Due to the subtle and physical body, it associates itself with the outer world and develops likes and dislikes. This is then called "self" with a small 's'. Self, with a capital 'S' is the Soul and it has no association with the body and the outside world.

The 'self' which is a reflection of the 'SELF' will associate itself with the world which is 'I'-ness in us.

PRĀṆA

The life-force, the energy which keeps us alive is *prāṇa*. It is the soul.

DVAITA (DUALISM)

Dvaita means two. It is a feeling of separateness. When one sees two in one, it is *dvaita*. Spiritually, the feeling of separateness of the Soul and *Paramātmā* or Universal Soul is *dvaita*.

ADVAITA (MONISM)

The feeling of oneness (non-two) is *advaita*. When one drops his ego and totally unites himself with the Lord and unites with such a thought, it is *advaita*. There is no more 'I'-ness in such a person. This will enable one to see *Paramātmā* sustaining the entire Universe. He sees *ātman* in all the creatures in the Universe. The milk in its original form is *advaita* but when broken into cheese and water, it is *dvaita*.

VIŚIṢṬĀDVAITA (QUALIFIED MONISM)

This is a school of thought which is not totally *dvaita* and not totally *advaita*.

It believes that after clearing one's *vāsanā*s, one will reach the abode of the Lord of one's devotion (but does not merge in Him) whence he does not return again to this world. The Lord of our choice will give us shelter and this state is experienced by transcendental meditation.

Examples:

(*a*) When I want to buy a fruit from the market, there are two separate objects: (1) we and (2) the fruit at a distance. This is *dvaita*.

(*b*) When I go to the market and take the fruit, in my hand, I get pleasure in having the fruit in my hand. This is *viśiṣṭādvaita*.

(*c*) When I eat the fruit, the fruit is in me. They are no longer two separate objects. It is *advaita*.

TAPAS

Tapas is an act performed towards purifying one's mind and *indriyas*. All our sense-organs, bring in stimuli to the mind. The mind, in turn, starts to develop likes and dislikes. These make one get attachment to the physical world. The process of detachment from the contact with the outer world is a means to purify our mind and this process is *tapas* which is described in Chapter 17.

For example, training our eyes in such a manner that objects of the world brought into the mind through our eyes do not tempt us, is *tapas* of the eyes.

In olden days, we were told, people went to the forest and performed severe austerities like standing in the sun for years together. Śrī Kṛṣṇa says that it is not *tapas*. *Tapas* is not physical torture of the body. *Tapas* means training of the mind and not letting it run towards desires.

TAPASVĪ

A person who has perfectly controlled his speech, mind and body (*vāk*, *manas* and *kāya*) is termed a *tapasvī*.

TAT TVAM ASI

Tat	—	That
Tvam	—	You
Asi	—	Art

Tat tvam asi means 'Thou Art That'

The essence of *Bhagavadgītā* is to make one realise *tat tvam asi* aspect of Him. We are really the *ātman* or 'divinity' with an outer covering of the physical body inside which is the subtle body consisting of the mind and the intellect.

Unfortunately, we get attached to the body and develop the 'ego'. Ego is the 'I' or 'My'-ness in us. It makes us believe that our physical body is real. We forget that we are living because of the life-force inside us. The life-force is the spiritual energy and is known commonly as the 'Soul' or the *ātman.*

The *Gītā* consists of 18 chapters. Experts say that

(1) The first six chapters deal with '*tvam*'
(2) The second six chapters deal with '*tat*' and
(3) The last six chapters deal with '*asi*'.

There are some other experts who give a different meaning to the three sections. They say

(1) The first six chapters deal with *karma-yoga*
(2) The second six chapters deal the *bhakti-yoga*, and
(3) The last six chapters deal with *jñāna-yoga*.

The commentary on the *Gītā* in this book is based on the theme of '*tat tvam asi*'.

'*Tat tvam asi*' is known as a *mahāvākya. Mahāvākya* means great sentence. The real 'TRUTH' is in realising one's own identity. To realise one's own divine status, to realise the same 'divine status' in all forms manifest in this Universe is to realise the oneness of the entire Universe.

This realisation of the oneness of the entire universe is *advaita*. It means 'NON-TWO'.

There are no two separate entities called the soul and the body. The 'Soul' is real and permanent and the body is not real and only a temporary suit on the soul. There are no two separate entities as Me and Him or Me and That. The entire Universe is part of the Supreme Reality (also known as *parabrahman*). This *advaita* philosophy is based on the teaching of Śrī Śaṅkarācārya.

This philosophy, if properly understood and followed, helps one to drop his ego or selfishness and contribute to the welfare of all in the Universe and helps one to leave a better tomorrow after death.

We shall now analyse the three words of *tat tvam asi* separately.

Tvam

Tvam—You

When we are in distress, when we want something to help us, we go and ask for help.

When do we ask the question, Who am I? We ask this question only when we are lost, and in grief of having been lost, we forget who we are.

We also want to know why we are suffering. We then would like to overcome the suffering.

In normal day-to-day events, we make use of local available resources to help us. For example, we go to the chemist and buy some pain-killing tablets like aspirin to relieve our body-aches. If we do not get better, we go to the doctor and ask for help. The end-result is relief from 'pain' and that would make us feel happy.

Certain diseases have no cure. They bring us a lot of pain and eventually kill us. Cancer is one such disease. Death or diseases to our beloved ones also brings us distress. Also, the loss of a part of our physical body or injury to beloved ones brings us distress. In such situations, we turn to various sources and try to get help.

When nothing in this world will help us, we fall at the feet of God and ask for His help, or We get angry and lose faith in God. We can try to read and understand the scriptures and try to find out what is the cure for our distress. *Bhagavadgītā*, properly learnt and understood is one of the sources to help us in distress.

Let us take another example. Let us imagine that a child has wandered off on a festival day like *dīpāvalī* (or Christmas). The child gets fascinated at the street decorations and colourful displays in the shop windows. The child gets fascinated on seeing many people merrily enjoying on the streets. Soon, the child gets hungry or may get hurt accidentally or may feel too hot or too cold. He will then realise where he is and try to trace his way back home.

OR

Imagine a child wandering to a railway station and out of curiosity getting on into a stationary train. If the train starts moving forward to its next destination, that child is truly lost. In distress, soon, he forgets his name and his address. Sometimes, he may not even remember his parents' details.

While the child was enjoying the beautiful well-decorated streets, while he was enjoying the comforts of a moving train, he was in a dream-world and enjoying the dream. As soon as he comes out of the dream world, when he is in distress, he starts crying. He would like to go back to his parents but the grief makes him forget his identity.

In the journey of life, similarly, we are lost and we have forgotten our real identity. We are living in a dream-world and we need help, and we are in distress. Losing track of our real identity is called ignorance.

We need to get knowledge of our true identity. We can get this knowledge by understanding *śāstras*. *Gītāśāstra* gives us that knowledge which expels the darkness of ignorance. First of all:

(1) we must realise that we are lost in our journey in our life;
(2) we must want to go back to our real home where we came from originally;
(3) we must find the right guide to guide us;
(4) we must have faith in the guide.

The Gītā is Such A Guide

The *Gītā* does not advocate blind faith. Śrī Kṛṣṇa, the teacher, says that every person must test the validity of the *śāstras* at every step. By finding out that what is said in the *śāstras* has been correct, one gets more faith in that *śāstra* and his future actions will be according to the *śāstras*.

When one goes to a doctor for help, the doctor gives him some medicine. By taking medicine as per directions, if he starts feeling better, his faith in the doctor and the medicine gets stronger. In future, he will go to the same doctor for help.

Lord Kṛṣṇa, wants us all to use our intellectual capacity (*buddhi*) and analyse our thoughts and actions. We must test the validity of the *śāstras* at every step and get more confidence in the *śāstras*.

The first chapter is an introduction to the discourse. It brings out the state of distress in Arjuna. Kṛṣṇa and Arjuna knew each other for several years. Arjuna had not realised the true identity of Kṛṣṇa and also was not aware of his true nature. In answer to Arjuna's request for help to overcome the grief which came out of distress, Śrī Kṛṣṇa gives the message of the *Gītā*. Kṛṣṇa did not teach the *Gītā* before. Why?

There was no reason for Arjuna to feel sorry for himself. Arjuna was a kṣatriya (warrior). Even though he had faced several problems before, his kṣatriya nature had not deserted him. He had a will to fight and survive.

But, the present war was of a different nature. It was a case of win or lose, die or survive. Not only that, he had to face the reality and be prepared to fight his respected elders like Bhīṣma, Droṇa and Kṛpa. They had to be killed. Feeling sorry for himself, frightened of committing the sinful act of killing elders, brought an immense sense of grief. He lost his kṣatriya instinct and dropped his bow Gāṇḍīva and he told Kṛṣṇa, 'I do not want to fight'. This was all due to ignorance. He wanted to forcibly change his kṣatriya nature and become a *saṁnyāsī*.

Arjuna had the sense to ask for help. He immediately requested Kṛṣṇa to guide him in the right path. Śrī Kṛṣṇa realising the earnestness in the request, realising the real capacity of his disciple, takes up the task of teaching the knowledge. He takes Arjuna as his student and helps him to overcome his ignorance.

Before describing various paths Arjuna could take, Śrī Kṛṣṇa gives Arjuna a detailed description of the 'Real Arjuna', the *ātman*. The second chapter is a description of the *ātman* (*tvam*) and ends up in a wonderful description of a *sthitaprajña* (man of steady wisdom).

Kṛṣṇa then takes up *karma-yoga* which deals with duties of all of us towards our '*tvam*' (Soul). Indirectly, they are duties of our universe and our society.

In the fourth chapter, he takes up *jñāna-yoga*. By performing right action how one could get real knowledge and by real knowledge how one should act, is taken up in this chapter.

The fifth chapter is *karmasaṁnyāsa-yoga* wherein he talks about renunciation of fruits of action which will help us to realise the *ātman* in us.

The sixth chapter is *dhyāna-yoga* which gives a detailed description of how to meditate and realise the 'REAL YOU' inside the 'FALSE YOU'.

Tat

'*Tat*' means 'That'. The second six chapters in the *Gītā* dwell on this Issue.

After describing 'who you are' in the first six chapters, Śrī Kṛṣṇa now points out what is 'That'. He says 'That' is '*ātman*' or the 'Soul' which is only a part of the Supreme *ātman*, known as the '*Paramātmā*'.

The seventh chapter is *jñāna-vijñāna-yoga*. By practically following *karma, jñāna* or *dhyāna-yoga*s mentioned before, one will be able to convert his knowledge into wisdom. He will become wise and realise '*tat*'.

The eighth chapter *akṣara-parabrahma-yoga* gives an exhaustive description of the imperishable. It describes '*tat*'.

The ninth chapter is *rājavidyā-rājaguhya-yoga*. "The knowledge of what is *tat*", 'Who one really is', the Lord says, should be given only to sincere seekers.

The tenth chapter is *vibhūti-yoga*. This describes the universal presence of '*tat*' in all forms of manifestation. It says that *tat* is omniscient (All-knowing) and omnipotent (All-powerful).

The eleventh chapter is *viśvarūpa-darśana-yoga*. It gives practical demonstration of '*tat*'.

The twelfth chapter is *bhakti-yoga*. Learning what is '*tat*', learning what is *tvam*, and actually visualising '*tat*' will give strength to develop *bhakti* (devotion) on '*tat*'.

In the earlier studies, *bhakti* would be of the blind type. After practical demonstration, one has seen the truth of what has been taught in theory. *Bhakti* on the Lord would reach Himālayan heights.

There is a beautiful comparison given in *Muṇḍaka Upaniṣad*. It describes an archer trying to hit the target with an arrow using a bow. Initially, the archer must want to hit the target. Towards achieving the desire, he must practice the art of archery. He will fit the arrow in the bow. He will then stretch the string to its maximum. All this time, he would be concentrating on the target. At the right tension, pointing in the right direction, he releases the arrow. No effort is needed after the arrow is released. One must develop this art so perfectly that he should be able to hit the target even by looking at the target's reflection in the water.

The bow is compared to the divine knowledge; The arrow is compared to the ego; The *ātman* is the target; The archer is the *sādhaka* trying to achieve liberation.

One should stretch the bow of divine knowledge to its maximum and release (surrender totally) his ego (arrow). During this process his mind should have single pointed concentration on the Lord. He should, when he is confident and ready, release the arrow (total surrender or ego). The arrow or ego without any further effort will reach the *ātman* and becomes one with the *ātman*.

Asi

Asi means 'Art' (The verb "are"). i.e., YOU ARE.

The last six chapters assert the importance of *tat* and *tvam* again and says "Yes, you are correct".

Four of its six chapters have the titles which include the word *vibhāga*. *Vibhāga* means division or separation. Separation of 'FALSE YOU' from 'THE REAL YOU' is what is expected from all of us if we want to realise the *Paramātman.*

The thirteenth chapter is *kṣetra* (field)-*kṣetrajña* (knowledge of the field)-*vibhāga-yoga*, it describes again what is false and what is real in all of us.

The fourteenth chapter is *guṇatraya-vibhāga-yoga*. It describes the characters of the false *tvam*, i.e., the body. It helps one to see at what level he is in his spiritual path. It describes characters of lowest order (*tamas*) to the highest order (*śuddha sattva*). By understanding it, we should be able to drop our *tāmasika* and *rājasika guṇa*s, should be able to go above *sattva* and even *śuddha sattva* state and reach a state beyond the *guṇa*s, i.e., to become a *guṇātīta*.

The fifteenth chapter is *puruṣottama-prāpti-yoga*. Dropping *guṇa*s and becoming *guṇātīta* means indirectly becoming one with the *Paramātmā*. We all have a divine right to become one with *Paramātmā* but to achieve it we must not have any trace of ego left in us.

The sixteenth chapter is *daivāsura sampad-vibhāga-yoga*. It tells us of the wealth we need in our journey in life to achieve salvation. To reach '*tat*', it tells us what bad qualities we must drop and what good qualities we must acquire.

The seventeenth chapter is *śraddhātraya-vibhāga-yoga*. It tells us that one needs faith to achieve what one wants. It gives us a detailed description of bodily and mental actions and thoughts which would help us to strengthen our faith in '*tat*'.

The eighteenth chapter is *mokṣa saṁnyāsa-yoga*. The *sādhaka* having understood the 17 chapters thoroughly, should be able to drop even the desire to achieve liberation. He is bound to achieve the final liberation and unite with '*TAT*'. He does not need to think of reaching that state. **Salt is bound to get dissolved in water it has to drop in the water and it will get dissolved. After all salt came from the water and it will get dissolved in it and loses its identity.**

(Note : See Page xvii, Addition to: **WHAT IS UPANIṢAD?***)*

Upaniṣads are sincere and serious attempts by the great scholars of the past who tried to express the meaning from the vast Vedas which are humanly impossible to read/grasp/implement in one's life. The Vedas are subjects in quest of the "Ultimate truth about the origin of life." The Upaniṣads are the culmination in such attempts. They are popularly known as "Vedantas" (end of the Vedas).

The seers who took up the Upaniṣads have used a portion of the Vedas and made it easy to bring out the message of the "Truth" in such statements.

The Upaniṣads do not bring reality to the seeker but suggest such reality which they can pursue. It depends on the individual seeker and the efforts he puts in if he is going to be successful in his efforts.

The Upaniṣads give us the key so that we can open the door and enter the temple of "Truth."

The word "Upaniṣad" can be split into "Upa Ni Sad". It means "To sit close by." It is to be understood as "The mind of the listener not deviating from the external influences of the world but concentrating on looking into one's own inner Self". The method of teaching these was from the "Preceptor" to the "Disciple." The disciple sat with rapt attention to what was taught by the guru and meditated on it.

In numbers, these are said to be over 200 Upaniṣads. Traditionally they are considered to be 108 in numbers and the principal ones are 10. Śrī Ādi Śaṅkarācārya has added meaning to the other one. The 11 Upaniṣads are:

Īśa, Kena, Kaṭha, Praśna, Mundaka, Mandūkya, Taittirīya, Aitareya, Chāndogya, Bṛhadāraṇyaka, and Śvetāśvatara.

Śrī Śaṅkara says that the Upaniṣads are those that burn away one's ignorance.

Volume I
(Chapters 1-10)

CHAPTER 1

ARJUNA-VIṢĀDA-YOGA

INTRODUCTION

The first chapter is *arjuna-viṣāda-yoga.* It means the *yoga* of Arjuna's despondency.

Yoga, philosophically, means union of *ātmā* with *Paramatmā.* The path leading to it is also termed as *yoga.* The branches that lead to the paths are also termed as *yoga.* In short, every aspect of spiritual progress towards Liberation is also *yoga.*

This chapter, after a brief introduction to the battle scene by Sañjaya to his King Dhṛtarāṣṭra, deals exclusively with the mental state of Arjuna.

Kṛṣṇa had tried mediation between the Pāṇḍavas and Kauravas. The Kauravas had taken by unrighteous means the kingodm belonging rightly to the Pāṇḍavas. They refused to give it back to the Pāṇḍavas. Duryodhana and his borthers made several unsuccessful attempts at killing the Pāṇḍava brothers. The Pāṇḍavas and Kauravas were cousins but it did not make any difference to Duryodhana. He even insulted Draupadī, the wife of the Pāṇḍavas by attempting to disrobe ḥer in the palace assembly hall.

Dhṛtarāṣṭra, the Emperor, was the father of Duryodhana and uncle to the Pāṇḍavas. He knew about the wicked deeds of his son and his ill-will towards the Pāṇḍavas, but his blind love towards his son made him turn a blind eye to his son's sinful acts.

The Pāṇḍavas under the guidance of Lord Kṛṣṇa attempted to get their fair share of the kingdom to which they were the rightful heirs. Unfortunately, the Emperor and his sons did not yield to the attempts at mediation and even insulted Lord Kṛṣṇa when he went to mediate. Therefore the Pāṇḍavas decided to fight to get back their kingdom.

There were a lot of senior members like grandfather Bhīṣma, the teacher Droṇa, family priest Kṛpa who all felt that they had a duty to the throne of the empire and not to him who actually was ruling at the time. They therefore, joined the Kaurava army and supported Duryodhana.

When the battle was about to begin, Arjuna requests Kṛṣṇa to take his chariot in between the two armies so that he could see the two armies and also give his respect to the elders. He was eager to fight his cousins and take revenge on their sinful acts towards his brothers and his wife. He was going to fight for righteousness. He also had a duty to the people of the kingdom to provide a righteous administration.

But suddenly he felt sorrow, pity and fear. He felt sorrow because during the war a number of people would be killed and their families would lose a bread-winner. He felt pity towards his cousins. He thought it was his duty to excuse his cousins who were ignorant. He felt greater pity towards Duryodhana, his wicked cousin. He was frightened because if the elders like Bhīṣma and Droṇa were to be killed, he would incur sin and he and his brothers would go to hell for such a sinful act.

Arjuna was a kṣatriya, warrior of the topmost order. He had received scriptural teaching by the best teachers. He was well-versed in the *Veda*s. He had a moral duty to fight. Suddenly ignorance, shameful to his kṣatriya state, came over him and he started looking at the army at personal, egoistic level. He forgot his duty to the land as described in the *śāstra*s and allowed his personal feelings to interfere in his actions. He totally forgot what he was taught so far and what he had to live for. He was in an utter state of despair and became hysterical. He wanted to become a *saṁnyāsī* and let the Kauravas rule the kingdom.

But even in despair he wanted liberation or *mokṣa* and requested guidance from his *guru*. He totally surrendered himself at the feet of Lord Kṛṣṇa. He asked him to be his guide towards *mokṣa*. Kṛṣṇa then delivered the great *Gītopadeśam*. Hence this chapter deserves the title of *yoga*.

Anybody, when they are in despair, can still try to attain *mokṣa* by surrendering at the feet of their *guru*s (teachers) or

God. They will still have a chance to get liberated in course of time.

धृतराष्ट्र उवाच
धर्मक्षेत्रे कुरुक्षेत्रे समवेता युयुत्सवः ।
मामकाः पाण्डवाश्चैव किमकुर्वत सञ्जय ॥१॥

dhṛtarāṣṭra uvāca
***dharmakṣetre kurukṣetre samavetā yuyutsavaḥ* ।**
***māmakāḥ pāṇḍavāś caiva kim akurvata sañjaya* ॥1॥**

Dhṛtarāṣṭra said

Having assembled together on the holy plain of Kurukṣetra, desirous of fighting the battle, O Sañjaya, what did the sons of Pāṇḍu and also my people do?

There are 700 verses in the 18 chapters of the *Gītā*. Of these, the first verse is the only one spoken by the blind king. The rest of the verses are the ones of Śrī Kṛṣṇa and Arjuna with an odd interception by Sañjaya.

It is interesting to note that the first word is *dharma-kṣetre*. It means the "field of *dharma*".

Dharma is a Sanskrit word and it has no English equivalent. In simple words it means 'righteousness'. The nearest definition of *dharma* is "The law of being". It is an essential quality of being without which being has no existence:

For example: Water has a number of qualities. It is fluid. It could be salty or sweet or insipid. It could be muddy. Of these qualities, fluidity is an essential quality. If it is not fluid, it cannot be called water. The *dharma* of water is therefore fluidity.

Similarly, the essential quality of human beings is divinity. As we will learn in course of the next 18 chapters, we have no existence without this divinity. This divinity in us is called *ātmā*. We really are the *ātman* inside but we have a covering of the physical and subtle bodies. Due to ignorance, we consider the physical and subtle bodies as real and forget our real nature.

Kurukṣetra: It is a holy plain in north India. It is said that in the past, a number of religious and righteous activities took place on that field. It is believed that Brahmā and Indra performed sacrifices (*yajñas*) is this place. Emperor Kuru, the ancestor of Pāṇḍavas and Kauravas ploughed the land in this holy place.

Actually, we can consider our own bodies as *dharma-kṣetra* and Kurukṣetra. As we have the divine *ātman* inside, our body is a *dharma-kṣetra.* We have a combination of divine and evil qualities in us. Our body is Kurukṣetra because it has two conflicting forces of righteousness and wickedness in it. In our battle of life we must know to which side we belong. If we want to attain *mokṣa,* we must strengthen our divine forces and know the strength of the enemy forces. By knowing one's enemy one can develop an action plan to overcome him.

Māmakāḥ: It means "my people". Dhṛtarāṣṭra considers Kauravas as his people. Pāṇḍavas are the sons of Pāṇḍu, the brother of Dhṛtarāṣṭra, but they are not his people. But Dhṛtarāṣṭra does not consider this to be a fault in his thinking.

The *śāstras* do want us to consider 'all' as 'one'. They do not want one to develop 'I'-ness (ego) which is the root-cause of all misery. What we have has to be shared by all. Dhṛtarāṣṭra was not willing to share his kingdom with his brother's children and was therefore acting against the doctrine of the *śāstras*.

Dhṛtarāṣṭra: It means 'The one who holds on to a kingdom (which is not his own)'. The king was holding on to the kingdom which was not his own.

Human body is to be considered as a temple with the Lord inside. It could be considered as a kingdom with the king inside. Forgetting this fact, holding on to the physical body, which we all do, makes us Dhṛtarāṣṭras.

Our body is a suitable medium for the performance of righteous deeds and hence it should be considered as *dharmakṣetra.* We have the power to intellect with which we can analyse our actions. This is not possible by any other form of life we know of. In this universe we should be considered as blessed by the Lord who has given us human life which we should make use of for doing righteous deeds.

Sañjaya: Literally it means 'he whose victory is decisive'. Sañjaya had mastery over his mind and senses and was straightforward. He used his intelligence and gave his king proper advice in all situations. Of course, the king did not make use of the suggestions given by his minister.

Śrī Śaṅkarācārya compares the attitude of Dhṛtarāṣṭra to that of a stone in water. The stone stays in water but does not let the water penetrate into it. Dhṛtarāṣṭra was like a stone in the water. Sañjaya gave him the right advice several times but the advice did not penetrate his intellect.

सञ्जय उवाच
दृष्ट्वा तु पाण्डवानीकं व्यूढं दुर्योधनस्तदा ।
आचार्यमुपसङ्गम्य राजा वचनमब्रवीत् ॥२॥

sañjaya uvāca
dṛṣṭvā tu pāṇḍavānīkaṁ vyūḍhaṁ duryodhanas tadā I
ācāryam upasaṁgamya rājā vacanam abravīt II2II

Sañjaya said

Having seen the Pāṇḍava Army arranged in a battle order, King Duryodhana approaching the teacher Droṇācārya spoke these words.

It is interesting to note that Duryodhana first approaches his teacher Droṇa. Why? Bhīṣma was the commander-in-chief of the Kaurava army but he did not go to the commander-in-chief but went to his teacher.

The reason is Duryodhana was frightened of Bhīṣma, his grandfather. He knew he would be rebuked by him. Bhīṣma would simply ask him to go and take his place in the battle array.

Another reason for his approaching his teacher was to show his respect and to raise the level of adrenaline in his teacher to fight for his side. Arjuna and the rest of the Pāṇḍavas were very dear to his teacher. Duryodhana was worried that his teacher may not put his best efforts in the battle.

One can understand the psychological state of Duryodhana. A frightened child automatically turns to his parent for protection. Droṇa was like a fatherly figure to Duryodhana. The fact that he went to Droṇa makes one feel that he was frightened on seeing the enemy forces. He looked for reassurance from his teacher.

> पश्यैतां पाण्डुपुत्राणामाचार्य महतीं चमूम् ।
> व्यूढां द्रुपदपुत्रेण तव शिष्येण धीमता ॥३॥
>
> ***paśyaitāṁ pāṇḍuputrāṇām ācārya mahatīṁ camūm |***
> ***vyūḍhāṁ drupada-putreṇa tava śiṣyeṇa dhīmatā ||3||***
>
> *O teacher, behold the great Pāṇḍava Army, formed in the battle order by the son of Drupada, your wise disciple.*

Droṇa and Drupada, both learnt under the same *guru* in the past. They were good friends. When they finished their studies, Drupada had given an open invitation to Droṇa to come and meet him anytime for any help or benefit.

Due to adverse circumstances, Droṇa became a poor man. Drupada on the other hand had become a king. Remembering the invitation of his friends, Droṇa goes to Drupada's court with a view to getting some help. Drupada, conscious of the difference in his present status chooses not to recognise his old friend. Droṇa felt insulted and swore he would take revenge.

Later on, Droṇa becomes the teacher for Pāṇḍavas and Kauravas. Arjuna was his best pupil. One day he asks Arjuna to go and catch and bring Drupada. Arjuna does so and ties Drupada to a bed in his teacher's house, as per his teacher's orders. Drupada on getting up sees his predicament and asks his friend to release him. Droṇa kicks his old friend on his chest and walks out of the house. Drupada then vows that he will get a son who will kill Droṇa and take revenge.

Dhṛṣṭadyumna was the commander-in-chief of the Pāṇḍava Army. He was the son of king Drupada who, by penance had got his son for the sole purpose of killing Droṇa who had insulted him. He was also a disciple of Droṇa in the early days.

Duryodhana was an extremely skilful warrior. He tries to rouse anger and hatred in his teacher. He specifically asks his teacher to see the battle-array of "Drupada-putra". The name of Drupada would raise the level of adrenaline in Droṇa and Duryodhana is trying to get his teacher exactly into that mood.

अत्र शूरा महेष्वासा भीमार्जुनसमा युधि ।
युयुधानो विराटश्च द्रुपदश्च महारथः ॥४॥

***atra śūrā maheṣvāsā bhīmārjunasamā yudhi* I**
***yuyudhāno virāṭaś ca drupadaś ca mahārathaḥ* II4II**

धृष्टकेतुश्चेकितानः काशिराजश्च वीर्यवान् ।
पुरुजित् कुन्तिभोजश्च शैब्यश्च नरपुङ्गवः ॥५॥

***dhṛṣṭaketuś cekitānaḥ kāśirājaś ca vīryavān* I**
***purujit kuntibhojaś ca śaibyaś ca narapuṅgavaḥ* II5II**

युधामन्युश्च विक्रान्त उत्तमौजाश्च वीर्यवान् ।
सौभद्रो द्रौपदेयाश्च सर्व एव महारथाः ॥६॥

***yudhāmanyuś ca vikrānta uttamaujāś ca vīryavān* I**
***saubhadro draupadeyāś ca sarva eva mahārathāḥ* II6II**

In the Pāṇḍava army, there are heroes and mighty archers equal to Bhīma and Arjuna. They are Yuyudhāna, Virāṭa, Drupada, of the first order of warriors.

Dhṛṣṭaketu, Cekitāna, the valiant king of Kāśī, Purujit, Kuntibhoja, Śaibya, the best of men, the strong Yudhāmanyu (Sātyaki), valiant Uttamaujā, Abhimanyu, the son of Subhadrā and Arjuna, and the sons of Draupadī, all of them, divisional commanders.

Mahārathī : One who can fight single-handed with 10,000 archers and also a master in the use of all weapons.

अस्माकं तु विशिष्टा ये तान्निबोध द्विजोत्तम ।
नायका मम सैन्यस्य संज्ञार्थं तान् ब्रवीमि ते ॥७॥

***asmākaṁ tu viśiṣṭā ye tān nibodha dvijottama* I**
***nāyakā mama sainyasya saṁjñārthaṁ tān bravīmi te* II7II**

O best of the twice-born, now I recall to you, for your information, the names of those who are the most distinguished amongst ourselves, the leaders of our army.

Droṇa was a brāhmaṇa by birth. Brāhmaṇas are usually known

as twice-born. It means those who after their physical birth, obtain knowledge and purify themselves of ignorance by scriptural reading and mastering the scriptures.

Droṇa is considered as the best of brāhmaṇas. Brāhmaṇas are generally teachers and are gentle by nature. They show love and compassion to all. Duryodhana, by reminding Droṇa that he is a brāhmaṇa, is probably trying to tease his teacher. "After all you are a brāhmaṇa. Brāhmaṇas are usually timid. Therefore, let me give you the names of mighty kṣatriya warriors on our side". This could be the reason for using the word 'twice-born'.

भवान् भीष्मश्च कर्णश्च कृपश्च समितिञ्जयः ।
अश्वत्थामा विकर्णश्च सौमदत्तिस्तथैव च ॥८॥

***bhavān bhīṣmaś ca karṇaś ca kṛpaś ca samitiñjayaḥ* I**
***aśvatthāmā vikarṇaś ca saumadattis tathaiva ca* II8II**

अन्ये च बहवः शूरा मदर्थे त्यक्तजीविताः ।
नानाशस्त्रप्रहरणाः सर्वे युद्धविशारदाः ॥९॥

***anye ca bahavaḥ śūrā madarthe tyaktajīvitāḥ* I**
***nānāśastrapraharaṇāḥ sarve yuddha-viśāradāḥ* II9II**

Yourself, Bhīṣma and Karṇa, and also Kṛpa the victorious in war, Aśvatthāmā, Vikarṇa and also the son of Somadatta, as also many other heroes who are prepared to give up their lives for my sake, armed with various weapons and missiles, all well-skilled in battle.

While naming the warriors on his side, Duryodhana, it is interesting to note, places Droṇa first in the list. Bhīṣma was the commander-in-chief of the Kaurava army. Instead of naming Bhīṣma first, Duryodhana places Droṇa's name first calling Droṇa a brāhmaṇa. He must have felt that he had gone too far in rousing the anger in his teacher. He is trying to correct his mistake and so puts Droṇa on top of the list of the warriors on his side.

अपर्याप्तं तदस्माकं बलं भीष्माभिरक्षितम् ।
पर्याप्तं त्विदमेतेषां बलं भीमाभिरक्षितम् ॥१०॥

aparyāptaṁ tad asmākaṁ balaṁ bhīṣmābhirakṣitam I
paryāptaṁ tvidam eteṣāṁ balaṁ bhīmābhirakṣitam II10II
This army of ours defended by Bhīṣma, is inadequate whereas that army of our enemies defended by Bhīma is quite adequate.

The two words *paryāptam* and *aparyāptam* have two different and contradictory meanings in Sanskrit. Hence different interpreters have given contradictory translations to this verse.

The first meaning:

aparyāptam: Unlimited.

paryāptam: Limited.

Taking this meaning, the verse on translation should read like this:

This army of ours defended by Bhīṣma is unlimited and the army of theirs defended by Bhīma is limited.

This is an encouraging statement. This is because the Kauravas had 11 battallions (*akṣauhiṇī*) of army and Pāṇḍavas had only 7 battallions (*akṣauhiṇī*). By looking at the numbers of warriors, Kauravas had a larger army.

The second meaning :

aparyāptam: Incomplete, insufficient, inefficient.

paryāptam: Complete, sufficient, efficient.

By taking this meaning, the verse should read like this:

This army of ours defended by Bhīṣma is inefficient and the army of theirs defended by Bhīma is efficient.

Mahatma Gandhi has given this interpretation to this verse. Why? Let us analyse it further. Duryodhana knew Bhīma's strength and also Bhīma's temper. He remembered that Bhīma vowed to drink the blood of his brother Duḥśāsana. He probably had a sense of fear that Bhīma by his physical strength would be capable of destroying the entire Kaurava army. He says, "That army of Pāṇḍavas protected by Bhīma". Bhīma was not the commander-in-chief but still he gives importance to Bhīma.

Also, in the previous verse, Duryodhana uses the word

madarthe tyaktajīvitāḥ. It means "the ones who have given up their lives for my sake". Duryodhana had a guilty conscience. He knew that war is about to take place because he alone insisted that the Pāṇḍavas should not get any land. He felt sorry for his army. By saying "The ones who have given up their lives", he is expressing the weakness of the army on his side.

अयनेषु च सर्वेषु यथाभागमवस्थिताः ।
भीष्ममेवाभिरक्षन्तु भवन्तः सर्व एव हि ॥११॥

***ayaneṣu ca sarveṣu yathābhāgam avasthitāḥ* I**
***bhīṣmam evābhirakṣantu bhavantaḥ sarva eva hi* II11II**

Therefore, do you all, standing firmly in your respective positions, in the divisions, guard Bhīṣma alone.

Bhīṣma had been given a boon by his father that he could die at his own wish at a time and place chosen by himself. In other words, nobody in the Pāṇḍava army could kill Bhīṣma. But he could of course get injured. If the commander-in-chief gets injured seriously in the battle, it would cause chaos and confusion and give extra strength to the opponents in the fight. Hence, Duryodhana is asking his teacher to make sure that Bhīṣma is protected all the time and does not get injured in the battle.

तस्य सञ्जनयन् हर्षं कुरुवृद्धः पितामहः ।
सिंहनादं विनद्योच्चैः शङ्खं दध्मौ प्रतापवान् ॥१२॥

***tasya sañjanayan harṣaṁ kuruvṛddhaḥ pitāmahaḥ* I**
***siṁhanādaṁ vinadyoccaiḥ śaṅkhaṁ dadhmau pratāpavān* II12II**

In order to embolden Duryodhana, Bhīṣma, the mighty grandsire, the oldest of the Kurus, now raised a lion's roar and blew his conch.

It was a rule that the eldest person on the battlefield must give the signal to start the war at the beginning of the day and to stop the war at the end of the day. Nobody should start fighting before and also should not continue fighting after the respective signals. Bhīṣma then decides that the time is right and blows his conch.

One can note that Droṇa did not say a word in reply to

Duryodhana's statements. He keeps silent and gets ready to fight. Why did he not reply?

One can assume that Droṇa was fighting for the Kauravas only as a matter of duty. He probably felt that there was no use in giving a reply. After all Duryodhana was a spoilt prince. He might have therefore decided to ignore the remarks of Duryodhana and waited for the war signal from Bhīṣma.

ततः शङ्खाश्च भेर्यश्च पणवानकगोमुखाः ।
सहसैवाभ्यहन्यन्त स शब्दस्तुमुलोऽभवत् ॥१३॥

tataḥ śaṅkhāś ca bheryaś ca paṇavānakagomukhāḥ **|**
sahasaivābhyahanyanta sa śabdas tumulo'bhavat **||13||**

(When Bhīṣma blew the conch) all the other warriors blew their conches, trumpets, drums and horns. The sound filled all sides and was tremendous.

ततः श्वेतैर्हयैर्युक्ते महति स्यन्दने स्थितौ ।
माधवः पाण्डवश्चैव दिव्यौ शङ्खौ प्रदध्मतुः ॥१४॥

tataḥ śvetair hayair yukte mahati syandane sthitau **|**
mādhavaḥ pāṇḍavaś caiva divyau śaṅkhau pradadhmatuḥ **||14||**

Then seated in the magnificent chariot, yoked with white horses, Kṛṣṇa and Arjuna blew their divine conches.

One should note that in this, the 14th verse, Kṛṣṇa and Arjuna make their appearance for the first time in the *Gītā*.

The white colour of the horses reflects *dharma*, and represents pure *sāttvika* state. The chariot and Gāṇḍīva were a gift to Arjuna by the God of Fire after burning of the Khāṇḍava forest. The horses were a gift to Arjuna by Citraratha, King of Gandharvas. They could move anywhere on the earth and sky.

Mādhava: It refers to Lord Viṣṇu who has a thousand different names. *Mā* refers to Lakṣmī, the consort of Lord Viṣṇu and *dhava* means "the husband". As Śrī Kṛṣṇa is the incarnation of Lord Viṣṇu, Mādhava, in this context refers to Śrī Kṛṣṇa. This word has a special reason to be used in this context. It should be understood that the Goddess of Wealth, Lakṣmī has showered her grace on the Pāṇḍavas.

The Pāṇḍavas, as followers of *dharma*, should win and rule the land. Whoever wins the war, is supposed to have been blessed by Vijaya-Lakṣmī and would get the kingdom, i.e., Rājya-Lakṣmī. Lakṣmī denotes abundance and wealth. Wealth could be of a number of varieties, of which Vijaya-Lakṣmī and Rājya-Lakṣmī are appropriate in this context. By the use of the word Mādhava, we should understand that Pāṇḍavas, as followers of *dharma*, have been blessed and assured of victory.

Kṛṣṇa though not fighting himself, was given the respectable task to blow the conch first on behalf of the Pāṇḍavas.

पाञ्चजन्यं हृषीकेशो देवदत्तं धनञ्जयः ।
पौण्ड्रं दध्मौ महाशङ्खं भीमकर्मा वृकोदरः ॥१५॥
***pāñcajanyaṁ hṛṣīkeśo devadattaṁ dhanañjayaḥ* |**
***pauṇḍraṁ dadhmau mahāśaṅkhaṁ bhīmakarmā vṛkodaraḥ* ||15||**

अनन्तविजयं राजा कुन्तीपुत्रो युधिष्ठिरः ।
नकुलः सहदेवश्च सुघोषमणिपुष्पकौ ॥१६॥
***anantavijayaṁ rājā kuntīputro yudhiṣṭhiraḥ* |**
***nakulaḥ sahadevaś ca sughoṣamaṇipuṣpakau* ||16||**

काश्यश्च परमेष्वासः शिखण्डी च महारथः ।
धृष्टद्युम्नो विराटश्च सात्यकिश्चापराजितः ॥१७॥
***kāśyaś ca parameṣvāsaḥ śikhaṇḍī ca mahārathaḥ* |**
***dhṛṣṭadyumno virāṭaś ca sātyakiś cāparājitaḥ* ||17||**

द्रुपदो द्रौपदेयाश्च सर्वशः पृथिवीपते ।
सौभद्रश्च महाबाहुः शङ्खान् दध्मुः पृथक् पृथक् ॥१८॥
***drupado draupadeyāś ca sarvaśaḥ pṛthivīpate* |**
***saubhadraś ca mahābāhuḥ śaṅkhān dadhmuḥ pṛthak pṛthak* ||18||**

Hṛṣikeśa blew the Pāñcajanya, and Dhanañjaya blew Devadatta, and Vṛkodara, the doer of terrible deeds, blew the great conch Pauṇḍra.

King Yudhiṣṭhira, son of Kuntī, blew Anantavijayam, Nakula and Sahadeva, blew Sughoṣa and Maṇipuṣpaka. The king of Kāśī, an excellent archer, Śikhaṇḍī, the mighty commander Dhṛṣṭadyumna, Virāṭa and the unconquered, Sātyaki, Drupada, the sons of Draupadī, Abhimanyu, the mighty-armed, all blew their respective conches.

These four stanzas describe the blowing of conches by Pāṇḍava army.

Hṛṣikeśa: This word refers to Kṛṣṇa. It means the one who is the lord over his mind and the senses. All his actions are righteous and according to the *śāstras*. He is not carried away by the turbulent senses.

Dhanañjaya: This word refers to Arjuna. It means a conqueror of wealth. The Pāṇḍavas were given a smaller portion of the land to rule by their uncle Dhṛtarāṣṭra. Arjuna, on behalf of his elder brother, king Yudhiṣṭhira, went round the country and won over many rulers. He expanded the kingdom by his battle skill and was given the title of Dhanañjaya.

Vṛkodara: (Bhīma) One who has a fire called Vṛka in his stomach and so can consume anything. He was once given poison by Duryodhana, but he did not die.

Pāñcajanyam: The conch of Kṛṣṇa. It was made from the bones of a demon called Pañcajana.

स घोषो धार्तराष्ट्राणां हृदयानि व्यदारयत् ।
नभश्च पृथिवीं चैव तुमुलो व्यनुनादयन् ॥१९॥

***sa ghoṣo dhārtarāṣṭrāṇāṁ hṛdayāni vyadārayat* I**
***nabhaś ca pṛthivīṁ caiva tumulo vyanunādayan* II19II**

The tumultous sounds of the Pāṇḍava army filling all sides reverberated through the earth and sky and rent the hearts of the Kauravas.

अथ व्यवस्थितान्दृष्ट्वा धार्तराष्ट्रान् कपिध्वजः ।
प्रवृत्ते शस्त्रसम्पाते धनुरुद्यम्य पाण्डवः ॥२०॥
हृषीकेशं तदा वाक्यमिदमाह महीपते ।

***atha vyavasthitān dṛṣṭvā dhārtarāṣṭrān kapidhvajaḥ* I**
***pravṛtte śastrasampāte dhanur udyamya pāṇḍavaḥ* II20II**

***hṛṣikeśaṁ tadā vākyam idam āha mahīpate* I**

Then, O Ruler of the Earth, seeing Dhṛtarāṣṭra's host being positioned and the fighting about to commence, Pāṇḍava, whose ensign badge is Hanumān, lifting his bow spoke the following words to Kṛṣṇa.

Kapidhvaja: The flag with the symbol of Hanumān on it. In *Araṇya-Parva* of *Mahābhārata,* Bhīma meets Hanumān. Hanumān gives a boon that he would be present on Arjuna's banner and help him to win the war.

It has a significant philosphical meaning. Hanumān is the symbol of *bhakti*. He is considered as *parama-bhakta*, the greatest devotee. It shows that Arjuna, in his duty while taking up the instrument of action—the bow, Gāṇḍīva, was actually first starting his journey in the battle-of-life following the path of devotion.

अर्जुन उवाच
सेनयोरुभयोर्मध्ये रथं स्थापय मेऽच्युत ।।२१।।
यावदेतान्निरीक्षेऽहं योद्धुकामानवस्थितान् ।
कैर्मया सह योद्धव्यमस्मिन् रणसमुद्यमे ।।२२।।

arjuna uvāca

***senayor ubhayor madhye rathaṁ sthāpaya me'cyuta* II21II**
***yāvad etān nirīkṣe'haṁ yoddhukāmān avasthitān* I**
***kair mayā saha yoddhavyam asmin raṇasamudyame* II22II**

Arjuna said

Place my chariot, O Acyuta, between the two armies so that I may behold the war-minded that stand here, with whom I must wage this war.

Acyuta: The one who does not fall. This refers to Kṛṣṇa. He never slips down from the state of Supreme Self.

योत्स्यमानानवेक्षेऽहं य एतेऽत्र समागताः ।
धार्तराष्ट्रस्य दुर्बुद्धेर्युद्धे प्रियचिकीर्षवः ।।२३।।

***yotsyamānān avekṣe'haṁ ya ete'tra samāgatāḥ* I**
***dhārtarāṣṭrasya durbuddher yuddhe priyacikīrṣavaḥ* II23II**

I will see these warriors assembled here for the fight, wishing to please the evil-minded Duryodhana.

On the Kaurava side there were a lot of people who should not be fighting against the Pāṇḍavas. Bhīṣma, Droṇa, Kṛpa were elders. They should not be considered as evil-minded. They felt they had a duty to fight for the Kauravas. Bhīṣma was sworn to protect the throne of Hastināpura whoever may be the king. Droṇa, and Kṛpa considered that they were employees of king Dhṛtarāṣṭra and they fought whomsoever Dhṛtarāṣṭra wanted to fight.

But Duryodhana was evil-minded and this war was unjust. Those who fight for him do not deserve any mercy from Pāṇḍavas, whatever the reason may be.

सञ्जय उवाच

एवमुक्तो हृषीकेशो गुडाकेशेन भारत ।
सेनयोरुभयोर्मध्ये स्थापयित्वा रथोत्तमम् ॥ २४॥

भीष्मद्रोणप्रमुखतः सर्वेषां च महीक्षिताम् ।
उवाच पार्थ पश्यैतान् समवेतान्कुरूनिति ॥ २५॥

sañjaya uvāca

***evam ukto hṛṣīkeśo guḍākeśena bhārata* I**
***senayor ubhayor madhye sthāpayitvā rathottamam* II24II**
***bhīṣma-droṇa-pramukhataḥ sarveṣāṁ ca mahīkṣitām* I**
***uvāca pārtha paśyaitān samavetān kurūn iti* II25II**

Sañjaya said

Thus addressed by Arjuna, Lord Kṛṣṇa placed the noble chariot in the middle of the armies, and in front of Bhīṣma, Droṇa and all the kings. He said: O Arjuna, behold the Kauravas gathered together.

These are the only words spoken by Kṛṣṇa in this chapter. Arjuna is addressed as Guḍākeśa, one who has conquered sleep. Sleep is the quality of *tamas*. While in spiritual learning the student should be constantly awake. Kṛṣṇa is teaching greater spiritual philosophy and he knew his student would understand what is taught.

Pārtha (Arjuna) is the son of Pṛthā. Pṛthā is another name for his mother Kuntī. Pārtha also closely resembles the Sanskrit word *pārthiva* which means "made of clay". Clay is perishable. Similarly, our physical body made of the five elements is perishable. We are all therefore, mortals. The *Gītā* is sung by Lord Kṛṣṇa, the immortal, to Arjuna, the mortal.

तत्रापश्यत् स्थितान् पार्थः पितॄनथ पितामहान्
आचार्यान्मातुलान्भ्रातॄन् पुत्रान्पौत्रान्सखींस्तथा ॥ २६॥
श्वशुरान् सुहृदश्चैव सेनयोरुभयोरपि ।

***tatrāpaśyat sthitān pārthaḥ pitṝn atha pitāmahān* I**
***ācāryān mātulān bhrātṝn putrān pautrān sakhīṁs tathā* II26II**
***śvaśurān suhṛdaś caiva senayor ubhayor api* I**

There, Arjuna saw father, grandfather, teachers, uncles, brothers, sons, grandsons, companions, fathers-in-law and friends in both armies.

तान् समीक्ष्य स कौन्तेयः सर्वान्बन्धूनवस्थितान् ॥२७॥
कृपया परयाऽऽविष्टो विषीदन्निदमब्रवीत् ।

***tān samīkṣya sa kaunteyaḥ sarvān bandhūn avasthitān* I**
***kṛpayā parayāviṣṭo viṣīdann idam abravīt* II27II**

Seeing all those relations, standing arrayed in the battle, Arjuna thus spoke sorrowfully, filled with deep pity.

Kṛpā means pity. Arjuna is said to be filled with sorrow and deep pity. He pitied the relations and old friends on either side who may get killed in the battle which had started because of the evil-minded Duryodhana.

Pity as such is a noble quality, but in the present situation it does not denote nobility. Kṛṣṇa had (before the war began) tried all methods of mediation to avoid the war. He failed to stop the war. Once the war started, the people on either side should not show any pity in killing the opponent, (this is specially so for the Pāṇḍavas who were following the path of *dharma).* This pity of Arjuna represents a mental weakness in him against the principle of *dharma*. Arjuna was a heroic warrior, but he began to weep as a child. This should be considered as weakness of mind, born out of ignorance. His mind needed to be cleansed of these faulty feelings and passions.

Spiritual knowledge is the only cure for this ignorance and that is what Arjuna got from his teacher, Kṛṣṇa. The first chapter, as we will see from now onwards, is the case-history of Arjuna's disease in full. It gives Arjuna's symptoms. Lord Kṛṣṇa gave him and mankind the 'Kṛṣṇa remedy', medicine in the form of *Gītopadeśam.*

अर्जुन उवाच
दृष्ट्वेमं स्वजनं कृष्ण युयुत्सुं समुपस्थितम् ॥२८॥
सीदन्ति मम गात्राणि मुखं च परिशुष्यति ।

arjuna uvāca
dṛṣṭvemaṁ svajanaṁ kṛṣṇa yuyutsuṁ samupasthitam **॥28॥**
sīdanti mama gātrāṇi mukhaṁ ca pariśuṣyati **।**

वेपथुश्च शरीरे मे रोमहर्षश्च जायते ॥२९॥
गाण्डीवं स्रंसते हस्तात्त्वक्चैव परिदह्यते ।
न च शक्नोम्यवस्थातुं भ्रमतीव च मे मनः ॥३०॥

vepathuś ca śarīre me romaharṣaś ca jāyate **॥29॥**
gāṇḍīvaṁ sraṁsate hastāt tvak caiva paridahyate **।**
na ca śaknomy avasthātuṁ bhramatīva ca me manaḥ **॥30॥**

Arjuna said:

O Kṛṣṇa, seeing these my own kinsmen gathered, eager to fight, my limbs fail, my tongue is dried up, my body trembles, my skin is burning all over and my hair stands on end, and even my mind is whirling. My Gāṇḍīva is slipping from my hand. I cannot stand up.

All these symptoms show the weakness, despair, and the sorrowful state of Arjuna's mind. This may be termed as 'anxiety-neurosis'.

Why did such a great man like Arjuna get it? One can see the preponderance of 'I'-ness here. He cries repeatedly: 'my' people, 'my' body. This is born of ignorance and the remedy should be *jñāna*—knowledge. Lord Kṛṣṇa gives him *ātma-jñāna*—knowledge of the Self.

निमित्तानि च पश्यामि विपरीतानि केशव ।
न च श्रेयोऽनुपश्यामि हत्वा स्वजनमाहवे ॥३१॥

nimittāni ca paśyāmi viparītāni keśava I
***na ca śreyo'nupaśyāmi hatvā svajanam āhave* II31II**

O Kṛṣṇa, I see many ill omens. I do not understand what good could come in killing my kinsmen in the battle.

Arjuna is in a state of hysteria. He has lost his intellectual capacity. Emotions have overtaken his capacity to analyse. He continues to use the words 'I' and 'mine' in a wrong context.

Arjuna initially went to the war with great determination. He had prepared himself to the task of fighting for *dharma*. But, suddenly his determination got weaker. His mind started ruling over his intellect. His intellect got clouded. Hence, his mind starts imagining things. When Arjuna says, he is seeing ill omens, it shows that he has become a weak-willed person and has lost his determination to fight. It is a subjective phenomenon and not objective. Because his mind is weak, his body also became weaker. The Gāṇḍīva slipped from his hand because of the weakness of his hands. Mental weakness has expressed itself as physical weakness.

न काङ्क्षे विजयं कृष्ण न च राज्यं सुखानि च ।
किं नो राज्येन गोविन्द किं भोगैर्जीवितेन वा ॥३२॥

na kāṅkṣe vijayaṁ kṛṣṇa na ca rājyaṁ sukhāni ca I
***kiṁ no rājyena govinda kiṁ bhogair jīvitena vā* II32II**

येषामर्थे काङ्क्षितं नो राज्यं भोगाः सुखानि च ।
त इमेऽवस्थिता युद्धे प्राणांस्त्यक्त्वा धनानि च ॥३३॥

yeṣām arthe kāṅkṣitaṁ no rājyaṁ bhogāḥ sukhāni ca I
***ta ime'vasthitā yuddhe prāṇāṁs tyaktvā dhanāni ca* II33II**

आचार्याः पितरः पुत्रास्तथैव च पितामहाः ।
मातुलाः श्वशुराः पौत्राः श्यालाः संबन्धिनस्तथा ॥३४॥

***ācāryāḥ pitaraḥ putrās tathaiva ca pitāmahāḥ* I**
***mātulāḥ śvaśurāḥ pautrāḥ śyālāḥ saṁbandhinas tathā* II34II**
O Kṛṣṇa, I do not desire victory or kingdom, or pleasures. Of what avail is this kingdom to us? Of what avail is the enjoyment or even life itself to us?

Those for whose sake we desire kingdom, enjoyment and pleasures stand here ready for the battle, having renounced their wealth and life.

Teachers, fathers, sons, grandfathers, maternal uncles, fathers-in-law, grandsons, brothers-in-law and other relatives.

One can see the signs of renunciation in Arjuna's mind. He is ready to receive *ātma-jñāna* medicine for his illness.

एतान्न हन्तुमिच्छामि घ्नतोऽपि मधुसूदन ।
अपि त्रैलोक्यराज्यस्य हेतोः किं नु महीकृते ॥३५॥
***etān na hantum icchāmi ghnato'pi madhusūdana* I**
***api trailokya-rājyasya hetoḥ kiṁ nu mahīkṛte* II35II**
O Madhusūdana, I do not wish to kill them, though they may kill me, even for the sake of dominion over all the three worlds, much less for a fragment of this earth.

Arjuna is trying to say that he is ready to renounce his kṣatriya (warrior) state. He, in this final great battle of *dharma*, decides that he does not want to fight at all. His ignorance shows itself here very vividly. It is philosophical truth that one's existing *vāsanā*s (mental impressions from the past) will come back at a later date if they are not burnt by proper action at the right moment.

निहत्य धार्तराष्ट्रान् नः का प्रीतिः स्याज्जनार्दन ।
पापमेवाश्रयेदस्मान् हत्वैतानाततायिनः ॥३६॥
***nihatya dhārtarāṣṭrān naḥ kā prītiḥ syāj janārdana* I**
***pāpam evāśrayed asmān hatvaitān ātatāyinaḥ* II36II**

What pleasure can be ours, O Janārdana, by killing these sons of Dhṛtarāṣṭra. Sin alone will be our gain by killing these felons.

Manu's *Dharmaśāstra* says *ātatāyī* is a felon and should be killed on the spot (whoever he may be). A felon is one who commits one of these crimes: (1) sets fire to another person's house; (2) poisons him; (3) falls on him with a sword to kill; (4) steals his wealth, or (5) land or wife. Duryodhana and associates had done not one but all these crimes.

Kṛṣṇa still has not made any remarks. He, like a good doctor, is listening to his patient's symptoms in full detail.

तस्मान्नार्हा वयं हन्तुं धार्तराष्ट्रान्स्वबान्धवान् ।
स्वजनं हि कथं हत्वा सुखिनः स्याम माधव ॥३७॥

tasmān nārhā vayaṁ hantuṁ dhārtarāṣṭrān svabāndhavān |
svajanaṁ hi kathaṁ hatvā sukhinaḥ syāma mādhava ||37||

O Mādhava, therefore we should not kill the sons of Dhṛtarāṣṭra who are our relations. How can we be happy by killing our own people?

Arjuna's 'I' and 'Myness' continues. Until this feeling goes, one cannot get Self-realisation. So long as one imagines himself to be the body and forgets his true identity with his Soul, the final truth cannot be revealed.

"What pleasure can one get by killing?" Arjuna asks. One does not work always to get pleasure. Work is a duty one does to society. Personal pleasure takes a back seat in one's duty to society, e.g., a judge passing death sentence or imprisonments all day, does not do it for his pleasure or sorrow.

यद्यप्येते न पश्यन्ति लोभोपहतचेतसः ।
कुलक्षयकृतं दोषं मित्रद्रोहे च पातकम् ॥३८॥

yady apy ete na paśyanti lobhopahatacetasaḥ |
kulakṣayakṛtaṁ doṣaṁ mitradrohe ca pātakam ||38||

कथं न ज्ञेयमस्माभिः पापादस्मान्निवर्तितुम् ।
कुलक्षयकृतं दोषं प्रपश्यद्भिर्जनार्दन ॥३९॥

***kathaṁ na jñeyam asmābhiḥ pāpād asmān nivartitum* |**
***kulakṣaya-kṛtaṁ doṣaṁ prapaśyadbhir janārdana* ||39||**

O Kṛṣṇa, though these men whose minds are overpowered by greed, see no evil in their destruction of families and the sin in hostility to friend, why do not we realise the evil of self-destruction and turn away from the path of sin?

The Hindu philosophical way of living is "active resistance to evil". If this is not followed, evil will destroy society. As a warrior, Arjuna's duty was to fight evil (even from his family members). He should not sit back nor retreat in such situations.

कुलक्षये प्रणश्यन्ति कुलधर्माः सनातनाः ।
धर्मे नष्टे कुलं कृत्स्नम् अधर्मोऽभिभवत्युत ॥४०॥

***kulakṣaye praṇaśyanti kuladharmāḥ sanātanāḥ* |**
***dharme naṣṭe kulaṁ kṛtsnam adharmo'bhibhavatyuta* ||40||**

अधर्माभिभवात् कृष्णा प्रदुष्यन्ति कुलस्त्रियः ।
स्त्रीषु दुष्टासु वार्ष्णेय जायते वर्णसङ्करः ॥४१॥

***adharmābhibhavāt kṛṣṇā praduṣyanti kula-striyaḥ* |**
***strīṣu duṣṭāsu vārṣṇeya jāyate varṇasaṅkaraḥ* ||41||**

संङ्करो नरकायैव कुलघ्नानां कुलस्य च ।
पतन्ति पितरो ह्येषां लुप्तपिण्डोदकक्रियाः ॥४२॥

***saṅkaro narakāyaiva kulaghnānāṁ kulasya ca* |**
***patanti pitaro hyeṣāṁ luptapiṇḍodakakriyāḥ* ||42||**

O Kṛṣṇa, when the family is destroyed, immemorial religious rites and rituals perish. When these perish, they fall into a state of impiety. By impiety the women of the family become corrupt, when women become corrupt, the purity of the caste is polluted by confusion and admixture. Caste pollution leads to hell for both the family and the slayers of the family, and the dead forefathers fall from the higher realms of existence, being deprived of the rites of śrāddha *and* tarpaṇa.

Cultural experiments were studies by our ancestors. They concluded that culture and tradition of each family was a unit of the total culture and integrity of the whole nation.

The caste system in the past was an intelligent division of available manpower in the community on the basis of intellectual and physical capacity of individuals. One should remember that there were no textbooks and colleges like what we have nowadays. Education was mainly for children learning the trade from their fathers.

Those intellectuals, having a passion for research, who study the scriptures, are brāhmaṇas. Those with political ambitions, and leadership quality, are kṣatriyas. Those interested in agriculture and trade are vaiśyas. The rest of the people—śūdras—do service and labour for the society.

दोषैरेतैः कुलघ्नानां वर्णसङ्करकारकैः ।
उत्साद्यन्ते जातिधर्माः कुलधर्माश्च शाश्वताः ॥४३॥
***doṣair etaiḥ kulaghnānāṁ varṇasaṅkarakārakaiḥ* I**
***utsādyante jātidharmāḥ kula-dharmāś ca śāśvatāḥ* II43II**

उत्सन्नकुलधर्माणां मनुष्याणां जनार्दन ।
नरकेऽनियतं वासो भवतीत्युनुशुश्रुम ॥४४॥

अहो बत महत् पापं कर्तुं व्यवसिता वयम् ।
यद्राज्यसुखलोभेन हन्तुं स्वजनमुद्यताः ॥४५॥
***utsannakuladharmāṇāṁ manuṣyāṇāṁ janārdana* I**
***narake'niyataṁ vāso bhavatīty anuśuśruma* II44II**
***aho bata mahat pāpaṁ kartuṁ vyavasitā vayam* I**
***yad rājyasukhalobhena hantuṁ svajanam udyatāḥ* II45II**
O Kṛṣṇa, by these evil deeds of the destroyers of the family, who can cause caste-pollution, the eternal laws of race and family perish. Men whose sacred rites and rituals are

destroyed are compelled to inherit hell for an unknown period. Thus have we heard.

Oh ! See, we have engaged in committing a heinous sin, as we are ready to kill our own kinsmen just for the sake of the pleasures of the sovereignty.

Religion in India was the spiritual culture, training for which was given in individual homes. Religious life in society comprised divine values of life in day-to-day living. Family-*dharma* means *kula-dharma* (this means rules of living). It means thinking and acting in a united, well-planned family. This made a better Āryan culture. After a war, there would be a sudden collapse of cultural values in any society.

When Arjuna says, 'men whose family-religion has broken down will go to hell', it means when unity of home-life is broken, purity of living and thought are destroyed in individual units. That generation is indirectly ordering life of hell for future generations.

यदि मामप्रतीकारम् अशस्त्रं शस्त्रपाणयः ।
धार्तराष्ट्रा रणे हन्युस्तन्मे क्षेमतरं भवेत् ॥४६॥

yadi mām apratīkāram aśastraṁ śastrapāṇayaḥ I
dhārtarāṣṭrā raṇe hanyus tan me kṣemataraṁ bhavet II46II

If the sons of Dhṛtarāṣṭra, weapons in hand, slay me in the battle, unresisting and unarmed, that would be better for me.

Arjuna uses the word *kṣema* instead of *mokṣa*. By escaping the battle, one would get physical security—*kṣema*. By fighting in the battle one would get liberation—*mokṣa*.

Arjuna thought by refusing to fight he would then not incur the sin of killing his own people. He would escape the sin of slaying families and be responsible for its evil effects described before. He also thought that it was a good act to spare the life of teachers/relations, and he would be climbing the ladder of spiritual achievement by such action.

This shows how Arjuna was eager for the fruits of action. This demoralised him. Instead, he should have followed his duty and fought the righteous war.

This great immortal universal philosophy given by Lord Kṛṣṇa was due to Arjuna's despondancy on facing the major crisis in his life. If Arjuna had fought the war bravely in the first instance or if he had decided to become a *saṁnyāsī*, we would not have had this *Gītā*. We therefore are indebted to Arjuna who asked Lord Kṛṣṇa for guidance and we hope the *Gītā* gives us similar strength to overcome the problems in our life.

सञ्जय उवाच

एवमुक्त्वाऽर्जुनः सङ्ख्ये रथोपस्थ उपाविशत् ।
विसृज्य सशरं चापं शोकसंविग्नमानसः ॥४७॥

sañjaya uvāca

***evam uktvā'rjunaḥ saṅkhye rathopastha upāviśat* I**
***visṛjya saśaraṁ cāpaṁ śokasaṁvignamānasaḥ* II47II**

Sañjaya said

Having spoken in this manner, Arjuna, distressed with sorrow, dropped his bow and arrows and sat on the seat of his chariot.

The beauty is that even though Arjuna was covered by ignorance of 'I' and 'Mine', he expressed his total grief to his teacher. He also told his teacher what he would rather do. The teacher (doctor) therefore got the full facts about his patient's weakness (symptoms). He could now take up his teaching (treatment). (The policy is "hit the iron when it is hot".)

Verses 29-46 express the mental weakness of Arjuna. These are the foundations for Kṛṣṇa's advice of *bhakti*, *jñāna* and *karma yogas*. Arjuna had fought several wars before. Why did he suddently get into such a state?

In all his previous battles, it was not a death-or-victory situation. Also, he did not see the relationship in the warriors. Arjuna suddenly felt, 'I am more than capable of killing the enemy and if I withdraw, I can save the kingdom from being ruined.' This sense of attachment is what Śrī Kṛṣṇa has tried to remove from

Arjuna's mind through the teaching of the *Gītā*. If we could drop our ego and do our worldly duties, we would be doing divine work in this universe.

As Arjuna wanted to know *dharma*, as he was confused in not knowing the right from the wrong action, and as he confided it fully to his teacher, this chapter deserves the title *arjuna-viṣāda-yoga*.

If for any reason, any man is prompted by a dispassion to worldly objects and at the same time is keen to know the truth, he would receive the grace of God.

इति श्रीमद्भगवद्गीतासूपनिषत्सु ब्रह्मविद्यायां योगशास्त्रे
श्रीकृष्णार्जुनसंवादे अर्जुनविषादयोगो नाम प्रथमोऽध्यायः ॥

***iti śrīmad-bhagavadgītāsūpaniṣatsu brahmavidyāyāṁ yogaśāstre śrīkṛṣṇārjunasaṁvāde arjunaviṣāda-yogo nāma prathamo'dhyāyaḥ* ॥**

Note : See Page 5, Addition to the second paragraph (Between 3rd & 4th line from the top).

The first two words "Dharmakṣetre and Kurukṣetre" of this verse have a subtle meaning to them. If the words are juggled around, one can read them as "Kṣetre Kṣetre Dharmam Kuru". It can then mean, "let there be adherence to Dharma in every soul." It is the only powerful tool for bringing about the "Peace and Prosperity" all round.

Another point of interest to note is the first word of the first śloka is "Dharma" and the last word of the last verse is "Mama". If we join the two together it would read as "Mama Dharma". It is "My acts of righteousness" from all the "Arjunas" of the world that would make the earth a heavenly place to live.

CHAPTER 2

SĀṀKHYA-YOGA

INTRODUCTION

Sāṁkhya-yoga is considered to be the summary of the philosophical content of the *Gītā*. The *Veda*s describe four paths to attain *mokṣa*. They are *jñāna*, *bhakti, karma* and *dhyāna*. *Veda*s are in three parts: (a) *karma-kāṇḍa,* (b) *upāsanā-kāṇḍa* and (c) *jñāna-kāṇḍa. Karma-kāṇḍa* deals with ritualistic actions which confer desired benefits on the devotee. *Upāsanā-kāṇḍa* deals with understanding the Supreme and ways of meditating on that Supreme. It makes one realise that fulfilment of desires should not be the aim of one's life. After studying and performing duties as described in *karma-kāṇḍa,* (which would purify the person), after learning the art of meditation on the Supreme, one would attain "realisation of the Supreme" and that is *jñāna-kāṇḍa*.

Unfortunately this led to various schools of thought and people got an impression that each of the four paths to perfecion was separate. Śrī Kṛṣṇa, through the *Gītā* has totally cleared this misconception and has said that all the four paths are intermingled with each other. The paths are given to help each individual so that he can take the path that suits his temperament.

Sāṁkhya is one of the six Hindu schools of philosophy and its author is sage Kapila. But, *sāṁkhya-yoga* here does not mean that. It is not a repetition of *Sāṁkhyan* philosophy but it is a word denoting "the logic of thought in a philosophy" (Swami Chinmayananda).

Sāṁkhya

Originally atheistic (*nirīśvara*), its purpose was to analyse the phenomenal world. *Sāṁkhya* distinguishes two fundametal constituents of existence:

- Spirit — *puruṣa* — Intelligence
- Matter — *prakṛti* — *jaḍa* (without life)

Prakṛti is composed of the three *guṇas: sattva, rajas* and *tamas. Saṁyoga* of the non-manifest *prakṛti* with the *puruṣa* leads to the evolution of the universe.

- *Sattva* — Light, knowledge, intellect,
- *Rajas* — Activity,
- *Tamas* — Passive, negativity.

Sāṁkhya philosophy believes that every effect is inherent in a primary cause. The *ātman* is a separate entity free from the body, ego, mind and the senses. Due to *māyā* man fails to realise this freedom and indentities with *prakṛti.* Lack of discrimination between Self and non-self is the cause of bondage. *Viveka* removes this bondage.

If viveka dawns,
In this life — *jīvanmukta*
In another life — *videhamukta*
Sam = Union, Completeness
Khyā = To be known, knowledge

Sāṁkhya means to have complete knowledge (or union with knowledge).

Sāṁkhya-yoga is concerned with the practical application of principles by which spirit becomes matter and about the means by which matter can be diverted towards spirit so as to achieve union with the spirit. The *Sāṁkhya* philosophy believes in the twenty-four *tattva*s of the evolutionary process of nature from spirit into matter and of matter getting back into a state of union with the spirit.

• [1] *Prakṛti*	Basic creative power in the field
• [2] *Mahān*	Cosmic intelligence (*citta*), individual intelligence (*buddhi*)
• [3] *Ahaṁkāra*	Egocentrism
• [4] *Manas*	Mind
• [5-9] *Jñānendriya*s	The eyes, ear, nose, tongue and skin

• [10-14] *Karmendriya*s	The hands, feet, speech, the excretory organ and the reproductory organs
• [15-19] *Tanmātrā*s	The abstract qualities of gross elements (*śabda, sparśa, rūpa, rasa, gandha*)
• [20-24] *Pañcamahābhūta*s	Space, fire, air, earth and water (the five gross elements)

From the subtle qualities of the *tanmātrā*s, *śabda*, *sparśa*, *rūpa*, *rasa*, *gandha*, the five gross matter (the *pañcamahābhūta*s) arise in solid, liquid and gaseous form. From the union of *prakṛti* (mother) with *puruṣa* (the creative power of the divine) evolves the *citta*. Inherent in this *citta* are *ahaṁkāra, buddhi* and *manas.*

The *citta* polarised by *manas* and *buddhi* gives rise to the *pañcamahābhūta*s. With the help of *guṇa*s they manifest as the *jñānendriya*s, *karmendriya*s, *tanmātrā*s and the five *prāṇa*s (*prāṇa*, *apāna*, *vyāna*, *samāna* and *udāna*).

Yoga is the union of the soul with the spirit. It is the withdrawal from the gross to the fine. In other words from consciousness from vibratory earth, vibratory water, vibratory fire, vibratory air, vibratory space, mind (*buddhi*).

It involves the dropping of the ego to enter into the *citta,* to *oṁ,* into spirit. It is initially achieved by reasoning (learning from the experiences of *dvandva*s in life). In the later stage, it is achieved by intuition and self-realisation.

Creation

Brahmā, from his mind, created Sanaka, Snandana, Sanātana, Sanatkumāra and asked them to create the universe and multiply. They refused and instead took the path to *nivṛtti.* This angered Brahmā and from this anger emerged Rudra.

Brahmā then created ten sons: Attri, Aṅgirasa, Pulastya, Pulaha, Kratu, Bhṛgu, Dakṣa, Marīci, Vasiṣṭha, Nārada. He also created: *dharma* and *adharma.*

His shadow took a form — 1st son, Kardama.
Developed four faces, i.e. the *Veda*s.
Divided the body into two.

Akūti married Ruci Prasūti married Dakṣa Devahūti married Kardama	} Their progeny is the various forms of life in this universe.

Brahmā asked Kardama to pro-create. Kardama meditated on Nārāyaṇa and as a boon asked for a perfect woman to help him pro-create. He also asked Nārāyaṇa for *mukti* after he had fulfilled his father's wish. Nārāyana asks Kardama to marry Devahūti. They then beget nine daughters who marry the nine *ṛṣi*s. In the end Nārāyaṇa is born as his son, Kapila Vāsudeva, who establishes *Sāṁkhya* or *Brahmavidyā.*

Kapila Vāsudeva preaches his mother on how the mind is the cause of bondage due to its inherent *guṇa*s.

The mind is also the route to freedom, *guṇātīta* (or *cittasamanvaya*), the first step to *mokṣa.*

Verses 11-46 in this chapter expound *sāṁkhya* philosophy. (*jñānā-yoga).* Verses 47-60 give a sketch of *karma-yoga.* Verses 61-70 give the idea on *bhakti-yoga.* Verses 71-72 indicate *saṁnyāsa-yoga.* Hence this chapter may be taken as the summary of, or an introduction to the entire *Gītā* philosophy.

The way the poet Veda Vyāsa has written the 18 chapters of the *Gītā* is perfectly systematic and orderly.

Śrī Kṛṣṇa's teaching starts from this chapter. Any good teacher will have to teach the subject to his student in a particular order. Initially he has to find out if he is a sincere student. Then he must start at the basics in that subject which is also the fundamental aspect of that subject. Later on he will go into different sections. It is similar to what a physician normally does. If a patient goes to the doctor, a good doctor is one that sits back and listens patiently to his patient's symptoms in detail. He will not interrupt his patient's description. He does get an insight into the diagnosis and thinks of methods of treatment. He will then outline to his patient what his plan of treatment will be.

It this chapter, Kṛṣṇa, having diagnosed his patient's disease, i.e., hysteria due to the ignorance of the Self, starts explaining about the Self (*ātman*) first.

Arjuna actually wants Kṛṣṇa to tell him what he has to do. He would have fought the battle if Kṛṣṇa had asked him to do so.

There are two ways of doing things. The first way is by someone telling you what to do and how to do a job. The second way is by finding out about the work, analysing it oneself and then doing it as one's intellect directs. Carrying out a job after analysing it oneself will be a better way because one would be putting more sincerity in his work. One would be answerable to one's conscience.

Anybody who is sincerely trying for spiritual progress must have belief in the *ātman*. He must believe that there is a soul in him and in all other living creatures. It is no use teaching or talking about scriptures to those who are not believers in the *ātman*. Of course a non-believer, sincerely wanting to know about *ātman* is also entitled to be told about it.

So, this chapter is in the right order. Instead of telling Arjuna to fight, instead of telling seekers in the path of liberation to do *karma-yoga*, *jñāna-yoga* etc., Śrī Kṛṣṇa, the teacher has beautifully given a description of the *ātman* (Soul).

सञ्जय उवाच
तं तथा कृपयाऽऽविष्टमश्रुपूर्णाकुलेक्षणम् ।
विषीदन्तमिदं वाक्यमुवाच मधुसूदनः ॥१॥

sañjaya uvāca
taṁ tathā kṛpayāviṣṭam aśrupūrṇākulekṣaṇam I
viṣīdantam idaṁ vākyam uvāca madhusūdanaḥ II1II

Sañjaya said

To him who was thus overwhelmed with compassion and was grieving, his eyes full of tears, Madhusūdana spoke these words.

In one simple statement Sañjaya has repeated the state of mind Arjuna was in. What was it? A state of mind overpowered by circumstances. Arjuna had nearly become a slave to the challenges of life. One should, on the contrary, be a master to the challenges of life.

Kṛpā means compassion. People who are in distress for some reason or the other usually look for compassion. Arjuna was in distress. He was not sure of what action to take. He therefore surrenders at the feet of the Lord and asks for compassion. He requests Lord Kṛṣṇa to clear his doubt.

Madhusūdana: This is another name of Śrī Kṛṣṇa. He got this name after killing the demon Madhu.

श्रीभगवानुवाच
कुतस्त्वा कश्मलमिदं विषमे समुपस्थितम् ।
अनार्यजुष्टमस्वर्ग्यम् अकीर्तिकरमर्जुन ॥२॥

śrībhagavān uvāca
kutas tvā kaśmalam idaṁ viṣame samupasthitam |
anāryajuṣṭam asvargyam akīrtikaram arjuna ||2||

The Lord said

O Arjuna! Whence is this perilous state come upon thee, this un-aryan, shameful and heaven-excluding?

Arjuna, in the beginning of the Great War, forgetting his own strength (he was the Great Archer), had dropped the Gāṇḍīva at his feet. His eyes were blurred with tears. For a kṣatriya this was an unthinkable, shameful act.

Kṛṣṇa therefore calls this state of Arjuna wretched. To bring Arjuna out of his hysterical state, the Lord had to use strong words to bring him round. (When one encounters somebody in a state of hysteria, one of the methods used to get them out of that state is by slapping that person hard.)

Śrī Kṛṣṇa says Arjuna's act is:

1. un-Āryan,
2. shameful,
3. heaven-excluding.

The word 'Āryan' has to be understood properly. Generally we use the word 'Āryan' to mean a particular race. It is not really so.

Manu-smṛti says this about Āryans:
kartavyam ācaran kāryam akartavyam anācaran ।
tiṣṭhati prakṛtācare sa ārya iti vai smṛtaḥ ॥

"Performing one's duty as per the *śāstras* and at the same time avoiding forbidden duties (as per the *śāstras*) is the way of an Ārya. Only such highly evolved, cultural men are entitled to be called Āryans."

Manusmṛti says that children born of parents who act with self-control and follow the *śāstras* are Āryans. The children born only out of lust are un-Āryans.

The *Vedas* tell us how to become and stay as Āryans. If one becomes and stays an Āryan, he is said to have understood *Vedānta*.

Śrī Kṛṣṇa does not say to Arjuna that he is not an Āryan. He said *anāryajuṣṭam*. It means "The one who does un-Āryan type of work". What was it that Arjuna did "un-Āryan like"?

Arjuna was fighting for *dharma*. His brother Yudhiṣṭhira loved peace. He decided to fight after making sure his brothers would give their full support. If Arjuna withdrew from the battle, he would have committed a sin on two grounds: (1) He would have helped *adharma* to win. The subjects of the kingdom needed a king who would follow *dharma* as dictated by the *śāstras*. (2) He would have been disloyal to his brother.

Let us take an example: Suppose we see an act of injustice going on before our own eyes. Suppose we hold a responsible position in the society. If we decide not to take any action against that act of injustice, it would be tantamount to supporting injustice. For a responsible person, in the society, an act of injustice is a sin.

Arjuna, a great warrior, should not run away from the battle. It would be like supporting *adharma*. Arjuna thinks that by not killing his family and friends, he would attain heaven. But Lord Kṛṣṇa does not agree. Lord Kṛṣṇa says that Arjuna would be subject to disgrace for his act. Arjuna may think that by killing his own people he would go to hell; but living in disgrace is worse than hell, says Lord Kṛṣṇa.

क्लैब्यं मा स्म गमः पार्थ नैतत्त्वय्युपपद्यते ।
क्षुद्रं हृदयदौर्बल्यं त्यक्त्वोत्तिष्ठ परंतप ॥३॥

klaibyaṁ mā sma gamaḥ pārtha naitat tvayy upapadyate |
kṣudraṁ hṛdaya-daurbalyaṁ tyaktvottiṣṭha parantapa ||3||

O Pārtha, do not yield to impotence. It does not befit you. Cast off this wretched weakness of heart. Arise, O scorcher of enemies.

Arjuna, was physically strong but now was mentally weak (two opposite characteristics in the same man). Hence Kṛṣṇa says, it is unmanly, throw this weakness off.

Uttiṣṭha: awake, arise till the goal is reached. This is a very strong *mantra* for those with mental weakness. This is the teaching of the *Upaniṣads*. Kṛṣṇa is asking Arjuna to stand up and do his duty.

Parantapa: scorcher of enemies. Kṛṣṇa is asking mankind to scorch the real enemies of man. Our enemies are mainly in our mind. They are sorrow and delusion. One should conquer these two to get on to the path of freedom.

Swami Vivekananda once said that the two key words in the *Gītā* are (1) *klaibyam* (wretchedness) and (2) *uttiṣṭha* (awake). They do contain the summary of the preaching of the entire *Gītā*.

There is an *Upaniṣadic* pronouncement: *nāyam ātmā balahīnena labhyaḥ*. It means "This *ātman* cannot be attained by the weak."

In the sixteenth chapter of the *Gītā*, verses 1, 2 & 3 enumerate twenty-six virtues of a person with divine qualities. The first quality is *abhayam*. One should not be frightened to follow the *śāstras*. One cannot attain peace with oneself if he acts against the principle of the *śāstras*.

The entire *Gītā* is meant to give one strength to overcome grief. Grief is a state of weakness of the mind. A man with a firm and determined mind will be strong enough to face any obstacles in his life, if he follows the *śāstra* way of life.

अर्जुन उवाच
कथं भीष्ममहं संख्ये द्रोणं च मधुसूदन ।
इषुभिः प्रतियोत्स्यामि पूजार्हावरिसूदन ॥४॥

arjuna uvāca
***kathaṁ bhīṣmam ahaṁ saṁkhye droṇaṁ ca madhusūdana* I**
***iṣubhiḥ pratiyotsyāmi pūjārhāv arisūdana* II4II**

Arjuna said

O Kṛṣṇa, Bhīṣma and Droṇa are fit to be worshipped. How shall I fight with them in the battle?

Indirectly, we can understand from this that Arjuna treated Bhīṣma and Droṇa, with the utmost respect. However, if the Pāṇḍavas were to win, these two must be killed. What Arjuna forgot was, these two are not just the persons he was supposed to fight. They were fighting under the banner of Kauravas who followed the unrighteous path. They had lost their respective names once they joined to fight for the Kauravas.

When the cause is glorious, when one follows the path of *dharma*, the names of the people in the enemy rank do not carry any meaning.

Vyāsa, in guiding generations of Hindus towards the path of 'freedom', is asking everyone to stop identifying himself with the little 'I' and 'Mine' in him. The problems of the world appear greater once this ego asserts itself.

One should discover the real identity of *ātman* or the Self which is the same in oneself and in all the creatures of this world. This is a Universal truth.

गुरूनहत्वा हि महानुभावान् श्रेयो भोक्तुं भैक्ष्यमपीह लोके ।
हत्वार्थकामांस्तु गुरूनिहैव भुञ्जीय भोगान्रुधिरप्रदिग्धान् ॥५॥

gurūn ahatvā hi mahānubhāvān
***śreyo bhoktuṁ bhaikṣyam apīha loke* I**
hatvārthakāmāṁs tu gurūn ihaiva
***bhuñjīya bhogān rudhirapradigdhān* II5II**

Better it is in this world to eat and live on the food of beggars than to kill the most noble of teachers. But if I kill them, I could enjoy only such pleasures as are stained with blood.

Arjuna had misread the situation totally and his understanding was clouded by sentiments. He was supposed to be fighting for *dharma*. Killing *adharma* was not evil. One will not get the stain of blood by killing *adharma*.

Arjuna uses the word *arthakāmān* in describing his elders. The word means wealth and desires. Arjuna says, ''Even if I consider that they are fighting for wealth and desires, they are still my respected elders and I should not be killing them''.

न चैतद्विद्मः कतरन्नो गरीयो यद्वा जयेम यदि वा नो जयेयुः।
यानेव हत्वा न जिजीविषामस्तेऽवस्थिताः प्रमुखे धार्तराष्ट्राः ॥६॥

na caitad vidmaḥ kataran no garīyo
***yad vā jayema yadi vā no jayeyuḥ* I**
yān eva hatvā na jijīviṣāmas
***te'vasthitāḥ pramukhe dhārtarāṣṭrāḥ* II6II**

I can hardly say which will be better for us, whether we should conquer them or whether they should conquer us. Those very people, sons of Dhṛtarāṣṭra, slaying whom we do not wish to live, stand facing us.

After first mentioning the names of his noblest elders, Arjuna is mentioning the rest of the Kauravas. He has come out of hysteria but is still trying to argue in his own way of thinking. He is still looking at the problem from the mental plane. What is needed was to look at it from his intellectual plane, i.e., wisdom *(jñāna)*. The worry about the fruit of action clouded the intellectual discrimination of Arjuna.

What one needs is tuning up one's mind to the right channel of discrimination and understanding. This would bring out his personality better and he can face the problems of day-to-day life and win them all. (A clear reception can be had from the radio if one tunes it to the right channel.)

कार्पण्यदोषोपहतस्वभावः पृच्छामि त्वां धर्मसंम्मूढचेताः ।
यच्छ्रेयः स्यान्निश्चितं ब्रूहि तन्मे शिष्यस्तेऽहं शाधि मां त्वां प्रपन्नम् ॥७॥

kārpaṇyadoṣopahatasvabhāvaḥ
pṛcchāmi tvāṁ dharmasammūḍhacetāḥ |
yacchreyaḥ syān niścitaṁ brūhi tan me
śiṣyas te'haṁ śādhi māṁ tvāṁ prapannam ||7||

O Kṛṣṇa, my mind is tainted with pity. I am ignorant of the right action. I am confused. I ask you to teach me what is good for me. I am your disciple, I take refuge in you.

Arjuna has now accepted his teacher's diagnosis of hysteria due to ignorance, but he also says, "I take refuge in you, I ask you to teach me what is good for me". He is also willing to get the treatment by his teacher. As Arjuna sought for light and guidance, the Lord at once took upon himself the responsibility to teach the highest wisdom.

Arjuna's mind was covered with dirt called ignorance. All of us have our minds covered with dirt. It means that our minds are pure underneath this dirt of ignorance. The attempt of religion is to give us a duster to wipe off the dirt. When Arjuna asked for guidance, his ego vanished and he became fit to receive spiritual teaching. If we have to understand the spiritual teaching of the rest of the *Gītā*, we must be prepared to kill our ego and clear the dirt of our mind. It is no use reading the scripture for the sake of reading. We should read it to understand and get the knowledge therein.

Arjuna uses the words *kārpaṇya* and *dharma*. We have discussed about *dharma* before. *Dharma* is "Law of the being".

A thing cannot be what it is without maintaining its own nature. That nature, which makes a thing what it is, is its *dharma*. For example, the *dharma* of fire is heat. Light, colour, flame are its other characters. But without heat it is not fire any more. Hence its *dharma* is heat. Our *dharma* is our true nature which is godly and our efforts in life should be to express godliness in our thoughts and actions.

Kārpaṇya means pity. *Kṛpaṇa* is one who is inclined to grieve due to self-pity. According to the *Upaniṣads*, if we do not strive for spiritual enlightenment, we are bound to grieve when we come across problems in our life. We will then be *kṛpaṇas*.

In life we strive to get or do something for two different reasons. The first reason is to get/do something which is 'good' The second is we can do or get something because it is 'pleasant'.

There is a world of difference between the two ways. Good actions, pursuit of good things make one develop divinity in oneself. We must remember that 'good' here means that which is in accordance with the *śāstras*, which have been written for the good of mankind. Eventually, good actions will lead one to the path of *mokṣa* from worldly attachments. In such situations, the good actions are for the *śreyas* (ultimate good) of the person.

If our pursuit is for things which bring pleasure, they will bind us to this life and we cannot attain *mokṣa*. Such actions are for the *preyas* of the person. Arjuna had wealth, kingdom and family which gave him pleasures of various kinds, but now, he has realised that they are of no avail.

He knows that his knowledge of the *Veda*s was insufficient and he asks for guidance from Lord Kṛṣṇa, his *sārathī*. He asks for knowledge that gives him *śreyas* which will lead him towards *mokṣa*. He does not want *preyas* which will bind him to this world and will not give him any peace of mind. Sometimes what is for our *śreyas* may not be pleasing. But, *preyas* will never be *śreyas*, e.g., the enjoyment from worldly objects can never be for our *śreyas*.

न हि प्रपश्यामि ममापनुद्याद् यच्छोकमुच्छोषणमिन्द्रियाणाम्।
अवाप्य भूमावसपत्नमृद्धं राज्यं सुराणामपि चाधिपत्यम् ॥८॥

na hi prapaśyāmi mamāpanudyād
yacchokam ucchoṣaṇam indriyāṇām ।
avāpya bhūmāv asapatnam ṛddhaṁ
rājyaṁ surāṇām api cādhipatyam ॥8॥

Even though possessing a prosperous kingdom free from rivals and holding even lordship over the Gods, I do not see that which would remove this sorrow of mine which burns up my senses.

This disease of Arjuna's mind cannot be cured by acquiring more wealth, power or fame. We can understand it better if we look for the meaning of the word *yogakṣema*.

Yoga means acquiring something. *Kṣema* means looking after what is acquired. Our entire life, unfortunately, revolves round *yoga-kṣema*. We acquire wealth, position in society etc. and we are always striving to carefully guard what we have acquired.

For Example, let us take two people who are on an overnight train. One of them has no luggage and the other person has two cases with him. The one who has no luggage can sleep without any worries. On the other hand, the second person who has his luggage will nod off to sleep but gets up several times to make sure his cases are still with him.

The first step in the spiritual path is to realise this truth. Evidently Arjuna realised this and Kṛṣṇa gave the cure. The cure being *ātma-jñāna*, knowledge of *ātman*.

सञ्जय उवाच
एवमुक्त्वा हृषीकेशं गुडाकेशः परन्तपः ।
न योत्स्य इति गोविन्दं उक्त्वा तूष्णीं बभूव ह ॥९॥

sañjaya uvāca
***evam uktvā hṛṣīkeśaṁ guḍākeśaḥ parantapaḥ* |**
***na yotsya iti govindam uktvā tūṣṇīṁ babhūva ha* ||9||**

Sañjaya said

Having spoken thus to Hṛṣikeśa, the Destroyer of Foes said to Kṛṣṇa, "I will not fight", and became silent.

Arjuna now as a good patient stops his description of symptoms. From now on whatever he says is meant to seek clarification regarding his understanding of the Lord's preaching.

Poet Vyāsa has used three words in this context which are very appropriate. One can see all through the *Gītā* that the poet has used words and names which are contextually appropriate.

1. **Hṛṣīkeśa:** it means the Lord of the senses and the mind. It refers to Kṛṣṇa.

2. **Guḍākeśa:** it means the conqueror of sleep. It refers to Arjuna.

Sleep is a *tāmasika* quality (*sattva* and *rajas* are the other two qualities of the mind). Arjuna, realising his ignorance of the *śāstras* and wanting to know what is for his *śreyas*, is correctly called Guḍākeśa. Whereas, Śrī Kṛṣṇa, the Lord incarnate, who is a *guṇātīta* is appropriately called Hṛṣīkeśa.

3. **Parantapa:** it means scorcher of enemies. It refers to Arjuna. Arjuna had in the past destroyed many enemies in the battlefield. But now, in his battle of life he has to destroy the most powerful enemy, i.e., "his ignorance of the *śāstras*". He is asking for help from his teacher to destroy his ignorance.

तमुवाच हृषीकेशः प्रहसन्निव भारत ।
सेनयोरुभयोर्मध्ये विषीदन्तमिदं वचः ॥१०॥

tam uvāca hṛṣīkeśaḥ prahasann iva bhārata |
senayor ubhayor madhye viṣīdantam idaṁ vacaḥ ||10||

O King Dhṛtarāṣṭra, seeing Arjuna lamenting in the midst of the two armies, Hṛṣīkeśa, as if smiling, spoke these words.

This is the scene of *Gītopadeśa* with which we are all familiar. There are two people who are facing each other here. One is Arjuna, who is depressed because he did not understand *dharma*. The other is Kṛṣṇa, who is the embodiment of *dharma*. He is smiling while Arjuna is crying.

Just as, for an ignorant man, a span of ground appears like an ocean—*goṣpadam sāgarāyate*—for the wise man the entire ocean appears like a small ground — *sāgaraṁ goṣpadāyate*.

The picture of *Gītopadeśam* brings this out clearly. Arjuna despondent and collapsed to the floor and Kṛṣṇa standing up smiling as if to say, "Is that all you are crying for?"

श्रीभगवानुवाच
अशोच्यानन्वशोचस्त्वं प्रज्ञावादांश्च भाषसे ।
गतासूनगतासूंश्च नानुशोचन्ति पण्डिताः ॥११॥

śrībhagavān uvāca
aśocyān anvaśocas tvaṁ prajñāvādāṁś ca bhāṣase |
gatāsūn agatāsūṁś ca nānuśocanti paṇḍitāḥ ||11||
The Lord said

You have grief for those for whom there should not be any sorrow. Yet you speak words of wisdom. The wise do not grieve for the dead or the living.

The *Gītā* so far has given us the state of Arjuna's mind. From this verse onwards starts the real teaching of the philosophy of the *Gītā*. Hence philosophers call this *śloka* '*bījamantra*'. It means it is the seed of *Gītopadeśam.*

The purpose of the *Gītā* is to help one overcome unhappiness. To overcome the grief we all have to face in our life, is the aim of the *Gītā*. Whatever happiness we get always ends in sorrow. There is no such thing as permanent happiness one can get from any objects of the world.

The first word in this verse is *aśocya*. It means, "Do not grieve".

We all have the conscience in us which is the spark of divinity. This is called variously as *ātmā*, Soul, Self etc. The *ātmā* is covered by mind, intellect, and the physical body. The physical body is made up of five gross elements (earth, air, space, fire and water). They together constitute *pañcabhūta*s. They are inert but come to life only when activated by the power of conscience (*ātman*). Mind-intellect and the body together constitute ego. The ego attaches itself to various objects of the world. It classifies objects into (*a*) those it likes; (*b*) those it does not like. Those it likes bring it a sense of happiness. When it loses contact with those it likes, it becomes unhappy.

Ātman is considered as:

sat	-	The Truth
cit	-	The Knowledge
ānanda	-	The Bliss

The truth behind every existence is *ātman*. Hence it is *sat*. *Ātman* is all-knowing. It is a witness to our bodily actions. To know and understand the nature of *ātman* means a perfect understanding of the *Veda*s. The real knowledge is knowledge of *ātman*. Hence it is known as *cit*. Knowing and understanding *ātman* brings a sense of bliss. This state is called *ānanda*. Knowing one's real identity brings great sense of happiness.

People with loss of memory go to psychiatrists to cure themselves. When they regain their memory they are very happy. We all have lost our memory. We have forgotten who we are. But, we give a name for our physical form, We call it *nāma* (name) and *rūpa* (form).

In sum we are:

sat *cit* *ānanda*	*Ātman* (real)
nāma *rūpa*	Body (unreal)

One should not grieve for changes in *nāma* and *rūpa* due to physical death of the body.

Arjuna did not want to kill his own people. He did not want his elders to die. He did not think that he would enjoy the kingdom obtained by killing so many of his own people.

First of all, it is only death of the body and not *ātmā*. Hence, Śrī Kṛṣṇa says, "Do not grieve for the dead."

Secondly, Arjuna's words of sorrow were not those of a man of wisdom. Arjuna had learnt *Veda*s and was considered as a wise man. A real wise man is one who should not grieve over the death of the physical body.

The Lord uses the word *paṇḍita* in this verse. We all consider men of knowledge as *paṇḍita*s. But according to Lord Kṛṣṇa, a *paṇḍita* is one who knows his true identity and has understood the meaning of the *Veda*s i.e., *tat tvam asi* (Thou art That). The person who has understood the real nature of the *ātman* is a *paṇḍita*.

The purpose of the teaching of the *Gītā* is to enable the person to attain union of the ego with the *ātman*. This is called *yoga*.

Kṛṣṇa is called Yogeśvara. He is the Lord of Yoga. The first step in *yoga* is harmony in thought, word and deed. Arjuna, unfortunately, had failed in his first step. He wanted to attain *mokṣa* and talked of the *Veda*s. But he had dropped his weapon of action and wanted to become a *saṁnyāsī*.

Ramakrishna Paramahamsa says: ''Do not create conflict between word and deed as nothing good comes out of it.''

न त्वेवाहं जातु नासं न त्वं नेमे जनाधिपाः ।
न चैव न भविष्यामः सर्वे वयमतः परम् ॥१२॥

***na tvevāhaṁ jātu nāsaṁ na tvaṁ ne'me janādhipāḥ* I**
***na caiva na bhaviṣyāmaḥ sarve vayam ataḥ param* II12II**

It is not that at any time indeed was I not, nor you, nor these rulers of men. Nor shall we all ever cease to be hereafter.

The Self or the *ātman* inside us is on a pilgrimage to merge into its original *Paramātmā*-state. In its journey on each birth, it gets attached to the physical body and becomes ego. It identifies itself in that birth as a separate individual. It also identifies itself with others as ''my people, my wife, my children, my enemies'' etc. When a beloved person dies, the ego thinks that it is the end of his beloved.

In truth, the *ātman* remains as witness to all our bodily changes. Egotistic desires leave an imprint on one's mind and they are called *vāsanā*s. They act as impurities and hinder the progress of *ātmā* in its journey to reach *Paramātmā*.

On the physical death of a name and form, that person's *ātmā* collects the subtle body and departs. The subtle body consists of the mind and the intellect. The subtle body keeps its unfulfilled desires (*vāsanā*s). The *ātman,* to fulfil the subtle body's desires, will find a new suitable environment. It finds a new set of *pañcabhūta*s and starts a new life. Unfortunately, by developing contact with the mind and intellect of the new form, it becomes ego again and forgets the past.

All the warriors who faced Arjuna did not come from nowhere. They will not disappear into nowhere after their death. This is true of Arjuna also. They were alive before the present birth and they will be reborn after their death. Birth and death take place due to *vāsanās*. *Vāsanās* do not let the *ātmā* free.

This is according to Hindu philosophy the re-incarnation theory. The Soul is immortal. The Soul is part of the Supreme Soul, i.e., God. All Souls merge back into the Supreme Soul.

The *Vedas* teach the great truth, viz., *tat tvam asi*. This is called a *mahāvākya*.

TAT	means	That
TVAM	means	Thou
ASI	means	Art

THOU ART THAT

'That' is the Lord, *Paramatmā*.
'*Tvam*' is the individual *ātmā* (not body).

As each *ātmā* comes as part of *Paramātmā* and merges back into *Paramātmā*, *ātmā* is nothing but *Paramātmā*. It becomes *Paramātmā* when it loses its ego. As the entire universe is the varied manifestation of *Paramātmā*, one should consider the universe as 'one'.

In our physical body, hands, feet and legs are different entities but are part of our body. They are all one.

This is the *advaita* Philosophy of the *Gītā*. This is called *brahma-jñāna*.

देहिनोऽस्मिन्यथा देहे कौमारं यौवनं जरा ।
तथा देहान्तरप्राप्तिर्धीरस्तत्र न मुह्यति ॥१३॥

dehino'smin yathā dehe kaumāraṁ yauvanaṁ jarā |
tathā dehāntaraprāptir dhīras tatra na muhyati ||13||

Just as man in this body passes through the various stages of boyhood, youth and old age, likewise he passes through another body after death. The wise man does not grieve at it.

Really speaking, we say all the time 'the past is dead' but do not really understand what we really mean. We are saying the truth without grasping its meaning.

The minute that is gone just now is dead. We cannot get it back. Similarly, we go through the developmental stages in this life. One stage dies and gradually merges into another stage without our recognising it.

The newborn baby is called a child, youth, adult, etc. in various stages of its development. The entity that experiences all these changes is the same. This entity is the *ātman* inside. One can say that the 'energy' behind that baby's modifications will be the same all through the modifications.

For example, we all have left behind our family and friends in India (or some other place). Suppose we see them after ten years. Some of those that we meet, have changed physically and we see a new person in them and do not recognise the old person. Similarly, a man of knowledge, should recognise the same soul inside all names and forms. Such a person will not grieve.

The Law of memory is that the experiencer and memoriser must be the same entity. I can remember my experiences only. I can remember my experiences of childhood and youth, when I reach my old age even though my childhood and youth have died to bring me to old age.

Similarly, my soul remembers the experiences (ego, *vāsanā*s) of the past and carries them even after my death till it gets purified. Just as I do not cry that my childhood is dead, my soul does not cry when my body dies a physical death. If one understands this, there should not be any grief for the dead.

The Lord calls that person a *dhīra* who does not grieve at any modifications of the physical body including death of the physical body. *Dhīra* is one who is firmly convinced of the knowledge he has attained. 'No physical body is immortal', is the basic law.

मात्रास्पर्शास्तु कौन्तेय शीतोष्णसुखदुःखदाः ।
आगमापायिनोऽनित्यास्तांस्तितिक्षस्व भारत ॥१४॥

mātrāsparśās tu kaunteya śītoṣṇa-sukha-duḥkhadāḥ |
āgamāpāyino'nityās tāṁs titikṣasva bhārata ||14||

The contact of senses with objects produce heat and cold, pain and pleasure. Those experiences come and go and are impermanent. Endure them, O Arjuna.

The pleasures experienced by the senses are not pure pleasures. They may last a few seconds—a few hours—a few days—a few months. Pleasure gradually decreases in intensity and disappears. It gets mixed with pain. Pleasure is only a state of the mind. Pure pleasure — bliss or *ānanda* will not have any pain before or afterwards. A certain thing can cause pain or pleasure in different circumstances. Pain and pleasure are different sides of the same coin and are termed as *dvandvas*.

Śrī Kṛṣṇa uses the word *mātrāsparśāḥ. Mātrāsparśa* means contact of the senses with the objects. Pleasures and pains are not commodities one can get from outside. They are the experiences at our mental level born out of union of objects with the senses.

Sound, taste, touch, smell and form are called *tanmātrās*. Ears, tongue, skin, nose and eyes respectively perceive these *tanmātrās*. The mind reacts to the contact between the two, as pleasure or pain. We feel happiness or sorrow depending on our mental reaction to the impulses received. There is another reaction which we do not usually recognise. The mind does not register the contact at all. In our day-to-day life, we come across a number of situations wherein our mind does not register the contact of sense-objects with the sense-organs. The ears will continue to receive the sound-waves from the space. But we do not hear everything. When we are fast asleep, our mind does not register the disturbances outside.

Pleasure at birth has to be mixed with sorrow at death of any person. There cannot be birth without death. Pleasures come and get felt because of attachment to objects. So, one should learn not to get attached. Our duty is to seek for truth in the midst of changes and reach the truth *(mokṣa)*.

So Kṛṣṇa says *titikṣasva*— 'endure'. It is the greatest medicine at the spiritual level. Be equal-minded in pain and pleasure is the Lord's advice to mankind. The external objects can convey their stimuli and give us experience only when our minds get attached to those contacts. Wise men should develop the attitude that 'even this will pass away' in course of time.

यं हि न व्यथयन्त्येते पुरुषं पुरुषर्षभ ।
समदुःखसुखं धीरं सोऽमृतत्वाय कल्पते ॥१५॥

***yaṁ hi na vyathayantyete puruṣaṁ puruṣarṣabha* I**
***sama-duḥkha-sukhaṁ dhīraṁ so'mṛtatvāya kalpate* II15II**

The firm man who is not affected by pain and pleasure, who remains equal-minded, is fit for immortality, O Arjuna, chief of mortals.

Immortality: State of deathlessness. This is a wide term and incorporates (a) destruction of body, (b) destruction at body/mind/intellectual level. To explain further:

(a) Destruction of body: One should start by asking 'What is the body?' Most of us consider that the physical body is real. Because we fail to realise that 'soul' is the real body and the physical body is a suit on the soul. Due to ego, we consider the outer the suit, as soul.

In other words, for a realised person, soul is the body and that is deathless.

(b) Deathless state of experiences: Any experience at physical, mental, and/or intellectual level gives an ordinary man a feeling of happiness or grief depending upon the circumstances. But these reactions are not permanent. They are short-lived. A realised person is one who is aware of this impermanency of the result of reaction to experiences, and who does not get elated or depressed, i.e., one who develops equanimity. He has transcended the level of reaction to experience and reached the intellectual plane.

An immortal is one who knows that the soul is deathless and is equal-minded in enduring all the pin-pricks of life's experiences.

If I get fired by the idea intellectually that I want to realise the Self, then I should be willing to endure or ignore comforts and pleasures at body and mind level. This should give me satisfaction of achieving something.

This state of happiness achieved is real *mokṣa.*

We all know that in our life we have to deserve to get what we want. It is no use saying, "I want such and such a thing". A student will not pass his exams merely because he has a desire to pass the exams. To deserve to pass, he must have been attentive in the classes, should have clarified his doubts from his teacher, referred to books of knowledge and worked hard all through his studies.

If we have to attain *mokṣa,* we must therefore deserve to get the first step. The Lord says that in the path to *mokṣa* the first step is to learn to bear equally pleasures and pains from contact with the outside world. We must be *dhīra*s, we must travel with firm determination in our path and face the obstacles bravely and not fall into nature's trap.

नासतो विद्यते भावो नाभावो विद्यते सतः ।
उभयोरपि दृष्टोऽन्तस्त्वनयोस्तत्त्वदर्शिभिः ॥१६॥

nāsato vidyate bhāvo nābhāvo vidyate sataḥ |
ubhayor api dṛṣṭo 'ntas tvanayos tattvadarśibhiḥ ||16||

The unreal has no being. The Real has no non-being. The final truth of these two has been seen indeed by those who have experienced the essence of things.

Continuing the theme of the last *śloka*, the Lord explains the outlook of the person who has realised the state of *ānanda* (*mokṣa).* Such a person looks upon the Self in him and all others as the real being.

The body and the world are subject to destruction and so they are not the truth, i.e., they are non-existent. Even if it appears as real, it is a mirage only. *Ātmā* is real. It was there in the past, it is there in the present and it will be there in the future.

For the ignorant, body and world are real and they deny the real (*ātman*). If one denies the existence of *ātman* that error is called *asaṁbhāvanā*. If one then asserts that the body and the world are real, that error is *viparīta-bhāvanā*.

Unreal is the one that was not in the past, that will not be in the future but seemingly exists in the present, i.e., physical body. This unreal has therefore been said to 'have no being'. The real is that which remains the same in all periods of time, past, present and future. So that real is said to "have no non-being".

The body, mind, intellect are ever-changing in us and so are unreal. But for these changes to take place, there should be a substratum.

When we go to the cinema, we see the continuous process of events on the screen. The screen was there before the film started, was there when the film was on (but not realised by us as we got immersed in the experience of the film) and will be there when the film is finished (we will not take notice of it and move out).

That substratum can be nothing other than *ātman* in us (pure consciousness). Experiences of childhood, youth and old age get illuminated on top of this consciousness and die away. This pure consciousness, unborn and undying is the one changeless factor, the infinite in us and this *ātman* is real. This is understood only by the realised ones (Men of Knowledge). *Tattva-darśana* means seeing into the real nature of things.

अविनाशि तु तद्विद्धि येन सर्वमिदं ततम् ।
विनाशमव्ययस्यास्य न कश्चित्कर्तुमर्हति ॥१७॥

***avināśi tu tad viddhi yena sarvam idaṁ tatam* |**
***vināśam avyayasyāsya na kaścit kartum arhati* ||17||**

Know that ātman *by which this whole universe is pervaded is indestructible. No one can cause destruction of 'That', the imperishable.*

Out of clay one can make a number of pots. The pots can be destroyed but the clay cannot be destroyed. This is the example one can give to explain the indestructivity of the *ātman*. Kṛṣṇa is telling us 'That *ātman*' is therefore indestructible. We can understand this by looking at an example: We all agree that we can destroy the various manifestations of electricity like bulbs of different forms but we cannot destroy the electricity behind the functioning of the bulbs.

> अन्तवन्त इमे देहा नित्यस्योक्ताः शरीरिणः ।
> अनाशिनोऽप्रमेयस्य तस्माद्युध्यस्व भारत ॥१८॥
>
> ***antavanta ime dehā nityasyoktāḥ śarīriṇaḥ* I**
> ***anāśino'prameyasya tasmād yudhyasva bhārata* II18II**
>
> *These bodies of the embodied Self, they are subject to destruction. The Self is eternal, indestructible, incomprehensible. Therefore, fight, O Arjuna.*

The *ātmā* is said to be incomprehensible. Why?

It is above the plane of body/mind/intellect. If it were in any of these planes, one could have described its physical structure, i.e., colour, height, etc. It is something which has to be realised by transcending the three planes of existence. To realise is to get absorbed in it and become one with it. That state where one says: "He entered into God", is the state of liberation — *mokṣa*.

Let us take an example. We all know that space is eternal. It was there yesterday, it is there today and will be there tomorrow. We can enclose the space by building houses. As soon as the building is destroyed, the enclosed space merges with the open space. One cannot destroy space at any time.

If one realises the truth that he is the *ātmā*, the same *ātmā* is in everybody and the physical body is just a suit on *ātmā* of all (conscious of universal *ātmā*) then one should carry out one's duty and fight the battle of life.

Here, Arjuna is asked to fight. Arjuna felt he could not kill the elders and members of his family and friends. Kṛṣṇa is asking Arjuna to look at it from a different plane. By killing others in the battle, he is only removing the suit over the real body and the real body does not get killed.

> य एनं वेत्ति हन्तारं यश्चैनं मन्यते हतम् ।
> उभौ तौ न विजानीतो नायं हन्ति न हन्यते ॥१९॥

***ya enaṁ vetti hantāraṁ yaś cai'naṁ manyate hatam* I**
***ubhau tau na vijānīto nāyaṁ hanti na hanyate* II19II**

He who thinks that Self is the slayer, or who thinks that Self is slain, both of these do not know the truth. Self, ātmā, *does not slay nor is slain.*

The *ātmā* which is inside us remains a witness to all our physical actions. During the battle, Arjuna will be killing so many soldiers. His *ātmā* is not the one that would be killing the soldiers. It is only the physical body of Arjuna that would kill the soldiers. Arjuna would be killing the name and form of the soldiers only. The *ātman* inside the soldier does not get killed.

If Arjuna thought that *ātman* inside him is the killer and if Arjuna thought that the *ātman* of the soldiers got killed by him, he would be wrong on both counts. Similarly, if we feel that our *ātman* does kill others or we kill the *ātman* in others, we are wrong on both counts. *Ātmā* is only a witness to all our bodily actions. (Of course, it does not mean that we can go and kill or injure anybody. This has been described later in the *Gītā*. We all have to work according to the *śāstras*).

There is a verse in *Kaṭhopaniṣad* similar to this verse.

न जायते म्रियते वा कदाचिन्नायं भूत्वा भविता वा न भूयः ।
अजो नित्यः शाश्वतोऽयं पुराणो न हन्यते हन्यमाने शरीरे ॥२०॥

na jāyate mriyate vā kadācin
***nāyaṁ bhūtvā bhavitā vā na bhūyaḥ* I**
ajo nityaḥ śāśvato'yaṁ purāṇo
***na hanyate hanyamāne śarīre* II20II**

It is not born, nor does it die. After having been, it does not cease to be; unborn, eternal, changeless and ancient. It is not killed when the body is destroyed.

Changes in the physical body are common to all, i.e., birth, existence, growth, disease, decay and death. Six modifications are attributed to the physical body; they are:

(*a*)	*jāyate*	-	is born
(*b*)	*asti*	-	exists
(*c*)	*vardhate*	-	grows
(*d*)	*pariṇamate*	-	changes, modifies
(*e*)	*apakṣīyate*	-	wears (as in wear & tear)
(*f*)	*vinaśyati*	-	is destroyed.

These do not apply to the *ātman*.

Self is unborn. Why? After physical death, the subtle body moves out to find another medium to re-establish itself. When it gets re-established another life starts but the Self is the same. It did not die and so was not born anew again. It only changed its physical covering.

As it was in the past, in the past of the past and so on and so on, the Self is ancient. As it will go on, and remain in the future, it is eternal. It does not change from youth to adult, from adult to old age and hence it is changeless. So it does not get killed when the body is destroyed.

वेदाविनाशिनं नित्यम् य एनमजमव्ययम् ।
कथं स पुरुषः पार्थ कं घातयति हन्ति कम् ॥२१॥

***vedāvināśinaṁ nityaṁ ya enam ajam avyayam* I**
***kathaṁ sa puruṣaḥ pārtha kaṁ ghātayati hanti kam* II21II**

O Arjuna, he who knows that ātmā *is birthless, real and imperishable, whom can he slay or cause to be slain?*

Kṛṣṇa wants Arjuna to remember the true nature of the *ātman*. *Ātman* is the constant factor present in all modifications of the body.

We go through various stages in our life—birth, childhood, teenage, adult, middle-age, old age, death. All these take place over the ever-changeless substratum of the *Ātman*. *Ātman*, the energy, the spark of life does not undergo any modifications. *Ātman* therefore cannot kill others nor can it be killed.

The Lord uses the word 'slain' so often. This is because of the context of the war Arjuna was in. In war, people get killed or kill others.

Any other modifications like disease, injury, also does not affect the *ātman*.

वासांसि जीर्णानि यथा विहाय नवानि गृह्णाति नरोऽपराणि ।
तथा शरीराणि विहाय जीर्णान्यन्यानि संयाति नवानि देही ॥२२॥

***vāsāṁsi jīrṇāni yathā vihāya navāni gṛhṇāti naro'parāṇi* I**
***tathā śarīrāṇi vihāya jīrṇāny anyāni saṁyāti navāni dehī* II22II**

Just as a man casts off his worn out clothes and puts on new ones, so also the Self throws away its worn out bodies and takes other fresh bodies.

Self, pure energy, gets to project into the outer world by using the physical matter of five elements earth, water, air,space, fire, called *pañcabhūta*s. At the end it casts off the five elements and goes out and then finds a new set of five elements again.

The plural word 'bodies' is used to indicate that it goes through several bodies birth after birth (so long as one is ignorant of the real Self).

A *jñānī* is not frightened of his death. He knows one day or the other he has to die. Similarly he is not frightened of the death of his beloved ones. On the other hand, the word death would bring pain and sorrow to the ignorant (ignorant of the existence of the *ātmā*). Evolution is therefore a phenomenon for the physical body, mind, intellect and is not for the Self.

नैनं छिन्दन्ति शस्त्राणि नैनं दहति पावकः ।
न चैनं क्लेदयन्त्यापो न शोषयति मारुतः ॥२३॥

***nainaṁ chindanti śastrāṇi nainaṁ dahati pāvakaḥ* I**
***na cainaṁ kledayanty āpo na śoṣayati mārutaḥ* II23II**

Weapons cannot cut, fire cannot burn, water cannot wet, wind cannot dry, this ātmā.

One can easily understand this if he has understood the earlier stanzas. *Ātmā,* pure Self, is subtlest of all. Can any body cut the air?

The five natural elements are: (1) earth, (2) air, (3) space, (4) fire, (5) water. Of these, space is not included in this verse. This is because the space is actionless. *Ātman* is subtler than space and hence it is also known as *cidākāśa*. Weapons are made of different constituents in the earth, weapon in this context means 'the earth'.

(Suppose we burn some wood in a room, the smoke that comes off might stain the wall but it does not affect the space—Sri Ramakrishna.)

When a thing is not seen, it is explained in terms of the seen so that one can understand it. Still one cannot see the unseen. As it is so subtle, when you throw water at it, water does not wet it. Water can wet things which have a form. *Ātmā* has no form and hence cannot get wet.

अच्छेद्योऽयमदाह्योऽयमक्लेद्योऽशोष्य एव च ।
नित्यः सर्वगतः स्थाणुरचलोऽयं सनातनः ॥२४॥

***acchedyo'yam adāhyo'yam akledyo'śoṣya eva ca* I**
***nityaḥ sarvagataḥ sthāṇur acalo'yaṁ sanātanaḥ* II24II**

The Self cannot be cut, nor burnt, nor moistened, nor dried up. It is eternal, all-pervading, stable, immovable and ancient.

It has a similar meaning as the last stanza. Self is not a composition of elements. Self is beyond time and place. It means it is eternal (*nitya*) and all-pervading (*sarvagataḥ*). Self is therefore not destroyed by time. If one can understand this, one will naturally develop universal love for all because the Self in him is the same as in others. It is formless, changeless (*sthāṇu*) subtle and not affected by elements.

The comparison of the film on the screen in a theatre can be applied to this verse. Many events like flooding, bombing, murder can take place in a film and films can change but the screen will be the same under all circumstances.

It is Existence	—	Truth, sat
It is Light		*cit*
It is Bliss		*ānanda*

The Truth is Eternal	—	*nityaḥ*
All-pervading	—	*sarvagataḥ*
Stable	—	*sthāṇuḥ*
Firm	—	*acalaḥ*
Ancient	—	*sanātanaḥ*

It is stable and firm because one cannot shift it from place to place as it has no form.

Self is not conditioned by time - it has no past, present and future because these three can be applied in relation to the time of its existence. If a thing has had a definite span of time, then you apply past and future to that span of time. Self, (truth, *ātmā*) is there all the time. Hence it is called ancient.

अव्यक्तोऽयमचिन्त्योऽयमविकार्योऽयमुच्यते ।
तस्मादेवं विदित्वैनं नानुशोचितुमर्हसि ॥२५॥

avyakto'yam acintyo'yam avikāryo'yam ucyate |
tasmād evaṁ viditvainaṁ nānuśocitum arhasi ||25||

The Self is unknowable by the senses, unthinkable by the mind and is not subject to any kind of change. Knowing this, you should not grieve.

When one can see, hear, touch, smell or taste, then it is said to be in a manifest form. These five great elements themselves become subtler to our perception as they go from earth to space. One can certainly feel and see the earth but space, one cannot see or feel. In this sense, space is almost unmanifest. The one beyond the five sense-organs is really the unmanifest, e.g., mango tree in a mango seed is in an unmanifest form.

Similarly, the truth (Self) is unmanifested and sense-organs cannot detect it.

This is the physical side of the explanation (unknowable by the senses).

The next plane is the mental level. The mind can only analyse what is brought to it by the sense-organs. If it is not perceived physically by the sense-organs, one has to conclude that it is unthinkable. The mind is powerless to know it. Similarly the intellect cannot comprehend it.

What then is the conclusion. When the mind is purified it merges in *ātmā*. It becomes one with *ātmā*. This is what one means when he says—so and so entered into God. Soul purified merges with the Universal Soul.

Soul is the eternal witness to this universe. Ultimately the universe dissolves into *ātmā* and *ātmā* remains alone.

Avikārya: It means unchangeable. The physical body undergoes modifications but the *ātman* does not.

"You should not grieve", is what Kṛṣṇa says. What makes one sorrowful? Disease, death, parting from beloved ones, losing a possession etc. If we have understood what we have read so far, should we be grieving? If we do, we have identified ourselves with the body—*dehadṛṣṭi*. If we go into a higher plane—*ātmadṛṣṭi*, we will then realise that the Soul is not affected by any of these.

So *śoka* (grief) is a direct consequence of ignorance of our real nature. Arjuna had the same disease. He was sorrowful because he thought a war would bring death to lots of people including the respected and beloved ones.

This sorrow evaporates on acquiring *jñāna* (knowledge) which has to be achieved by the study of *śāstra*s, by the grace of the teacher and of God. Realisation of Self would kill the evils of *śoka* and *moha*. Hence Kṛṣṇa has in this chapter so far emphasised on the *ātmā*.

Arjuna was not an illiterate. He had studied scriptures under a *guru* but had not understood it when it was taught (he was not ready to grasp it). The iron was not hot, as one says. He was trained to fight because he was a kṣatriya.

But during the war, facing the enemy, he suddenly got the feeling of the worst calamity that would follow and this total despair gave him the capacity to understand what was taught by Kṛṣṇa.

A patient can understand the benefit obtained by medical treatment better than an ordinary, physically fit person.

If Kṛṣṇa had explained this *Gītā* to Arjuna at any other time Arjuna might not have understood it. So Kṛṣṇa in this chapter, immediately after Arjuna's grief, is talking about *ātmā*.

अथ चैनं नित्यजातं नित्यं वा मन्यसे मृतम् ।
तथापि त्वं महाबाहो नैनं शोचितुमर्हसि ॥२६॥

***atha cainaṁ nityajātaṁ nityaṁ vā manyase mṛtam* I**
***tathā'pi tvaṁ mahābāho nainaṁ śocitum arhasi* II26II**

O mighty-armed, even if you think of Him as being constantly born, constantly dying, even then you should not grieve.

When Kṛṣṇa says 'mighty-armed' of Arjuna, he is both praising and ridiculing him. He is praising him by saying, "you have killed so many brave warriors before and surely you will kill many enemy forces now".

He is ridiculing him by saying, "What is the use of your physical strength? Develop mental courage and overcome this ignorance, get spiritual light and knowledge to fight the enemy within you."

जातस्य हि ध्रुवो मृत्युर्ध्रुवं जन्म मृतस्य च ।
तस्मादपरिहार्येऽर्थे न त्वं शोचितुमर्हसि ॥२७॥

***jātasya hi dhruvo mṛtyur dhruvaṁ janma mṛtasya ca* I**
***tasmād aparihārye'rthe na tvaṁ śocitum arhasi* II27II**

For certain is death to the born and certain is birth for the dead. Therefore you should not grieve about this inevitable.

This is an argument from the materialistic view. The materialists do not believe in *ātmā*. They believe that life arises from nowhere and disappears to nowhere. They also believe that what is born has to die.

Arjuna was taught in his *gurukula* that there is birth after death; Kṛṣṇa is asserting the same truth. "Even if you do not know the *ātmā*, the process of birth and death is the same; so do not grieve" — says Kṛṣṇa.

अव्यक्तादीनि भूतानि व्यक्तमध्यानि भारत ।
अव्यक्तनिधनान्येव तत्र का परिदेवना ॥२८॥

avyaktādīni bhūtāni vyakta-madhyāni bhārata I
avyakta-nidhanāny eva tatra kā paridevanā II28II

O Arjuna, beings are of unknown origin, known middle and of unknown end. Why then lament for it?

Kṛṣṇa says: What was not before and what does not exist hereafter, cannot be real, and take it therefore as non-existent.

The present life is like a bubble in the ocean. The bubble has a short span of life. It emerges from the water, appears for a short while and merges back into the water. During its short stay, it moves with other bubbles and waves of the ocean. Various bubbles burst and merge in water at different times.

We can consider the single bubble to be ourselves and other bubbles and waves to be family and friends and the entire universe of manifest object.

I dreamt while in sleep and then woke up. In the dream I was a millionnaire and lost everything. On waking up I realised I was not a millionnaire and I did not lose anything. I therefore felt contented.

Similarly, in our life, the universe is an illusion, it is a dreamstate because of the projection of Self via mind/intellect. On knowing *ātmā*, the illusion disappears and the man is said to be awakened, to be a new spiritual man.

आश्चर्यवत्पश्यति कश्चिदेनं आश्चर्यवद्वदति तथैव चान्यः ।
आश्चर्यवच्चैनमन्यः शृणोति श्रुत्वाप्येनं वेद न चैव कश्चित् ॥२९॥

āścaryavat paśyati kaścid enam
āścaryavad vadati tathaiva cānyaḥ I
āścaryavac cainam anyaḥ śṛṇoti
śrutvāpyenaṁ veda na caiva kaścit II29II

One sees this as a wonder, another speaks of it as a wonder, another hears of it as a wonder, yet having heard, none understands this at all.

There are many who have read or heard of the Self through reading or listening, but still they do not understand. They just feel wonder and nothing more. Very rarely one can find a person who has understood it. It does not mean that a spiritual seeker should despair. The seeker has to undergo the process of purification, may be several births to realise the truth.

By our ignorance, we think that the truth is something far away for us to reach. But the truth is in us. We forget we have not cleansed ourselves of our ignorance. This process of cleansing to remove ignorance is called spiritual practice. Practised constantly it is just like cleaning the mirror (polishing it to see a beautiful reflection of oneself).

Man awakened to the Self's glory is 'God'. One can say that God forgetful of his own glory is "the deluded man". This is so when we forget that our *ātman* is real but consider this physical body to be real.

देही नित्यमवध्योऽयं देहे सर्वस्य भारत ।
तस्मात्सर्वाणि भूतानि न त्वं शोचितुमर्हसि ॥३०॥

dehī nityam avadhyo'yaṁ dehe sarvasya bhārata |
tasmāt sarvāṇi bhūtāni na tvaṁ śocitum arhasi ||30||

This Self existing in the body of all beings is never killed. You should therefore not grieve for any creature, O Bhārata.

Dehī : This word refers to the *ātman* encased in the physical body.

Bhārata : It means Lover of Light. Light is knowledge of Self. Anyone who loves this *ātmā*, (knowledge of Self) is then fit to be called Bhārata.

This verse is the summary of Kṛṣṇa's description so far of *ātmā*'s immortality. Arjuna is therefore asked not to identify the *nāma, rūpa* of people in the war but see *sat, cit, ānanda* behind everyone. *Sat, cit, ānanda* or *ātmā* never dies and so no need to grieve on the death of *nāma* and *rūpa*.

स्वधर्ममपि चावेक्ष्य न विकम्पितुमर्हसि ।
धर्म्याद्धि युद्धाच्छ्रेयोऽन्यत्क्षत्रियस्य न विद्यते ॥३१॥

svadharmam api cāvekṣya na vikampitum arhasi |
dharmyād hi yuddhāc chreyo'nyat kṣatriyasya na vidyate ||31||

And moreover, looking at your own duty you should not waver, for there is nothing higher for a kṣatriya than a righteous war.

Lord Kṛṣṇa now is focusing on the duty of an individual. Every individual has to work according to the law of nature. No one can stay without doing some work or other. Even to keep the minimum requirements of the body one has to work.

In *karmayoga* and *karmasaṁnyāsa-yoga*, Kṛṣṇa elaborates on the theme of *karma*. He is strongly reminding Arjuna that it is a kṣatriya's duty to fight an agressor. The Kauravas were aggressors and were not also righteous. Arjuna is not fighting any names and forms here. He is only fighting aggressors. He will fail in his duty if he does not fight to defend his sacred culture (*dharma*).

Arjuna had asked the question before: *yacchreyaḥ syānniścitaṁ brūhi tanme* ("tell me that, which is definitely for my *śreyas*").

Holding on to one's *dharma* is a sure means of gaining *śreyas*. Our *dharma* is that duty which is best suited to our temperament which is due to our existing *vāsanā*s. We have to burn all our existing *vāsanā*s, if we have to attain *mokṣa*. (This theme is described later in the *Gītā*.)

यदृच्छया चोपपन्नं स्वर्गद्वारमपावृतम् ।
सुखिनः क्षत्रियाः पार्थ लभन्ते युद्धमीदृशम् ॥३२॥

yadṛcchayā copapannaṁ svargadvāram apāvṛtam |
sukhinaḥ kṣatriyāḥ pārtha labhante yuddham īdṛśam ||32||

For a kṣatriya, O Pārtha, a righteous war of this type which has come of itself, is the open gateway to heaven.

Every kṣatriya is born to defend his king and kingdom and he gets an opportunity ever so often to do so. Even now, every soldier who joins the army is dedicated to defend his country. In olden days when areas of land were ruled by kings, kṣatriyas were looked upon as the protectors of that land. As a matter of fact, Pṛthā (Kuntī) asks Kṛṣṇa before the war started, to tell her sons Arjuna and Bhīma that the time has come to justify why any kṣatriya mother desires to have sons. A kṣatriya's quality (*vāsanā*) is an ever-bubbling enthusiasm to defend the weak and poor from threats of aggression.

Kṛṣṇa has come down from the *ātmic* plane to individual, physical plane and comes to the same conclusion, i.e., to fight to destroy *adharma*, aggression.

We too, should be like kṣatriyas and be always alert to fight *kāma*, *krodha* and their associates who envelop us with a veil of ignorance.

In every walk of life, we come across moments when we have to prove ourselves. What we do at the opportune moment will decide our future.

Every student knows that, every year he has to face examinations to prove that he has learnt and understood what was taught so far. Preparing all through a course of studies and then deciding not to sit for the exams is not the *svadharma* of any student.

We too get opportunities to discharge our duties ever so often. We should do so to the best of our capacity at that time and achieve *śreyas* in our path to *mokṣa.*

अथ चेत्त्वमिमं धर्म्यं संग्रामं न करिष्यसि ।
ततः स्वधर्मं कीर्तिं च हित्वा पापमवाप्स्यसि ॥३३॥

atha cet tvam imaṁ dharmyaṁ saṁgrāmaṁ na kariṣyasi |
tataḥ svadharmaṁ kīrtiṁ ca hitvā pāpam avāpsyasi ||33||

But, if you will not fight this righteous war, then, having abandoned your own duty and fame, you would incur sin.

Arjuna was a great and famous warrior. It was his duty to protect the people of the land. If he had abandoned the duty to protect the subjects of his land, he would lose his fame. He would be subject to ridicule. For a famous man, life of ridicule is very hard. Having attained a position in life, one must discharge the duties appropriate to that position.

Kṛṣṇa also says that it is a sin if one does not discharge his duties. According to the *śāstra*s, sin is an act contrary to the essential nature of the 'Self'.

We all have a bundle of *vāsanā*s in us. Every thought of ours leaves an imprint on our mind. When the thought is put into action, that imprint gets wiped off. This imprint is called *vāsanā*. In performing actions to fulfil the desires, we again accumulate more *vāsanā*s. *Mokṣa* is a state of mind where there are no desires of any kind. To achieve this state, one has to burn all existing *vāsanā*s.

What we are now, is due to the *vāsanā*s which we are carrying now. We must therefore be prepared to act to fulfil the desires of the past which we are carrying.

Arjuna's *vāsanā*s made him to be born as a kṣatriya warrior. His duty was to act as a kṣatriya. He had to protect the people of his land. Also, in his path to *mokṣa*, he had a duty to his *ātman* and he had to burn all existing *vāsanā*s so that his *ātman* would join *paramātman*. His *ātman* would not have to incarnate again. Instead, if he did not perform the duties of a kṣatriya, his *ātman* would have to take on a new birth. Sin, then, is an act contrary to the essential nature of the Self.

Arjuna wanted to be a *saṁnyāsī* and go to the forest to learn knowledge, acquire purity and attain liberation. By that act he would not have obtained purity. His kṣatriya *vāsanā*s would bring him back to the world and he would be living a life of restlessness by his thoughts of guilt at a later date in his life.

अकीर्तिञ्चापि भूतानि कथयिष्यन्ति तेऽव्ययाम् ।
संभावितस्य चाकीर्तिर्मरणादतिरिच्यते ॥३४॥

akīrtiṁ cāpi bhūtāni kathayiṣyanti te'vyayām |
saṁbhāvitasya cākīrtir maraṇād atiricyate ||34||

People too, will speak of your everlasting dishonour and

to one who is honoured by his country, dishonour is worse than death.

Death is only for the physical body. Disgrace, on the other hand, stains the name of a man for generations. A great man who is honoured by his country will go down in history with disgrace if he does any shameful act. Similarly, in a small unit such as a family, if one commits a shameful act, generations in that family would remember their ancestor's sinful act.

Also, looking now at the *ātmic* level, our identification with the physical body and sinful acts will disgrace us for generations of our births and deaths (which we need to purify ourselves).

भयाद्रणादुपरतं मंस्यन्ते त्वां महारथाः ।
येषां च त्वं बहुमतो भूत्वा यास्यसि लाघवम् ॥३५॥

bhayād raṇād uparataṁ maṁsyante tvāṁ mahārathāḥ I
yeṣāṁ ca tvaṁ bahumato bhūtvā yāsyasi lāghavam II35II

Moreover, these great warriors from whom you received honour formerly, would think you turned away from the battle out of fear and regard you with little respect.

Arjuna as we know was a highly respected warrior. He earned his respect by brave deeds. He even fought Lord Śiva once. Lord Śiva gave him the weapon "Pāśupata". If he withdrew from the battlefield, his opponents would use the opportunity to ridicule him. They would not want to know why he did not fight. They would look at the end result. Later on he would not be able to carry the same respect with him.

अवाच्यवादांश्च बहून्वदिष्यन्ति तवाहिताः ।
निन्दन्तस्तव सामर्थ्यं ततो दुःखतरं नु किम् ॥३६॥

avācyavādāṁś ca bahūn vadiṣyanti tavāhitāḥ I
nindantas tava sāmarthyaṁ tato duḥkhataraṁ nu kim II36II

Your enemies will belittle your ability and in various ways speak words of ill fame. What is more painful than this?

In these two verses, Kṛṣṇa is painting to Arjuna the future if he did a cowardly act. He is continuing the theme of asking him to fight at the individual, physical level.

हतो वा प्राप्स्यसि स्वर्गं जित्वा वा भोक्ष्यसे महीम् ।
तस्मादुत्तिष्ठ कौन्तेय युद्धाय कृतनिश्चयः ॥३७॥

***hato vā prāpsyasi svargaṁ jitvā vā bhokṣyase mahīm* I**
***tasmād uttiṣṭha kaunteya yuddhāya kṛtaniścayaḥ* II37II**

O Arjuna, if killed in the battle, you will obtain heaven, if you win, you enjoy the world. Therefore arise, determined to fight.

So far, Lord Kṛṣṇa has taken pains to explain what happens if the war is not waged. Now, he is trying to explain what good will come out of waging the war.

Spiritually speaking, Kṛṣṇa is asking us to face boldly the game of our life and meet the challenges of life by doing one's best following the path of righteousness. If at any time we get dejected in life, when we cannot face a challenge, we should then remember this sacred verse (*mantra*).

For a spiritual seeker, then, if successful, it would be the reward in the form of liberation (*mokṣa*); if not successful, he would get more chances to purify himself and attain liberation.

Uttiṣṭha: Arise. Arise, awaken and stop not till the goal is reached, i.e., face the problems of life, the ills and shocks of life with the sword of knowledge and devotion. This word *uttiṣṭha* is an extremely potent medicine in the *Gītā*. One must remember it constantly in one's life.

सुखदुःखे समे कृत्वा लाभालाभौ जयाजयौ ।
ततो युद्धाय युज्यस्व नैवं पापमवाप्स्यसि ॥३८॥

***sukhaduḥkhe same kṛtvā lābhālābhau jayājayau* I**
***tato yuddhāya yujyasva naivaṁ pāpam avāpsyasi* II38II**

Having an equal mind in pain and pleasure, gain and loss, victory and defeat, engage in battle and thereby you will not incur sin.

This is the secret of *karma-yoga*. Vyāsa has beautifully brought it out by these examples of experience at different levels of perception.

Pain and pleasure	—	at intellectual level
Gain and loss	—	at mental level
Victory and defeat	—	at physical level

At each level of experience of the opposites, one should develop a sense of equilibrium. This is meant as an advice for spiritual seekers. By following this advice, one will not incur sins.

Detachment and equanimity are essential in the path of spiritual progress.

Work in itself does not bind man to the wheels of birth and death. It is due to the attachment to the fruits of action, that binding takes place. No binding if one works without attachment to the fruits of action.

Life is full of waves as in an ocean. Whether we want it or not, we are here, in this world. Similarly, whether we want it or not, we expect plenty of waves in our life, of painspleasures, gains-losses, victories-defeats.

Just as a swimmer, going to swim in the ocean is expected to know the art of sea-bathing to survive, we should also know the art of swimming in the ocean of life. This method of developing steadiness and equipoise of mind and intellect is *yoga*.

One should assess every challenge in his life at the three planes of intellect/mind/physical body and from spiritual plane as well. Then one gets a chance to learn to travel in the path of spiritual liberation.

Arjuna's fault was that he evaluated his thought at the level of sentiments. If one has to be successful in developing equanimity, then he must know what is *ātmā* and what is ego, and detach himself (i.e., to lose 'I', 'mine'ness). This will give him equanimity of mind. Once this is achieved one must then fight (work).

Work becomes worship automatically.

एषा तेऽभिहिता सांख्ये बुद्धिर्योगे त्विमां शृणु ।
बुद्ध्या युक्तो यया पार्थ कर्मबन्धं प्रहास्यसि ॥३९॥

eṣā te'bhihitā sāṁkhye buddhir yoge tv imāṁ śṛṇu |
buddhyā yukto yayā pārtha karmabandhaṁ prahāsyasi ||39||

O Arjuna. This, which has been taught to you, is sāṁkhya-yoga, *about* ātmā. *Now listen to* karma-yoga, *having known which, you shall cast off the bondage of work.*

So far, Kṛṣṇa has described in detail all about the *ātmā*. *Sāṁkhya-yoga* means the one that deals with the knowledge of the *ātman*. From this stanza onwards, he goes on to teach Arjuna the secret of work.

In all branches of knowledge, theory and practice form part of the training. So far Śrī Kṛṣṇa has dealt with the theory. Now, he has taken up the practice.

To understand the secret of work is termed *buddhi*. Working thus, one does get liberated in course of time. Devotion through work is *buddhi-yoga*.

If one learns to detach oneself from body, mind, and intellect, he will then automatically be killing his ego. As the ego is the one that thinks he is the sufferer in this world, if ego is dead, automatically the fruits of action do not bind that person. He would ultimately attain liberation.

नेहाभिक्रमनाशोऽस्ति प्रत्यवायो न विद्यते ।
स्वल्पमप्यस्य धर्मस्य त्रायते महतो भयात् ॥४०॥

nehābhikramanāśo'sti pratyavāyo na vidyate |
svalpam apy asya dharmasya trāyate mahato bhayāt ||40||

There is no loss of effort in this karma-yoga. *Even if it is stopped in the middle, no harm is produced. Even a little of this knowledge, even a little practice of this yoga, protects man from great fear.*

It is a common saying, "I am ignorant of the *śāstra*s. I cannot swim this ocean of *saṁsāra*. I am not a saint. How can I attain *mokṣa* (liberation)?".

Man's great fear is death, diseases, parting from those he is attached to.

One can cross the ocean in a small ship provided he has all the necessary equipment to keep it steady, and he looks out for obstacles, and uses his tools properly. Sooner or later he is bound to cross it. Similarly, the Lord says that a little practice of *karma-yoga* will protect man from the ills of life. The method of practising is *sādhanā*. The end result to be obtained is *sādhya*. By constant practice one can attain liberation. One knows by experience that when one practises anything sincerely, that practice automatically becomes a habit. For example, if one practises to get up at 5 every morning, that habit in course of time becomes his nature. Later he automatically gets up at that time. Similarly, Kṛṣṇa is saying that even a little sincere practice of equanimity will become one's nature in course of time and that will help him in spiritual progress.

व्यवसायात्मिका बुद्धिरेकेह कुरुनन्दन ।
बहुशाखा ह्यनन्ताश्च बुद्धयोऽव्यवसायिनाम् ॥४१॥

***vyavasāyātmikā buddhir ekeha kurunandana* I**
***bahuśākhā hy anantāś ca buddhayo'vyavasāyinām* II41II**

O Arjuna, there is only one faith and thought for those who practise this karma-yoga. *The minds of others are divided into various branches and their thoughts are endless.*

The word *vyavasāya* has various meanings. In this context it means "single-pointed determination".

It is common knowledge that anyone who works with steadfast, single-minded approach towards a goal, will succeed in reaching it. At the same time if that object is a worldly object, it means he still has 'I'-ness in him—his ego is still there. Ego is expression of mind/intellect.

We know that the mind is an ocean and thoughts arise as millions of waves. These thoughts are described as endless branches.

For the man with single-pointed dedication to a worldly object, his ego will develop other thoughts as well and later on he might want to go for another object. In other words, you get one and to protect it you start looking for others. This becomes endless and gets into a whirlpool.

For the person, who has faith in *ātmā* (God), there is only one goal. When he achieves it, he gets absorbed into it and he becomes one with it, he becomes God. This is liberation (*mokṣa*). There is nothing else to get after this absolute bliss.

In all he does, his mind is fixed on *ātmā* and he sees the same *ātmā* in all he does. Having faith in this spiritual truth, one should practise *karma-yoga*. Having faith in this is *buddhi-yoga*.

यामिमां पुष्पितां वाचं प्रवदन्त्यविपश्चितः ।
वेदवादरताः पार्थ नान्यदस्तीति वादिनः ॥४२॥
***yām imāṁ puṣpitāṁ vācaṁ pravadanty avipaścitaḥ* I**
***vedavādaratāḥ pārtha nānyad astīti vādinaḥ* II42II**

कामात्मानः स्वर्गपराः जन्मकर्मफलप्रदाम् ।
क्रियाविशेषबहुलां भोगैश्वर्यगतिं प्रति ॥४३॥
***kāmātmānaḥ svargaparā janmakarmaphalapradām* I**
***kriyāviśeṣabahulāṁ bhogaiśvarya-gatiṁ prati* II43II**

भोगैश्वर्यप्रसक्तानां तयापहृतचेतसाम् ।
व्यवसायात्मिका बुद्धिः समाधौ न विधीयते ॥४४॥
***bhogaiśvaryaprasaktānāṁ tayāpahṛtacetasām* I**
***vyavasāyātmikā buddhiḥ samādhau na vidhīyate* II44II**

O Arjuna. The unwise utter flowery speech. They take pleasure in the eulogising words of the Vedas, *and say, "There is nothing else but pleasures".*

They are full of desires, their highest goal is heaven, leading to new birth as the reward for their actions, and engage themselves in specific works for the purpose of acquiring enjoyments and prosperity.

The minds of such men who are drawn away by attachment

> *to pleasure and wealth cannot be concentrated to remain fixed in divine contemplation and* samādhi.

There are three parts in the *Veda*s. The end result to be attained by the *Veda*s is *mokṣa* (liberation, absolute bliss). The three parts are a means towards the liberation. The three parts are: (1) *karma-kāṇḍa,* (2) *upāsanā-kāṇḍa,* (3) *jñāna-kāṇḍa.*

There are those who have read the *Veda*s but not understood them completely. There are those who read only the beginning and think it enough.

Karma-kāṇḍa deals with the rites and rituals and speaks of the various rewards one would get by these rites and rituals. As these rewards are tempting, they stop at this part of Vedic teaching, and do not proceed to learn the other two parts. *Upāsanā* and *jñāna-kāṇḍa* are a higher level of teaching and take one to higher levels of spiritual progress.

If one looks at schools, colleges in a similar way, education at various levels is meant to give higher and higher knowledge in that field selected by the person. At the end of GCSE's, one can find satisfaction in thinking, "I can get such and such jobs from getting GCSE's and enjoy my life". Going to the university, acquiring a degree is one step higher in the field of knowledge. Going to do post-graduate work gets one the title of Doctor and the person would have reached the highest level in that speciality. He can then go for Post-Doctoral fellowship also. Higher education brings its own rewards. It is a great satisfaction to have received the highest degree in any speciality.

Similarly, in spiritual progress, stopping in earlier stages of education will not bring its full rewards. *Karma-kāṇḍa* when followed properly and practised would bring a number of rewards. They are temporary. They do not bring permanent happiness. Learning *upāsanā-kāṇḍa* and *jñāna-kāṇḍa* and practising them will help one to achieve *mokṣa. Mokṣa* is a state of absolute bliss. The verses tell us not to stop in the spiritual path until we achieve *mokṣa.*

Heaven is a term wrongly understood by many. It is not a separate place as such. Similarly, hell is not a separate place either. Both are in this world, in this life only. Heaven and hell are only states of experiences of one's mind. The degree of happiness and suffering is equivalent to a place in heaven or hell. Vedic rituals in *karma-kāṇḍa* speak of results to be obtained by the rites. When they say one goes to heaven, they mean one gets certain things that make him feel as though he is in heaven. Similarly, they say that certain actions lead one to hell, they mean that one suffers.

As we have learnt so far, these pleasures and pains are not permanent. You cannot be in heaven forever. When you finish your quota of enjoyment which you deserve for your good work, you lose your heavenly position, i.e., you come back to the earth. Similarly, when you finish your term of punishment for your sins, you come back to earth again. Life has to continue. Therefore, those who misunderstand *Vedas* and look for rewards in heaven are termed *svargaparāḥ*. It is a foolish sentiment. The real goal for mankind is to realise the Eternal Truth.

Desires that make one go to heaven, i.e., 'to enjoy' crop up in the mind always. They disturb the balance of the mind. So 'give up desire' is Kṛṣṇa's teaching. Do not say "I want to go to Heaven" because you will then have to go the hell as well.

Sri Ramakrishna Paramahamsa gives a beautiful example which summarises the meaning of these three verses.

Vultures fly high in the sky, but what are they looking for? They are always looking out for dead bodies below. As soon as they find one, they come down and attack it.

So, real seekers of *mokṣa*, should not be like vultures and look for pleasures they get from worldly actions.

त्रैगुण्यविषया वेदा निस्त्रैगुण्यो भवार्जुन ।
निर्द्वन्द्वो नित्यसत्त्वस्थो निर्योगक्षेम आत्मवान् ॥४५॥

traiguṇyaviṣayā vedā nistraiguṇyo bhavārjuna |
nirdvandvo nityasattvastho niryogakṣema ātmavān ||45||

The Vedas *deal with three* guṇas *O Arjuna. Transcend the three* guṇas, *become free from the pairs of opposites and ever remain in pure* sāttvika *state and be firmly established in* ātmā.

*Guṇa*s are three *sattva, rajas* and *tamas*. They are the attributes of the mind. The world perceived by us is influenced and conditioned by the state of our mind at any one time (see chapter 14).

As we have learnt before, the world is an experience perceived by the mind and the intellect from the contact of sense-organs with the external world. That means the three *guṇa*s are below the level of *ātmā* (Self). Worldly bondage is for those who are subject to the influence of the *guṇa*s.

One should ascend from the lowest of the three *guṇa*s, *tamas* (darkness-ignorance-laziness), to the level of *rajas,* (action/activity), to the level of *sattva* (pure calm state of mind), and later to the level of pure *sattva*. Pure *sattva* is the state of experience of pure bliss. Lastly, one will not be in any state because one gets absorbed into the Self and becomes one with the Self (no ego, no mind, no intellect, pure bliss) and attains liberation. So, the word *nityasattva* is used here to indicate that one should strive for the pure state of mind always.

Yoga is gaining new things. The true meaning of *yoga* is gaining union of *ātmā* with *paramātmā*, i.e., liberation. At the physical level it means gaining new things. *Kṣema* is retaining what one has gained.

We are always revolving round these two, gaining and retaining. Gaining what? One may ask. Wealth, name, fame, etc. Once we get it, we struggle hard to retain it. So, Kṛṣṇa is teaching us to drop these two at the physical level only. True *yogakṣema* is acquiring union of *ātmā* with *paramātmā* and preserving that state. That is what we should all be aiming at in our spiritual path to progress.

Detach oneself from the pairs of opposites, keep constant awareness of one's divine nature, strive to realise the truth is *Gītā*'s message to mankind.

यावानर्थ उदपाने सर्वतः संप्लुतोदके ।
तावान्सर्वेषु वेदेषु ब्राह्मणस्य विजानतः ॥४६॥

***yāvān artha udapāne sarvataḥ saṁplutodake* |**
***tāvān sarveṣu vedeṣu brāhmaṇasya vijānataḥ* ||46||**

To an enlightened person, who has known the Self, all the Vedas *are as useful as a reservoir of water in a place where there is a flood.*

Vyāsa has used a beautiful simile to describe and stress his point. Tanks are areas wherein one collects water for use as needed. One builds a tank at the top of his house and gets water from it when he needs it. One builds a reservoir in a village so that villagers go and get water from it when needed. If the village is submerged in floods, there is no need for the tank or the reservoir anymore.

One can get the same water from the tank in his house or the reservoir in the village. Both serve the same purpose. One need not go to the ocean to get water. Similarly, for a *jñānī,* there is no stipulation that he must know all the *Veda*s. For a thirsty man, a few glasses of water will do. For a hungry man all the food in the world is not needed.

*Veda*s are like a big ocean. A wise man, who has understood the *ātman* properly, does not need to know the entire *Veda*s. A few practices given in the *Veda*s will be enough to attain Self-perfection. Thousands of *mantra*s are given in the *Veda*s. One can choose what suits him best and destroy his ignorance and attain liberation. Not knowing all the *Veda*s is not a barrier in the path of liberation.

Kṛṣṇa is advocating mankind not to be trapped in ritual processes which offer heaven. 'Carry on doing your duty without looking for fruits of work', is his advice.

कर्मण्येवाधिकारस्ते मा फलेषु कदाचन ।
मा कर्मफलहेतुर्भूर्मा ते सङ्गोऽस्त्वकर्मणि ॥४७॥

karmaṇy evādhikāras te mā phaleṣu kadācana |
mā karmaphalahetur bhūr mā te saṅgo'stv akarmaṇi ||47||

You have the right to work only but never to its fruits. Let not the fruit of action be your motive, nor let your attachment be to inaction.

There is a definition of *karma* in this verse. This is different from the meaning of *karma* in the *Veda*s.

Śrī Kṛṣṇa says *karma* means 'all activities in both the social and personal life of any person, without the desire in the person for its results'. Single-pointed, dedicated work thus becomes divine work. This is called *niṣkāma karma.* Whereas in the *Veda*s, on reading the *karma-kāṇḍa* one gets the meaning that it is all about religious and ritual activities. One has to read *upāsanā-kāṇḍa* and *jñāna-kāṇḍa* to understand the real meaning which is given by Śrī Kṛṣṇa in his *Gītopaniṣad.*

On the other hand, there may be some who think that by actions one gets attachment. So why not inaction (not act at all), they may say.

No one can live without work even for a second. To give up work is a sign of laziness. It is *tāmasika* character.

The spiritual seeker must realise that by not acting, he is not burning his existing *vāsanā*s. His mind due to his past *vāsanā*s, will automatically turn to action sooner or later.

Arjuna wanted to escape action, go to the forest and become a *saṁnyāsī*. This verse tells him and mankind not to do so.

Kṛṣṇa is informing Arjuna that he has to,

(*a*) perform his *karma* to the best of his capacity;
(*b*) not to have any desire for the fruits of action.

At the same time, he is also warning Arjuna not to escape from his *karma.*

Good always comes from detachment and not from attachment. One gets *śreyas* in his path to *mokṣa* by such an action. This aspect is taken up in detail in chapter 3.

The great philosopher Tilak has divided this verse into four quarters and says the four quarters are the four doctrines in *karma-yoga.*

(1) *karmaṇyevādhikāraste:* you have the right to work only;
(2) *mā phaleṣu kadācana:* you have no right to its fruits;
(3) *mā karma-phala-heturbhūḥ:* let not the fruits of action be the motive.

(4) *mā te saṅgo'stvakarmaṇi:* let one not be attached to in-action.

Bring out your best every moment and the future will take care of itself, is Kṛṣṇa's advice to mankind.

योगस्थः कुरु कर्माणि सङ्गं त्यक्त्वा धनञ्जय ।
सिद्ध्यसिद्ध्योः समो भूत्वा समत्वं योग उच्यते ॥४८॥
yogasthaḥ kuru karmāṇi saṅgaṁ tyaktvā dhanañjaya I
siddhy-asiddhyoḥ samo bhūtvā samatvaṁ yoga ucyate II48II

O Arjuna, Do you work, be steadfast in yoga, *giving up all attachment, unmindful of success or failure. Such equanimity of mind is* yoga.

The Union of *ātmā*, with *Paramātmā* is *yoga*. Towards this object the union of the ego with *ātmā* is needed. That is also *yoga*. To reach this state, equanimity of mind is needed. This is also *yoga*. By keeping one's identity with the universe, one should bring Godliness and spirituality into one's work. Do this by cultivating the habit of remaining steadfast in *ātmā* is the meaning here. *Yoga* in this context means *karma-yoga*, *saṅga* means attachment to the fruits of action. A *yogī* is one who considers that he is doing God's work as the servant of the Lord.

We can understand this by looking at an example. A boss in an office would want someone to go to the bank, encash a cheque and bring it in. He delegates this duty to his assistant. The assistant goes to the bank, encashes the cheque, and brings it and gives it to his boss. He has no sense of 'I'-ness in any of his actions performed in discharging his duty. He is satisfied that he has discharged his duty as per the instructions. On the other hand, when the assistant goes and finds that the bank is closed, he is not disappointed. He simply comes back and informs his boss of the reason for not getting the cash. The assistant should not be elated when he brings the money nor should he be depressed when he does not brings the money.

Let us take it a step further. Suppose the boss says, go to the bank and bring a large sum of money and I will reward you with a gift. The assistant should not have a different attitude towards the task delegated to him. He should consider that it was nice of the boss to have trust in him for such a large sum of money. He should not be looking for the gift he is going to get. There should not be any disappointment for not getting the cash if the bank were closed. "I lost out on getting the reward" should not be the attitude. If at all he is sorry, it should be for the boss. "Oh, what a pity, I do not know what he wanted the money so badly for. I hope it does not matter to him because the bank is closed" can be the attitude of the assistant for not cashing the cheque.

One should keep two facts in his mind constantly on doing any *karma:*

(1) I am not the doer; I am only an agent;
(2) I have no right to the fruits of action.

To worry for the results is the same as worrying for the future. To live in the future is not to live in the present. One has to live in the present and not in the future and such action then brings a special feeling of happiness in that person.

दूरेण ह्यवरं कर्म बुद्धियोगाद्धनञ्जय ।
बुद्धौ शरणमन्विच्छ कृपणाः फलहेतवः ॥४९॥

dūreṇa hy avaraṁ karma buddhiyogād dhanañjaya |
buddhau śaraṇam anviccha kṛpaṇāḥ phalahetavaḥ ||49||

O Arjuna, work with attachment is far inferior to niṣkāma karma. *Seek refuge in desireless action with equanimity of mind. Those who work for fruits are wretched.*

Buddhi is the intellectual capacity of discrimination. The spiritual seeker must think beyond his mental capacity. He should think properly of rights and wrongs of any action and then perform the action properly. Desireless action opens the door to knowledge and liberation.

The attitude to work is more important than the actual value of the work. When the thoughtflow to work is single-pointed, calm and serene it is called 'the intellect' (*niścayātmikā*, the clear mind). When the thoughtflow is agitated it is called 'the mind' (*saṁśayātmikā,* doubting mind). *Buddhi-yoga* therefore can be defined as 'establishing in the devotion to the intellect'. Work with your mind and keep it under the control of your intellect. Be a master of your own mind.

The mind can be used as a searchlight. If we direct it towards sense-objects, it is aimed at desires and one accumulates more *vāsanā*s and gets trapped in the wheel of *saṁsāra.*

The mind can be directed towards the *ātman* by using the intellectual capacity. This brings in *ānanda* and leads to *mokṣa.*

Kṛṣṇa calls those who work for small rewards for their work as *kṛpaṇa*, i.e., wretched. By working for fruits of action one automatically will incur new *vāsanā*s and his spiritual realisation will become that much farther away. It is a great shame that having been born as men and women in this world, we do not use our intellect in full but we make ourselves slaves to the play of Nature.

> बुद्धियुक्तो जहातीह उभे सुकृतदुष्कृते ।
> तस्माद्योगाय युज्यस्व योगः कर्मसु कौशलम् ॥५०॥
> **buddhiyukto jahātīha ubhe sukṛtaduṣkṛte |**
> **tasmād yogāya yujyasva yogaḥ karmasu kauśalam ||50||**
>
> *Endowed with the wisdom of evenness of mind one releases himself both from good and bad even in this life. Therefore strive for* niṣkāma karma *with an equal mind. Skill in action is* yoga.

Another definition for *yoga* is given here. It is 'skill in action'. It just means action, using one's intellect. Developing equanimity at all times itself becomes *yoga*, because ultimately this leads to union with *Paramātmā.*

An action performed with equilibrium of mind gives the best results. If the mind thinks of the result, the action will not have same efficiency.

We accumulate both good and bad from our actions. Good

actions will result in a better future and bad actions lead to future suffering. A real *karma-yogī* is not affected by *karma* of any kind. He does not look at any action as good or bad. He discharges the duty as per the *śāstras*.

Let us take the example of a Judge. He listens to arguments in any case and decides the accused to be guilty or not guilty. He has no personal interest in the case. He then orders the right punishment to the accused if he is found guilty. If necessary, he is not afraid to order the death penalty. He is not accumulating any sin by such an action. If, by thinking it is a sin to order the death penalty, he does not order it, he is actually committing a sin.

In the above case, he kept a constant equilibrium of mental composure and heard the arguments from the defence and the prosecuting lawyers. If the accused were a relative, the Judge would not have had the same composure of mind.

Śrī Kṛṣṇa says, be always alert and work with equanimity of mind and look upon every work as God's work and discharge it to the best of your capacity. A perfectly discharged duty then becomes a *yoga* and such a *yogī* will achieve *mokṣa* eventually. A spiritual seeker in his first step should avoid all evil work. The next step would be to do good work. The further step would be to do good work without desiring the fruits of work.

Buddhi-yukta means one whose actions are guided by his vision of a higher and diviner goal. Kṛṣṇa is calling us all to work at the intellectual level at all times. 'Go beyond the world of sense-objects, physical body and mind', is the message.

Arjuna was in a hysterical state. He is asked by his teacher to be a master of his mind and get the grip over external situations.

कर्मजं बुद्धियुक्ता हि फलं त्यक्त्वा मनीषिणः ।
जन्मबन्धविनिर्मुक्ताः पदं गच्छन्त्यनामयम् ॥५१॥

***karmajaṁ buddhiyuktā hi phalaṁ tyaktvā manīṣiṇaḥ* I**
***janmabandhavinirmuktāḥ padaṁ gacchanty anāmayam* II51II**

Wise men, possessed of knowledge, having abandoned the fruits of action, go to the abode beyond all sorrow and evil.

Wise men will attain final liberation, is the Lord's promise here.

Maniṣī means 'possessing wisdom' (wise men, men of knowledge). A man of knowledge is one who has no desire for fruits of action. He knows the principle of right action. The wise always develop the habit of saying *kṛṣṇārpaṇam astu* while they are discharging their duties and also say *kṛṣṇārpaṇam astu* for the results of their actions. This applies only for actions performed according to the *śāstra*s. It means that everything is dedicated to God (Kṛṣṇa).

By considering that one is doing God's work, by not keeping the 'I'-ness in any work, one can develop the attitude of *kṛṣṇārpaṇam astu* in discharging his duties. By doing so, automatically he would know that he has no right to the fruits of such action. Such wise men do attain *mokṣa.*

Egotistic actions always bring new *vāsanās*. New *vāsanās* plunge one into the whirlpool of *saṁsāra*, i.e., birth and deaths. If one desires spiritual freedom one should act wisely. There is only one state we can reach where there is no pain or sorrow. That state of pure bliss, is *mokṣa* (liberation). It is possible to reach this state if one acts wisely.

यदा ते मोहकलिलं बुद्धिर्व्यतितरिष्यति ।
तदा गन्तासि निर्वेदं श्रोतव्यस्य श्रुतस्य च ॥५२॥

***yadā te moha-kalilaṁ buddhir vyatitariṣyati* |**
***tadā gantāsi nirvedaṁ śrotavyasya śrutasya ca* ||52||**

When your mind crosses the mire of delusion, you will attain to indifference as to what has been heard and what has to be heard.

Nirvedam means indifference. Indifference to what? To *śrotavyam* and *śrutam.*

Śrotavyam: What has to be heard. Correctly expressed, it would mean, "all sense-experiences that are yet to be experienced."

Śrutam: What has been heard. It means, "all experiences that have been experienced already."

When one develops such an indifference, he will be eligible to attain the end result of *mokṣa*. Śrī Madhvācārya says *nirvedam* means "maximum profit". One can get maximum profit from one's life by following the principle of indifference to worldly experiences experienced in the past and to be experienced in the future. One can cross over *māyā* by this method.

Crossing the mire of delusion means crossing the darkness of ignorance (*māyā*). *Ātmā* is beyond ignorance. The *śruti* declares "*tamasastu pāre*", to reach the Self one has to go beyond the ocean of darkness of sorrow (*śoka*) and delusion (*moha*).

Māyā, (delusion) is like electricity. It is not perceptible. It manifests itself in different ways. It is realised in life's various expressions. *Māyā* at the intellect level acts as a film of obstructing the understanding of the Self in us. This power of *māyā* is termed as *āvaraṇa-śakti.* Because of this, the Self reflects itself as the ego, and the intellect forgets the Self and believes the reflection to be the real self. But, by pure devotion through work, one can unveil the mask of ignorance and see the real Self behind. The aspirant comes to live in his own real nature of Bliss.

श्रुतिविप्रतिपन्ना ते यदा स्थास्यति निश्चला ।
समाधावचला बुद्धिस्तदा योगमवाप्स्यसि ॥५३॥

***śrutivipratipannā te yadā sthāsyati niścalā* I**
***samādhāv acalā buddhis tadā yogam avāpsyasi* II53II**

When your intellect, though perplexed by what you have heard, becomes steady and immovable in the Self, then you shall attain Self-realisation.

When Kṛṣṇa says "by what you have heard" it means what Arjuna has learnt so far in this chapter. Arjuna had been taught the *Veda*s in his *Gurukula-āśrama.* He has heard conflicting views so far. It is time for Arjuna to make up his mind and develop a steady composure of mind.

By hearing the *karma-kāṇḍa* on rites and rituals, one initially gets distracted and perplexed. But on hearing the *upāsanā-kāṇḍa* and *jñāna-kāṇḍa,* the intellect gets clearer. The veil of ignorance lifts off and one can attain the union of Self with *Paramātmā*. When that union (*yoga*) takes place, there is no mind or ego separate from the Self. The mind has become one with 'That'.

To develop the immovable steadiness of mind (*niścalatva*) one should hear of *ātmā*, think of *ātmā* and meditate on *ātmā*. This gradually helps one to merge his mind in *ātmā*. This state is called *ātma-samādhi*. (When the mind is merged into the *ātmā* that state is called *samādhi*—Śrī Śaṅkarācārya).

अर्जुन उवाच
स्थितप्रज्ञस्य का भाषा समाधिस्थस्य केशव ।
स्थितधीः किं प्रभाषेत किमासीत व्रजेत किम् ॥५४॥

arjuna uvāca
***sthitaprajñasya kā bhāṣā samādhisthasya keśava* |**
***sthitadhīḥ kiṁ prabhāṣeta kim āsīta vrajeta kim* ||54||**

Arjuna said

O Kṛṣṇa, what are the characteristics of a man of steady wisdom while he is merged in the 'super-conscious state'? How does such a man speak, sit and move.

Samādhi means grave. It means that no physical activities are left. In this context *samādhi* is actually 'this state' of having reached *ātmā*. When one merges into this superconscious state he is said to have reached the state of *samādhi*. This is so because the awareness of the world of sense-objects through his sense-organs does not agitate his mind. Arjuna wants clarification on this point. He wants to know how such a person can get along in his day-to-day activities? How can one recognise such a person in society. *Sthitaprajña* means the man of steady wisdom, who through direct realisation comes to experience and live his Godly life.

From this verse to verse 72 we get the answer to this question. Mahatma Gandhi used to recite these verses everyday. These verses will help any sincere spiritual seeker to find out what type of values and mental development one needs in order to become a *sthitaprajña*.

श्रीभगवानुवाच
प्रजहाति यदा कामान् सर्वान् पार्थ मनोगतान् ।
आत्मन्येवात्मना तुष्टः स्थितप्रज्ञस्तदोच्यते ॥५५॥

śrī bhagavān uvāca
***prajahāti yadā kāmān sarvān pārtha manogatān* |**
***ātmany evātmanā tuṣṭaḥ sthitaprajñas tadocyate* ||55||**
The Lord said

When a man renounces completely all the desires of the mind, when he is fully satisfied with his mind fixed in ātmā, *O Pārtha, he is then declared to be a* sthitaprajña.

This verse gives the mental make up of such a person.

We all enjoy worldly pleasures in some form or other. We have a desire to obtain the pleasures. Desire is a capacity of the mind to see ahead of itself. This craving is because of the ignorance of our true Self—*sat, cit, ānanda* (blissful state). We need not go searching for peace in any nook and corner or in a far off place. The light of knowledge has its switch in our own intellect. By practice, one will find out where the switch is, and automatically his mind does not run after desires.

When one goes to a holy man asking for the means of liberation from the ills of life, the holy man will repeat this verse. Getting the liberation is in one's own hands. To reach the point, the first step is to give up desires fully and the second step is to realise that worldly pleasures are momentary. The bliss that one gets on finding out the true nature of oneself is permanent. There is no sorrow to experience after achieving that state.

When all the desires are fully cast off permanently one experiences the sense of bliss, oneness with *ātmā.* This is a spontaneous reaction after casting off all desires. This takes a very long, long time, but it is not impossible. One should first of all know that he has a Soul inside him and should have a desire for spiritual progress. Then the task is much simpler. Liberation is not something to be achieved after death. It is liberation from the ills of life and to be achieved in the present life by casting off all desires fully and permanently.

The aim of *Vedānta* is to remove the impure covering and discover the natural *ānanda*.

You look in a mirror to see what you are. A perfectly clean, spotless mirror gives a true reflection of you. If there is a covering of dust on the mirror the reflection will be hazy; and you need to wipe and polish the mirror. It is true that external dust will keep on collecting on the mirror. But if you keep on cleaning, you will see a clear reflection.

The example should make it clear as to how the dust of desire causes obscurity (ignorance). Practising renunciation of desires is the first step and that is, *sādhanā*. Experiencing the goal of *ātmānanda* is the result; that is *sādhya*.

दुःखेष्वनुद्विग्नमनाः सुखेषु विगतस्पृहः ।
वीतरागभयक्रोधः स्थितधीर्मुनिरुच्यते ॥५६॥

duḥkheṣv anudvignamanāḥ sukheṣu vigataspṛhaḥ |
vītarāgabhayakrodhaḥ sthitadhīr munir ucyate ||56||

He whose mind is not troubled by sorrow, who does not go after pleasures, who is free from attachment, fear and hatred, is called a sage of steady wisdom.

A few more mental characteristics of the *sthitaprajña* are enumerated here.

Ātmā is above the mind, like the sun. Troubles are natural reactions of the mind to the phenomenon of the outer world, like the clouds obscuring the sun. Any situation that brings sorrow would agitate the mind of an ordinary person, but not of a *jñānī*. There are three types of situations that might bring sorrow to any person:

(*a*) Situations due to problems of the physical body, i.e., disease, injury etc. These are types of problems one has to face in life. These are *ādhyātmika* problems.

(*b*) Situations due to problems of the surroundings, i.e., problems concerning the loved ones. These are called *ādhibhautika* types of problems.

(*c*) Situations due to adverse situations in the world, i.e., lightning, thunder, earthquake etc. These are called *ādhidaivika* types of problems.

In any such situation, the *sthitaprajña* remains very calm and does not get perturbed. Equanimity in pleasure and pain is an essential character.

Attachment	-	*rāga*	Remove these three handicaps in you and you will be a master of all situations.
Fear	-	*bhaya*	
Anger	-	*krodha*	

Attachment: It is a fact of life that one collects things in life as an ongoing thing. They could be simple things like toys in childhood, good clothes and jewellery when young, family and possessions of material wealth as one grows older.

Yoga means to get united with something (real meaning is union with *Paramātmā*). That brings happiness.

Desire as we mentioned above is the first step towards attachment. When one wants a thing badly, a sense of fear also develops within himself, the fear that he might not get it. This is *bhaya*. Or else when one gets the object of his desire, he might fear he may lose it and is worried about the security of the object. This is also *bhaya.* One gets married and attached to his spouse and gets children and gets attached to them. He would then automatically not want to let go off them. As one gets older and has more attachment, he would be inwardly frightened of losing the spouse, e.g., by death.

It does not mean you should not love your spouse and children. As long as you have got them it is your duty to love them and look after them. Give them what you should be giving them to share your life and wealth. Look after them in sickness and get the best you can to treat them. If still death comes, do not be frightened. This is detachment in attachment.

Also, when one gets the objects of deep attachment, one would get angry at losing it. If he does not get it then also he gets angry. This is *krodha*. Duryodhana wanted the entire kingdom for himself and he got more and more angry when he found that at every attempt he failed. This anger is the object between him and the desire. In the case of Duryodhana the obstacle between him and his desire were the Pāṇḍavas.

A *sthitaprajña* is one who has developed this equanimity—who is free from attachment, fear and hatred.

यः सर्वत्रानभिस्नेहस्तत्तत्प्राप्य शुभाशुभम् ।
नाभिनन्दति न द्वेष्टि तस्य प्रज्ञा प्रतिष्ठिता ॥५७॥

yaḥ sarvatrānabhisnehas tat tat prāpya śubhāśubham |
nābhinandati na dveṣṭi tasya prajñā pratiṣṭhitā ||57||

He who has no attachment to anything and anywhere, who does not rejoice or hate, his wisdom is fixed.

There should be a sense of detachment to every material thing in this world. This is called detachment in attachment.

It is easy not to be attached to unpleasant things. The same attitude should develop towards pleasant things as well. It is the law of nature that both pleasant and unpleasant things happen in our daily lives.

Kṛṣṇa does not mean that one should run away from these. Running away is not a sign of perfection. The challenges of life should be met with courage, equanimity and the knowledge of the Self.

Arjuna wanted to give up the war, and the pursuit of kingdom. He would then have committed two mistakes. Arjuna was fighting *adharma* (unrighteousness). If he ran away he would have given a free run for *adharma* to rule the land. This would cause harm to mankind. This is therefore a sin. And that would be his first mistake.

One is supposed to, in his path of spiritual progress, burn existing *vāsanā*s and not accumulate new *vāsanā*. This can be achieved by *niṣkāma karma* and not by running away to live in the forest. One's *vāsanā*s will not give peace to that person and he will have to come back from his retreat. This therefore would be the second mistake in his progress.

Mere detachment is only a negative existence of escaping from life. To live in attachment is like being a slave to the pleasures of the world. Arjuna asked Kṛṣṇa how does a *sthitaprajña* speak.

This is the answer. He does not complain or cry at unpleasant things. He does not boast or compliment himself on pleasant things. To him everything is pure bliss.

यदा संहरते चायं कूर्मोऽङ्गानीव सर्वशः ।
इन्द्रियाणीन्द्रियार्थेभ्यस्तस्य प्रज्ञा प्रतिष्ठिता ॥५८॥

yadā saṁharate cāyaṁ kūrmo'ṅgānīva sarvaśaḥ |
indriyāṇīndriyārthebhyas tasya prajñā pratiṣṭhitā ||58||

When the yogī, *like the tortoise drawing back its limbs into its own shell, withdraws all the senses from the sense-objects, his wisdom is fixed. He is a* sthitaprajña.

It is a very beautiful, and an appropriate example. The tortoise as we know, on encountering obstacles, immediately withdraws itself into its shell. One can throw a stone and it does not get injured.

Our senses always go after pleasures. They send their message to the mind. We should withdraw our organs of actions, that means, our mind should be educated not to react to the impulses from the sense-organs.

This is at the physical plane of one's character-assessment. Like the three monkeys, do not hear, do not see, do not speak ill in any form is another way of expressing it.

Even if we keep one door open, it is enough to let the burglar in, is another way of explaining it.

In each of us, five distinct beams of light go out of our mind through the five sense-organs and find the objects and receive the message. The mind then sends messages to the organs of action to obtain the objects of desire. The messages from the sense-organs provide disturbances to the mind.

A deaf person is not worried about abuses thrown at him. He keeps on smiling even if people surrounding him are ridiculing him. This capacity to withdraw from the field of objects is called *pratyāhāra* in *yoga-śāstra*.

This is possible by developing single-pointed concentration on the *ātman* (*vyavasāyātmikā buddhi*). The sense-organs should withdraw into the mind, the mind should withdraw into the intellect and the intellect should withdraw into the *ātman*. It is then that nothing from the outer world would harm the person (cf., *nainaṁ chindanti śastrāṇi. . .*).

विषया विनिवर्तन्ते निराहारस्य देहिनः ।
रसवर्जं रसोऽप्यस्य परं दृष्ट्वा निवर्तते ॥५९॥

***viṣayā vinivartante nirāhārasya dehinaḥ* |**
***rasavarjaṁ raso'pyasya paraṁ dṛṣṭvā nivartate* ||59||**

When a man rejects the sense-objects by withdrawing the senses, he becomes free from the sense-world only. Even his longing also is removed on intuiting upon the Supreme.

For those in the spiritual path it is important that objects of the outer world do not tempt them. This is what is meant by rejecting the sense-objects.

Rasavarjam: giving up longing. *rasam* means taste.

This verse explains the mental make up of the beginner in austerity. An austere person might decide not to eat. Even though he wants to give up the longing for food, the taste for food remains. This longing for taste will disappear only on realisation of the *ātman* (*paraṁ dṛṣṭvā nivartate*).

The mind of such a person has experienced several objects in the past and there will be a latent longing for them still. This is known as *rāga*. What is meant here is, that apart from rejecting the objects, one should also not be contemplating on the objects in his thoughts. The *vāsanā*s or imprints of thought-action-processes of the past have to be burnt also.

When they are burnt, it means the mind is destroyed, (*manonāśa*) and at that time, direct experience of the Self takes place automatically. Destruction of *vāsanā*s is the only way to *mokṣa*.

Vāsanās work through the senses, and the senses function by contact with sense-objects in the world.

The word *nirāhāra* is used here. It means 'restraining from food'. Here food means all sense-objects of the world which bring happiness to a person.

In spiritual progress, thinking of *ātmā*, meditating on *ātmā* frequently and intensely, helps one to develop less taste for worldly objects. By constant application to work without looking for fruits of action (as long as the physical body remains) the bliss of Self-experience becomes more and more and finally the mind merges into *ātmā*, the ego (self) is dead and the person is said to be liberated.

यततो ह्यपि कौन्तेय पुरुषस्य विपश्चितः ।
इन्द्रियाणि प्रमाथीनि हरन्ति प्रसभं मनः ॥६०॥

***yatato hy api kaunteya puruṣasya vipaścitaḥ* I**
***indriyāṇi pramāthīni haranti prasabhaṁ manaḥ* II60II**

O Arjuna, the turbulent senses do violently carry away the mind of a wise man, though he is striving to control them.

The power of the mind and senses (*māyā*) is phenomenal. The mind always tries to push itself out as it were through the senses and attaches itself to the world. Even for a wise man (i.e., the man in the path of spiritual liberation) this is not easy.

The mind is said to be objective because it runs after the objective world. Using the power of intellectual discrimination it is possible to stop the mind running outwards and make the mind run inwards to the Self. This is what one calls 'trying to attain divinity'.

God is Divine and totally pure. He has no qualities of *sattva, rajas* and *tamas*, i.e., he is above *māyā* or illusion. The three qualities are due to the veil of *māyā* covering the Self. If one has to develop divinity, he must transcend the three *guṇas*. A spiritual seeker has to fight between the divinity within and the sense-world outside. To merge into God, to become one with God, is the aim. This is achieved by strict self-control and developing necessary power within.

One can never say that one achieves total mastery over the senses. One can see a clear sky when he goes to work. It is possible that within a short period the sky might get overcast and covered by clouds. Similarly, our *vāsanās* of the past can come as a cloud and cast a veil over the *ātmā* (Mother Sarada Devi). If the seeker, after some years of practice, relaxes in his *tapas* (effort) then the mind might go out again and he will find it difficult to restrain it. This is the meaning of this verse. If it is difficult even for such a person, how much harder it will be for a beginner to develop control over the senses?

तानि सर्वाणि संयम्य युक्त आसीत मत्परः ।
वशे हि यस्येन्द्रियाणि तस्य प्रज्ञा प्रतिष्ठिता ॥६१॥

***tāni sarvāṇi saṁyamya yukta āsīta matparaḥ* I**
***vaśe hi yasyendriyāṇi tasya prajñā pratiṣṭhitā* II61II**

Having restrained all the senses, he should sit steadfast, intent on Me. His wisdom is steady, whose senses are under control.

It is a continuation of the last verse. It suggests that the practice of total sense-control has to become a regular way of living for such a person. There should be control of all the senses constantly and also contemplation on divinity constantly.

It is no use controlling only a few sense. That sense which is not controlled would be strong enough to pull the person down from his path of spiritual progress. This can be understood if one looks at an earthen pot with five holes. If one has to carry a potful of water, all the holes must be closed. Leaving one hole open is enough to let the collected water flow out from the pot.

It means 'reject the objective world' (*dṛśya*) and 'identify with the subject' (*draṣṭā*). Just rejecting the objective world does not make one 'a man of knowledge'. If it were true, all of us would be men of knowledge when we are asleep.

The control of all senses is emphasised repeatedly in the *Gītā*. As we said before, one open door or window is enough for a burglar to enter into the house.

One has to develop harmony with the Self or the superconscious state. If one has to achieve liberation, one must unite with the Soul (Self) in him. Kṛṣṇa is suggesting the ultimate *advaita* philosophy here through *dvaita* philosophy.

Dvaita is two—You (or Self) and God. *Advaita* is non-two, i.e, one— You in the Self/You in the God. Initially one has to contemplate on the God in him and automatically he becomes one with the God, i.e., becomes God. So, these two are not two different philosophies.

Dvaita leads to *advaita. Bhakti* leads to liberation.

A sthitaprajña is one who has not suppressed his *indriyas* by sheer excessive force. He is one who has developed a natural habit of self-control and allowed his sense-organs to lie tamely at his feet and rediscover his infinite perfection in himself. He has exposed his mind to the quiet atmosphere of meditation upon the Self. He has used his mind to develop blossoms of divinity. He who has developed divinity is said to have "divinity blossomed" in him.

These blossoms can become fine flowers if no weeds are allowed to grow, and water and manure are given as needed. This is what is achieved by total sense-control and by concentrating on the Lord.

ध्यायतो विषयान्पुंसः सङ्गस्तेषूपजायते ।
सङ्गात् सञ्जायते कामः कामात्क्रोधोऽभिजायते ॥६२॥

***dhyāyato viṣayān puṁsaḥ saṅgas teṣūpajāyate* I**
***saṅgāt sañjāyate kāmaḥ kāmāt krodho'bhijāyate* II62II**

क्रोधाद्भवति संमोहः संमोहात्स्मृतिविभ्रमः ।
स्मृतिभ्रंशाद्बुद्धिनाशो बुद्धिनाशात्प्रणश्यति ॥६३॥

***krodhād bhavati saṁmohaḥ saṁmohāt smṛti-vibhramaḥ* I**
***smṛtibhraṁśād buddhināśo buddhināśāt praṇaśyati* II63II**

Brooding on the objects of senses, man develops attachment to them; from attachment comes desire; from desire anger sprouts forth.

From anger proceeds delusion; from delusion, confused memory; from confused memory the ruin of reason; due to the ruin of reason he perishes.

Śrī Kṛṣṇa now gives the consequence of yielding to sense-pleasures. As a man thinks of sense-objects, attachment for them arises. From attachment desire for them will be born. From desire arises anger. From anger comes delusion. From delusion comes loss of memory and destruction of discrimination. From this he perishes.

The path of destruction (path to hell) is described here in consequential order. Each fall takes one down to the next step in the path of destruction. The seed of destruction is wrong thinking or contemplation on an object of desire. The more one thinks of an object the more he gets attached to it. This is true both of spiritual progress and spiritual destruction. Once he starts thinking more on a particular thing, it becomes an object of attachment. His thoughts then flow towards such attachment and this state is called desire. The first sprout from the seed is desire (*kāma*).

Because of desire, one would want desperately to get its object. The stronger the desire, that much stronger will be the desperation to get it. If one does not get it, he then gets angry (*krodha*). Anger acts like alcohol in a man. The man of anger trembles and shivers in his whole body; his eyes become blood-shot and his speech becomes incoherent.

The man of anger experiences delusion. The intellect loses the power of discrimination. He indulges in abuse and violence. In short, man becomes an animal possessed by an evil spirit. This state is delusion—*saṁmoha*.

A deluded man forgets his environment and his status. He does not remember who he is dealing with (wife, father, friend or teacher). This is loss of memory (*smṛtivibhrama*) of one's self. Once the memory is lost, the man perishes (*praṇaśyati*).

Here the word 'perishes' does not mean death. It means that he perishes in his path to attain *brahma-jñāna*. He will not attain liberation.

This downward contemplation may be any object—wealth, fame, wine, sex, etc.

In a different way, one can say that contemplation of the divine constantly would develop a desire for divinity. This would bring peace and permanent happiness in its progress.

The process of Duryodhana's destruction is a beautiful example for these verses.

Sri Ramakrishna Paramahamsa says, "Beware of your thoughts and everything will be all right with you".

रागद्वेषवियुक्तैस्तु विषयानिन्द्रियैश्चरन् ।
आत्मवश्यैर्विधेयात्मा प्रसादमधिगच्छति ॥६४॥

rāgadveṣaviyuktais tu viṣayān indriyaiś caran I
ātmavaśyair vidheyātmā prasādam adhigacchati II64II

But the self-controlled man, free from attraction and repulsion, with his senses under restraint, though moving among objects, attains peace.

Rāga and *dveṣa* are the two causes for attachment to the world of *saṁsāra*. *Rāga* is sense of attraction for what one likes. *Dveṣa* is sense of hatred for what one dislikes.

It is very difficult to avoid attachment to family, friends and possessions. Similarly, it is very difficult not to show hatred in action to what we dislike most. Both *rāga* and *dveṣa* tie us to this world. We need the sense-organs for our continuation of life in this world and also we need them towards our spiritual progress.

If we want to listen to the discourse on the *Gītā* by a *guru*, we need our ears and if we want to say prayers we need our tongue. We need eyes to see the beautiful idol of the Lord in the temple. Directing the sense-organs and the mind towards attaining *ātma-jñāna* will give a sense of tranquillity. This tranquillity of the mind is called *prasāda*.

The sense-organs are the instruments in our own hand. We can either let them free or let them stay at our feet doing their duty. We can use them to sustain our life and for this purpose not get tainted.

The senses are like the horses of a chariot. When the horses are under control, the charioteer can move freely in the world. He does not fall into ditches on the road nor does he fall on the wayside. This is the meaning one should get on seeing Kṛṣṇa holding the reins of the horses in the *Gītopadeśa* picture. The horses will then take the master to the destination without danger. The senses therefore do help when they are under control. Controlling self, means controlling the mind and the senses. This means, 'Be a master over yourself'. Without self-mastery Self-realisation is impossible.

प्रसादे सर्वदुःखानां हानिरस्योपजायते ।
प्रसन्नचेतसो ह्याशु बुद्धिः पर्यवतिष्ठते ॥६५॥

prasāde sarvaduḥkhānāṁ hānir asyopajāyate |
prasannacetaso hy āśu buddhiḥ paryavatiṣṭhate ||65||

When a man attains peace, all pains caused by an unbalanced mind come to an end. By peace and purity the mind is soon fixed in ātmā.

Peace is attained by control of all sense-organs constantly and by constant meditation on the Self. This gives the mind purity. In course of time, such a mind dissolves in *ātmā* and that is called liberation.

The first half of the verse says that equanimity in pain and sorrow makes one peaceful. Happiness is peace. Peace is happiness. This peace of mind is also termed *prasāda* because it is the grace of God.

All the turbulent rivers lose their turbulence when they merge into the ocean. Similarly, a man who can control the agitations caused by the sense-organs and the mind (by absorbing himself in the contemplation of the *ātman*) will attain peace. He is said to have merged himself in the ocean of bliss.

नास्ति बुद्धिरयुक्तस्य न चायुक्तस्य भावना ।
न चाभावयतः शान्तिरशान्तस्य कुतः सुखम् ॥६६॥

nāsti buddhir ayuktasya na cāyuktasya bhāvanā |
na cābhāvayataḥ śāntir aśāntasya kutaḥ sukham ||66||

To the unsteady mind there is no knowledge of the Self. To the unsteady there is no meditation. To the unmeditative no peace, and to the man without peace, how can there be happiness?

Yoga as we have understood so far is union of the ego with the *ātmā*. A *yogī* is one who has attained such union; such a *yogī* is a *yuktaḥ*. *Ayuktaḥ* is that person who has not united the ego with his *ātman*. In other words, his senses and mind look for worldly pleasures. Such a person will not have steady *bhāvanā*.

Bhāvanā means contemplation. In spiritual terms it means "contemplation of Self-knowledge". The main features of good *bhāvanā* (*sadbhāvanā*) are four:

maitrī (friendship)
karuṇā (compassion)
mudita (happy and pleased)
upekṣā (indifference)

Maitrī: Universal friendship is *sadbhāvanā*. Such a person looks upon all equally. He loves all. He does not say "my people, mine" etc. There is no room for *dveṣa* in such a person. He does not hate others.

Karuṇā: Such a person has compassion for others who are in distress. He begs God to help people in distress.

Muditaḥ: Such a person has respect and praise for good actions. Any person who is performing good deeds that are for the welfare of the community is respected by the person with *sadbhāvanā*.

Upekṣā: This means indifference. The person with *sadbhāvanā* is indifferent to his critics. He continues to perform his duty as per the *śāstras*. He has no thought of revenge on those who criticise and try to harm him.

Ayukta is one who has no *buddhi* and no *bhāvanā*. He is an egotistic person.

If we feel sorry for ourselves because someone criticises us, if we are looking for taking revenge on others, if we are jealous of others, can we find any peace in ourselves? If we are not peaceful can we be happy? If we are not happy and peaceful, what is the use of having all the worldly pleasures? By becoming a millionnaire one cannot find peace and happiness in himself. One cannot buy his way to attain liberation.

Peace and happiness are close associates of the person who has dropped his ego and merged his mind in the contemplation of the divine *ātman.*

इन्द्रियाणां हि चरतां यन्मनोऽनुविधीयते ।
तदस्य हरति प्रज्ञां वायुर्नावमिवाम्भसि ॥६७॥
indriyāṇāṁ hi caratāṁ yan mano'nuvidhīyate I
tad asya harati prajñāṁ vāyur nāvam ivā'mbhasi II67II

For, the mind which follows the wandering senses, carries away the discrimination, just as the wind carries away a boat on the waters.

The mind can be directed to worldly pleasures or turned towards contemplation on the divine. This verse describes the state of the mind that is directed towards worldly pleasures. Our sense-organs are those that take the mind towards the worldly pleasures.

Our sense-organs are constantly on the look out for objects that please us. This search is never ending. Instead of attaining liberation, such a person is caught in the cycle of births and deaths. This is compared to a boat on the waters in a river. One needs a sail to hold the boat steady. The boat has to be steady to take the passenger to his distination. If there is no sail, the winds will push the boat hither and thither. Instead of reaching the destination, the boat will reach a different destinaion or will capsize. Therefore, just like the sail, the mind should contemplate on the *ātman* and no let the senses dictate.

तस्माद्यस्य महाबाहो निगृहीतानि सर्वशः ।
इन्द्रियाणीन्द्रियार्थेभ्यस्तस्य प्रज्ञा प्रतिष्ठिता ॥६८॥
tasmād yasya mahābāho nigṛhītāni sarvaśaḥ I
indriyāṇīndriyārthebhyas tasya prajñā pratiṣṭhitā II68II

Therefore, O Arjuna, his knowledge is steady whose senses are completely restrained from sense-objects.

The Lord says, "control the senses from all sides if you have to develop a steady wisdom of the *ātmā*."

What does "from all sides" mean? It means, (1) control via the sense-organs and (2) control through the mind.

(1) **Control via sense-organs:** We all need sense-organs. They can take us to *śreyas* or *preyas*. For example, we can see a body with lustful eyes. We can also see the same body as a temple of God. In other words, how we see an object is important. What we see is also important. We can shut our eyes to sensual things but we can open our eyes for divine objects. It does not mean that we should walk with our eyes closed. We should keep our eyes open and train them to look for those that do not harm us in our path to attain liberation. The same principle applies to other sense-organs.

If we compare our senses to the horses of the chariot, we should not blindfold the horses, but we only need to put blinkers on them. They should be seeing the road ahead and not get distracted by wayside distractions.

(2) **Control through the mind:** The mind as we have learnt before, is a treasure-house. Its main character is memory. It remembers the events of the past. Even when we close all sense-organs, it can dwell on its past and live in its own dream-world. Such a mind cannot contemplate on the *ātman*. This state of mind is sometimes called mental prostitution (*manovyabhicāra*).

Let us take the example of a student who has an important topic to study for the next day's classes. He is in his room that night; and also suppose, that he is working with a candlelight. He, first of all, gets all his books in one place, closes all doors and windows, draws the curtains and then starts reading. He then gets absorbed in his studies. If he follows all these steps, he will make progress in his work and prepares properly for the next day's classes.

If he had left the doors or windows open, the wind would put the light out. If he had not drawn the curtains, he would be distracted by the events outside. Even after closing his doors, windows, and drawing the curtains, his mind could dwell on some other topic.

Similarly, if we have to develop contemplation on the *ātman*, we must control our senses from all the sides.

या निशा सर्वभूतानां तस्यां जागर्ति संयमी ।
यस्यां जाग्रति भूतानि सा निशा पश्यतो मुनेः ॥६९॥

***yā niśā sarvabhūtānāṁ tasyāṁ jāgarti saṁyamī* I**
***yasyāṁ jāgrati bhūtāni sā niśā paśyato muneḥ* II69II**

That which is night to all, in it the sage is awake. Where all beings are awake, that is the night for the sage who sees the Self.

This is to explain the difference of outlook on life between egocentric persons and the men-of-wisdom. The night in this context refers to darkness. Ignorance has *tāmasika* character, it is dark like the night. A *jñānī* lives in the light of knowledge and an *ajñānī* lives in darkness. The egocentric person is an *ajñānī*.

We consider it as day when we start seeing and experiencing the world around us. Day and night are only physical states due to presence or absence of the sunlight. What we do in day and night differs from person to person. For a thief, the night is like a day. He is wide awake to what he is going to steal.

For us, ordinary men, therefore our senses dictate what is day and what is night. Being bound to our senses, we consider that worldly objects are real. This is what is meant by, "when all beings are awake, that is night for the sage who sees the self".

A sage is a *brahma-jñānī* who has learnt the art of contemplation on the divine *ātman*. A sage does not see the world as we see. He does not see names, forms, likes, dislikes, but he sees divinity in all. He is not immersed in pleasures of the world and so, day is like night for him.

We consider worldly knowledge as the real knowledge and

consider those who do not have it as ignorant. In our view, such knowledge is day and ignorance is night.

For a *brahma-jñānī*, the real knowledge is the knowledge of *Paramātmā*. The light of knowledge (Sun) is day and everything else is night as far as he is considered.

Therefore, that which is night for us, is daytime for the sage. He sees knowledge of *Paramātmā* and is awake whereas we see the world and are not aware of *Paramātmā*. For those who have no knowledge of the *ātman* and *Paramātman*, such knowledge is like darkness because they cannot see "the *ātman*".

> आपूर्यमाणमचलप्रतिष्ठं समुद्रमापः प्रविशन्ति यद्वत् ।
> तद्वत्कामा यं प्रविशन्ति सर्वे स शान्तिमाप्नोति न कामकामी ॥७०॥
>
> ***āpūryamāṇam acalapratiṣṭhaṁ***
> ***samudram āpaḥ praviśanti yadvat* |**
> ***tadvat kāmā yaṁ praviśanti sarve***
> ***sa śāntim āpnoti na kāmakāmī* ||70||**
>
> *He attains peace into whom all desires enter as waters enter the ocean, which is filled from all sides, and remains unmoved. But not for the desirer of desires.*

The Lord stresses the point of sense-control constantly in his teaching.

The sense-organs provide the mind a craving for getting the objects that bring pleasure. This is desire. We constantly desire something or the other and some desires are stronger than others. If one examines the example of an ocean our understanding becomes clearer.

The sun draws up the waters of the ocean but the ocean does not reduce in size. The rivers join it from all sides and yet it does not expand. It remains the same, immovable. Similarly, a sage-of-wisdom is not moved when desires flood into him. The desires get merged into him but he continues to meditate on the Self. He is indifferent to earthly pleasures even if he is brought into such situations. His reality is the state of blissful experience of the Self.

In the modern society, there is a constant increase of the awareness of more and more objects of worldly pleasures (desires). We are bombarded through the media; new products all the time tempt us. We are like small wells and tanks. Small wells and tanks when they overflow with water, burst and cause damage. But a man-of-wisdom is like an ocean—no overflowing occurs in him.

So, "develop the spirit of detachment to worldly desires", is the Lord's command here.

In the earlier description the Lord discussed the same theme (verse 55) "He is the one, the man of steady knowledge, who completely casts off all the desires of the mind."

विहाय कामान् यः सर्वान् पुमांश्चरति निःस्पृहः ।
निर्ममो निरहंकारः स शान्तिमधिगच्छति ॥७१॥

***vihāya kāmān yaḥ sarvān pumāṁś carati niḥspṛhaḥ* I**
***nirmamo nirahaṁkāraḥ sa śāntim adhigacchati* II71II**

That man who, abandoning all desires, lives without longing for them, without the sense of 'I' and 'mine', attains peace.

How does one attain *mokṣa* and become one with *Brahman*? By dropping his 'ego' and uniting with the Self. How can one drop his 'ego'? By abandoning all the desires which are the real cause for attachment. At the same time one should develop the desire to merge with the Self. When one abandons all desires, automatically the feeling of 'I' and 'Mine' disappears. Such a person does not even have a desire to achieve liberation. He does not boast that he is a *jñānī*. He is then fit to be called an *ātma-jñānī* or *jīvanmukta*.

This verse deals with renunciation and hence it is taken as a summary of *saṁnyāsa-yoga* in this chapter.

Renunciation (*saṁnyāsa*) does not mean running away from life which is a very common misunderstanding. *Saṁnyāsa* means to renounce completely one's ego and egocentric desires. In sleep we "escape" from life and our ego is dead in sleep. But it awakens when we wake up from sleep. That is therefore not *saṁnyāsa*. One should be constantly asleep to the experiences of the phenomenal world by not keeping egocentric attitude, and then he is called a true *saṁnyāsī*. It is no use giving up all desires and running away because our minds may still contemplate the desires. That longing for desires must go as well.

> एषा ब्राह्मी स्थितिः पार्थ नैनां प्राप्य विमुह्यति ।
> स्थित्वाऽस्यामन्तकालेऽपि ब्रह्मनिर्वाणमृच्छति ॥७२॥
>
> ***eṣā brāhmī sthitiḥ pārtha naināṁ prāpya vimuhyati* I**
> ***sthitvā'syām antakāle'pi brahmanirvāṇam ṛcchati* II72II**
>
> *O Arjuna, having obtained this* brāhmī *state, man is not deluded. Being established in this even at the end of life, man attains oneness with Brahman.*

As one learns the art of dropping the ego, one should also develop the art of meditating on the Self. Just by dropping egocentric desires one does not get liberated. By developing meditation on the Self, one will not get deluded.

The final goal of *Vedānta* is liberation—'oneness with Self' (*mokṣa*). This state is called '*brāhmī*-state' or 'the state of *Brahman*'. Once he reaches that *brāhmī*-state, it does not mean physical death. Life in him cotinues till physical death but he remains in the same state till death, i.e., worldly objects do not cause disturbances any more. Even if he reaches this state at the last lap in his life, he would still get liberated. He has no rebirth. He is in a state of absolute bliss. This state cannot be explained, as it is above the mind and intellect level. It can only be experienced by becoming one with it.

One should therefore start on the path to spiritual progress early in life and keep constanly in it (*sādhanā*). One does not know when death or dementia will hit him.

To work without attachment and desires, without ego and vanity, ever steady in perfect equilibrium in success and failure, is, in other words, unconsciously 'to assert the great truth' (the Self). The negation of the false and assertion of truth is the path to realise the Self.

This state of experience is called *brahma-nirvāṇam. Nirvāṇam* means 'oneness'. Any experience concerning the physical world is possible at one's mental and intellectual level of thinking. They are *parokṣa anubhūti* (experiences of the physical world).

Brāhmī experience is *aparokṣa anubhūti.* It is not an experience one learns with the help of his *indriyas* (sense-organs) and hence it is above the level of the mind and intellect. It cannot be explained; but it is not impossible to attain it. This attempt to experience the state that cannot be explained should be the goal for the spiritual seekers.

इति श्रीमद्भगवद्गीतासूपनिषत्सु ब्रह्मविद्यायां योगशास्त्रे
श्रीकृष्णार्जुनसंवादे सांङ्ख्ययोगो नाम द्वितीयोऽध्यायः ॥

iti śrīmad-bhagavadgītāsūpaniṣatsu brahmavidyāyāṁ yogaśāstre
śrīkṛṣṇārjuna-saṁvāde sāṁkhyayogo
nāma dvitīyo'dhyāyaḥ **॥**

CHAPTER 3

KARMA-YOGA

INTRODUCTION

This chapter is termed *karma-yoga. Karma* means action, and so it can be called Yoga of Action. It is one of the four main paths towards liberation.

By following and performing the duties one is born into (due to his previous *vāsanās*) one can attain liberation. But, to achieve liberation, one must perform duties as prescribed by the *śāstras*.

Karma-yoga applies to the majority of people. To lead a family life is not contradictory to the laws of the scriptures. One can discharge his duties to society by being a family man. We have to discharge our duties to society. Only then a society can survive. We are part of the society we live in. We must do the duties that will help to make the world a better place to live in for the future generations.

There are a few people who say, "I do not want to have anything to do with the world", and they stay within the four walls of the house. They think that they will attain liberation by disassociating themselves from the world around them. Unfortunately, such persons do not realise that even for bare necessities for survival, one has to work and depend on others. What are our bare necessities?

We have to breathe and we have to eat. To breathe, we need fresh air. Polluted air brings in diseases. Unless society acts as a whole, one cannot provide fresh air. If the members of the society make the environment healthy, it will be safe for such a community because everybody will breathe fresh air. So even to breathe, we have to work using our lungs and we have to become part of the society.

To survive we have to eat also. Food does not come from nowhere. One has to harvest the crops. Even to live on milk and dairy products, one needs cows and someone has to look after them. To get the food one has to at least walk to the shops or to the vegetable garden. One can buy food or grow his own food or depend on charity. Roads have to be built and kept clean for one to walk upon.

So, each one of us has to do certain jobs in our community and be interdependent on the community. This chapter deals with ways of working and at the same time achieving liberation. One need not be a *saṁnyāsī* to get liberated.

Every human being has a mind. The mind is the centre for thoughts. It has connection with the outside world through the sense-organs. The sense-organs send in the stimuli from the outer world to the mind. The mind sends its reaction via the organs of action. Every action is brought about via this channel. Of course animals also have a similar channel. What is the difference between the two?

We have been blessed by something superior to the mind. It is called 'intellect'. We have the capacity to analyse the input into our minds before we act. Animals have an instinct only to survive. We have an intellect to understand and analyse what we have to do and also what we have done. Śrī Kṛṣṇa is teaching us to remember that we have the intellect and asks us to make use of it.

The majority of people are not well-versed in scriptures. If one has to be a *jñānī* and understand the scriptures to get *mokṣa*, then *mokṣa* would be only for a handful.

Doing *karma* (action) is also a path to liberation. Our scriptures have given us a full description of duty to be done by all members of the society. By performing the assigned duties and working sincerely one could achieve liberation.

One must know something about *vāsanās* at this stage.

Vāsanā is an imprint on our mind. When we think of something it leaves an imprint on our mind. This in turn leads to an action. There is always a reaction to every action. Once the reaction takes place that original imprint vanishes. Because of the constant flow of thoughts in our mind, we have millions of imprints, i.e., *vāsanās*, in us. We have to act to clear them. Only by doing selfless, sincere action without anticipating any rewards (*karma-phala-tyāga*), no further imprints gather. For this one needs to concentrate on things other than the material world, i.e., look inwards and think of the Self (this will be discussed later). In simple words, we all have to work to get rid of our *vāsanās*. Hence *karma-yoga* is an essential path for the majority.

Karma is sometimes defined as fate. If it is fate that is responsible for my being what I am or what I suffer, then there is nothing I can do. I have to live with that fate. If I still want liberation, I have to accept my fate as a blessing from God and live my life. I have to live as part of the society for mutual welfare. This will lead me towards the path to liberation.

In chapter 2, verse 47, Śrī Kṛṣṇa strongly stresses the point: "*karmaṇyevādhikaraste. . . .*". He stresses on performance of one's duty. Arjuna, not having clearly understood what was told, puts a question which starts this chapter on *karma-yoga*.

अर्जुन उवाच
ज्यायसी चेत्कर्मणस्ते मता बुद्धिर्जनार्दन ।
तत्किं कर्मणि घोरे मां नियोजयसि केशव ।।१।।

arjuna uvāca
jyāyasī cet karmaṇas te matā buddhir janārdana |
tat kiṁ karmaṇi ghore māṁ niyojayasi keśava ||1||
Arjun said

O Kṛṣṇa, if your belief is that knowledge is superior to action, why do you engage me in dreadful battle?

Arjuna in his heart of hearts still wanted to run away from the battle. He had heard Kṛṣṇa telling him that action was superior (in the middle of the second chapter) but then Kṛṣṇa elaborately described a man of steady wisdom. He now sees some flicker of light in his ignorance but still wants to clarify his doubts. He therefore asks him this question.

व्यामिश्रेणेव वाक्येन बुद्धिं मोहयसीव मे ।
तदेकं वद निश्चित्य येन श्रेयोऽहमाप्नुयाम् ।।२।।

vyāmiśreṇeva vākyena buddhiṁ mohayasīva me |
tad ekaṁ vada niścitya yena śreyo'ham āpnuyām ||2||

You confuse my intellect as it were with speech which appears paradoxical. Therefore tell me that 'one' path, by which I may attain the Highest.

Kṛṣṇa had dwelt on *karma* and *jñāna* in detail so far and also mentioned renunciation briefly.

In chapter 2, Kṛṣṇa had said that for a kṣatriya, righteous war was the only path to liberation (*dharmyādd hi yuddāc chreyo'nyat* . . . verse 31) Then, Kṛṣṇa had asked Arjuna to go beyond the three *guṇas* (*traiguṇya-viṣayā. . . .*) Arjuna thought that it meant, "Do not work". But Śrī Kṛṣṇa said *karmaṇyevādhikaras te* which stressed on performance of one's *karma*. But finally Śrī Kṛṣṇa ends with the description of a *sthitaprajña*. These apparently contradictory terms caused confusion. By knowledge (*jñāna*) one can realise *ātmā*. It helps to take one away from the world of the senses. Whereas *karma* keeps one in the world of the senses.

Arjuna, asks Kṛṣṇa as to which path would take him to *śreyas*. His aim was noble. He wanted to attain the highest, i.e., *mokṣa*. As he was in a state of hysteria to start with, probably his mind was not clear when Kṛṣṇa was teaching *sāṁkhya-yoga*.

Of course, poet Vyāsa is really putting the words in Arjuna's mouth. He is indirectly putting the question on behalf of every ordinary person. Why take a minor road to reach salvation? Why not take the best?

श्रीभगवानुवाच
लोकेऽस्मिन्द्विविधा निष्ठा पुरा प्रोक्ता मयानघ ।
ज्ञानयोगेन सांख्यानां कर्मयोगेन योगिनाम् ।।३।।

śrī bhagavān uvāca
loke'smin dvividhā niṣṭhā purā proktā mayā'nagha |
jñānayogena sāṁkhyānāṁ karmayogena yoginām ||3||

In this world there is a two-fold path, O sinless Arjuna, the path of knowledge of the Sāṁkhyans *and the path of action of the* Yogins.

Kṛṣṇa says that men fit for spiritual discipline fall under two separate categories. They have been in existence since ancient times.

Sāṁkhya, as we have learnt, is the description of the Soul; hence it is a study of knowledge. It is *jñāna-yoga.* A *karma-yogī* is one who believes that he is born to do his duty in the world. He looks upon work as worship.

A *jñāna-yogī* is considered as an *antarmukhī* and a *karma-yogī* is considered as a *bahirmukhī* by some philosophers. An *antarmukhī* is one whose knowledge stands out first, he still would be doing his duty. In other words, in him knowledge of *ātmā* will be in front and his duties follow behind his knowledge. Saint Sanaka is considered as an *antarmukhī.* A *bahirmukhī* is one whose duty stands out prominently. He will be recognised as a man of action, though he is also going to become a *jñānī* in course of time. His *karma* is in front and knowledge is a shadow behind his *karma.* King Janaka is considered as a *karmaniṣṭha.*

Even though Kṛṣṇa says that there are two distinct paths, he means, as we learn later on, that the people of Arjuna's time had read the *Veda*s and had thought *karma-kāṇḍa* and *jñāna-kāṇḍa* of the *Veda*s to be two separate paths to attain *mokṣa.*

The *Veda*s were misunderstood. The *Veda*s have never said so. They did offer rewards for performing various ritual acts of worship. It was in a way to encourage people to work according to the *śāstra*s. The *Veda*s are vast, and it is difficult for men to master them totally. Men had clear and strong opinions on the benefits one would get from the *Veda*s (from what they heard and understood).

To avoid this confusion and bring out the best in the *Veda*s, Śrī Kṛṣṇa has taught this *Gītā* to mankind. Kṛṣṇa, the cowherd, milked the cow (*Veda*s) and got the milk (*Gītā*) which is such a sweet and healthy product. It nourishes our brain.

Kṛṣṇa addresses Arjuna as sinless. As he was sinless, Kṛṣṇa choose to teach him. It means that the person fit to receive this teaching should have a pure mind, a sincere mind. One does not go to the teacher to test the teacher. This would be a sinful act.

One goes to the teacher to get knowledge only. The more sincere one is, the more one gets of the teacher. Arjuna, whenever he put a question to Kṛṣṇa, did so to clarify his doubts and not to test his teacher.

The Lord says that he taught the two-fold path in ancient times. He is already declaring his immortal state, i.e., he is beyond time and place.

Men of different types existed from the very beginning of creation. Some were meditative and the path of knowledge was fit for them. Others (the majority) were active men and for them was the path of action.

न कर्मणामनारम्भान्नैष्कर्म्यं पुरुषोऽश्नुते ।
न च संन्यसनादेव सिद्धिं समधिगच्छति ॥४॥

na karmaṇām anārambhān naiṣkarmyaṁ puruṣo'śnute |
na ca saṁnyasanād eva siddhiṁ samadhigacchati ||4||

Man does not reach the actionless state of Brahman *by non-performance of actions. Man also does not attain 'perfection' by renunciation only.*

The path of action is a means to an end because it prepares the person to go to the higher path of knowledge. Once having reached or gained the state of knowledge, it leads to liberation without any further help. This applies to the temperament of a majority of individuals. We are all really men of action.

What is *karma*? The first quarter of this verse begins with the word *na karmaṇām anārambhāt*. It means not from not starting the work in the beginning. What is the beginning of *karma*? To understand these two words, one must understand *vāsanās* (see Introduction for description of *vāsanās*).

The actions performed because of our thoughts are *karma*. These actions if performed according to the *śāstra*s do not leave further reactions behind (by *niṣkāma karma* and *karma-phala-tyāga* as we will understand later).

We have come from God and we have to merge into Him. The day we came from God we started to do our duties. *Karmārambha* is therefore the day we first came from God and not the day we were born in this birth. Once we realise that we have come from Him and that we have to return to Him, we will then have to clear our sins and the desires of our past. Our duty is:

(*a*) To purify our minds of past thoughts and actions,

(*b*) To obtain *jñāna*, and

(*c*) To attain union with *Paramātmā*.

Actions performed to fulfil the above three criteria are then known as the *karma* we have to perform. Such action is then known as *yajña*.

The *Veda*s describe various *yajña*s. *Yajña*s in simple terms mean duties one has to perform. The *Veda*s have prescribed duties to different types of men. Man is part of the community in which he lives and he has to live in harmony with one and all. The *Veda*s, in trying to keep the communities in order, prescribed duties to all. They realised that temperaments were different and so prescribed duties to fit the temperament. Whenever *karma* or action is mentioned in the *Gītā*, one must think of it as prescribed duties.

Nobody in a community has a right not to work and still expect benefits from the community. (The society had prescribed duties to look after the handicapped and sick people and children also). Hence the assertion that 'by not working one does not get liberated'. It is a statement to motivate every individual to do his duty to his community.

We all have desires of some kind or the other in varying proportions. As the desire is, so our thoughts are in our mental zone. These thoughts are expressed and projected in the world towards fulfilling some desires. All these are out of ignorance of the Soul in us. So, by simply declining our duties, we cannot attain *mokṣa*. By renunciation also one cannot attain *mokṣa*. What is needed is purification of the mind.

Let us take an example. We all want ourselves to be clean. We do not want to appear dirty, or unkempt in front of others. So, what do we do? We bathe daily to clean ourselves physically. We have to get along with our work every day. We cannot sit back and not do our work. After work, at the end of the day there is accumulation of sweat and dirt which we have to wash off. We cannot lock ourselves in a room so that no dirt falls on us. We therefore get along in our daily work, try not to get ourselves dirty, keep up a clean appearance. We repeat it everyday in our life.

Similarly, we must wash our mind and intellect everyday. This is to get self-development and re-discover the Self in us. The issue here is how to get inner purity of mind and not whether to work or give up work.

न हि कश्चित्क्षणमपि जातु तिष्ठत्यकर्मकृत् ।
कार्यते ह्यवशः कर्म सर्वः प्रकृतिजैर्गुणैः ॥५॥

na hi kaścit kṣaṇam api jātu tiṣṭhaty akarmakṛt |
kāryate hy avaśaḥ karma sarvaḥ prakṛtijair guṇaiḥ ||5||

No one can ever remain, even for a moment, without performing work. Everyone, without his will, is made to do work by the qualities born of Prakṛti.

In the first half, the point brought out is, that we as individuals have some essential duties to our physical body and towards achieving if we have essential duties to the community we live in.

We have to breathe, eat, sleep etc. We cannot survive without these acts. We breathe fresh air if all of us in the community keep the air clean. We have to eat and food is obtained from various sources in the community. We cannot say we do not depend on others for our basic needs. Hence, as a member of the society we have to do our duties towards society. We can be milkmen, roadsweepers, engineers, doctors, etc. We need people of different qualities to do the varied work in our community. It is for our mutual existence.

In the second half, we are told that we are made to act helplessly by the qualities born of nature and this is known as *prakṛti*.

Our qualities born according to nature fall into three categories called *sattva*, *rajas* and *tamas*. These will be described in detail later on (chapter 14). They are known as *guṇas*.

We are all a mixture of the three *guṇa*s. One *guṇa* predominates over the others, at any one time. The *guṇa*s in us make us do some work or the other and it becomes our nature.

Once one realises there is a soul in him, then he should start aiming at purification by disciplined work (using his intellect).

Hospitals admit patients with various ailments. They are kept in until they get better. Similarly, those who suffer from ignorance of the Self, are admitted in the hospital known as *prakṛti*. Their treatment is in the form of various *karma*s to suit their temperament. Once they achieve enlightenment, they can quit *prakṛti* and attain union with the *Brahman* (Sri Ramakrishna).

कर्मेन्द्रियाणि संयम्य य आस्ते मनसा स्मरन् ।
इन्द्रियार्थान्विमूढात्मा मिथ्याचारः स उच्यते ॥६॥

***karmendriyāṇi saṁyamya ya āste manasā smaran* |**
***indriyārthān vimūḍhātmā mithyācāraḥ sa ucyate* ||6||**

He who, restraining the organs of action, sits contemplating the sense-objects with mind is called a hypocrite.

We already know that actions are the results of thoughts. Thoughts originate in the mind.

The mind is an ocean of thoughts. An idle mind is known as a devil's workshop. By tying one's hands and feet, or by blindfolding the eyes or by putting cotton wool in the ears, one cannot stop the mind from thinking. On account of previous thoughts and experiences the mind has the capacity to dwell on itself. It can recollect its past experiences and live in its own world.

Our mind therefore can contemplate on worldly objects despite our controlling the sense-organs. The way to overcome this is to give the mind some food of our choice, (to think). It could be divine contemplation or worldly actions. Do the actions selflessly, is what we will be told later on.

Kṛṣṇa is using a strong word of criticism — 'hypocrite' in this verse. In India, we come across many people with saffron (priestly) clothes. An ordinary, ignorant man may take such a person as a *jñānī* (spiritual person). Just by wearing such clothes and not doing the duties, those men have no right to expect others to consider them as pure. They are hypocrites.

In spiritual progress, restraining the mind is essential. This is called *sādhanā*, or practice. This has to be constantly practised to achieve liberation (*sādhya*).

Sense-control is a means to mind-control, the end result is purity of the mind.

Two friends wanted to have a night out. On the way they came across an assembly of men where there was a spiritual discourse. One of the friends decided to stay back and listen to the discourse. The other one said to his friend that he would go to see an 'X' film. When they met the next day, they asked each other how they had enjoyed their evening. The friend who stayed back to listen to the discourse complained that his mind was on his friend who had gone to see the 'X' film. He asked him for all the details of the film. He was sorry that he did not go to see the film. The friend who went to the film could not explain the film at all to the other friend. He had not seen the film. All through the film he sat feeling guilty at not listening to the discourse.

It was an act of *mithyācāra* (thinking of one thing but doing something contrary to the *śāstras*) to sit at the discourse and think of the 'X' film.

As the mind is the only instrument we have to attain *mokṣa* we must keep it under constant control. All the senses should be restrained like the reins on the horses and the reins should be held by our conscience. The mind should be constantly under the control of one's *buddhi* (intellectual capacity of discrimination between right and wrong action and thought).

यस्त्विन्द्रियाणि मनसा नियम्यारभतेऽर्जुन ।
कर्मेन्द्रियैः कर्मयोगमसक्तः स विशिष्यते ॥७॥

***yas tv indriyāṇi manasā niyamyā-rabhate'rjuna* |**
***karmendriyaiḥ karmayogam asaktaḥ sa viśiṣyate* ||7||**

But O Arjuna, he who controls the senses with his mind and engages his organs of action of karma-yoga, *without attachment, is the best.*

What are the conditions of *karma-yoga* to attain liberation is discussed in this verse.

As we learnt before, the mind projects out through the five sense-organs of perception towards the field of sense-objects in the world. The first half of the verse says that one should be able to control the mind and not allow it to run away towards sense-objects. The mind should be under one's control. For example, we have all experienced that when an artist is deeply immersed in drawing or when a student is seriously reading, he does not seem to hear the arrival of someone else into the room until the visitor goes and nudges them. That person's hearing did not register the footsteps of his friend arriving into the room. Naturally, as the mind entertains several thoughts, by controlling it one would conserve a lot of energy. What should be done is explained in the second half of this verse.

The senses and the instruments of action should be under the control of the mind. In other words, it means one should do his worldly activities. But, then, one may ask, if we do worldly activities we get attached to them and get desire to possess. Hence Śrī Kṛṣṇa specifically says the actions should be without attachment. So, real *karma* has three components:

1. Mind should be under one's control (control by the intellect).
2. Senses and sense-organs should be under the control of the mind.
3. The action done should be done without attachment.

Such a person can walk easily on the path towards achieving *mokṣa*. If the mind is pure, any work done by the person does not affect him in his progress towards achieving liberation.

By doing actions without attachment two results are achieved. The first one is burning of the old *vāsanā*s (which is also a must towards *mokṣa*). The second is we do not get new *vāsanā*s by pure actions. And we burn existing *vāsanā*s by actions without attachment.

This should be the way of life of any *karma-yogī*. A *karma-yogī* is one who performs *niṣkāma karma* and shows equanimity towards opposites in his actions (e.g. pains and pleasures).

नियतं कुरु कर्म त्वं कर्म ज्यायो ह्यकर्मणः ।
शरीरयात्रापि च ते न प्रसिद्ध्येदकर्मणः ॥८॥

***niyataṁ kuru karma tvaṁ karma jyāyo hy akarmaṇaḥ* |**
***śarīrayātrāpi ca te na prasiddhyed akarmaṇaḥ* ||8||**

Do the obligatory work prescribed by śāstras*. It is superior to inaction. By inaction even the maintenance of the body is not possible for you.*

"What should I be doing in this world?" is a question by the beginner in his spiritual path.

Our *śāstra*s have been written by great men who realised that everyone has a duty—

(*a*) to himself,
(*b*) to his family,
(*c*) to his society,
(*d*) to his country,
(*e*) to his universe.

By doing so, we can name the work as dedicated work. Work for its own sake and universal benefit, is what the *śāstra*s prescribe.

There are four types of *karma*:

(1) *nitya-karma,*
(2) *naimittika-karma,*
(3) *kāmya-karma,*
(4) *niṣiddha-karma.*

This verse speaks of *nitya-karma*. It means obligatory, daily activities. To survive we have to eat, sleep, have a bath etc. One cannot survive without these activities. One can be a *saṁnyāsī* but still he has to perform his obligatory duties to his physical body. One falls ill if he does not follow his obligatory duties. Our *śāstra*s are very particular about physical purity of one's body and the surroundings.

Naimittika-karma is the continuation of *nitya-karma*. One cannot just eat, sleep and have a bath; one needs a place to sleep. One needs to earn to buy food and clothes and shelter. To earn, one has to be member of the community. One cannot be a Doctor,

Engineer, Minister in isolation. One has therefore to perform duties to fulfil his role according to his nature. These are *naimittika-karmas*.

Unfortunately, by forgetting this doctrine, we, having fallen into *saṁsāra*, perform duties to fulfil our desires. These can be selfish desires and are known as *kāmya-karmas*. Performing duties to achieve something for ourselves is contrary to the *śāstras*. As members of the community, one gets rewards as a matter of course on the merits of one's work. One should therefore perform his duties to the best of one's capacity. *Śāstras* prohibit us from certain actions. They are *niṣiddha karmas*. Stealing, raping, murder etc. are *niṣiddha-karmas*.

In the process of evolution from manhood to Godhood—

(1) we must do our *nitya-karma* to survive,

(2) we must do *naimittika-karma* to be part of the universe,

(3) we must not do *kāmya-karma* as we will get more new *vāsanās*,

(4) we must refrain from *niṣiddha-karma*.

Kāmya-karma and *niṣiddha-karma* bind us to this world and we will fall down the ladder from Godhood to manhood and further down to animal existence.

To work for himself and his family is the work at an individual level. To carry out the professional work is the work for the society and the country. By doing both diligently is to work for the universe.

Śāstras say that as the work reaches higher steps of the ladder, from work to your family to that of the nation, the works done at higher steps take priority and one will not be accruing sin by not doing work at the lower steps of the ladder. As an example, a soldier is both a householder responsible for his family and a soldier responsible for his country. By carrying on the work for the nation he may have to leave his family for a long time and may even get killed. Even though he had a duty to his family he could not do it when he was away at the battlefield. If he got killed his family may have lost the breadwinner. The soldier, according to the *śāstras*, is not a sinner and the nation takes over such duties as are necessary to look after the soldier' family.

This dedicated work, if carried out by all, constantly remembering their *dharma*, would uplift the nation and such a nation becomes a great nation. National output grows by leaps and bounds and everbody would enjoy the harvest. On the other hand, a nation full of idlers and philosophers who do not do the prescribed duties, will not progress. It may even get ruined. There are armchair philosophers. Practical philosophers, however, help a nation to be prosperous. Every person must do the work in his field of activity to the best of his capacity.

यज्ञार्थात्कर्मणोऽन्यत्र लोकोऽयं कर्मबन्धनः ।
तदर्थं कर्म कौन्तेय मुक्तसङ्गः समाचर ॥९॥

***yajñārthāt karmaṇo'nyatra loko'yaṁ karma bandhanaḥ* |**
***tad arthaṁ karma kaunteya muktasaṅgaḥ samācara* ||**

O Arjuna, work other than those performed for the sake of sacrifice (yajña) binds this world; so perform the work for sacrifice without attachment.

Arjuna, when he learnt the *Vedas*, had understood that *yajña* means a certain form of ritual, accompanied by sacred-fire oblations and *mantras*. This is what most of us understand even now. But Lord Kṛṣṇa gives a different interpretation to the word *yajña* (for meaning of *yajña* see chapter 4).

Śāstras say that *karmas* performed to achieve the end-result of *yajña* (i.e., *mokṣa*) do not bind a person to this life. All other *karmas* bind one to this life. Kṛṣṇa asks Arjuna to perform *karma* without attachment.

There are five types of *yajñas*. *Nitya-karma* and *naimittika-karma* are two of the five *yajñas*. The other three *yajñas* are the worship of God. They are:

(1) Worship of a deity using the sacrificial fire; this is *deva-yajña*.
(2) Worship of ancestors is *pitṛ-yajña*.
(3) Giving food as charity to fellow-beings is *manuṣya-yajña*.

The *Upaniṣads* declare that *yajña* is Viṣṇu. We come across three classes of existence in this universe:

(1) competitive existence,
(2) cooperative existence,
(3) self-dedicated existence.

Competitive existence is existence for survival. The animal kingdom is an example. Cooperative existence is human existence for the welfare of the group of people. Self-dedicated existence is divine existence. It is the highest law of life. It is an act of *yajña*. (*a*) Offering the best and the most useful thing one has to others is self-dedicated *yajña*. (sacrifice for others). (*b*) Offering due wages to a labourer is *yajña*. (*c*) To do the best work for wages is *yajña*. (*d*) Dedicating oneself to spiritual life and imparting spiritual knowledge is *yajña*. (*e*) Upholding *dharma* is *yajña*. (*f*) Working for increasing national wealth is *yajña*.

What has been said before, is the physical side of *yajña*—it was an act towards a goal. The goal is, "perform actions with no selfish motive" for the service of humanity and attain liberation. Any type of work dedicated to God and the universe becomes a *yajña*.

The Pāṇḍavas performed *aśvamedha yajña*. It involved leading a sacred and sacrificial horse to go wherever it wanted to go. The people of the land who walked on the path taken by the horse were expected to join the Pāṇḍavas. They had a choice either to join or fight the Pāṇḍavas. The Pāṇḍavas, by acquiring more land, would of course become more powerful. The duty of the Pāṇḍavas (and other kings at that time) was to spread *dharma* (righteousness). By acquiring more land, they would be spreading their *dharma* to more people of the newly acquired land. The emperors and kings of the olden days were all expected to follow the path of *dharma*.

At the individual level, any dedicated work is also *yajña*. The symbolic representation of this is the sacrificial fire and oblations and *mantra*s. Fire and *mantra*s need not be there but dedicated work still becomes a *yajña*.

Arjuna got attached to the people on both sides in the war and forgot at what level, in the ladder of *dharma,* he was. His duty to protect *dharma* was to fight for his country and forget personal level relationships. To act at the national level was his duty.

Arjuna was ignorant of his duty. Likewise, we are all ignorant of our duty (as prescribed by *śāstras*) and that is the reason why we see the moral and intellectual decline of our nation. Kṛṣṇa clearing the ignorance of Arjuna and of mankind says this: Understand the work first and then start working.

(1) Perform your *yajña* as an act of dedication to God and service to humanity. If you know that the same God is in all, service to humanity is service to God.

(2) Perform your *yajña* without any attachment to the fruits thereof.

सहयज्ञाः प्रजाः सृष्ट्वा पुरोवाच प्रजापतिः ।
अनेन प्रसविष्यध्वमेष वोऽस्त्व् इष्टकामधुक् ॥१०॥

sahayajñāḥ prajāḥ sṛṣṭvā purovāca prajāpatiḥ |
anena prasaviṣyadhvam eṣa vo'stv iṣṭakāmadhuk ||10||

The Prajāpati (Creator) having created mankind in the beginning with yajña, *said "By this shall you prosper". Let this be to you the milk-cow of desires, the wish-fulfilling heavenly cow, 'Kāmadhenu'.*

Prajāpati means Lord of the people. The Lord who created us is Prajāpati. Having created the universe, He has also provided the means for its survival.

We can take *pravṛtti-mārga* or *nivṛtti-mārga. Pravṛtti-mārga* means the path one takes with attachment to the worldly objects. *Nivṛtti mārga* means the path that involves detachment from worldly objects. The majority of us belong to the former class. Hence our needs are many. As the resources cannot keep on multiplying, we have to impose control on our wants and how much we want; and also, we must know how to get what we want. Towards fulfilling this, to help in sustaining the universe, to make the universe a prosperous place to live in, *yajñas* were introduced by our elders.

A *yajña*, as we discussed in the last verse, is any type of dedicated work. Kāmadhenu is the mythological cow that belonged to the sage Vasiṣṭha. It is said to give any object one desires. The *yajña* is compared to Kāmadhenu. It will fulfil one's desire.

When the world was created first, the cosmic forces came into existence first. These function instinctively in the service of all. The creative force of nature is an aspect of the Lord. They prepared the field by their unselfish, dedicated work for the arrival of life-on-earth. When life developed and multiplied, they kept up harmonised growth of existence.

But now, we humans, having intellect but not using it, working ego-centrically, are destroying the harmony of existence. It is a call of service to us all by Lord Kṛṣṇa to avert the imminent danger of disaster by our egotistic acts.

"Work unselfishly, work without expecting the fruits of work and work constantly and vigilantly and then you would all be performing *yajñas*. You will automatically prosper and the work will bring you the Kāmadhenu", is the Lord's teaching, again, in this verse.

The creator has created us with the capacity for service. No achievement is impossible for man, if he knows how to act in discipline and co-operation without attachment to the fruits thereof.

देवान्भावयतानेन ते देवा भावयन्तु वः ।
परस्परं भावयन्तः श्रेयः परमवाप्स्यथ ॥११॥

devān bhāvayatānena te devā bhāvayantu vaḥ |
parasparaṁ bhāvayantaḥ śreyaḥ param avāpsyatha ||11||

Cherish the devas *with* yajña. *They shall cherish you. Thus cherishing one another you shall attain the highest good.*

The universe is made up of five elements collectively. They are known as *pañcabhūtas*. They are: earth, water, fire, space, air.

These five are represented in all bodies. They are:

(1) **Tongue**: for taste, "represents water".

(2) **Eyes**: for light, "represents fire. The Sun is taken as representing fire".

(3) **Nose**: for smell, "represents earth".

(4) **Ears**: for hearing, "represents space".

(5) **Skin**: for touch, "represents air".

The eyes, tongue, nose, ears and skin together constitute the five sense-organs. Each sense-organ performs only one specialised task. Eyes can only see, ears can only hear, nose can only smell, tongue can taste and skin can touch and feel.

As one cannot hear without space,
one cannot see without light,
one cannot touch without air,
one cannot smell without earth,
one cannot taste without water,

the *pañcabhūtas* are considered as *devas*. The *deva* of eye (Sun) blesses the eyes to see, the *deva* of ears (space) blesses the ears to hear (and so on for other sense-organs).

When we work, we all have to work in the field of any one or any combination of *pañcabhūtas*. *Deva* is considered as the presiding deity in any field. The *deva* will bless the worker. There is productivity dormant in any type of work. This productivity is also called *deva*. The effort one puts in his work when he uses it for dedicated work then becomes a *yajña*.

For example, the farmer working hard will be invoking the Mother Earth. Mother Earth will be his *deva* for his activity. The crop he will harvest is said to be the blessings of Mother Earth. The deva (Mother Earth) blessed the farmer for his efforts. Similarly, in any field of work, there is a potential to achieve more. This productivity-potential is called *deva*. The more effort we put in that field, the more sincere our efforts are, the more benefits will we get.

Do your selfless, sincere work	—	*yajña*.
You will invoke the *deva*	—	productivity.
The *deva* will bless you	—	product of your work.

Man is given the choice of acting the way he likes because he has been endowed with a mind. But man has also been endowed with an intellect to discriminate between his true Self and his body. One may ask the question: "If I give away what I have, what will I get? I will only be losing what I have and I will become poorer". The *Vedas* tell us that those who sacrifice what they have in the service of the Universe, will get their reward accordingly.

We all use firewood. We light the fuel. What happens to it? The fuel becomes fire. The fuel has potential energy in it and it manifests as fire. In other words, by lighting the fuel with fire, the fuel becomes the fire. Similarly, those devotees who surrender everything they have to the Lord (by saying *kṛṣṇārpaṇam astu*), will become divine by their actions. They attain Godhood.

Yajña therefore, as described in the *Vedas* brings Godhood to man. But, unfortunataly, we have forgotten our true nature and the purpose of our existence. Spiritualists want to awaken us (before we ruin ourselves).

इष्टान्भोगान्हि वो देवा दास्यन्ते यज्ञभाविताः ।
तैर्दत्तानप्रदायैभ्यो यो भुङ्क्ते स्तेन एव सः ॥१२॥

iṣṭān bhogān hi vo devā dāsyante yajñabhāvitāḥ I
tair dattān apradāyaibhyo yo bhuṅkte stena eva saḥ II12II

Cherished by sacrifice, the devas *give you desirable enjoyments. He who enjoys objects given by the* devas *without offering them is verily a thief.*

If we consider that there is God (divinity) in all, the society of gods gives us the reward for our work, i.e., our pay and their contributions to our welfare. If we receive a few benefits from society, we must return some benefit to society.

Initially when I was born into this world, my 'society' would be mainly my parents. They gave me more than what I gave them. When I went to school and college, my 'society' increased. I had teachers, who taught me. Again, that society gave me more than what I gave them in return. Society in a way, sacrificed more for my sake, and my parents sacrificed more for my sake. I was mainly a receiver, rather than a dispenser of benefits. So, when I grow up, I should be asking, ''What am I giving to the society? How much useful I am going to be for society?'' Our actions must always be beneficial to others and then only our actions become *yajña*s.

This can be done by our continued work (*yajña*) and by giving benefit to those members of society who cannot look after themselves, i.e., charitable work. Charitable work can be on a one-to-one basis or as a group. One can give charity to an individual or to a group who do charitable work.

If we give more than we take, then we will be doing righteous *karma*. If we take more than what we give, we will be committing sin. We suffer for our sins sooner or later. A thief is one who takes from others but does not give. If we have had benefits from the *deva*s by their blessing, we must return it to the *deva*s in one form or another. As the *deva*s are inside all forms of existence, giving to those in need is like giving to the *devas*.

So the advice is, share your rewards amongst all.

A member of the society who consumes without producing is a liability to the nation. A nation of idlers, with idlers expecting benefit from the nation without returning benefits given in some other form will not prosper.

This law applies to all countries. Also, it is a Universal Law. We must return a part of our benefits to the welfare of the universe.

यज्ञशिष्टाशिनः सन्तो मुच्यन्ते सर्वकिल्बिषैः ।
भुञ्जते ते त्वेघं पापा ये पचन्त्यात्मकारणात् ॥१३॥

yajñaśiṣṭāśinaḥ santo mucyante sarvakilbiṣaiḥ I
bhuñjate te tv aghaṁ pāpā ye pacanty ātmakāraṇāt II13II

The righteous who offer food to the Gods in sacrifice and eat the remnants, are freed from all sins. But those who cook food to satisfy their own needs, are sinners and verily eat sin.

This is another way of elaborating on 'share and survive or be selfish and go to hel'.

Those who share their food (wealth) with *deva*s and gods (fellow creatures of the universe who are in need) will not incur sin.Why do we elaborate on "sin"? What is sin? What happens to sinners?

Sin is an act done wilfully or without one's knowledge, which is against the *śāstras*. It could be a major act like murder, rape etc. or a simple act like telling a lie. Because it is an act it will have a reaction in course of time. What we suffer now as pain, is, according to scriptures, the result of our sins of the past. For the sins we do now, we pay later (*vāsanā* — reaction). Also, if it is a sin of thought, an act which is only a thought in the mind and not put into action. We will be punished for that also.

If one does not share his food (wealth), he has committed a sinful act and will pay the fine later (it could mean next birth also). How to get rid of sins of the past?

Every action has a reaction. Good action now, in the form of action in the spirit of worship of God or service to the members of the universe, will help to neutralise the past sins. Later on, once all sins of the past are paid up either in fines or by good acts, the same selfless work will accumulate good points and that will take one to a higher plane of existence.

Karma as such is neither good nor evil but the motive behind it makes it good or bad. Eating the remnants of *yajña* means accepting the benefits of *yajña* as God's grace. Offering the food to Gods means sharing the benefits of *yajña* with others.

Yajña, as we have learnt before, means any dedicated work. So any *karma* that has no selfish motive is *yajña*. Whatever we think or do or speak should always be directed to the good of the world and praise of the Lord. Whatever I have done (only acts not prohibited by *śāstra*s) should be done in the spirit of *kṛṣṇārpaṇam astu.* "Lord made me do the *karma* and its results go back to the Lord", should be the spirit behind all thoughts and actions.

We eat food daily. We do so to keep our body in good trim. The *ātman* is inside our body. So, it is not wrong to eat to sustain oneself. But we should think of those who are in need of food. Forgetting this and eating only for one's personal needs is a sinful act.

The *śāstras* direct us to perform *yajñas* everyday. Basically there are five types of *yajñas*.

(1) **Deva-yajña:** We must remember the Lord who created us. We must remember the Lord who sustains us. We must therfore spend certain times of the day thinking and praising the Lord's glory. The *śāstras* give us some special auspicious days when we do the same worship with family and friends. There are times in the day when we actually do not do anything special. For example, when going to school or work or coming back from school or work, or on a long journey, we actually do not do anything particular. Instead of letting other thoughts into our mind we can be saying prayers. Learning, memorising prayers and repeating such prayers when we are not doing anything, is also *deva-yajña.*

(2) **Ṛṣi-yajña:** This is respect towards *ṛṣis*. *Ṛṣis* or sages are those who impart *śāstric* and divine knowledge to the ignorant. We may not see them daily but we can attend the discourses given by them. We could read scriptures like *Rāmāyaṇa, Gītā, Bible* etc. They are written by great sages. We should not only listen and study them but should also understand what is said and put it into practice.

(3) **Pitṛ-yajña:** This is respecting *pitṛs*. *Pitṛs* are parents. Respecting one's parents and pleasing them according to *śāstras* is *pitṛyajña*. Parents of parents and their parents are also *pitṛs*. They are departed souls or manes. The parent of all is Pitāmaha Brahmā, the creator. Worshipping departed souls is also *yajña*. This is to remind us that we are part of somebody. This is to take away the 'Self' or 'I'ness in us.

(4) **Nara-yajña**: All fellow beings are *naras*. Acts for the welfare of the needy welfare of the society are considered as *yajñas*. Public interest must always take priority in one's acts.

(5) **Bhūta-yajña**: All other creatures other than man are *bhūtas*. The Universe is a combination of man, animals and plants. We

are interdependent on each of these. All creatures after all are still God's creation and we have a duty to look after them. By giving some food to birds and insects is *bhūta-yajña*. Also, taking care of the environment to make the birds and animals survive is *bhūta-yajña*.

These five *yajña*s are considered as *nitya-karma*s by the *śāstras*. They are our daily, obligatory duties. Any act to the contrary is a sin.

The verses 10-13 are considered to be *the arthavāda*. It means explaining the reason for any action (*artha*) to those who argue on "what and why" of *karma*. It is like the teacher or mother explaining something which the child does not know but is curious to know. *Arthavāda* is in four sections.

(1) **Stuti**: This means praise. Saying good things about the work is *stuti*. Saying what will profit you or fulfil your desires, is *stuti*. The word used is *eṣa vo'stviṣṭakamadhuk*.

(2) **Nindā:** Saying the evil or harm that comes out of not doing the work is *nindā*. That you are to be considered as a thief (*yo bhuṅkte stena eva saḥ; stena:* thief) is the *nindā* used in this *arthavāda*.

(3) **Prakṛti**: It is God's act and hence you must do it, is the third part of *arthavāda*. "*Purovāca prajāpatiḥ*"*:* Prajāpati, the creator said so, I am not saying it myself, so do the *karma,* is what is meant by *prakṛti*.

(4) **Purākalpa:** You will be blessed by different *deva*s for different acts is another way of explaining the need to perform *karma*. The *deva*s shall bestow on you all your desires. There are some who may not believe in existence of one supreme God. For them, we can say, mother earth will bless you, Sun-god will bless you etc.

अन्नाद्भवन्ति भूतानि पर्जन्यादन्नसंभवः ।
यज्ञाद्भवति पर्जन्यो यज्ञः कर्मसमुद्भवः ॥१४॥

***annād bhavanti bhūtāni parjanyād annasaṁbhavaḥ* |**
***yajñād bhavati parjanyo yajñaḥ karma-samudbhavaḥ* ||14||**

कर्म ब्रह्मोद्भवं विद्धि ब्रह्माक्षरसमुद्भवम् ।
तस्मात् सर्वगतं ब्रह्म नित्यं यज्ञे प्रतिष्ठितम् ॥१५॥

karma brahmodbhavaṁ viddhi brahmā'kṣara-samudbhavam |
tasmāt sarvagataṁ brahma nityaṁ yajñe pratiṣṭhitam ||15||

From food, beings are born. Food is produced from rain. Rain comes from sacrifice. Sacrifice is born of action.

Know that action arises from the Vedas. *The* Vedas *are born from the imperishable* Brahman. *Therefore know that the Supreme being is established in* yajña.

What is *yajña*? It is a dedicated act towards purification of oneself. Even though one is already pure, one can still perform pure acts. Though we might become one with *Brahman*, though we have attained the state of a *jīvanmukta*, we still will have to live till the death of the physical body. We should still be doing selfless work for the welfare of society, e.g., educate the ignorant.

*Yajña*s usually have a sacrificial fire into which are offered oblations. These oblations involve the Deity of fire who will help the performer of the *yajña* to get his object of desire.

In olden days *yajña*s included sacrifice of animals. This was because of a false interpretation of the *Veda*s. The *Veda*s do not ask us to sacrifice animals in *yajña*s. The sacrifice of animals should be understood as 'sacrifice of animal instincts'. In our sacred duties in this world, we must sacrifice our selfish animal instincts. Such acts immediately become pure. By pure acts one gets higher rewards for his work. We should stop the ritual of animal sacrifice which unfortunately is done even today by some ignorant people.

God, *Brahman* without form, having a desire to create, projected himself as Brahmā with form. He developed intellect and mind and physical body. Through these he developed contact with the physical world. He brought forth life on earth initially from his mind. The earlier sages who were born thus were called *mānasaputra*s (born of the mind of Brahmā).

The sages gave ideas of pure thoughts and pure living to the subsequent generations. They have given us the sacred texts, *Vedas*, which are our ancient treasure. The *Vedas* contain a number of *mantras*. During some inspired moments, the sages came out with these *mantras*. They attributed the origin of the *mantras* to a divine force. They did not accept authorship of the *mantras*.

All the *mantras* recited by a number of ancient *ṛṣis* were compiled together into four texts. They became the four *Vedas* (*Ṛg*, *Yajur*, *Sāma*, and *Atharva*). Hence in this verse it is said that the *Vedas* are born from *Brahman*.

The *Vedas* describe the various actions one can undertake and the benefits one would get from such action (*karma*). They also describe the method of concentrating on the *Brahman* and obtaining knowledge of the *Brahman*. As *Brahman*, through the *Vedas*, has given the foundation for the welfare of the Universe, it is said the *Brahman* is established in *yajña*.

Good actions, in large numbers, give showers of good results. It is symbolised as rains produced from *yajña* (rains : *parjanya*).

These good results would benefit society and society would live longer and happily. This is what is meant by saying that food is produced from rain and beings are born of food.

Dharmacakra is

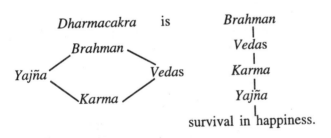

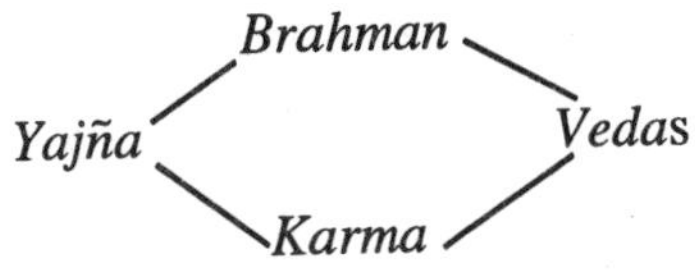

Brahman
|
Vedas
|
Karma
|
Yajña
|
survival in happiness.

एवं प्रवर्तितं चक्रं नानुवर्तयतीह यः ।
अघायुरिन्द्रियारामो मोघं पार्थ स जीवति ॥१६॥

evaṁ pravartitaṁ cakraṁ nānuvartayatīha yaḥ |
aghāyur indriyārāmo moghaṁ pārtha sa jīvati ||16||

The man who does not follow the cycle thus set revolving, is a sinner, rejoicing in the senses. He lives in vain, O Pārtha.

This verse is meant to emphasise that one should do good deeds. It is like saying, "you go to jail for stealing", repeatedly in different ways.

The entire universe is surviving on the principle of this cycle of *Brahman-Vedas-Karma-Yajña-Brahman*. It is our duty to see that the cycle is revolving constantly. Those that do not help in keeping the cycle revolving are considered as sinners.

In this cycle, we come in at the *karma*-stage. If we do not perform *yajña* (i.e., if we all work selfishly), our society will have a majority of selfish people in course of time who will not take part in the welfare of society. This is what is meant by, "He lives in vain". Of course this will lead to ruin for the person and entire society eventually.

Those who do not follow this *cakra* are people who have forgotten 'God'. They are living in sin (*aghāyu*), rejoicing in senses (*indriyārāmāḥ*), work for personal pleasures.

So, "live the life of *ātmārāma* (live in Godhood), rejoice in *ātmā*", is the meaning here.

यस्त्वात्मरतिरेव स्यादात्मतृप्तश्च मानवः ।
आत्मन्येव च संतुष्टस्तस्य कार्यं न विद्यते ॥१७॥

yas tv ātmaratir eva syād ātmatṛptaśca mānavaḥ |
ātmany eva ca saṁtuṣṭas tasya kāryaṁ na vidyate ||17||

But the man who rejoices in ātmā *who finds satisfaction in* ātmā, *who is contented in* ātmā, *has no work to perform.*

Desires are the first enemy for us. Desire to possess brings in thoughts and action. It is an endless circle. If one can cut the desire, there will be no more thought-waves and actions to follow. Such a person lives in contentment.

The next step is to divert the mind towards the Self and finding pleasure in the Self. Such a person who rejoices in *ātmā*, finds satisfaction in himself. *Rati* means pleasure. Pleasure in *ātman* is *ātmarati*. Finding satisfaction in *ātman* is *ātmatṛpti*.

The mind concentrating on worldly objects automatically is more active. There are far too many desirable objects in the world.

The mind concentrating on the *ātman* is comparatively less active. There is only one point of concentration and that is the *ātman*. Of course, the task is difficult in the initial stages. Once it is merged in the *ātman*, it has no more work to do. It remains in a state of bliss.

Rivers are very active till they join the ocean. When they merge in the ocean, they have no individuality left and are said to be inactive.

For such an *ātmatṛpta* person, it says, there is no work to perform—the person is still living but works involuntarily for the welfare of the community (divine work). He is not working to satisfy himself but he is fulfilling "God-realisation" (doing the work of God, i.e., becomes 'the God'). He is a *jñānī*.

The opposite to this is *ajñānī*, the ignorant, covered by *māyā*. He is one who forgets his divine nature and lives selfishly.

नैव तस्य कृतेनार्थो नाकृतेनेह कश्चन ।
न चास्य सर्वभूतेषु कश्चिदर्थव्यपाश्रयः ॥१८॥

naiva tasya kṛtenārtho nākṛteneha kaścana |
na cāsya sarvabhūteṣu kaścid arthavyapāśrayaḥ ||18||

For him, there is in this world, no interest whatsoever by work done or not done. He does not depend upon any being for any object.

This is again re-emphasising the merits of good work. The prize is 'Godhood'. He is called *jīvanmukta*. Even while living he has attained 'Godhood'.

The *jñānī* who has attained the status of *jīvanmukta*, will spend the rest of his life performing divine work for the welfare of society. He has no personal interest to achieve anything. He will propagate the teaching of the *Veda*s to those who want to better themselves. His way of living becomes an example for others to follow.

It is important to note that Śrī Kṛṣṇa has said that such a person has nothing to gain and nothing to lose. But he has not said that such a person will not perform or should not perform any work.

Kṛṣṇa, later on tells Arjuna, "I have told you what *Vedas* say, it is up to you to do what you want."

If he had asked Arjuna to fight, it would have meant that Śrī Kṛṣṇa also had a 'desire' to fulfil. Kṛṣṇa, the human manifestation of God, did not ask Arjuna to fight. *Brahman* has given intellect to humans and He has also given *Vedas*. He has left it to individual humans to do what they want. He has given us the means to purify ourselves and it is up to us whether we make use of it or not.

तस्मादसक्तः सततं कार्यं कर्म समाचर ।
असक्तो ह्याचरन्कर्म परमाप्नोति पूरुषः ॥१९॥

tasmād asaktaḥ satataṁ kāryaṁ karma samācara |
asakto hy ācaran karma param āpnoti pūruṣaḥ **||19||**

Therefore do the work that has to be done, do it always without attachment. For, by performing action without attachment, you will attain the Supreme.

How should one do his duties? This question is answered in this verse. One has to perform his obligatory duties. We all have to do our *nitya* and *naimittka karmas*. We should do so without any sense of attachment and this will aid us to attain liberation.

Niṣkāma karma is action performed without attachment to the results. This is considered as *sāttvika* action. If an action is performed with a desire for gaining results, it becomes *sakāma*. This then becomes *rājasika* action. *Akarma* is laziness wherein one does not do any work. This is *tāmasika* action.

How can one develop detachment in attachment? We have to work but should not be attached to our work. We should not work for the results of our work.

I am a government employee working as a teacher. There are two ways in which I can look at my job.

(*a*) I am performing my *naimittika karma*. I am doing a co-operative work. By doing so, I do get paid. The salary I get will help me to perform duties for my body (*nitya karma*) and also to look after my family. Without the salary I will have no shelter and I cannot maintain my family. I am therefore indebted to my society for having given me the job of the teacher and giving me my salary. By having such a frame of mind, I will look upon my pay packet as a *prasāda* from society. I feel indebted to society. I will therefore do my best as a teacher and will work to earn my salary. This is *niṣkāma karma* or working without attachment.

(*b*) I feel proud to be a teacher. I look forward to my pay packet as something that society owes me. I look forward to my monthly pay and think of what I can do with the pay. I will plan to buy a variety of goods that will please me and my family. I look forward for the pay to fulfil my desires (not my *nitya karma* and my duty to my family). In the process I overspend (credit card as in the present society, or buying first and paying later etc.). Every month, I am intent on getting the pay so that I can repay my debts and will continue spending on fulfilling the desires. This is *sakāma karma*.

Of course, I may not work at all. I may be physically fit or at least capable of doing some work, but still will not work. I depend on my rich parents or on help from society. This then becomes *akarma*.

We should look after our family with love and affection. Even in this work, we must develop detachment in attachment. We should provide the necessary comforts to our dependents but this should fulfil the following requirements:

(*a*) Provide comfort within our means.

(*b*) Get the means to provide maximum comfort, i.e., work according to *śāstras* to the best of one's capacity.

(*c*) Let our dependents realise what our earning capacity is and live within our means.

(*d*) After performing duties to our family in the above manner, we should not be frightened to let go of them. We should not be so attached to our family that we are frightened of losing them (i.e., death). We should be prepared to part company from them. We should not be totally disheartened and shattered by the death of our beloved ones. We still have to live and be part of the cooperative society. Hence, we must develop the spirit of detachment in attachment.

We must do our worldly activities but even in the midst of them, keep the mind fixed on the Lord. We should not deviate from the Godly path. We must work in the spirit of work as God's work. The work we do must please our master (God) and He will automatically reward us in one form or another. We must not work for the reward. There should not be any desire in the work we do. This is *niṣkāma karma.*

कर्मणैव हि संसिद्धिमास्थिता जनकादयः ।
लोकसंग्रहमेवापि संपश्यन्कर्तुमर्हसि ॥२०॥

karmaṇaiva hi saṁsiddhim āsthitā janakādayaḥ **।**
lokasaṁgraham evāpi saṁpaśyan kartum arhasi **॥20॥**

King Janaka and others attained perfection by action only. Even with a view to protecting the masses you should perform actions.

Śrī Kṛṣṇa gives examples of great men of the past who attained liberation by *niṣkāma karma.* King Janaka was one such. He was a great scholar and a learned man. He had the title *rājarṣi.* A *rājarṣi* is a *rājā* (king) and *ṛṣi* in one. He was a great administrator and ruled his kingdom well. He took steps to improve the welfare of his subjects and at the same time worked at gaining *ātma-jñāna.*

There was no need for him to be the king. He could have gone to the forest to meditate and attain *mokṣa.*

If all knowledgeable people decide not to work and not to pass on their knowledge to others, there will be very few leaders in society to set an example to the rest of the community. A knowledgeable person could be a teacher to teach or be an example for others to follow.

In ancient times, the land was ruled by kings, who were advised by their ministers and family priests. The children of the royal family and of the priest went in their learning days to *āśrama*s to learn scriptures, including rules on governing a country. A very learned person would be the *guru* of the *āśrama*. In this way the king who would rule later would be trained to rule for the welfare of his subjects under the guidance of his ministers. Arjuna being a kṣatriya was therefore reminded by Kṛṣṇa about king Janaka.

Service to humanity has the highest place in our philosophy. One can help a single individual, a group or a community or a nation. Arjuna, belonging to the royal family was in a position to set an example not only for other kings but also to all the subjects in the kingdom.

यद्यदाचरति श्रेष्ठस्तत्तदेवेतरो जनः ।
स यत्प्रमाणं कुरुते लोकस्तदनुवर्तते ॥२१॥

***yad yad ācarati śreṣṭhas tat tad evetaro janaḥ* |**
***sa yat pramāṇaṁ kurute lokas tad anuvartate* ||21||**

Whatsoever a great man does, that other men do (imitate). Whatever he sets up as the standard, that the world follows.

Yathā rājā tathā prajā is an ancient saying in Hindu philosophy. As is the King, so are his subjects. An evil king leaves behind a lot of evil men in his kingdom. He will constantly have the company of evil people who will perform evil deeds.

The majority of people do not try to read and analyse the scriptures. They tend to follow the persons whom they consider great. It is therefore the duty of gifted people to set an example for others. They can do so by teaching or by setting a personal standard of life for others to follow.

In a household, one tends to say that the son should get into the shoes of his father. They say children should follow the footsteps of their parents. If parents themselves do not know the *śāstra*s and do not follow the rules of society, how can the children learn? What will happen to that household?

Similarly, Arjuna, being a great warrior had a duty to set examples for others. If he ran away in his fight agains *adharma*, what would the weaker men be expected to do?

Kṛṣṇa is asking Arjuna to be a practical man of action. It is no use talking philosophy without following it in one's daily action.

न मे पार्थास्ति कर्तव्यं त्रिषु लोकेषु किञ्चन ।
नानवाप्तमवाप्तव्यं वर्त एव च कर्मणि ॥२२॥

na me pārthāsti kartavyaṁ triṣu lokeṣu kiñcana |
nānavāptam avāptavyaṁ varta eva ca karmaṇi ||

There is no duty for me to do in the three worlds, O Pārtha. There is nothing unattained or to be attained for me, and yet I am also engaged in work.

Kṛṣṇa is God himself. He incarnated himself for the protection of righteousness. He could have killed the Kauravas easily and given the kingdom to the Pāṇḍavas, but he did not do so. Why?

In the past he had killed several wicked people like Kaṁsa and others. But he did not rule the country after killing them.

He has now taken up the work as *sārathī* to Arjuna. He could have annihilated the Kauravas by his *Sudarśana cakra*. He did not do so. His only aim is to protect righteousness and in the process, he has sided with the Pāṇḍavas and guided them. The action of Śrī Kṛṣṇa and the Pāṇḍavas was to uphold righteousness and set an example for others. Evil will be rooted out sooner or later; the evil-doers must realise it.

He therefore taught Arjuna the greatest philosophy that mankind should be proud of and let Arjuna decide what was right and do accordingly. Every person has to decide for himself as to what is right and wrong and do what his intellect says.

Kṛṣṇa showed the right path for mankind and it is still followed even after 5000 years. His *niṣkāma karma* has been followed and kept alive for 5000 years. There is no more one can say. Action speaks for itself.

यदि ह्यहं न वर्तेयं जातु कर्मण्यतन्द्रितः ।
मम वर्त्मानुवर्तन्ते मनुष्याः पार्थ सर्वशः ॥२३॥

yadi hy ahaṁ na varteyaṁ jātu karmaṇy atandritaḥ |
mama vartmā-nuvartante manuṣyāḥ pārtha sarvaśaḥ ||23||

If I am not engaged in action relentlessly, without relaxation, men would follow my path in every way, O Arjuna.

This is the other side of the coin, the other aspect of the previous verse. Kṛṣṇa is saying that if he were not doing *karma* always, others who observe him would do the same. He would then be responsible for ruining the life in the universe.

One cannot say how many follow the good example set by great men. On the other hand, it is true that one lazy action, or momentary indiscretion by such men will remain in the memory of others.

In the case of Śrī Kṛṣṇa, suppose he relaxed for a short period from his duties, it is possible people would say: "After all, a great man like Śrī Kṛṣṇa did not do it. There must be some reason for doing so. Let us not do it then." People's nature is to look for excuses.

Some people have a divine gift and become great. They have a special responsibility in guarding themselves against anything they do or say which will be a bad influence on others.

We, ordinary folks, should be on our guard always and keep a control on our sense-organs. We should not let them disturb our minds.

उत्सीदेयुरिमे लोका न कुर्यां कर्म चेदहम् ।
सङ्करस्य च कर्ता स्यामुपहन्यामिमाः प्रजाः ॥२४॥

utsīdeyur ime lokā na kuryāṁ karma ced aham |
saṁkarasya ca kartā syām upahanyām imāḥ prajāḥ ||24||

These worlds would perish if I did not perform action. I would be the author of confusion and would destroy these people.

In continuation of the last verse, Śrī Kṛṣṇa emphasises that universal stability will be lost if he does not work. After all, Śrī Kṛṣṇa is God Himself. If He, the God, does not work, the world would perish. (Verse 16 *dharmacakra*, the wheel, should be constantly in motion. Even Brahmā cannot stop it for a minute).

This verse can be read in another form.

God is in every living being in this world. If, we, the representatives of God do not do our work as per the *śāstras*, then the world we live in will perish eventually. We are seeing examples of destruction in various parts of the world by undivine and selfish work of the people. Because of actions of a lot of good people on earth, the universe is still surviving.

"I would be the author of confusion" Śri Kṛṣṇa says. The inner world of thoughts and emotions in each of us could make us into kṣatriyas, brāhmaṇas, vaiśyas, or śūdras and our actions would be according to the thoughts we carry. If our thoughts are not proper, there would be confusion in our actions. So, always keep divine thoughts, would be the advice for mankind.

सक्ताः कर्मण्यविद्वांसो यथा कुर्वन्ति भारत ।
कुर्याद्विद्वांस्तथासक्तश्चिकीर्षुर्लोकसंग्रहम् ॥२५॥

saktāḥ karmaṇy avidvāṁso yathā kurvanti bhārata |
kuryād vidvāṁs tathāsaktaś cikīrṣur lokasaṁgraham ||25||

As the 'ignorant' men act from attachment to action, O Bhārata, so, should the 'wise man' act without attachment, wishing the welfare of the world.

One, on closer analysis, can see a deeper meaning here.

(1) We all have to work and perform *nitya* and *naimittika karmas*. This is the common rule for both the wise and the ignorant. Who are the ignorant and who are the wise?

The majority of us work with egotistic feelings and work always for fruits of action (gains). We all work because we have to earn. We earn because our aim is fulfilment of our personal desires. The wise are those who also work, but they do not work for the fulfilment of their desires.

The mind needs to contemplate on something. It cannot be idle. So, one should, instead of attachment to 'personal fulfilment of desires', attach himself to 'nobler' thoughts.

(2) Śrī Kṛṣṇa is advising the wise people here. "Just as the ignorant work, you, the wise, also, work". But he says "work with a wish for the welfare of the world." The wise should not get attached to the fruits of action, i.e., should do divine work.

(3) Bhārata: A member of Bharata family. Also, *bhā* means 'light'. Bhārata means one who is desirous of light, i.e., 'those desirous of knowledge' are Bhāratas.

न बुद्धिभेदं जनयेदज्ञानां कर्मसङ्गिनाम् ।
जोषयेत्सर्वकर्माणि विद्वान्युक्तः समाचरन् ॥२६॥

na buddhibhedaṁ janayed ajñānāṁ karma saṅginām |
joṣayet sarva-karmāṇi vidvān yuktaḥ samācaran ||26||

The wise men should not disturb and confuse the minds of the ignorant attached to action, and should perform all actions with yogic equanimity. They should make the ignorant do accordingly.

Śrī Kṛṣṇa is continuing the advice to the wise men. He is asking Arjuna to be wise and act wisely. Do not make people believe that 'action' is wrong. If the wise run away from action and become *saṁnyāsins*, ordinary people would think that that would be the proper way and stop actions and become *saṁnyāsins*.

Not everybody is a *jñānī* and one cannot make everybody a *jñānī*. Not all wise people are good as teachers. Teaching is a special art. By trying to teach, if one is not a good teacher, one would cause confusion in the minds of his students.

It would be wiser that wise men should still work wisely. How? By continuing to work with yogic equanimity. *Yoga* means the union of the ego with the soul, and *ātmā* with *Paramātmā*. Divine actions done with a balanced mind, which is not perturbed by success and failures, is the way to work.

Arjuna should therefore not run away from battle but fight for protecting *dharma*. Instead of telling Arjuna what to do, Kṛṣṇa says, "Wise men do this, wise men should not do this". He wants Arjuna's ego to assert that he is a wise man and therefore work wisely.

प्रकृतेः क्रियमाणानि गुणैः कर्माणि सर्वशः ।
अहङ्कारविमूढात्मा कर्ताहमिति मन्यते ॥२७॥

**prakṛteḥ kriyamāṇāni guṇaiḥ karmāṇi sarvaśaḥ ।
ahaṁkāra-vimūḍhātmā kartāham iti manyate ॥27॥**

By the qualities of nature, all actions are performed, in all cases, but one whose mind is deluded by egotism thinks, "I am the doer".

The qualities of nature are called *guṇa*s and they are of three types. They are *sāttvika* (good), *rājasika* (dynamic) and *tāmasika* (dull). (They are described in detail in chapter 14).

These qualities arise out of one's desires. The *ātman* inside each of us has no desires as such. But the same *ātman*, falsely gets attached to the mind, intellect and the physical body. By this false attachment, it gets in contact with the outer world. The *ātman*, which thus seemingly gets attached to the body is then called ego. Ego is also known as *jīva*.

Ego attributes actions to himself. He considers that 'He, the ego, is the doer'. Ego considers some objects he gets in contact with as pleasures. He likes them. He wants more of such contacts. They become his desires and he wants to fulfil such desires. These desires leave an imprint on the mind and they are called *vāsanā*s. *Vāsanā*s have to become actions at a later date to fulfil the desires. The *vāsanā*s become one's inborn nature. They are the *guṇa*s.

Because of desires entertained, one performs action in course of time to fulfil such desires. It is not the Self within who does such actions, but it is the ego who feels that he did so. The Lord attributes egotistic feeling to a deluded mind.

Identification with the body is known as *dehātma-buddhi*. If one identifies himself with the body, he would incur the joys and sorrow of life. If, on the other hand, one identifies himself with the Soul inside, he will get the bliss of the Absolute. He will attain *mokṣa.*

तत्त्ववित्तु महाबाहो गुणकर्मविभागयोः ।
गुणा गुणेषु वर्तन्त इति मत्वा न सज्जते ।।२८।।

tattvavit tu mahābāho guṇa-karma-vibhāgayoḥ ।
guṇā guṇeṣu vartanta iti matvā na sajjate ।।28।।

But, he, who knows the Truth, understands the divisions of qualities and functions, O mighty-armed Arjuna. He knows that the guṇas *function through the senses amidst sense-objects and are not affected by them. Thus knowing, he remains unattached.*

What is the attitude of a wise man? Who is a wise man?
— What are *guṇas*?
— What are senses?
— What are sense-objects?
— Who is the knower of the truth?

The wise man knows that he is the *ātman* with a covering of the subtle and physical body. He also knows that the physical body with the mind and sense-organs is in contact with the sense-objets. He knows also that the sense-objects send in the impulses through the sense-organs. If they please the mind, his mind would consider them as desirable objects. It would send the organs of action to obtain them. Desires bring in more desires and in turn they bring unhappiness in course of time. One would not like to lose the objects that would give pleasure.

The wise man knowing this, does not get attached to the sense-objects. He knows it is the false self (ego) that gets the attachments. But he will remain unattached constantly.

Arjuna is addressed as *mahābāhu.* Why? *Mahābāhu* means ''mighty-armed''. Arjuna was mighty-armed and he could face strong enemies in the battlefield. But in this situation, he is facing the strongest enemy-force. Who is the enemy? Ignorance. Ignorance of his true nature is his own enemy.

Tattvavit means the one who knows the 'truth' in essence of what has been said in the *Vedas*. The wise man, described so far in this verse, is *tattvavit*.

Guṇa-karma-vibhāga: One should understand this word clearly. It means division of *guṇa*s and division of *karma*s.

*Guṇa*s as we know, are three: *sattva*, *rajas* and *tamas*. At any one time we all have the preponderance of one *guṇa* over the other two and due to this we do either, (*a*) *satkarma*—good acts, or (*b*) *duṣkarma*—bad acts.

We are all born with certain *guṇa*s due to our past thoughts (*vāsanās*). Even a *tattvavit* is born with *guṇa*s. But, he knows that he is born as such and will perform duties which will burn the *vāsanā*s and he will not accumulate new *vāsanā*s. Śrī Kṛṣna asks Arjuna to be a *tattvavit*.

प्रकृतेर्गुणसंमूढाः सज्जन्ते गुणकर्मसु ।
तानकृत्स्नविदो मन्दान्कृत्स्नविन् न विचालयेत् ॥२९॥

***prakṛter guṇasaṁmūḍhāḥ sajjante guṇakarmasu* |**
***tān akṛtsnavido mandān kṛtsnavin na vicālayet* ||29||**

The man of knowledge should not confuse the minds of those men of imperfect understanding, who, deluded by the guṇas *of nature, are attached to actions in the material world.*

The meaning implied in this verse is similar to that in verse 26 of this chapter.

An artist draws a picture, goes back and observes it and comes back to add a few strokes with his brush and goes back to see it again. He repeats it till he gets satisfied that he has got what he wanted to express through his drawing. Similarly, the words are altered to give a better meaning and emphasising the same truth in a different way.

The majority of men in this world are not well-versed in *śāstra*s. They have a predisposition to perform *karma* due to their inherent *guṇa*s. Also, a number of those who are ignorant of the *śāstra*s perform actions blindly. Very few think that what they perform is due to their *guṇa*s. They attribute their individuality to their actions. Suppose they perform Gaṇeśa-*pūjā* or *vratam*, they would say, 'I did the *vratam*'.

As a matter of fact, there is no harm in their performing their duties with attachment. The wise, instead of trying to change their nature, should try to instil *śraddhā* (dedication) in their work. Such people, will mature in course of time. They will get *jñāna* eventually and understand the true nature of their *ātman*.

There is a saying, "one should not teach *Brahma-vidyā* just because one asked for it" (Purandara Dāsa). To receive this knowledge the recipient should have maturity of mind. The wise man, should be like a good teacher (or a good doctor) to know when his student is ready to receive his teaching (or to receive the treatment).

मयि सर्वाणि कर्माणि संन्यस्याध्यात्मचेतसा ।
निराशीर्निर्ममो भूत्वा युध्यस्व विगतज्वरः ॥३०॥

mayi sarvāṇi karmāṇi saṁnyasyādhyātmacetasā |
nirāśīr nirmamo bhūtvā yudhyasva vigatajvaraḥ ||30||

Surrendering all actions in Me, with the mind fixed in Self, free from hope and egotism, fight without fever (mental agitation).

The minds of people are of two kinds : troubled minds and peaceful minds. Troubled minds are those that are immersed in actions in the pluralistic world, with egotistic attachment to their actions and the fruit of actions. Peaceful minds are those that surrender their fruits of action to the Self and work without attachment.

A troubled mind is full of ferish passions. Hence, the Lord uses the word *jvara*. (fever of mind). That mind tosses restlessly about because of the fever.

When one gets physical illness, one goes to the Doctor for cure. Similarly, when one gets fever of the mind, one should seek spiritual knowledge. What is 'fever of the mind'?

'Fever of the mind' is that state of mind where one tosses

restlessly due to agitations in the mind. When does one get such agitations of the mind?

When one does his work with the feeling of 'I', and 'Mine', he feels happy when the work is finished satisfactorily. He feels sad when the work does not get done. During such states his mind will toss hither and thither. How then should one get over it?

Nirāśirnirmamo bhūtvā: By abandoning egotism, by dropping the 'I'-ness in one's action, by feeling that it is God's work (only such work as is accepted by the *śāstras*) and by surrendering fruits of such work at the feet of the Lord. Victory over passions like 'I'-ness, by developing detachment in attachment is the real victory in one's battle of life. How can one achieve this victory.

Adhyātmacetasā mayi karmāṇi saṁnyasya: You fix your mind on the Self (i.e., Lord) and let your mind dissolve and merge into the Self and you are then a victor. When there is no trace of *ahaṁkāra* ('I'-ness) one can achieve such victory.

Vedic scriptures repeat this advice to mankind several times. They do not recommend non-action, but recommend action with proper understanding (*karma-yoga*).

ये मे मतमिदं नित्यमनुतिष्ठन्ति मानवाः ।
श्रद्धावन्तोऽनसूयन्तो मुच्यन्ते तेऽपि कर्मभिः ॥३१॥

ye me matam idaṁ nityam anutiṣṭhanti mānavāḥ |
śraddhāvanto'nasūyanto mucyante te'pi karmabhiḥ ||31||

Those men who constantly practise this My teaching with faith and being free from ill-will, are also freed from bondage to the actions.

What has been said by the Lord in the previous verse, will help the person to achieve victory provided he follows the two basic rules:

(1) should have *śraddhā*;
(2) should not have jealousy.

It is a common experiene that we think of God and ask for

his help only when we are in distress. When things go wrong with our body or in our relationship with the world, we ask for God's help.

Śraddhā is a state of mind wherein one pursues an act with faith. This faith should not be a blind faith. Ever so often one must question his actions. ''Am I doing it properly or am I going the wrong way by doing such work?'', he should ask himself.

What does *śraddhā* in the *Gītā* mean? One should try to read and understand the *Gītā*. This should be an earnest effort. While putting one's effort in learning, one should hope that one day the difficult passages in the *Gītā* will become clear and the *Gītā* will help him to achieve peace of mind. One may need years of repeated reading of the *Gītā* and it will be surprising to note that every new attempt at reading will give a better meaning of what is said in it.

One should not have *asūyā*. *Asūyā* is jealousy. One will feel jealous only when one compares himself to others. This comparison will come when one looks upon himself as a separate entity (*ahaṁkāra*, 'I'-ness). ''So and so owns a car and I have not got it'', is an example of *asūyā*.

Let us consider two bright students in a class. When one gets higher marks, the other will feel jealous. The Lord says that jealousy is an obstacle to progress. It makes one's mind impure. Instead of being jealous, the other student should look at it this way:

(1) He should feel happy at the other's progress.
(2) He should question himself: ''Where did I go wrong?'' He should see what were the faults in his work. He should put more *śraddhā* in his work and try to improve his knowledge.

Only with *śraddhā* and *anasūyā*, one will be liberated from bondage to actions and will attain *mokṣa* in course of time.

ये त्वेतदभ्यसूयन्तो नानुतिष्ठन्ति मे मतम् ।
सर्वज्ञानविमूढांस्तान्विद्धि नष्टानचेतसः ॥३२॥

ye tv etad abhyasūyanto nā-nutiṣṭhanti me matam |
sarvajñānavimūḍhāṁs tān viddhi naṣṭān acetasaḥ ||

But those who carp at my teachings and do not practise, know them as men deluded of knowledge, devoid of discrimination and doomed to destruction.

This is a warning to non-believers in the Self. They have 'I'-ness in all their actions. The Lord uses two simple words for such people.

(1) They are ignorant.

(2) They are doomed to destruction.

The subtle mind is the intellect. Ignorant men do not use the intellect and hence lose the power of discrimination in their actions.

The path of ascent from manhood to divinity is for spiritual seekers. Man has the blessing of the Lord in having been given the intellect.

The path of descent from manhood to animalhood is for the ignorant. They would have wasted their precious birth as men and would continue to live like animals. They destroy themselves.

The *śāstras* and scriptures are written by our learned ancestors for the welfare of the Universe. By following them, one would prosper; by ridiculing them and going contrary to their teaching, one would ruin oneself and ruin others also.

सदृशं चेष्टते स्वस्याः प्रकृतेर्ज्ञानवानपि ।
प्रकृतिं यान्ति भूतानि निग्रहः किं करिष्यति ॥३३॥

sadṛśaṁ ceṣṭate svasyāḥ prakṛter jñānavān api |
prakṛtiṁ yānti bhūtāni nigrahaḥ kiṁ kariṣyati ||33||

Even a wise man acts according to his own nature. Beings will follow nature, what can restraint do?

Our nature is our *guṇas*. *Guṇas* are the *vāsanās* we carry from our previous existence. The *vāsanās* are due to our thoughts and action. We are all born with different *guṇa*s and we act according to our *guṇa*s.

A wise man would still be acting according to his *guṇa*s. But, when he commits a mistake, he realises it and tries to correct his mistakes. He does not stop his actions but his attitude to actions change. He will develop *niṣkāma karma* and *karma-phala-tyaga* by *śraddhā* and *anasūyā*.

The ignorant also have to work according to their nature.

Before the realisation of *jñāna*, one should not restrain his senses. The inherent *vāsanā*s in one's mind (subtle body) will hinder one's progress. Arjuna, would not have attained *mokṣa* by becoming a *saṁnyāsī*. He would have to burn his kṣatriya *vāsanā*s and use his kṣatriya *vāsanā* to fight evil.

Restraining the senses will have to be practised at a later stage in one's path to *mokṣa* and not in the earlier stages. This is explained further in the following verse.

इन्द्रियस्येन्द्रियस्यार्थे रागद्वेषौ व्यवस्थितौ ।
तयोर्न वशमागच्छेत्तौ ह्यस्य परिपन्थिनौ ॥३४॥

indriyasyendriyasyārthe rāgadveṣau vyavasthitau |
tayor na vaśam āgacchet tau hyasya paripanthinau ||34||

In each of the senses abide attraction and repulsion for the object of the senses. One should not come under their sway, for they are man's enemies.

We all have five sense-organs (eyes, ear, nose, skin and tongue) which bring in light, sound, smell, touch and taste sensations. They bring in impulses from our surroundings. Surroundings being the same, the reaction to them is decided by our mind and intellect.

The impulses that bring in a sense of happiness are called *rāgas*; *rāga*s are those that please us. The impulses that bring in unpleasant feeling are called *dveṣas*. *Dveṣa*s are those that we dislike and hate. Depending on the reaction, our organs of action are brought into action. They are mouth, hands and feet, organs of excretion and genital organs.

Both *rāga* and *dveṣa* bind us to this world. For example, love for our family members bind us strongly. We do not want to be separated from them. If they are ill we get upset. Similarly, if we hate somebody, that hatred will stay in our mind for a long time and we are bound by it also. Arjuna did not want to fight. Why? Because of his love for his elders and teachers. He did not want them killed or hurt. *Rāga* was binding him and stopping him from fighting for justice.

If the mind is directed towards the *ātman*, the senses will then be his friends. Desire for worldly objects brought in by the senses become our enemies to progress on the spiritual path. Desire towards divinity, brought in by the same sense-organs, will act as our friends in our progress to *mokṣa*.

The difference between animal and man is in the subtle mind of man, i.e., the power of discrimination. If one does not use his intellect, he is like an animal and he gets carried away by the impulses brought in by the sense-organs. Hence, sense-organs are called his enemies.

So, when the Lord recommends restraining, it is not restraining from any actions. It means restraining the impulses from the sense-organs and using the intellectual capacity of discrimination. This can be achieved by making proper use of the mind to receive impulses. The intellect should order the mind what it should do in reaction to those impulses. The mind should be like a postman following the order of the Post Master (intellect). The mind should be subordinate to the intellect. This is the only way to kill the ego.

श्रेयान् स्वधर्मो विगुणः परधर्मात्स्वनुष्ठितात् ।
स्वधर्मे निधनं श्रेयः परधर्मो भयावहः ॥३५॥

śreyān svadharmo viguṇaḥ paradharmāt svanuṣṭhitāt |
svadharme nidhanaṁ śreyaḥ paradharmo bhayāvahaḥ ||35||

One's own dharma, *though devoid of merit, is better than the* dharma *of another even if well-discharged. Better is death in one's own* dharma, *the* dharma *of another is fraught with fear.*

What is *dharma*? What is *svadharma*? *Dharma* is not easy to translate into English. It means righeousness, good conduct, duty etc. But it does not give the real meaning. *Dharma* is "the essential quality of an object without which it cannot exist." For example, the *dharma* of fire is 'heat'. Fire's other characters could be colour of the flame, height of flame etc., but without heat none of the others exists.

The divine nature of *ātman* in us is our *dharma*. Without the *ātman* we cannot exist. When the vital energy (life-force) leaves our body, we are considered as dead.

Our mind is full of *vāsanā*s of the past and these determine the texture of thoughts in us. These determine our actions at any given time. The nature of actions at the physical level (of the body) due to our existing *vāsanā*s, is *dharma* in the context of action of the physical body.

Owing to our nature, we all have our *vāsanā*s. They determine our future actions. Some may have philosophical minds (brāhmaṇa). Some may have warrior (fighting) quality (kṣatriya). Some may have knowledge in business and trade enterprise (vaiśya). Others who may not have any, come under the class called labourers (śūdra). At any given time one of these qualities dominates in all of us and we show such qualities outwardly. But, basically, one such quality dominates in any one person more than other qualities.

Arjuna's quality was of the kṣatriya type. His *vāsanā*s determine that he is a person to fight. He had shown it in the past. Now he was trying to suppress his kṣatriya quality by force. Arjuna was going contrary to *svadharma*, his inherent quality. It would be better if he died in war. If he wanted to be a *saṁnyāsī*, he would fail utterly, because his *vāsanā*s would not give him peace of mind. He did not know about *saṁnyāsa*. Even though he may think that he can be a good *saṁnyāsī*, he is bound to make mistakes as a *saṁnyāsī*.

Let us take an example. An electrician fully qualified is fit to do the duty of an electrician. A plumber fully qualified, is fit to do the duty of a plumber. If the electrician then changes his trade, wants to become a plumber, even if he does it to his best, the job is fraught with danger. He is prone to commit major mistakes sometime or the other.

So, it is better to stick to *svadharma*. Philosophically, it has another meaning. We all have to follow *ātma-dharma*, that is, the *dharma* towards Self-realisation. Our *svadharma* is the law of the Self and is for Self-realisation. *Paradharma* is the law of the objective world, i.e., pleasures, the pluralistic world.

Our duty to *ātmā* is difficult to practise but will help us to attain *mokṣa*. Our duty to our physical body is easy to follow, but fraught with dangers. If we live a life of sensual pleasures, we will also have to bear with the pains that follow pleasures. We will also have to follow the law and be born with animal instincts. We will waste our human birth.

One has to burn the *vāsanās* and not collect new *vāsanās*. To burn is easier. That is, by acting according to his inborn nature due to his *vāsanās*. By going against nature, one will be doing wrong things, it will be difficult and will lead to accumulation of more *vāsanās*. More *vāsanās* mean no early entry to the path of liberation. One should work without desire for fruits of action.

There are few more angles from which one can look at *svadharma* and *paradharma* (*paradharma* means an alien *dharma*).

Brāhmaṇa, kṣatriya, vaiśya, śūdra are the four basic groups of people classified according to their inherent nature. The four castes have some special prescribed duties to perform. But all classes of people have some common duties to perform (*sāmānya dharma*). They are: Devotion to God, a truthful way of living, devotion to parents, control of senses, *ahiṁsā*, compassion, alms-giving etc. By performing duties according to the caste and also performing common duties, one would attain liberation.

Another interpretation of *svadharma* and *paradharma*

Hindu religion advocates different duties at different stages in one's life. They are known as *āśrama-dharmas*: (a) *brahmacarya,* (b) *gṛhasthāśrama,* (c) *vānaprastha,* (d) *saṁnyāsa*

Brahmacarya is practised when one is in his teens. In teenage, our religion advocates celibacy. It considers that the teenager has a duty to learn. It considers that he is immature and not capable of standing on his own legs or to take responsibility of the family. Concentration on studies is not easy if a student is not a celibate.

Gṛhasthāśrama means married life. This period is for settling in one's professional duties and looking after the family. One gets married and has responsibility to his family.

Vānaprastha is withdrawing from the family affairs and concentrating on *śāstras* and imparting the knowledge acquired in life to sons, grandsons, and other young members of the family. It involves guiding the youngsters in their family and professional life.

Saṁnyāsa āśrama: Once the youngsters have grown up to *vānaprastha āśrama* stage, the older members can withdraw from family duties and go to sacred places. They should give family responsibilities to their youngsters.

At each level it will be one's *svadharma* and other levels are *paradharma*. One should always stick to duties of that stage in life. Due to problems at home, running away from its responsibility will not be considered as *saṁnyāsa*. The person may run away but he will carry with him the nature of the *gṛhastha*. He will have longing for family pleasures. He therefore will not survive as a true *saṁnyāsī*.

Arjuna's duty was the kṣatriya's duty of *karma*, i.e., to fight. He had no right to take over the duties of a *saṁnyāsī*. He could not jump from *karma-yoga* to *jñāna-yoga*. He had to walk on his path of *karma* and eventually he would attain *jñāna*.

अर्जुन उवाच

अथ केन प्रयुक्तोऽयं पापं चरति पूरुषः ।
अनिच्छन्नपि वार्ष्णेय बलादिव नियोजितः ॥३६॥

arjuna uvāca

atha kena prayukto'yaṁ pāpaṁ carati pūruṣaḥ ।
anicchann api vārṣṇeya balād iva niyojitaḥ ॥36॥

Arjuna said

O Vāsudeva, constrained by force as it were, by what does man commit sin even against his wish?

Arjuna has now started to look introspectively. He has heard his teacher. As a sincere student, he is asking questions to clear his doubts. He is a sincere spiritual seeker. He does not wish to do wrong, or do evil acts. He is asking for help.

There are people who know it is evil to do certain acts but still do it.

Arjuna's question is—what is this mysterious power that drives one to sinful acts? He wants to know about it, so that he can correct his ways and achieve liberation. It is always better to know the cause and source of evil. It becomes easy to avoid and counteract it.

Most of us intellectually (probably) know what is right. But when it comes to actual action, sensual pleasure-gratification will make us do the wrong things. Human nature is such that, though we know it is wrong to tell a lie we still tell lies. Not only that, we try to cover it so that others will not recognise it as a lie. What is this force that makes us do it?

In other words, the divine and the devil are both in us. The devil in us forces us to do evil. There is a constant battle for spiritual seekers to fight the devil in them. The devil's qualities are explained now by the Lord.

श्रीभगवानुवाच
काम एष क्रोध एष रजोगुणसमुद्भवः ।
महाशनो महापाप्मा विद्ध्येनमिह वैरिणम् ॥३७॥

śrī bhagavān uvāca
kāma eṣa krodha eṣa rajoguṇa-samudbhavaḥ ।
mahāśano mahāpāpmā viddhy enam iha vairiṇam ॥37॥

Lord said

It is desire. It is anger, born of rajoguṇa. *It is all-devouring and sinful. Know this as the enemy here.*

There are evil tendencies in man. *Kāma* (desire), *krodha* (anger), *lobha* (greed), *moha* (delusion), *mada* (pride) and *mātsarya* (envy).

Kāma is the leader of the team and he is the devil in us. *Krodha* is his close associate and others are his team-mates. They all work in unity and take one downward in the path of spiritual progress.

Desire is an agitation of the mind to gain something. All our actions are related to the degree of agitation. The stronger the agitation, the greater is the desire.

The objective world is in between the person and his desire. It may give easily what one wants or it may refuse to give it. The stronger the possibility of not getting the object of desire, the stronger the desire — the reaction is anger. When one cannot get what he wants, he gets angry.

Kāma can be compared to fire. Whatever one offers to fire to satisfy its hunger, it burns and consumes it all (all-devouring). Hence it is called *mahāśanaḥ*—big devil.

The attempt to satisfy desire makes it stronger and it wants more satisfaction. Also, to preserve what one gets, one gets more agitated, frightened that he may lose it. Sin increases in direct proportion to desire. We should, therefore, try not to get attached to the objective world and not be frightened of parting company with what we possess in the physical world. Pull the seed of evil out as soon as it sprouts. The weed may kill the plant if left unchecked. "Know that desire is your enemy and kill it instantly", is the Lord's teaching.

King Yayāti, when he reached his old age, felt he had not fulfilled his sense-gratifications of youthful life. He requests his family priest Śukrācārya to grant him a second youth. With the help of his family priest, he exchanges his old age with his son's youth. Unfortunately, on reaching old age second time round, he finds he still wants more enjoyments. He realises his mistake. He comes to know that there is no end to desires of lust and one has to know how and when to control it. One can start fire to keep one warm in his house. If he is careless, and goes very near the fire, he may catch fire and the house may be burnt.

धूमेनाव्रियते वह्निर्यथादर्शो मलेन च ।
यथोल्बेनावृतो गर्भस्तथा तेनेदमावृतम् ॥३८॥

dhūmenāvṛyate vahnir yathādarśo malena ca |
yatholbenāvṛto garbhas tathā tenedam āvṛtam ||38||

As fire is enveloped by smoke, as a mirror by dust, as the embryo by the amnion, so is the knowledge of the Self enveloped by kāma *and* krodha.

Ātmā, the light of knowledge is shining in everyone of us. The different examples given here are: (1) light in the fire, (2) mirror, (3) embryo.

Smoke (the evil in fire) covers the fire and obscures the light. One can fan away the smoke or open the windows to drive the smoke away. Then only one can see the light. Dust covers the mirror. It obscures reflection. The greater the amount of dust, the greater is the distortion of the reflection. The embryo is covered by the amnion and on breaking of the waters of the amnion, the infant comes out of the womb.

In all these cases, the light inside is obscured, but not swallowed up by darkness. What was needed was : (*a*) to fan away the smoke, (*b*) clean the mirror with a duster and polish it, (*c*) break the water of the amnion.

The discriminative capacity in us is not used to clear away the dust accumulated due to attachment of the mind to the pleasures of worldly objects which brings *kāma* first and *krodha* next. They are the initial dust on the light of knowledge. *Lobha*, *moha* etc., accumulate more dust over it. They hide the divine in us. But they cannot destroy the divinity. What is needed for us is the duster: i.e., the capacity in us or our intellectual ability to clear the dust.

Each of these examples is related to the three qualities (*guṇas*). Fire and smoke are for *sattva-guṇa*. Fire needs only fanning away of the smoke to make the fire visible. Mirror and dust is for *rajo-guṇa*. Dusting is slightly harder than fanning the smoke. Amnion and embryo is for *tamo-guṇa*. It is the hardest of the three tasks. Similarly, it is hard to come out of *tamo-guṇa*. The embryo takes 40 weeks to mature and come out of its cavity. We need several births to come out of *tamo-guṇa*.

Even an ignorant man has the *ātman* inside. It exists by its own right.

Śrī Kṛṣṇa uses the word *idam* which means 'this'. 'This' is, knowledge of the Self. In the next few verses he takes up the topic of knowledge and follows it up in *jñāna-yoga* in the next chapter. In most of the chapters of the *Gīta*, the last few verses are an introduction to the next chapter.

आवृतं ज्ञानमेतेन ज्ञानिनो नित्यवैरिणा ।
कामरूपेण कौन्तेय दुष्पूरेणानलेन च ॥३९॥

āvṛtaṁ jñānam etena jñānino nitya-vairiṇā ।
kāmarūpeṇa kaunteya duṣpūreṇānalena ca ॥39॥

O Arjuna, knowledge of the Self is covered by this everlasting enemy of the wise in the form of desire, insatiable like fire.

The Lord here makes three definitive statements and gives an example.

In the last verse, he said *idam* and here he says 'knowledge' of the Self. He is clearing the doubt some may have on what was *idam* in the last verse. He clearly states that 'this' is covered by desires. He categorically states that desires are the everlasting enemy of the wise.

Who are the wise? The wise are the ones who are students in the path to spiritual progress. They are aware of the *ātman* inside and are looking to reach it. Who are their enemies? Normally when we say 'enemy', we mean those that we hate. The enemy of today can become a friend tomorrow. We may not hate the person at a later stage. But, for the wise man, desires can never become friends any time. Hence the adjective "everlasting" is used.

He uses the example of fire. *Analena* is — by fire. *Alam* means 'enough'. *Analam* means 'not enough'. Fire is never satisfied. It never says "enough". You put *ghī* on it and it glows strongly again. Similarly desires of the mind never satisfy the mind. The mind immediately looks for more desires. Fire burns any one who touches it. Desires burn anyone who goes for them.

इन्द्रियाणि मनोबुद्धिरस्याधिष्ठानमुच्यते ।
एतैर्विमोहयत्येष ज्ञानमावृत्य देहिनम् ॥४०॥

***indriyāṇi mano buddhir asyādhiṣṭhānam ucyate* |**
***etair vimohayaty eṣa jñānam āvṛtya dehinam* ||40||**

The senses, the mind, and the intellect are said to be its seat. By these it deludes the embodied by veiling the wisdom.

Arjuna was a true warrior. A warrior always wants to find out (*a*) who his enemy is, (*b*) how powerful he is, (*c*) where does he hide, (*d*) how does he come out, and (*e*) who are his friends. The wise, as true warrior also must know the details of their enemies. This verse gives those details.

The senses, mind and intellect are the seat of desires, it says. The senses bring impulses from the outside world to the brain. They are the first outward path for the desires to reach the brain. The mind receives the impulses and knows by physical enjoyment, what it likes. Later on when senses do not bring any more pleasures, the mind can still recollect the experiences. Hence the mind is the main seat for the desires. It is its house and the doors of the house are the senses. Both are the seats for desires.

How can one say the intellect is also the seat? Intellect is not really the seat, but the intellect is hidden by the enemy, *kāma*. The desire is so strong, that the mind loses its subtler intellectual capacity. It fails to use its discriminative power. When the discriminative power tries to come out, the force of desire pushes it down and hides it.

The power of discrimination has to be brought out to wipe the enemy off.

तस्मात्त्वमिन्द्रियाण्यादौ नियम्य भरतर्षभ ।
पाप्मानं प्रजहि ह्येनं ज्ञानविज्ञाननाशनम् ॥४१॥

tasmāt tvam indriyāṇy ādau niyamya bharata-ṛṣabha |
pāpmānaṁ prajahi hy enaṁ jñānavijñāna-nāśanam ||41||

O Best of Bharatas, therefore, control the senses first, kill surely this kāma, *the sinful destroyer of knowledge and self-realisation.*

Kṛṣṇa reaffirms that for the followers of the spiritual path to self-realisation, the killer is *kāma*. The seekers therefore, have to kill 'desire'. As desires are the objects of the external world and they can only reach the mind *via* the senses, the first act of the spiritual warrior is to close the gates of entry for the desires. If one controls the gates of entry, the enemy will not be able to gain entry.

Kṛṣṇa again confirms that desires are sinful and are the destroyers of knowledge. Desires have two effects: (1) They make the person go downward on the path of spiritual realisation. One accumulates sins in his eagerness to acquire the desired object. Man commits some heinous sins under the influence of *kāma*. He forgets what is right and what is wrong. (2) Even people who are on a higher level of progress on the spiritual path are taken off the guard by desires and get ruined. In Hindu mythology there are a number of stories where great *ṛṣi*s and even Indra (Lord of heaven) have been bitten by the snake of desire and have fallen down from their high position. Only *jīvanmukta*s can escape from this devil.

इन्द्रियाणि पराण्याहुरिन्द्रियेभ्यः परं मनः ।
मनसस्तु परा बुद्धिर्यो बुद्धेः परतस्तु सः ।।४२।।

indriyāṇi parāṇy āhur indriyebhyaḥ paraṁ manaḥ |
manasas tu parā buddhir yo buddheḥ paratas tu saḥ ||42||

They say that senses are superior to the body. Superior to the senses is the mind. Superior to the mind is the intellect. One who is superior to the intellect is He (the Self).

Kṛṣṇa is giving the names of superior officers, in order of rank in the fight against the enemy.

The first soldier, is the senses. It is the first line of defence. He is an officer of the first rank.

The second line of defence is the mind. He is an officer of the second rank. The mind receives the impulses and gets the feeling of happiness. The greater the desire achieved, the mind is that much happier. It has the capacity to go into a dream-world of imagining enjoyment even when the senses are not functioning. How to control this officer? By the intellect (the duster, to clean).

But strong desires can hide this capacity. If the intellect is killed then man is ruined. Desires destroy him. One can no more protect the king (*ātman*) inside.

Really speaking one can never kill the *ātman*. One must know who his king is and how much he loves him and how much he wants others to see his king. Then his work becomes that much stronger and powerful. He can then kill his enemy and uproot him from the source.

When we are masters of our own emotions, we can live efficiently in our divine spirit. Knowledge of the Self is the sword that can cut the knot between *ātmā* and *anātma* and kill the enemy. *Ātman* automatically shines in such a person.

We are all, indirectly, Arjunas in our daily life. We are hesitant in facing our problems. We want to run away and something in us is telling us not to run away.

Most of us are *rājasika* type of men, men of action. This chapter tells us how to act and hence *karma-yoga* is its title. The union of the lower self (ego) to the higher Self in us by proper daily actions is *karma-yoga*. It is our own Self that remains in darkness if the intellect is destroyed. If the intellect functions well it will destroy *kāma* and his friends and *ātman* gets glorified in that person.

Ātman is the king and the Lord, ever present, and by killing the enemy, the Lord is seen by all who look at Him.

एवं बुद्धेः परं बुद्ध्वा संस्तभ्यात्मानमात्मना ।
जहि शत्रुं महाबाहो कामरूपं दुरासदम् ॥४३॥

evaṁ buddheḥ paraṁ buddhvā saṁstabhyātmānam ātmanā |
jahi śatruṁ mahābāho kāmarūpaṁ durāsadam ||43||

O Arjuna, mighty-armed, thus having known what is greater than the intellect namely ātmā, *and restraining the mind and intellect, conquer the foe in the form of desire which is indeed hard to overcome.*

The concluding words in this chapter again remind Arjuna to act. Physically Arjuna is mighty-armed. But mentally, due to his ignorance, he feels he has no strength to fight. All our contacts with the outside world are only up to the level of the mind, the intellect has the discriminating capacity.

Our *ātmā* is stronger than our intellect. Through our conscience we should restrain the mind and intellect which are sources for desires to breed. It is very hard to overcome desires.

In a war, one is usually fighting for his country or as in the olden days, fighting for the kingdom ruled by his king. Every soldier does his best to protect his king and his country. In our body, the king is our *ātmā* and the enemy fighting the king are our *guṇas*. Our intellect has to fight for and protect the king and kill the *guṇas*. This has to be achieved at the mental level. The mind is a store-house of all memories of the past and it also constantly receives impulses from the outer world. Kṛṣṇa is asking Arjuna to wipe the dust off his mind with the help of a duster (intellectual capacity). Arjuna is asked to discriminate the right from the wrong and kill the evil.

Kṛṣṇa concedes that this process is very difficult and the enemy is hard to overcome. We can overcome it by constant practice. We have the weapons to fight. We can collect new weapons in the form of divine virtues and use them to fight against the evil.

We must remember always that our *ātmā* is reality and the physical and the subtle body are not real, i.e., they are *anātma*. The ignorant tie a knot between *ātmā* and *anātma*. The wise ones try to cut the knot and free the *ātmā*.

इति श्रीमद्भगवद्गीतासूपनिषत्सु ब्रह्मविद्यायां योगशास्त्रे श्रीकृष्णार्जुनसंवादे कर्मयोगो नाम तृतीयोऽध्यायः ॥

iti śrīmadbhagavadgītāsūpaniṣatsu brahmavidyāyāṁ yogaśāstre śrīkṛṣṇārjunasaṁvāde karmayogo nāma tṛtīyo'dhyāyaḥ ||

CHAPTER 4

JÑĀNA-YOGA

INTRODUCTION

Karma, carried out according to the *śāstras* ends in knowledge of the *ātman* and of *Paramātman.* This chapter is entitled *jñāna-yoga* which means it is *yoga* of Knowledge. What is Knowledge?

One can obtain knowledge in various sciences. Of all knowledge, spiritual knowledge is the best. This knowledge gives happiness which does not end in sorrow. Knowledge in any other field brings success and happiness only in relation to material possessions. Such happiness does not last long.

Using such knowledge towards welfare of society would confer spiritual knowledge in course of time. Realising the presence of *ātman* in oneself and in all others helps one to overcome the ego. Actions which do not have ego in them are for the welfare of others. To see the Self (*ātman*) in one's own self (ego) is the real knowledge one can get.

We can sit in the car and drive it to where we want. We cannot do so without the power of the petrol. The energy from the petrol is the real force behind the movement of the car.

Similarly, the power of the Soul inside us makes us function. We, the mind and the body, think that it is we who are functioning and forget the force behind that body. Without the *ātman* (life), the mind and the physical body are considered as dead.

Jñāna is the main gate of entry into the temple of knowledge. The temple with the idol of *ātmā* inside is our body. The inner *sanctum sanctorum* of the temple is our 'Soul'. This is ever shining but is enveloped by ignorance. Apparently, it is not seen by the naked eye.

Just as in a temple, where one lights a lamp to illumine the God who is inside, we should illumine our *ātman* with the Light of Knowledge. This can be achieved by developing divine virtues and by dropping the senses of 'I'-ness in actions. In such a person, in all his activities, the divinity shines through.

When one is asked to light the lamp of knowledge, it means dropping the ego in all one's thoughts and actions. To attain that knowledge, one has to work (*karma*), worship (*bhakti*) or meditate (*dhyāna*).

Kṛṣṇa, in this chapter tells Arjuna that He is not Kṛṣṇa, the son of Devakī but He is *Paramātmā*. He has re-incarnated Himself for upholding *dharma* and rooting out evil. He says, He has come down to show the path of liberation to all. He makes it clear that what He has said is only the teaching of the *Veda*s but put in a simplified way to make it easier to understand and follow.

This chapter, in continuation of *karma-yoga* (chapter 3) explains how one attains knowledge by *karma*. By reincarnating himself on this earth as Kṛṣṇa to uproot evil, Śrī Kṛṣṇa is showing the way to *jñāna* through *karma*. He has himself set a great example of *karma-yoga*.

श्रीभगवानुवाच
इमं विवस्वते योगं प्रोक्तवानहमव्ययम् ।
विवस्वान्मनवे प्राह मनुरिक्ष्वाकवेऽब्रवीत् ॥१॥

śrī bhagavān uvāca
***imaṁ vivasvate yogaṁ proktavān aham avyayam* I**
***vivasvān manave prāha manur ikṣvākave'bravīt* II1II**
The Lord said

I had taught this everlasting yoga *to Vivasvān. Vivasvān taught it to Manu who declared it to Ikṣvāku.*

The Lord is making a clear statement that He first taught this *yoga* to the Sun-god at the beginning of creation.

The *yoga* taught at the time of creation consisted of the *Veda*s. It therefore means that the *Veda*s were taught by *Brahman* to Vivasvān.

Vid means 'to know'. *Veda* means 'knowledge'. Knowledge of the Self, (divinity in us) and the technique of bringing the divinity out for the welfare of other individuals and the universe is the theme of the *Vedas*.

The path of *jñāna* and *karma* ultimately lead to attain *mokṣa*. *Mokṣa* is that state of mind where there would be no sorrow to follow happiness. This state of happiness is also known as *ānanda* and one does not have to undergo any more births and deaths. Hence it is a state that is *avyaya*, the one that does not perish, the "Imperishable".

In the earlier Vedic period, the mode of teaching was oral transmission from father to son. Later on, it was from the teacher to his disciple. Vivasvān taught it to his son Manu. King Manu provided us with the earliest ancient laws. Even now, Indians follow a number of laws dictated by Manu. Manu taught it to his son Ikṣvāku, who was the ancestor of the solar dynasty rulers. They ruled from Ayodhyā and Lord Rāma was born in this dynasty.

The *Vedas* are masterly descriptions of scriptures. They are very vast and difficult to understand. Common men were finding it hard to understand them and they were losing their effect on the public.

Hence Lord Kṛṣṇa brought it out again in the form of *Bhagavadgītā*. It is a lot simpler and clearly explains step by step the various paths to liberation.

एवं परम्पराप्राप्तमिमं राजर्षयो विदुः ।
स कालेनेह महता योगो नष्टः परंतप ॥२॥

***evaṁ paramparāprāptam imaṁ rājarṣayo viduḥ* I**
***sa kāleneha mahatā yogo naṣṭaḥ paraṁtapa* II2II**

This knowledge was handed down in regular succession from generation to generation. The royal sages knew this yoga. *But by long lapse of time it has been lost here, O Arjuna.*

This knowledge of the Self given by *Brahman* is *Brahma-vidyā*.

In olden days kings ruled the land. They were supposed to be well-read in scriptures and were fit to rule for the welfare of their subjects. Those kings who mastered and practised the *Vedas* came to be known as royal sages or *rājarṣis*. King Janaka is one of the famous royal sages.

Rājarṣis practised *karma-yoga*. They performed *niṣkāma karma* and *karma-phala-tyāga*. Unfortunately, some of the kings instead of practising *karma-yoga*, indulged in *karma-bhoga*. They worked for enjoying the benefits of their actions.

Kṛṣṇa therefore says, "by long lapse of time, it has been lost here". It does not mean 'lost' in the real sense (stolen during certain periods). Men, being what they are, at certain periods of time, became very materialistic and lost track of the spiritual quest for knowledge. During such times, this knowledge got locked up in the cupboard, as it were, accumulating dust.

Some great person or persons ever so often are born to bring the knowledge out for the benefit of mankind and revive spiritualism. This knowledge is imperishable and only by negligence of people gets forgotten at times.

स एवायं मया तेऽद्य योगः प्रोक्तः पुरातनः ।
भक्तोऽसि मे सखा चेति रहस्यं ह्येतदुत्तमम् ॥३॥

sa evāyaṁ mayā te'dya yogaḥ proktaḥ purātanaḥ I
bhakto'si me sakhā ceti rahasyaṁ hyetad uttamam II3II

This same ancient yoga has now been taught by Me to you for you are My devotee and friend. It is indeed a supreme secret.

Arjuna was a well-learned man. He knew the *Vedas*. He accepted Kṛṣṇa as his teacher and did not realise that Kṛṣṇa was God.

Kṛṣṇa knew Arjuna very well because of their friendship. He knew that Arjuna was a gentleman, always willing to learn and respect his elders.

Arjuna wanted Kṛṣṇa to be his *sārathī* (i.e., charioteer). He wanted Kṛṣṇa to guide him in the battle. Charioteers played an important role in the warfare of olden days.

At the greatest moment of crisis, instead of abandoning the battle and running away, Arjuna bows at the feet of Kṛṣṇa, gives

Him his symptoms and asks for His guidance.

Kṛṣṇa therefore says, "I have taught you this *karma-yoga*, because you are My devotee and friend. It is a supreme secret". Why call it 'supreme secret?' A thing can be called secret for one of the following two reasons:

(*a*) Because one does not want others to know it now as it should spring as a surprise at a later date. This is a selfish reason. Christmas and birhday presents are hidden from the recipient till the actual day of the celebration. One might come across some hidden wealth or stolen goods and naturally he tries to keep it away from others. This is secrecy for selfish reasons.

(*b*) A thing can be kept as a secret because it may be harmful. Nuclear installations, military documents are such examples.

What Śrī Kṛṣṇa is saying does not fall into either of these categories. It is simply because of man's incompetence to understand, follow and impart it. It is like a diamond that has fallen into the hands of a monkey.

It is not really a secret as such. What it means is, this knowledge has to be imparted to the right student at the right time. This makes sure that the knowledge is intact and will pass on to the next generation of people who will use it for the welfare of mankind. If, by chance, it falls into wrong hands, i.e., people who understand it wrongly and misinterpret, it would cause confusion in the mind of the next generation. They will not understand *dharma*. Hence it is a secret that has to be explained to the right people.

अर्जुन उवाच

अपरं भवतो जन्म परं जन्म विवस्वतः ।
कथमेतद्विजानीयां त्वमादौ प्रोक्तवानिति ॥४॥

arjuna uvāca

***aparaṁ bhavato janma paraṁ janma vivasvataḥ* I**
***katham etad vijānīyāṁ tvam ādau proktavān iti* II4II**

Arjuna said

Later was your birth, earlier the birth of Vivasvān. How then am I to understand that you taught him in the beginning?

This is not a prying question to test the statement of the teacher. Arjuna honestly wanted to know who Kṛṣṇa is. "Who are you?" is his question. If a great man suddenly appears before you and gives you the greatest gift, you would like to know, who he is and what is his ancestry.

Arjuna is doing exactly the same here. He had seen Kṛṣṇa at body-plane (*dehadṛṣṭi*) before. He had known the physical characteristics of Kṛṣṇa and knew him to be the son of Devakī and Vasudeva.

श्रीभगवानुवाच
बहूनि मे व्यतीतानि जन्मानि तव चार्जुन ।
तान्यहं वेद सर्वाणि न त्वं वेत्थ परंतप ॥५॥

śrī bhagavān uvāca
bahuni me vyatītāni janmāni tava cārjuna |
tāny ahaṁ veda sarvāṇi na tvaṁ vettha paraṁtapa ||5||

The Lord said

O Parantapa, many births of mine have passed as well as yours. I know them all, but you know them not.

The Lord is God. He created the Universe for His *līlā*. He created *Māyā* which put mankind into ignorance of divinity. He is the controller of *māyā*. The individual, or *jīva* is subject to *māyā* which makes him forget his past. From times immemorial many people have tried to transcend *māyā* and reach the Self. Very few have succeeded in doing so.

Kṛṣṇa, the controller of *māyā*, is therefore aware of all his past, i.e., creation of the Universe, creation of *Veda*s etc. Arjuna, of course is not aware of it. Kṛṣṇa is not chiding His student for questioning His status. He is kindly explaining to him what his background is.

One should understand the secret of the difference between the past births of Śrī Kṛṣṇa and those of Arjuna. Arjuna's previous births were due to his past *karma*s and now *māyā* has obscured that knowledge from his mind. But Śrī Kṛṣṇa took several births in the past out of his divine free will. He did so, as we will learn later, to protect righteousness. He, the *māyātīta*, therefore knows his past births.

It is a blessing to be born as human beings. We have got the intellect, or the capacity to discriminate between right and wrong. We can look at any object at mental and intellectual plane and not just at body-plane. We must make use of this human birth to question ourselves and better ourselves.

अजोऽपि सन्नव्ययात्मा भूतानामीश्वरोऽपि सन् ।
प्रकृतिं स्वामधिष्ठाय संभवाम्यात्ममायया ॥ ६॥

***ajo'pi sann avyayātmā bhūtānām īśvaro'pi san* |**
***prakṛtiṁ svām adhiṣṭhāya saṁbhavāmy ātmamāyayā* ||6||**

Though I am unborn and eternal in My being, the Lord and controller of all beings, controlling my own nature, I take birth by my own māyā.

Kṛṣṇa is asserting that He is not born as an ordinary human being. We are all born because of our *vāsanā*s and our present birth is to burn our *vāsanā*s and attain Self-hood. Kṛṣṇa was not born because of his *vāsanā*s. He used his creative power to be born in Devakī's womb. Devakī must have been a very fortunate woman to give birth to Kṛṣṇa. Kṛṣṇa has no *vāsanā*s to burn. His divinity is eternal. So, He is said to be unborn and eternal.

He says that He is the Lord and controller of all beings. He is the Supreme Power. He makes His presence felt at certain times for the purpose of doing good to the world. He is the Lord of all situations. He is a master of Himself. In other words, He is absolute divinity, who comes out ever so often to uproot evil and open the minds of people and remind them to follow the spiritual path. He has no duty to perform. But he wants every human being to do his own duty and realise his divinity. To set an example, He takes birth, goes through the whole apparent life-process, only for others to see, observe and follow.

यदा यदा हि धर्मस्य ग्लानिर्भवति भारत ।
अभ्युत्थानमधर्मस्य तदात्मानं सृजाम्यहम् ॥७॥

yadā yadā hi dharmasya glānir bhavati bhārata |
abhyutthānam adharmasya tadātmānaṁ sṛjāmy aham ||7||

O Bhārata, whenever there is decline of righteousness and rise of evil, I manifest Myself.

There are two words of importance to note here, *dharma* and 'manifest'.

Dharma is the 'law of the being', the principle of man's existence. There is a famous saying *dharmo rakṣati rakṣitaḥ*. '*Dharma* protects the person who protects *dharma*'. (See introduction for the meaning of *dharma*.)

Dharma can also be defined as the *karma* that is conducive to man's progress. *karma* becomes *adharma* when it impedes such progress. Righteousness is, "acts by the majority of the members of any given community, to give peace and prosperity to that community". These acts should be according to the *śāstras*.

On the other hand, if the majority are not righteous or if there is a very strong evil element in the society forcing and leading to evil, that society is doomed to anarchy and self-destruction. When evil has risen its head, like a snake, Kṛṣṇa says, He manifests himself .

Sṛjāmi: manifest. Manifest means "show his/its presence". If God is considered as good and divine, if God is said to manifest Himself, it means good and divine manifest. This will kill evil and bring prosperity in course of time.

As we have seen before, the man who works selflessly and without looking for fruits of action, eventually becomes a *jīvanmukta*, and merges into his Soul (merges into God). He then continues to live till his physical death working for the welfare of all. That man is then said to be God Himself.

During evil times, there will arise someone who will reach

Godhood, become God Himself and destroy that evil. (Kṛṣṇa says He manifests Himself presumably as *jīvanmukta* also.) Why does He manifest?

परित्राणाय साधूनां विनाशाय च दुष्कृताम् ।
धर्मसंस्थापनार्थाय संभवामि युगे युगे ॥८॥

paritrāṇāya sādhūnāṁ vināśāya ca duṣkṛtām |
dharma-saṁsthāpanārthāya saṁbhavāmi yuge yuge ||8||

For the protection of good, for the destruction of the wicked and for the establishment of righteousness, I am born in every age.

Man being what he is, very often the animal in him dominates. This happens all the time. History has shown us several such instances.

In Hindu philosophy, we talk about four ages. *Kṛtayuga, Tretāyuga, Dvāparayuga* and *Kaliyuga*. Our mythological stories tell us that the forms of Narasiṁha and Vāmana *avatāras* (forms) of the Lord manifested in *Kṛtayuga*, Rāma *avatāra in Tretāyuga* and Kṛṣṇa *avatāra* in *Dvāparayuga*. They also say that in this present age of *Kaliyuga*, the Lord will come as Kalki (in the form of a sword-weilding man on a white horse) to kill evil.

We have learnt before that desire is the seed of action. If there will be no desire, there is no action. Even the Supreme has a 'desire' to kill the evil and manifest in some form to achieve the result. He does so only for the welfare of all. He sets an example of righteous living which men start following in greater numbers and as a result peace and prosperity prevail again.

The word *sādhūnām* is used in this verse. Generally *sādhu* means a *saṁnyāsī*. Many people call *saṁnyāsī*s as *sādhu*s. This is a wrong notion.

A *sādhu* is a righteous person. In the profession he is born into (due to his *vāsanā*s), he will perform the duties in that profession for the welfare of others. As a brāhmaṇa he will perform *yajña*s and *tapas* and impart spiritual knowledge to others. As a kṣatriya he will rule righteously for the welfare of his subjects. As a vaiśya, he sees that the items of food, clothing etc. are available to all at affordable prices, accumulates wealth by righteous means and uses his wealth righteously. As a śūdra, he will do the duty of a loyal servant to his master. Also, a *sādhu* spends his time in praise of the Lord in the form of reading scriptures or attending spiritual discourses.

Contrary to this nature of the *sādhu* is *duṣkṛta,* i.e., 'wicked person'. A wicked person is one who harms innocent people, who hurts a *sādhu,* dwells in lies, cheating, prostitution and such bad habits and who does not believe in the *Veda*s and God.

Whenever wickedness prevails in a community, whenever a wicked person dominates in society and harms the whole community, the Lord says He will incarnate to "uproot the wicked".

Destruction of evil is either killing it totally or removing the evil tendencies in the individuals. One extremely bad person may influence evil tendencies in others who follow his way of life. By killing the leader, in course of time, some of his evil followers will lose their evil tendencies and would turn over a new leaf in their lives. If one kills the enemy, *kāma,* then his followers *krodha, lobha* etc. will automatically lose their influence and the person becomes righteous.

Kṛṣṇa had to describe Himself to an extent and that is what He did now. He has sown the seed of thought in Arjuna's mind that he is Divine Supreme.

जन्म कर्म च मे दिव्यमेवं यो वेत्ति तत्त्वतः ।
त्यक्त्वा देहं पुनर्जन्म नैति मामेति सोऽर्जुन ॥९॥

***janma karma ca me divyam evaṁ yo vetti tattvataḥ* I**
***tyaktvā dehaṁ punarjanma naiti māmeti so'rjuna* II9II**

O Arjuna, he who thus knows my divine birth and action, having abandoned the body, is not born again, but to Me he comes.

There is a hint here on meditation (*upāsanā*). Meditation is a means to attain purity of mind (purity of thoughts). To divert the mind from the pluralistic world, one needs to concentrate on the divine. This is *bhakti mārga.*

In the Vedic period, there were no forms of God to meditate upon. They performed *nirguṇa upāsanā* (*nirguṇa* means without *guṇas*). This was achieved by repeating the sacred word *Oṁ*.

It was hard to concentrate on the formless *Brahman*. It was slighly easier to concentrate on *Oṁ* than on the formless *Brahman*. Later even this proved to be difficult. To help ordinary people to develop concentration on meditation, in later ages, (i.e., the Purāṇic period) the same *Oṁ* was given various forms, in the form of stories of those who did carry out great divine acts. Thus the names of Viṣṇu, Rāma, Kṛṣṇa etc. came to be attributed to represent the formless *Brahman*. Kṛṣṇa is suggesting that one should meditate on divine forms, see divinity in those forms and eventually become divine.

Śrī Kṛṣṇa wants us to understand who He really is. Kṛṣṇa is not simply the son of Vasudeva and Devakī. Duryodhana thought that Kṛṣṇa was a magician and hypnotist who hypnotised others. One should see the divine in Kṛṣṇa. We should understand that he is birthless, deathless, *guṇātīta*, God Himself who came to uproot unrighteousness. The person who can meditate on this aspect of Kṛṣṇa is bound to attain liberation in course of time.

The one who knows *Brahman* becomes *Brahman*. *Tattva* means the 'essence'. The person who knows the essential principle in life (of *Brahman*) is the real knower. It is not theoretical knowledge. It has to be by self-realisation (*tattvavit* : verse 28 chapter 3).

One must see divinity in all, it is the same principle in all forms. The action of divine is to uproot evil. The person who knows this is the knower.

वीतरागभयक्रोधा मन्मया मामुपाश्रिताः ।
बहवो ज्ञानतपसा पूता मद्भावमागताः ॥१०॥

vīta-rāga-bhaya-krodhā manmayā mām upāśritāḥ |
bahavo jñānatapasā pūtā madbhāvam āgatāḥ ||10||

Free from desire, fear and hatred, absorbed in Me, purified by the fire of knowledge, many have attained Me.

If one studies this verse closely, one can see the three paths and it also gives the end result of *sādhanā.* The free paths are a follows.

Karma: We have read in the third chapter, that by performing *niṣkāma karma* one can be free from the triple evils of attachment, fear and hatred. This part of it therefore is about the path of action of *karma-yoga.*

We have seen in verse 37, chapter 3 what the evils of *kāma* are. Our attachment to our desires, our attachment to what we want to get from our desires is *rāga.* The fear of not getting what we want or losing what we get, is *bhaya.* One tends to hate whoever or whatever that stops one from getting what he wants or takes away what he has. This is *dveṣa.*

Due to *rāga, bhaya* and *dveṣa,* one gets angry, gets deluded and perishes. Living a life of detachment in attachment and performing *karma,* one would attain purity of mind.

Bhakti: Absorbed in Me. In the last verse, the lord has hinted at the 'path of *bhakti*'. Divert your thoughts from worldly affairs by meditating on My form is what is meant by 'absorbed in Me'. This is *bhakti-yoga.*

Jñāna: *Tapas* is an act of purification. There are various methods of purification of the mind. One method is by knowledge of the Self. This is *jñāna-yoga* . Know the essential divinity in you, know that it is the same divinity in all, and live a life of divinity and you will achieve liberation.

The three paths are no distinct, separate paths. Each one mingles with the other. A person following *karma-yoga* eventually becomes a *jñānī* and realises the Self. A *jñānī* eventually is the one who is free from attachment, fear and hatred and lives that life. A man of *bhakti* eventually sees God in all and becomes a *jñānī* and still leads the life of *karma-yoga.* The end-result is the realisation of the Self and attaining *mokṣa* (the state of birthlessness).

ये यथा मां प्रपद्यन्ते तांस्तथैव भजाम्यहम् ।
मम वर्त्मानुवर्तन्ते मनुष्याः पार्थ सर्वशः ॥११॥

***ye yathā māṁ prapadyante tāṁs tathaiva bhajāmy aham* |**
***mama vartmānuvartante manuṣyāḥ pārtha sarvaśaḥ* ||11||**

O Arjuna, in whatever way men approach Me, even so do I reward them, for the path that men take from every side is Mine.

This is symbolised in our *Sanātana Dharma* by the symbol of *svastika.*

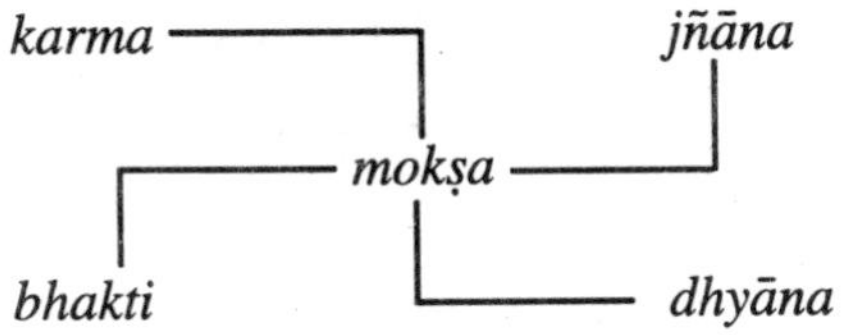

The Lord admits that men have different temperaments. He wants people to achieve the final goal. He does not want them to change their way of life. Every type of living, if aimed at the Lord, will eventually lead to Him.

The reward for men who worship God would srictly be in relation to the aim and object of worship. The purpose, the manner to achieve it, the intensity of effort will determine the type of reward in any action.

Petrol in the car gives the energy for the car using the machinery in the car. But it depends on the driver of the car where it goes. The driver, by driving carelessly will end in an accident. It is not the fault of the force of energy called petrol.

What we wish, God gives. But how we pursue it, is important. One has to approach Him, He says, to obtain the reward. It is no use just wishing for things to happen. One must act and strive towards obtaining the result. Depending on the wish, how one works towards it, one gets appropriate results.

If one wants wealth, the result depends on his actions. Proper actions to get wealth will achieve the result. If one wants to achieve self-realisation, it all depends on his efforts to achieve it. At the end, eventually he will attain liberty, the Lord says. There is a verse in *sandhyāvandanam* prayers which has the same meaning:

ākāśāt patitaṁ toyaṁ yathā gacchati sāgaram I
sarva-deva-namaskāraḥ keśavaṁ prati gacchati II
"Just as the drops of water from the sky do end in ocean, the salutations to various Gods reach Me."

काङ्क्षन्तः कर्मणां सिद्धिं यजन्त इह देवताः ।
क्षिप्रं हि मानुषे लोके सिद्धिर्भवति कर्मजा ॥१२॥

***kāṅkṣantaḥ karmaṇāṁ siddhiṁ yajanta iha devatāḥ* I**
***kṣipraṁ hi mānuṣe loke siddhir bhavati karmajā* II12II**

They, who long for satisfaction from actions in this world, make sacrifices to the gods, because satisfaction is quickly obtained from actions in this world of men.

In *karma-kāṇḍa* of the *Vedas*, it is said that there are different sacrifices to please different Gods. Different sacrifices bring different results.

Those who perform such sacrifices, enjoy the fruits of such actions. Many of us believe that there are different places of rewards, like heaven, *indraloka*, *brahmaloka* etc. After the benefits are used up, they come back to earth. The earth is considered as the world of action (*karma-bhūmi*). Similarly, many of us believe that evil actions here would result in our going to hell. Either way, fruits of actions are obtained very quickly in this world. It is up to us what actions we do. Just as it is easy to get rewards for good actions, it is as easy to get penalised for bad actions.

If we want to achieve something great, we have to work that much harder. Spiritual knowledge and attainment of *mokṣa* are the highest goals and to achieve them we have to forego the pleasures of the world. We are blessed with an intellect which gives us *buddhi*. Using our *buddhi*, we can attain *mokṣa*.

चातुर्वर्ण्यं मया सृष्टं गुणकर्मविभागशः ।
तस्य कर्तारमपि मां विद्ध्यकर्तारमव्ययम् ॥१३॥

cāturvarṇyaṁ mayā sṛṣṭaṁ guṇakarmavibhāgaśaḥ |
tasya kartāram api māṁ viddhy akartāram avyayam ||13||

The four-fold caste-system has been created by Me according to the differentiation of qualities and actions. Though I am the author, know Me as non-doer, eternal.

We are what we are; that is, the result of what thoughts we entertain and what actions we do.

Our actions are determined by the thought-process in our minds. This, as we have discussed before, is due to the *vāsanās*. (imprints of thought-processes). Our qualities can be broadly divided into:

(1) Pure — *sāttvika*
(2) Passionate — *rājasika*
(3) Lazy — *tāmasika.*

We possess all these qualities in different proportions. The qualities depend on the desires we entertained in the past. These qualities are also known as *guṇas*. We all show a predominant *guṇa* at any one time. When we go to the temple, we automatically show *sāttvika* temperament. When we are involved in the battle of day-to-day life, we tend to be automatically passionate. We tend to fight and quarrel with others. We passionately act to obtain what we want. This is *rājasika* temperament. Sometimes we are lazy, heedless in our actions. This is *tamas.* It is also a fact that we generally have one predominant *guṇa* and that makes us what we are.

On this principle, the four-fold caste system was introduced in the olden days. A brāhmaṇa is one whose thoughts and actions are pure. A kṣatriya is one whose thoughts and actions are passionate. A vaiśya is a person with a mixture of *rājasika* and *tāmasika guṇas*. A śūdra is that person whose thoughts and actions are lazy and idle.

The Lord says that this classification is made by Him only to differentiate the qualities in the person. Each quality suits a person for a particular post. The brāhmaṇa quality suits one to be a priest and scholarly person. The kṣatriya quality suits one to be a warrior and protector of the land and its people. The vaiśya quality suits one to be a trader by profession. The śudra quality suits one to be a labourer.

We belong to the caste which are determined by our *guṇa*s, we are in turn our past desires. Our *vāsanā*s make us what we are. God does not make us a brāhmaṇa, a kṣatriya, a vaiśya or a śūdra. We are that in ourselves.

There is a description of the four-fold case system in ancient scriptures. In *Śānti-Parva* of *Mahābhārata*, there is a verse in which Bhīṣma prays to Virāṭa Puruṣa:

brahma vaktraṁ bhujau kṣatraṁ kṛtsnam ūrūdaraṁ viśaḥ I
pādau yasya śritaḥ śūdras tasmai varṇātmane namaḥ II

The meaning of this is:

"My salutation to *varṇātma* (Virāṭa Puruṣa) who has brāhmaṇa as his face, shoulders as kṣatriya, stomach and thighs as vaiśya and feet as śūdra."

We have to understand that all the four castes belong to God. All parts of the body constitute one person. All actions by different parts of the body keep one going. Each part of the body has to do its duty. The feet cannot do the job of the stomach, and the stomach cannot do the job of the feet.

The one who uses his head is a clever person. The head is therefore considered as brāhmaṇa. Shoulders are needed for one to lean on to in distress. Shoulders are needed also to show one's strength. Hence the shoulder is considered a kṣatriya. The stomach holds food and releases energy. A vaiśya is compared to the stomach because he holds stocks, releases them and makes profits. He wants to make sure he has enough food (i.e., wealth). The feet do manual work such as walking. The śūdra is therefore compared to the feet.

Unfortunately, in course of time, somewhere in the past, man used this class-system for personal gains. It came to be attributed as a birthright (i.e., child born to a brāhmaṇa is a brāhmaṇa). This birthright is acutally due to the desires we entertained in the past. It is man who made the caste-system a birthright. Śrī Kṛṣṇa gave the caste-system as "*guṇa*-right" (*vāsanā*-right).

न मां कर्माणि लिम्पन्ति न मे कर्मफले स्पृहा ।
इति मां योऽभिजानाति कर्मभिर्न स बध्यते ॥१४॥

***na māṁ karmāṇi limpanti na me karmaphale spṛhā* |**
***iti māṁ yo'bhijānāti karmabhir na sa badhyate* ||14||**

Actions do not taint me. Nor have I desire for the fruits of actions. He who knows Me thus, is not bound by karma.

Really speaking, any person who wants liberation, while he is in his spiritual path to progress must say to himself, "these actions do not taint me. I have no desire for the fruits of action." He should work in that spirit. When Kṛṣṇa says: "He who knows me thus", it should read as "He who knowing this, lives thus." Such a person is bound to get *mokṣa* as his reward.

The Self inside, if reflected as ego and if attains the status of "I", "mine" etc. will look for individual desire-gratification.

Let us take the example of the moon. The moon is reflected in ponds, wells, in pots of water etc. When there is movement in such waters, the reflected moon also gets shaken. Though the original moon is still, its reflection shakes in the pond. Similarly, the reflected self (ego) is the one who feels the reaction to the ripples of movements by the desires.

Śrī Kṛṣṇa in His status as Kṛṣṇa, the son of Vasudeva, is performing a number of actions. All His actions are for the welfare of mankind. He desires no personal gain from His actions. His action is *niṣkāma karma.* Also, he is not looking for fruits of His actions.

We all should understand that we, who are after all part of Śrī Kṛṣṇa, must work in the same spirit. We should not be egotistic in our actions. We should do our work for its sake and contribute to the welfare of society.

Such actions will not taint us. It means they do not leave any further imprints on our mind. We will no more acquire any new *vāsanās*. On burning our existing *vāsanās,* on burning our old desires, we will become *jīvanmuktas* and will attain *mokṣa.*

एवं ज्ञात्वा कृतं कर्म पूर्वैरपि मुमुक्षुभिः ।
कुरु कर्मैव तस्मात्त्वं पूर्वैः पूर्वतरं कृतम् ॥१५॥

***evaṁ jñātvā kṛtaṁ karma pūrvair api mumukṣubhiḥ* |**
***kuru karmaiva tasmāt tvaṁ pūrvaiḥ pūrvataraṁ kṛtam* ||15||**

Thus knowing, the ancient spiritual seekers also performed actions. Therefore you shall do the same actions as performed by the ancestors in the olden times.

Lord Kṛṣṇa is saying that his teaching of *niṣkāma karma* is not a new idea. He is just reasserting its importance in the maintenance of this universe. He is asking Arjuna to do what his ancestors and great *ṛṣis* of the past did and attain liberation.

We should understand that this path is open to all of us, and will be open to all in future. The principle is the same—*niṣkāma karma.*

किं कर्म किमकर्मेति कवयोऽप्यत्र मोहिताः ।
तत्ते कर्म प्रवक्ष्यामि यज्ज्ञात्वा मोक्ष्यसेऽशुभात् ॥१६॥

***kiṁ karma kiṁ akarmeti kavayo'py atra mohitāḥ* |**
***tat te karma pravakṣyāmi yaj jñātvā mokṣyase'śubhāt* ||16||**

What is action? What is inaction? In this matter even the wise are deluded. I will teach you that action knowing which, you shall be liberated from the evil.

Evil here means *saṁsāra*, the cycle of births and deaths. Those who do not want the evil, will have to work for liberation. These are people who are wise, they do realise that *saṁsāra* is evil.

Such wise people should know how to act in this world. Just saying "I want Liberation. I do not want to fall into *saṁsāra*" and not doing any work is wrong. They do not yet understand what right actions they should perform and what wrong actions they should not perform.

Actions are always related to the "motive" behind such actions. The wise on the spiritual path must know the motives behind actions and develop the tendency for right actions.

कर्मणो ह्यपि बोद्धव्यं बोद्धव्यं च विकर्मणः ।
अकर्मणश्च बोद्धव्यं गहना कर्मणो गतिः ॥१७॥

karmaṇo hyapi boddhavyaṁ boddhavyaṁ ca vikarmaṇaḥ |
akarmaṇaś ca boddhavyaṁ gahanā karmaṇo gatiḥ ||17||

The nature of right action and of wrong action and also of inaction should be known. Deep and difficult to understand is the path of action.

What is *karma*? What is *vikarma*? What is *akarma*? It is difficult to undersand *karma*. One should know what these three words mean. There are different explanations by philosophers for these words.

1. Karma

All actions as prescribed by the *śāstra*s are *karma*s. Actions are *karma*s (chapter 3 verse 8). The various duties prescribed for the four castes are *karma*s. Also the duties prescribed for different states in life (*bramacarya, gṛhastha, vānaprastha* and *saṁnyāsa* (verse 35 chapter 3) are *karma*s. *Karma* therefore means actions of various types mentioned above.

All actions performed with a motive for the result, pure *bhāvanā* actions and those done according to *śāstra*s such as *yajña, dāna, tapas* are considered as *karma*s. A doctor working for somebody performing surgery on a patient is doing his *karma*. It is his *naimittika*, professional *karma*. He is paid to do the job by his employer.

2. Vikarma

These are actions prohibited by the *śāstra*s for all classes of people. They are *niṣiddha karma*s (chapter 3 verse 8). They are also actions prohibited by the *śāstra*s for each of the four classes of people. (A person with vaiśya tendency should not be the ruler. He will then be looking for personal gains rather than the welfare of the public.) All actions that bring sorrow in this world are also *vikarma*.

All actions performed with a motive for the result thereof but with impure *bhāvanā* are considered as *vikarma.* (A doctor who is an employee for a firm, performing surgery on a patient but accepting additional gift for his work would be doing *vikarma.* He should not be accepting a reward from the patient.)

3. Akarma

This is a state of actionlessness. When one does any work without looking for any result (according to *śāstras*), he is doing *akarma.* A *jñānī* is one who performs action in this spirit. That action which does not give a feeling of happiness or sorrow in his world or in the other world, is *akarma* (i.e., work done by a *jīvanmukta* who has nothing to gain or lose). All actions, performed with no desire for the fruits and with feeling of *kṛṣṇārpaṇam astu* (only those actions according to the *śāstras*) are considered as *akarmas*. The surgeon who is self-employed, performs surgery on a patient who has no means to pay. He is performing *akarma.* He does so out of compassion, with a feeling of its being God's work.

Kṛṣṇa admits that it is difficult to understand *karma-mārga.*

> कर्मण्यकर्म यः पश्येदकर्मणि च कर्म यः ।
> स बुद्धिमान्मनुष्येषु स युक्तः कृत्स्नकर्मकृत् ॥१८॥
> ***karmaṇy akarma yaḥ paśyed akarmaṇi ca karma yaḥ* I**
> ***sa buddhimān manuṣyeṣu sa yuktaḥ kṛtsnakarmakṛt* II18II**
>
> *He who sees actions in inaction, and inaction in action, he is the wise man; the* yogī, *the doer of all actions among men.*

To understand this verse, it will help if one looks upon action as *prakṛti* and inaction as the *ātman. Prakṛti* is perishable and *ātman* is imperishable.

No action in "action": This is the *sāttvika* type of work. Actions are at physical level. If one realises that he is really the Self and Self is just a witness to the actions, then even when he is acting, he is not acting. He sees himself as the Soul and attributes actions to the physical body which he is not. As for example, the screen in a cinema theatre. The screen is essential, without which the film cannot be shown. The screen is not tainted by the various scenes in the film. Without the screen, the film could not be shown.

A *jñānī* is one who knows the secret of work. He works without any sense of doership. As far as the *jñānī* is concerned, there is no action at all in him. He has the capacity to keep himself as an actor on the stage of life and is not happy or grieved at life's modifications.

Action in "no action": Actions sprout from thoughts. Thoughts originate in the mind. Hence by not showing outward actions, a person can still be active. 'An idle mind is a devil's workshop' is a common saying. This is the path to destruction and one must avoid it. The thoughts entertained in an inactive state incur *vāsanā*s and have to be burnt at a later stage.

That person who can realise and see intense activity in inaction, and action in inaction, is the wise man. The Lord says, he is fit for liberation. For example, while on a train journey, a passenger on the moving train, comes across another stationary train on the platform, gets the wrong notion that the stationary train is moving. This is seeing action in inaction. It is ignorance.

While we are standing on a shore, a moving ship at a distance looks like a stationary ship. It is seeing inaction in action.

Arjuna on the battlefield dropped his bow and said, "I do not want to fight". But his mind was full of thoughts of sorrow, uncertainty etc. He was showing action in inaction. His actions were at the mental level.

Śrī Kṛṣṇa holding on the reins of the chariot was still performing his *karma*. He had no desire for action nor desire for the fruit of action. He gives Arjuna the knowledge Arjuna asks for, but does not tell him to fight. He wants to uphold righteousness but does not take up arms himself nor does he order Arjuna to fight. He is imparting knowledge to Arjuna and mankind. This is inaction in action.

यस्य सर्वे समारम्भाः कामसंकल्पवर्जिताः ।
ज्ञानाग्निदग्धकर्माणं तमाहुः पण्डितं बुधाः ॥१९॥

***yasya sarve samārambhāḥ kāmasaṅkalpa-varjitāḥ* |**
***jñānāgni-dagdhakarmāṇaṁ tam āhuḥ paṇḍitaṁ budhāḥ* ||19||**

He whose undertakings are all free from desires and purposes, whose actions have been burnt by the fire of knowledge, him, the wise call a pandit.

Here another definition of pandit (wise man) is given. A *pandit* is not one who is learned in theoretical knowledge. A real *pandit* is that person whose actions do not include egotistic feelings, who has no desire for the fruits of action. He continues to perform practical work in his daily life.

Kāma-saṁkalpa-varjitaḥ: It means free from desire and purpose, *kāma* as we know is passionate desire.

Saṁkalpa: It means egotistic thoughts like 'I will do', 'I will fight', 'I will get this' etc. A real wise man should not have any egotistical feeling in his actions. He considers his body as a vehicle (*upādhi*) for execution of actions by the power of Self, and has no personal identity in that work.

During rituals one is asked to say, 'I am going to do this *pūjā* or ceremony.' During weddings one is aksed to say, "I will perform this wedding."

A real and wise man will not say such words. He is aware that whatever he is doing is *nimittamātram.* He is an agent for the action. The owner is the Self.

A *jñānī* (wise) is one whose actions are burnt in the fire of knowledge.

One should remember, that actions arise out of desires. So, this statement means, one whose desires are burnt in the fire of knowledge. Once a person has developed the knowledge of *ātmajñāna* in his daily actions, his actions do not produce any further reactions and so they do not accumulate further *vāsanā*s. He will then be a free or liberated soul. A *jñānī* gets this state by *niṣkāma karma*, which purifies his mind, and by *karma-phala-tyāga*.

त्यक्त्वा कर्मफलासङ्गं नित्यतृप्तो निराश्रयः ।
कर्मण्यभिप्रवृत्तोऽपि नैव किञ्चित्करोति सः ॥२०॥

***tyaktvā karmaphalāsaṅgaṁ nityatṛpto nirāśrayaḥ* ।**
***karmaṇy abhipravṛtto'pi naiva kiñcita karoti saḥ* ॥20॥**

He who has given up attachment to the fruits of work, who is ever content, who does not depend upon anything, though engaged in actions, does not verily do anything.

Here is the definition of a liberated man and the way he works. It is the state of the mind that indicates action and inaction. If we take three characteristics of such a person and analyse them we will understand it better.

(1) He has given up attachment to the fruits of action: Every word is important in this sentence. Everybody is entitled to fruits of action. Even a man on the spiritual path is entitled to liberation.

What is suggested is, "give up attachment to the fruits of action. Renounce your desire to obtain the fruits of action", is what it means. Do not be a slave to desires.

A student wanting to pass his 'A' levels and go to the university is expected to put in great efforts in his 'A' level career. He will surely get his reward and get into the professional course he wants, if he puts in proper efforts at studies. On the other hand, if he dreams on what college he is going to, what friends he would make, how he is going to be independent and how he will enjoy earning money later, his efforts will diminish and he would spend his time dreaming while he was expected to study hard.

A true spiritual *sādhaka* will not work with the aim of ultimate liberation. In the early stages he might do so. But, as he ascends the ladder of progress in his effort, by his *sāttvika* actions he is expected to drop the feeling of obtaining success in his efforts.

Looking for success in spiritual efforts is a reflection of the remnants of ego in the *sāttvika* person. The moment ego is dropped, the moment he continues to perform divine acts, he will reach the *śuddha-sattva* state. *Śuddha-sattva* is the state which is very near to achieving *mokṣa*.

One should not consciously work for achieving *mokṣa*. It will come ultimately. It will depend upon the person's efforts.

(2) Ever content in himself : Wise ones experience the bliss of Self and are content with it. They do not look at *nāma* or *rūpa,* but are aware of *sat*, *cit* and *ānanda* in everything they perceive. Their contentment is not conditioned by time, place or circumstances. It is called the state of *nityatṛpta.*

(3) He does not depend on anything (*nirāśrayaḥ*): We all cling to something or the other in the materialistic world. We cling on to our wealth, family or to our own physical body (ego). The wise ones do not cling to anything. They have no ego in their actions and are content in their Self.

The wise ones are those with the above three characterisitics. They will still do their daily activities and yet they are not doing anything at all. One does not see the 'I'-ness in their actions. Actions only flow out of such a person without producing any reaction.

निराशीर्यतचित्तात्मा त्यक्तसर्वपरिग्रहः ।
शारीरं केवलं कर्म कुर्वन्नाप्नोति किल्बिषम् ॥२१॥

***nirāśīr yatacittātmā tyaktasarvaparigrahaḥ* |**
***śārīraṁ kevalaṁ karma kurvan nāpnodi kilbiṣam* ||21||**

He who is free from hope, who is self-controlled, who has abandoned all possessions, though working merely with the body, does not incur sin.

Three more attributes of a *jīvanmukta* are given here. To stress the point, Śrī Kṛṣṇa explains the same both in a negative and a positive way. He has said before "do not live for desires".

1. Nirāsīḥ: A *jīvanmukta* does not have any desires, he does not wish to enjoy the pleasures of the materialistic world, and he does not also have desires to enjoy the "Self". He automatically gets the bliss, but does not work to get that bliss.

His desire not to enjoy the possessions include also desire not to look for fame and credit for himself.

2. Self-controlled (yatacittātmā): It is not the control of the real Self (*ātman*). But it is the control of the reflected self, i.e., ego. Ego works through the mind and the physical body. "Self-control" is control of one's mind and body when they run towards desirable objects in the materialistic world.

3. Aparigraha: *Parigraha* is "to receive". *Aparigraha* is "non-receiving". When one wants to abandon all possessions, it also includes his not receiving anything from others. He does not obtain anything without having worked for it.

The person who gives a gift to others, is incidentally giving away a part of his *karma* to the recipient. A person, who is a thief, who has given a party to others from the process of the theft, is really distributing his sin among others. One should think carefully before receiving anything free from others.

Our *śāstras* are very particular on this point. We come across some rare people who do not accept any food in the houses of others.

If one looks a bit more deeply, what we receive (from God) is just the reward for our actions, no more and no less. Similarly, one receives from others the reward he is entitled to for his work. (It applies only to works done according to the *śāstras*.)

Such a person, working as per the *śāstras* and receiving benefit for his just work, does not accumulate sin. For example, a judge does not incur sin for sentencing a murderer to death, and the hangman does not incur sin for hanging the murderer.

यदृच्छालाभसंतुष्टो द्वन्द्वातीतो विमत्सरः ।
समः सिद्धावसिद्धौ च कृत्वापि न निबध्यते ॥२२॥

***yadṛcchālābha-saṁtuṣṭo dvandvātīto vimatsaraḥ* I**
***samaḥ siddhāv asiddhau ca kṛtvāpi na nibadhyate* II22II**

Content with what he gets without efforts, free from the pairs of opposites, free from malice, balanced in success and failure, though acting, he is not bound.

These characteristics are seen in that person who has conquered his ego. He has got himself absorbed in *ātman*. His thoughts are above the plane of his mind.

The worldly pleasures and pains reach only up to the mind and the intellect reacts to them. But in that person who is above the level of the mind, these things do not affect him. He knows that it is his body that is living and feeling the world and takes everything in a balanced way. He does not go after worldly pleasures. He does his duty to the best of his capacity and what he gets in return, he accepts it as God's grace. When it is said, "content with what he gets without effort", one must not misunderstand the sentence. Because he is above the plane of mind, what he does with his body is not an effort for him. He just does his best, that is all. He does not for a moment think, 'I have done so much'. He is not an idler receiving an offering by sitting on the wayside.

He is free from malice. He does not hate ohers or begrudge others, again because his thinking is above the plane of mind. He has no envy for those who are in a higher or better position than himself.

When he is working like this, success and failure do not affect him. He is not looking for fruits of his actions. Sometimes unforeseen circumstances may spoil the success of any work. But he does not sit and cry. Nor does he get elated if he achieves success. Even if he has reached perfection, he is not elated. "I"-ness (ego) is dead in him. He automatically has developed a state of contentment called *tṛpti* in his own Self. Nothing else affects him.

Knowledge and action go hand in hand. The man of knowledge does his action in the above spirit. A true *karma-yogī* is actually a *jñānī*.

A *jñānī* is one who knows that the body is just an *upādhi* (vehicle) for his Self and he lets the vehicle do its best without getting attached to the results of the function of the vehicle.

There is a verse in *Bhajagovindam* by Śrī Śaṅkarācārya with a similar meaning:

mūḍha jahīhi dhanāgamatṛṣṇāṁ
kuru sadbuddhiṁ manasi vitṛṣṇām ।
yallabhase nijakarmopāttaṁ
vittaṁ tena vinodaya cittam ॥

(O, you ignorant, drop your thirst for wealth. Attain that state of the mind which is free from thirst for wealth. Develop the habit of letting your mind be satisfied with what you get from your personal effort).

गतसङ्गस्य मुक्तस्य ज्ञानावस्थितचेतसः ।
यज्ञायाचरतः कर्म समग्रं प्रविलीयते ॥२३॥

gatasaṅgasya muktasya jñānāvasthitacetasaḥ **।**
yajñāyācarataḥ karma samagraṁ pravilīyate **॥23॥**

Of the man who is devoid of attachment, who is liberated, whose mind is established in knowledge, the whole action performed in the spirit of sacrifice is dissolved .

The first half of the verse gives three qualities of the *jñānī.*

1. Gatasaṅgasya: Devoid of attachment to the world of plurality. Nothing in the material world is his. He stays with it as long as it stays. If any member of his family is ill, he is not distressed and does not get into despair. He continues in his fixation on the Self. He does his duty to his family, he gives them love and affection but is not attached to them. He has detachment in attachment.

2. Muktaḥ: (Liberated man) He is liberated from desires and hatred which are the two main reasons for action. Because of desires one acts to possess. His mind does not get enslaved in any emotions. He has no hatred to others and does not harm others because of hatred.

3. Jñānāvasthitacetasaḥ: Whose mind is established in knowledge. The light of knowledge is burning consantly in him. He is not living in ignorance. He does not have any dark spots in his mind. The whole mind is illuminated. He therefore sees the *āman* inside and gets fixed in the *ātman.* Such a person, who is working, gets his actions dissolved in the spirit of *yajña.*

Śrī Madhvācārya gives the following meaning to these three words:

Gatasaṅgasya: Free from friendship from fruits of action.

Muktasya: Free from bodily attachment. The one who is free from *ahaṁkāra.*

Jñānāvasthitacetasaḥ: The one who constantly keeps the mind immersed in the knowledge of *Parameśvara.*

Normally desires lead to actions. Actions lead to reactions and more desires and actions. One keeps on accumulating *vāsanā*s (thought-processes which result in action). These actions are responsible for one's fall into the *saṁsāra* of birth and death.

But in a *jñānī*, this does not happen. All his actions, because they are selfless works, become acts of devotion for the welfare of mankind. *Yajña* is defined as "self-dedicated activity in the spirit of service". One pours his actions in the fire of *yajña* (offer his services to the universal welfare). Automatically his actions do not cause new *vāsanā*-imprints in his mind.

Of course, a *jñānī* will still have his *vāsanā*s of the past to burn away. These are called *prārabdha karma*. He would have inherited these *vāsanā*s from the past *karma*s. They have to be burnt away by fruitless actions of the present. While the body is living, one has to perform *karma* to destroy existing *vāsanā*s and also to perform dedicated activities.

ब्रह्मार्पणं ब्रह्म हविर्ब्रह्माग्नौ ब्रह्मणा हुतम् ।
ब्रह्मैव तेन गन्तव्यं ब्रह्मकर्मसमाधिना ॥२४॥

brahmārpaṇaṁ brahma havir brahmāgnau brahmaṇā hutam |
brahmaiva tena gantavyaṁ brahmakarma-samādhinā ||24||

The oblation is Brahman, *the offerings are* Brahman, *the sacrifice is* Brahman *and absorption in action is* Brahman. *This can be called spiritual or divine energy.* Brahman *shall be reached by him who cognizes* Brahman *alone in his action.*

This is a famous verse in the *Gītā*. It summarises the teaching of the *Vedānta.*

Brahman: The primordial energy which is responsible for creation is *Brahman* (This can be called spiritual or divine energy). The energy which is needed for survival is also *Brahman* and is termed as *ātman. Nāma-rūpa* have enveloped this reality and have given diversity to it. Basically *ātman* is the substratum.

If one is indebted to someone or something for survival, it is natural that one's actions are dedicated to that 'factor'.

This prayer is to remind us of the truth and how to act keeping the truth in mind constantly.

Yajña: In Vedic periods it was a ritualistic act. They had a sacred fire in which oblations and sacrifices were offered to invoke and satisfy the deity. In return they expected rewards from the deities. In other words, it was an act to fulfil a desire.

Yajña has four factors:

(1) the deity invoked,

(2) the fire,

(3) the material for oblation,

(4) the individual performing the *yajña.*

What this verse says is that all the four factors are *Brahman.*

For the performer of the sacrifice, the essential factor is the truth behind this plurality.

He, the *ātman,* is invoking the creator *Brahman.* He has lit the fire which is *Brahman.*

Firewood is used to ignite the fire. Fire is inside the wood but is not manifest. Unmanifest energy in the wood is the fire. (When the wood is burnt, the greater portion of that energy is burnt and small portions of ash remain.) So the fire is *Brahman.* Materials of oblation like oil, *ghī* are also *Brahman.* It is similar to saying that all waves in the ocean are ocean. Man should realise *Brahman* everywhere and in all things by contemplating on this truth.

This verse is repeated before every meal as a tradition in many Hindu families, similar to "the grace before meal" uttered by pious Christians. Food is the main source of energy for survival and without food we cannot survive. It is a daily act. It is therefore one's duty to remember where this energy for survival comes from and where it should go.

brahmāgnau brahmaṇā hutam: In the fire of *Brahman*, by Brahman is *offered*. The fire is *Brahman*. The energy is *Brahman*. The food is *Brahman*, the feeder is *Brahman* and the act of eating is *Brahman*. Everything and every act is *Brahman*.

What this verse means is, eating and digesting the food is for the survival for any person. It is *nitya karma*. What we eat, what we are, and what we digest are all nothing but *Brahman*. If I do not consider myself as an agent for the performance of an action (sacrifice) and if I look at the "Lord in all living and non-living", then I see only *Brahman* in all. Hence, we are asked by sages to remember this verse in every action we perform and live the life accordingly.

दैवमेवापरे यज्ञं योगिनः पर्युपासते ।
ब्रह्माग्नावपरे यज्ञं यज्ञेनैवोपजुह्वति ॥२५॥

daivam evāpare yajñaṁ yoginaḥ paryupāsate |
brahmāgnāv apare yajñaṁ yajñenaivopajuhvati ||25||

Some yogīs *perform sacrifice to gods only while others, by the union of the self with* Brahman, *offer the self as sacrifice in the fire of* Brahman.

In the next seven verses Kṛṣṇa is explaining the different types of *yajña*s performed by those *yogī*s who wants to unite with *ātman*.

There are two ways of understanding the word *deva*s used in this verse. The forms of God which different individuals worship depending on their choice like Gaṇeśa, Gaurī, Satyanārāyaṇa etc. are *deva*s. Such people are *bhakta*s and perform sacrifices to those Gods with devotion. This helps in the spiritual growth of a person.

The power behind each of the sense-organs is also known as *deva*. For example, the *deva* for the eyes is fire. The light of fire in the sun-god is seen by the eyes. Eyes cannot see in darkness. Similarly, The *deva* for the ears is space. The *deva* for the nose is earth. The *deva* for the mouth is water. The *deva* for the skin is air.

Fire, space, earth, water and air are the five great elements. They are represented as the five sense-organs in our bodies. Each sense-organ represents one element.

''Sacrificing'' the eyes, (invoking the Sun), means, one offers as a sacrifice whatever one sees into the fire of *yajña*. In other words, one develops a way of living where he does not see anything that morally or spiritually wrong and sinful. He has sacrificed it. What he sees and recognises is only light, only that which is morally right. Wherever he sees anything, he only sees that which gives him spiritual satisfaction and not which gives mere physical pleasure. The same applies to all the sense-organs. The particular *deva*s bless him and fulfil his desires.

2. Other type of *yogī*s offer as sacrifice their total individuality into the fire of *yajña*. Their ego, mind and body are offered in the sacrifice. They do not have 'I'-ness any more. Every act is *kṛṣṇārpaṇam astu— bhāvanā* in such people. They are *jñāna-yogī*s. They have inquired into their real nature, and realised what they really are. They carried on working only to kill the existing *vāsanā*s and purify their mind. They have lost their ego. They have lost their duality and have become *Brahman*. They do not use sense-organs for seeking the pleasures of the world. They have gone above the plane of senses, mind and intellect. They dedicate their sense-life to the service of the world. They realise that it is the physical body that has to stay alive till death and they make use of the body for the welfare of the society.

श्रोत्रादीनीन्द्रियाण्यन्ये संयमाग्निषु जुह्वति ।
शब्दादीन्विषयानन्य इन्द्रियाग्निषु जुह्वति ॥२६॥

***śrotrādīnīndriyāṇy anye saṁyamāgniṣu juhvati* I**
***śabdādīn viṣayān anye indriyāgniṣu juhvati* II26II**

Others sacrifice the senses like the organ of hearing etc., in the fires of sense-restraint. Some othrs offer sense-objects like sound etc., in the fires-of-the-senses.

Sense-restraint: It is the first method of progress to spiritual freedom. *Mokṣa* is nothing but freedom from pains and pleasures. The first source of these pleasures and pains is from the objects of the world perceived by the sense-organs. If one can restrain the sense-organs, the objects of the world have no way of reaching the mind. It is like going to sleep, in which state the sense-organs do not function.

Be awake but let the sense-organs go to sleep. Do not let the sense-organs take objects to the mind. This is achieved by following several vows, rules of conduct and getting the senses under control.

Some people in India go to Kāśī, the most sacred place in order to visit the temple of Kāśī Viśvanāth and to have a bath in the Ganges river. They take a vow that they will give up one of the things they like when they make such a visit. For example, if they like a particular vegetable like aubergine, they will vow not to eat aubergine any more. The idea behind this is sense-control.

Mind-control is also self-control: It is the next step in the progress. From the time of birth till death, the sense-organs will take impulses from the outer world to the mind which registers them. It realises pleasures and pains obtained and keeps a memory of those events.

At different times it recapitulates these reactions. Then it wants to go out and enjoy the pleasures again. It sends its organs of action in search of that pleasure. It is like a child opening its box of assortments when she is alone to find out what she likes best and then play with it.

By ''self-control'' one means, the mind using its intellectual capacity and rejecting the objects of the world. It is like examining objects, understanding how painful they are at the end and realising their worthlessness (like the child saying 'I do not like any toys in my box' and forgetting the existence of the box altogether). Once the mind has rejected an object, evem when the senses perceive them, the mind does not get any pleasure from them. When such a mind which is calm is working in the physical world, nothing disturbs it.

In addition to making senses ineffective by sense-restraint, self-control makes the same senses more effective. Because of the control one achieves, one uses the senses for adoration of the Lord. Anything perceived, any sound heard etc. will register in the mind only if they are in relation to the *ātman*. Nothing pertaining to the ego and material objects registers in such persons. In course of time, their mind will be a treasure-house of thoughts on *ātman* only. Such minds can dwell on *ātman* and find eternal bliss.

Sense-control is negative discrimination and self-control is positive discrimination. Sense-control is dropping 'Bad' and self-control is taking in 'Good'.

सर्वाणीन्द्रियकर्माणि प्राणकर्माणि चापरे ।
आत्मसंयमयोगाग्नौ जुह्वति ज्ञानदीपिते ॥२७॥

sarvāṇīndriyakarmāṇi prāṇakarmāṇi cāpare |
ātmasaṁyama-yogāgnau juhvati jñānadīpite ||27||

Others again sacrifice all the functions of the senses and the functions of breath (vital energy) in the fire of yoga *of self-control, illumined by knowledge.*

Some people have acquired knowledge by constantly questioning about the Self in them. They have inquired into as to what is the reality behind the existence. Having realised "That", their mind ceases to run after the outer world and goes into its own Self.

These people have discriminated and distinguished the Self and the ego. They then live more and more in the Self. Such people are said to have self-control by the Self (ego-control by the *ātman*).

After this, it is easy to control sense-organs (*jñāna-indriya*s) and organs of action (*karma-indriya*s). This path is called the *yoga* of self-restraint (*ātma-saṁyam-yoga*). Breath-control is called *prāṇāyāma*. This idea is described as sacrificing the senses and vital energy in the fire-of-self-control.

The identification of the mind with the *ātman* is possible by dropping the ego. This identification is referred to as the "fire of self-control". Only by knowledge one can control the senses by sense-organs, sense-organs by the mind, mind by the intellect and intellect by conscience. In such cases, the individual has no mind, it is merged in the glory of *ātman*. *Prāṇāyāma*, *pratyāhāra*, *dhyāna* etc. are means to achieve this end result.

Prāṇāyāma: Control of inspiration and expiration (inhalation and exhalation).

Pratyāhāra: The state of the mind where in sense-organs have no influence on the mind in respect of matters relating to the body and its connections with the outer world.

Dhāraṇā : Constant flow of thoughts on an object.

Dhyāna : Constant flow of thoughts on the object of *dhāraṇā.*

Samādhi : When the mind merges into *ātman* by *dhyāna*, there are no two entities. There is no objective world, no ego. It is a state of total merging into *ātman.*

Saṁyama : When *dhyāna*, *dhāraṇā* and *samādhi* are only on the *ātman*, it is known as *saṁyama*.

द्रव्ययज्ञास्तपोयज्ञा योगयज्ञास्तथापरे ।
स्वाध्यायज्ञानयज्ञाश्च यतयः संशितव्रताः ॥२८॥

***dravyayajñās tapoyajñā yogayajñās tathāpare* I**
***svādhyāya-jñānayajñāś ca yatayaḥ saṁśitavratāḥ* II28II**

Others offer wealth, austerity and yoga *as sacrifice. Some others, the ascetics of self-control and rigid vows, offer study of knowledge as sacrifice.*

Five forms of *yajña*s are described in this verse.

(1) Dravya-yajña

Acquiring wealth by proper means and utilising it for the welfare of the needy is a form of *yajña*. It is wealth offered to the needy. It is also called *dāna*. Scriptures do give a detailed description of whom to give the *dāna*, when to give it, where to give it, and how much to give etc.

(2) Tapo-yajña

Austerity means subjecting the body and senses to discipline by vows of fasting, silence etc.

(3) Yoga-yajña

Yoga is controlling various diversions of the mind. This is to help union of the ego with the self.

There are eight steps in *yoga*. They are: *Yama, niyama, āsana, prāṇāyāma, pratyāhāra, dhāraṇā, dhyāna* and *samādhi.*

Of these the five latter are described in the last verse.

Yama : *Ahiṁsā*, truthfulness, *brahmacarya*, non-receiving of gifts (*aparigraha*) are all acts that come under *yama.*

Niyama : Cleanliness, purity, peaceful *tapas*, *svādhyāya*, devotion to God are *niyama*s.

Āsana : A posture wherein one can sit peacefully in contemplation of the Lord. Various *āsana*s are mentioned in the *śāstra*s, e.g., *padmāsana*, *vīrāsana*, *bhadrāsana* etc.

(4) Svādhyāya-Yajña

The study and recitation of scriptures is a form of sacrifice. Study of the Self (*ātman*) is *svādhyāya-yajña.*

(5) Jñāna-Yajña

Pursuit of spiritual knowledge is another form of sacrifice. *Dravya-yajña* can be discusssed in some detail. One can offer material wealth. Even the poor man can also offer wealth. What wealth?

The wealth of his own treasures. That is, the treasure of love, kindness, sympathy and affection. These are an inexhaustible wealth. The more we give them, the more it fills up again in us. The actions of giving love, kindness, sympathy and affection can bring more satisfaction to the receiver than the giving of money. These can be given to anybody in need. Just holding the hands of a terminally ill person, can give more satisfaction to that person.

Jñāna-yajña consists of rejecting the false (ego-body) and uniting with the *ātmā* and knowing the nature of the Self.

All these are obtained by *saṁśita-vrataḥ* (men of rigid vows). One has to try hard at these. *Sādhanā* is practice and *sādhya* is the goal. By constant practice one can achieve freedom. Spiritual realisation is a great reward. If one practises to run daily for a few months at least to train to win a race, to win the race of life how much training is needed? An athlete, if he stops training, finds it hard to get into the habit later. Similarly, for *brahma-jñāna*, one cannot really relax even for a moment. One has to constantly remember the goal and purify the mind always. The above methods, all in their own way purify the mind in their own time. The ripe time is when all *vāsanā*s are burnt away and no new *vāsanā*s have come in.

The word *yatayaḥ* means ascetics, but it does not mean *saṁnyāsins*. Ascetics constantly work to burn the *vāsanā*s and walk in the spiritual path.

अपाने जुह्वति प्राणं प्राणेऽपानं तथापरे ।
प्राणापानगती रुद्ध्वा प्राणायामपरायणाः ॥२९॥

***apāne juhvati prāṇaṁ prāṇe-pānaṁ tathāpare* I**
***prāṇāpāna-gatī ruddhvā prāṇāyāma-parāyaṇāḥ* II29II**

Others offer as sacrifice the outgoing breath in the incoming, and the incoming in the outgoing, restraining the sources of the outgoing and incoming breaths, solely absorbed in the restraint of breath.

The verse describes the technique of breath-control as a form of sacrifice.

In states of passion and agitation, one can observe changes in the breathing pattern. Breathing then gets heavier, noisy and irregular. Intake of oxygen and exhaling carbon-dioxide is disturbed. Oxygen is, as we know, required for proper functioning of the body. It is needed for survival. Diminished oxygen to the brain results in a state of confusion. A steady, well-developed, well-planned form of breathing regulates the proper flow of oxygen to the brain. This is achieved by *prāṇāyāma* (breath control).

Details on *prāṇāyāma* should be learnt from proper texts and experts on the subject. A brief description of it is as follows:

Steady intake of breath is *pūraka*.

Holding the breath for a short while is *kumbhaka*.

Steady breathing out is *recaka*.

Repeating this cycle, accompanied by the chanting of *Oṁ*, is regular *prāṇāyāma*.

Controlling the mind where thoughts arise due to desire, and controlling the response to incoming stimuli from the sense-organs is an important step in spiritual progress.

Even though *prāṇāyāma* means breath-control, *prāṇa* really means life, not just breath. All manifestations of life are *prāṇa*; to sustain these manifestations, oxygen is needed (i.e., breathing). Breathing regulates life's activities.

अपरे नियताहाराः प्राणान्प्राणेषु जुह्वति ।
सर्वेऽप्येते यज्ञविदो यज्ञक्षपितकल्मषाः ॥३०॥

***apare niyatāhārāḥ prāṇān prāṇeṣu juhvati* I**
***sarve'py ete yajñavido yajñakṣapitakalmaṣāḥ* II30II**

Others with well regulated diet, sacrifice life-breaths in the life-breaths. All these are knowers of sacrifice whose sins are destroyed by sacrifice.

In the previous verse breath-control was discussed. In this verse diet is discussed. We cannot survive without food and air.

The food we eat turns into energy, which is needed for all our activities, including spiritual practice. Wrong habits in eating, and eating wrong types of food, upset the health of the person. An unhealthy person finds it hard to concentrate his mind on spiritual progress. If health is upset, that would be one more obstacle to spiritual progress. Good health will help in spiritual *sādhanā*.

Later on Śrī Kṛṣṇa discusses food habits of persons (chapter 17) of different *guṇa*s. For example, eating garlic and spices in excess induce indulgence in actions of passion.

Food we eat has to be—

(1) pure,
(2) moderate in quantity,
(3) earned by righteous means,
(4) eating at the proper time of the day, and
(5) should have been offered to God before eating.

All the types of sacrifices discussed so far are means to purify the mind which in turn kills all sins (burns up *vāsanās*) and leads one to liberation. They are all techniques which help the mind turn inwards looking for the Ultimate Truth (i.e., increase the divinity in us).

The verse says "sacrifice life-breaths in the life-breaths". What does this mean? It is a fact of life that life lives on life. We should dedicate our life to the service of the cosmic life which is the universe we live in, which is nothing but the various modifications of the Lord.

यज्ञशिष्टामृतभुजो यान्ति ब्रह्म सनातनम् ।
नायं लोकोऽस्त्ययज्ञस्य कुतोऽन्यः कुरुसत्तम ॥३१॥

***yajñaśiṣṭāmṛtabhujo yānti brahma sanātanam* I**
***nāyaṁ loko'sty ayajñasya kuto'nyaḥ kurusattama* II31II**

Those who eat the remnants of sacrifice which is nectar go to eternal Brahman. *To the non-sacrificer, even this world is not, how can he get a higher world, O best of the Kurus.*

The Lord has enumerated various types of self-dedicated *karma*s in the previous verses. These *yajña*s help one to overcome selfishness.

Every act we perform with no *ahaṁkāra* in it, leads us one step higher towards liberation. Even our *nitya* and *naimittika karma*s, if performed according to the *śāstra*s for the welfare of others and not for personal gains, will help us to achieve *mokṣa*.

Total destruction of "I"-ness is equivalent to merging of the mind in the *ātman*. This state wherein one realises *Brahman* is the state of *ānanda*. This is described by the Lord as 'The Nectar' which one gets by eating the remnants of sacrifice. First is the welfare of all beings and then welfare of the individual's family and finally of the individual himself.

If we consider every man as a composition of man and divinity, our aim then would be to kill "the man-part" of the individual and leave only the divinity to live. We, "the man-part", are known as *jīva*. We should offer jīvahood as oblation to gain *Brahman*.

To the non-sacrificer—This word means a self-seeking person. The person who performs any work which is only for his selfish needs, eventually destroys himself. He cannot and will not attain *mokṣa*. When one does both daily (*nitya*) and professional (*naimittika*) acts with a view to gaining personal ends and with no wish for the welfare of others, one cannot thrive at all. If he cannot thrive even in this world, how can he attain *Brahman*.

एवं बहुविधा यज्ञा वितता ब्रह्मणो मुखे ।
कर्मजान्विद्धि तान्सर्वानेवं ज्ञात्वा विमोक्ष्यसे ॥३२॥

evaṁ bahuvidhā yajñā vitatā brahmaṇo mukhe |
karmajān viddhi tān sarvān evaṁ jñātvā vimokṣyase ||32||

The various forms of sacrifice are spread out in the storehouse of the Vedas *(which are the faces of* Brahmaṅ). *Know them all to be born of action. Thus knowing, you will be liberated.*

What has come out of Brahman? The *Veda*s. So, the first line means that all these *yajña*s are described in the four *Veda*s. It can also mean that they all lead us to *Brahman*. They are described in *karma-kāṇḍa*. They are all different types of actions one can pursue. Actions are born of desires to achieve the desired objects. They are the means and not an end in themselves.

The means is the action. The end is the knowledge. Do not just think about the means. Achieve the end, i.e., *jñāna*. *Jñāna* leads to liberation.

In the *Vedas*, the final section is *jñāna-kāṇḍa*. One should not just be performing one or the other sacrifices. He must try to achieve the ultimate *jñāna*.

Individual effort is essential for right action. Action, well-planned and executed, is the means. Inactivity will lead us nowhere. Everyone of us must use our faculties of senses, body, mind and intellect to uplift us. And by that process we should help in the prosperity of society.

If one knows what *Brahman* is, he would know what the "faces of *Brahman*" means. Such a person knows the *Vedas*. The one who knows *Vedas*, knows how nature functions. Any person, who converts his *karma* into *yajña*, is fit for liberation. If *karma* is not converted to *yajña*, it binds the person to his *saṁsāra*.

Arjuna had thought that by running away from the battlefield, he would attain *mokṣa*. Kṛṣṇa is now declaring that action is an essential pre-requisite for knowledge.

श्रेयान्द्रव्यमयाद्यज्ञाज्ज्ञानयज्ञः परन्तप ।
सर्वं कर्माखिलं पार्थ ज्ञाने परिसमाप्यते ॥३३॥

śreyān dravyamayād yajñāj jñānayajñaḥ parantapa |
sarvaṁ karmākhilaṁ pārtha jñāne parisamāpyate ||33||

O Parantapa (scorcher of enemies), knowledge-sacrifice is superior to wealth-sacrifice. All actions in their entirety, O Arjuna, end in knowledge.

Kṛṣṇa, through this verse, brings out the fact that both *karma* and *jñāna* are excellent paths in spiritual progress. The final result is attainment of the knowledge of the Self. To attain that knowledge one has to follow one or the other paths mentioned above.

Jñāna-yajña is sacrificing one's ignorance in the altar of knowledge. To know 'the Truth', to know what is *ātmā* and what is *anātma* is *jñāna*. The ability to control the mind and senses from running towards material objects in the world is *jñāna*. To be able to use intellectual capacity to discriminate between the Soul and the ego is *ātma-jñāna*.

Dravya-yajña is sacrifice of material objects. This is a step towards achieving the knowledge. Once the person performs *dravya-yajña* with no desire for personal benefits (*niṣkāma karma*) he is said to be on the path to attain *jñāna*. *Jñāna-yajña* is superior to *dravya-yajña*.

In the second half of the verse, Kṛṣṇa declares that all actions culminate in knowledge. *Karmas* done according to *śāstras* end in knowledge. The *karmas* help to purify the mind. Knowledge in course of time develops to wisdom (*vijñāna*) and by *vijñāna*, man attains liberation.

Karma is *sādhanā* — to achieve knowledge.
Jñāna is *sādhya* — knowledge achieved.

Liberation is not something that suddenly dawns one fine morning. It is the end result of a continuous process of action, and devotion to God.

Our ignorance is our misunderstanding of our true nature. Our desires are born of ignorance. They force us to follow the ego and not the Self. Desires lead to action. Worldly desires lead to the bondage of *saṁsāra*. By right knowledge, we can reverse the process. We can turn the materialistic desires into the desire of the Self and perform actions in that spirit.

"Burn away past *saṁskāra* tendencies,
achieve knowledge and continue
spreading the divine glory", is the
Lord's message to spiritual seekers.

तद्विद्धि प्रणिपातेन परिप्रश्नेन सेवया ।
उपदेक्ष्यन्ति ते ज्ञानं ज्ञानिनस्तत्त्वदर्शिनः ॥३४॥

***tad viddhi praṇipātena paripraśnena sevayā* |**
***upadekṣyanti te jñānaṁ jñāninas tattvadarśinaḥ* ||34||**

Know that by full prostration, question and service, the sages who have realised the Truth will instruct you in that knowledge.

Methods of learning from the *gurus* (knowledgeable persons) and the qualities necessary in the teacher are discussed in this verse. The first line is about, how to approach the *guru*. The method described here is 5000-years-old. This method is still applicable in the present-day for sincere seekers of the Truth.

It is true that the modern technology of audio-visual presentation and distant learning have altered the approach to any subject. There is still nothing superior to learning directly from the master of any particular field of the subject.

By prostration: Physically falling flat at the feet of any person is prostration. In approaching the *guru*, one must be ready to surrender oneself at the feet of the *guru* with respect and obedience. It is a mental and intellecutal attitude. One has to drop his ego at the feet of the master if one wants sincerely to learn the best. This method is known as *sāṣṭāṅga namaskāra*. Hands, feet, knees, chest, head, eyes and speech are the *aṣṭāṅga*s eight limbs) with which the disciple surrenders himself at the feet of the *guru*.

By question: Unless one is ready to clarify any doubts, one cannot really understand any subject. Towards this object one should and must ask questions. To think that ''what would he think of me if I ask this question'', is wrong. To feel that one exposes one's ignorance by asking questions is also wrong. After all one goes to the teacher to learn. If the student does not ask questions the teacher gets the feeling that he has done a good job and that his student has understood it. But, questioning by the student should not be to probe the teacher's knowledge nor should it be to show off one's knowledge before the teacher.

By service: In olden days, any one who wanted to learn, whether it be the king, emperor, minister etc. had to go to the teacher's *āśrama* and serve the master. After sometime if the teacher was satisfied, then he would accept the student. This was to make it clear to the student that material or physical wealth of a person does not make one superior.

If one approaches the teacher who is intellectually wealthy, one has to be humble. He has come to learn the knowledge for the welfare of mankind and not for personal gain. The real knowledge has to be passed on to the right people. That is one of the reasons why Hinduism has survived all the onslaughts and hard times in its long history.

Real service to the teacher lies in the attempt of the student to live the life indicated by the teacher. This method is also known as *satsaṅga*. *Sat* is truth, *saṅga* is attachment. The attachment between the teacher and students for learning the truth is *satsaṅga*. Together they explore the truth.

Total dedication of body, speech and mind (*mana*, *vāk*, *kāyā*) to the *guru* (teacher) is offered by the student by prostration, by question and service. There is no place for commercial attitude. The *guru* does not physically give *jñāna* to the student. *Jñāna* is the inherent nature of all of us, but it is clouded by ignorance (*māyā*). The *guru* helps to tear the mask of ignorance in his disciple. This is best achieved by considering the *guru* as God and prostrating before him. Just as a burning candle lights another candle (that is taken to it), the *guru* lights the knowledge in his student.

What are the qualities of the teacher? This is answered in the second half of the verse. The sage must have realised the truth. He must have a perfect knowledge of scriptures, must have realised the Self and should be far above the pleasures of worldly life. They are not just masters in theory, but they are also practical followers of what they know.

यज्ज्ञात्वा न पुनर्मोहमेवं यास्यसि पाण्डव ।
येन भूतान्यशेषेण द्रक्ष्यस्यात्मन्यथो मयि ॥३५॥

yaj jñātvā na punar moham evaṁ yāsyasi pāṇḍava |
yena bhūtāny aśeṣeṇa drakṣyasy ātmany atho mayi ||35||

O Arjuna, having obtained that knowledge, you will not be deluded again like this. You shall see all beings in yourself and also in Me.

Having obtained that knowledge of the Self (knowledge of *atmā* is the highest knowledge, that is, *Brahma-jñāna*) one clears all doubts about the illusory world. One can see and realise the *ātman* in himself and in others all over. One's delusion is cleared.

Let us take the example of a mango. An unripe mango is sour. When it ripens, the same mango becomes sweet. The sourness will have disappeared totally. The unripe mind of a person is sour and hence the person sees the diversity of the world. A ripe mind is sweet. It sees unity in diversity of the world.

Arjuna's delusion was his 'I'-ness, 'my'-ness. He recognised his relationship to the warriors. As a soldier, his duty was only to know who the enemy was and who the warriors on his side were. Kṛṣṇa wants him to develop the knowledge to see Self in all (including in Kṛṣṇa). Kṛṣṇa emphasises the practical way of living in truth. We should all learn to approach others in the following way:

(1) See what good there is in the other person. Then question ourselves, "have I got that quality? If I have not got it, can I develop that quality?"

(2) See what is bad in that person. Then question oneself, "have I got the same bad quality in me? If so, can I get rid of that bad quality?"

By this technique one can purify oneself. It is no good trying to point out bad qualities in others. We should correct our own bad habits and let others see the good in us and set an example for others to follow. We have no right to point out the bad in others. Each one of us has to develop and this is possible by: (1) learning from the teachers, scriptures, and (2) by living that life to set an example for others to follow.

A *jñānī* is one who has understood that Self is not delusion. It is there now, it was in the past and will be there in the future. All the world is in the Self and the Self is not in any world. See the Self in all and see the Self in God, is implied in the second half of the verse. Kṛṣṇa is saying that a *jñānī* and Himself are one and the same. The devotee and the God are one. This is *Advaita* Philosophy as mentioned by Lord Kṛṣṇa.

Knowledge leads to Unity, and ignorance to diversity. (Sri Ramakrishna)

अपि चेदसि पापेभ्यः सर्वेभ्यः पापकृत्तमः ।
सर्वं ज्ञानप्लवेनैव वृजिनं संतरिष्यसि ॥३६॥

api ced asi pāpebhyaḥ sarvebhyaḥ pāpakṛttamaḥ |
sarvaṁ jñāna-plavenaiva vṛjinaṁ saṁtariṣyasi ||36||

Even if you are the most sinful of all sinners you shall cross over all sins by the raft of knowledge.

The Lord, out of kindness has also dwelt upon sinners. Do they go to hell? How do they get liberated? Is there a way out for sinners.

The *Vedas* do not condemn sinners. They just point out good and bad. They explain what happens due to good and bad actions. They say it is up to the person to do what he wants.

We have, in the past, due to ignorance, committed sins. They have accumulated and become an ocean. If we have to cross the ocean, we need a raft.

One need not be frightened that he is a sinner and that he cannot attain *mokṣa*. The moment he realises that he is a sinner he is on the boat to travel to *mokṣa*. He needs the raft of knowledge to make him travel easily on the ocean.

Sin and virtue are two sides of the same coin. *Karma* performed in ignorance of the Self becomes sin and the same *karma* performed with full knowledge of the Self becomes a virtue. Once knowledge dawns, then further sins will not accumulate. One will then continue to live, accepting life, paying penalties for past sins without despair, till he clears all his *vāsanās*. Finally, he lives the life of a *jīvanmukta*.

यथैधांसि समिद्धोऽग्निर्भस्मसात्कुरुतेऽर्जुन ।
ज्ञानाग्निः सर्वकर्माणि भस्मसात्कुरुते तथा ।।३७।।

yathaidhāṁsi samiddhognir bhasmasāt kurute'rjuna |
jñānāgniḥ sarvakarmāṇi bhasmasāt kurute tathā ||37||

O Arjuna, just as the blazing fire reduces fuel to ashes, so does the fire of knowledge reduce all actions to ashes.

It is another example of knowledge and its powers. One cannot recognise different types of fuel in the ashes once they are burnt. It is simple ash. Any type of sin committed, once knowledge is obtained, will be burnt and one gets pure ash, at the end. One clears any type of sin if he has kindled his fire of knowledge.

Our sins are due to our actions. Accordingly, the actions (*karma*s) fall into the following three categories.

1. *sañcita karma*
2. *prārabdha karma*
3. *āgāmī karma*

Sañcita is the cumulative effect of all *karma*s done in the past. *Prārabdha* is the result of a portion of *sañcita karma*, and that is the cause of our present birth. *Āgāmī* is the future actions and their effect.

What sins we have committed in the past, is stored in our 'fate'. We have to pay for those sins sooner or later. Similarly, what good we have done in the past is also stored in our 'fate'. We enjoy the benefits of it sooner or later. As they are actions of the past, we have no control over them. We accept our fate. We suffer or enjoy sooner or later due to our *sañcita karma*.

What sins we commit now, will be stored as well and we will pay for it in future. What good we do now will also be stored and will pay its rewards in future. If we realise the presence of *ātman*, the knowledge of it will act as fire and burn our past sins and also help to give us a better future. This *prārabdha*, the present state, is very important. If we realise we are groping in the dark, we should make attempts to light the candle of knowledge. If not, we do not know how many more obstacles are in our path.

Our sinful acts of the present and the past will make us suffer in future. Similarly, our good acts of the present and the past will give us a good life for the future. What happens to us in future, which will be the result of our present actions, i.e. *āgāmī,* is known only to us. We do not need a gypsy to tell us our future. *Āgāmī* means not seen. We do not see our future due to our ignorance. By lighting the light of knowledge we can see our own future. Of course, we do not know what we have done in the past. We should be prepared to face difficulties in future which are the result our actions in the past.

The fire of knowledge will destroy *sañcita* and *āgāmī karma*s and make *prārabdha* ineffective. For example, a child runs home in the dark because he is late and is afraid that his parents will scold him. He takes a dark, unlit road because it is quicker to reach. In his hurry he has forgotten to wear his slippers. Unfortunately he runs over some thorns and sharp stones on the road. He feels pain and stops. He now begins to think, because he is in pain. What he did so far was *sañcita karma*. It was mistakes in the past. He cannot retrace it. He has to suffer now and also for some more time in future. If he gets infection, he will suffer longer in future. This is *āgāmī*.

The pain he is suffering now is *prārabdha*. He can now see where he is running, avoid the obstacles and get the wound washed with antiseptic. He can try to prevent future problems by his present actions. He may still get infection and have pain, but he still has to suffer. He will walk in pain, but he will accept it as his *prārabdha*, i.e., fate. He made a mistake and so is suffering.

By the light of knowledge, he would develop such will-power as will help him to bear the present calamity and will try to make the future less painful. At the end, the boy gets the infection under control and is free from pain.

Similarly, we can make our future blissful by our present actions and learn to accept the present as the result of our past actions. We can leave a better world for our children (who are after all, part of our body) by our present actions.

न हि ज्ञानेन सदृशं पवित्रमिह विद्यते ।
तत्स्वयं योगसंसिद्धः कालेनात्मनि विन्दति ॥३८॥

***na hi jñānena sadṛśaṁ pavitram iha vidyate* |**
***tat svayaṁ yogasaṁsiddhaḥ kālenātmani vindati* ||38||**

Certainly there is nothing so pure as knowledge in this world. He who is himself perfected in yoga *finds it in the Self by himself in due season.*

There are different types of knowledge. Of these the knowledge of the Self is most pure. There is no other knowledge in the world that is purer than the knowledge of *ātmā*.

In our house, I have my family who love me. My friends come to my house and love me. They invite me to their house. Why? Because I am an individual. If I die, my body will not be in this house for long, because 'I' am no more warm and I putrify. I will not be allowed into other's house as a dead person.

So, what is it they loved in me? They loved my physical body which was blessed by the Self or *ātmā* inside.

This knowledge of the Self, who He is, where is He from, etc. is the purest knowledge.

Who is perfected in yoga: It means the one who has mastered the art of *niṣkāma karma yoga*. Such person has the qualifications to receive such knowledge of the Self. He must practise *niṣkāma karma* regularly.

If we are hungry we have to eat to satisfy our hunger. If somebody else eats the food, it does not fill our stomach. We also have to masticate the food and digest it ourselves. Similarly, Self-knowledge has to be learnt by oneself. One has to attempt and practise (*sādhanā*). To acquire that knowledge, *guru*s and scriptures can show the way, but the *sādhanā* (practice) must be by the *sādhaka* (practitioner) himself to obtain the *sādhya* (the goal or the object).

This knowledge is not in any secret place in this universe. If it were, it would have been available for searching eyes and ears.

This Self-knowledge is in oneself. It is beyond mind/intellect. It is not perceived by the sense-organs or grasped by the organs of action. By using the inner intellectual eye, by inquiry into the Self, by constant *niṣkāma karma*, one sees it in himself. It means that the knowledge shines out in such a person. Though he cannot see it himself, he shines brightly in his surroundings. By his actions, he finds bliss in himself and lives in that bliss. One cannot describe it, because it is beyond the senses; it is not possible to see, hear, smell, touch or taste the bliss of *ātmānanda*. It can only be experienced by entering into that state. This knowledge liberates us from worldly sorrows and delusion. It is in everybody and it can be attained.

Lastly, the Lord declares that one will find it in due season. There is no time limit. It depends on the sincerity of one's actions and *sādhanā*. Just as a polished mirror shines brightly, a person on whom knowledge dawns in course of time also shines.

Kṛṣṇa did not impart magic into Arjuna. He taught him the *śāstras* and made him decide on the future course of action. Learning the hard way makes one perfect in course of time.

श्रद्धावाँल्लभते ज्ञानं तत्परः संयतेन्द्रियः ।
ज्ञानं लब्ध्वा परां शान्तिमचिरेणाधिगच्छति ॥३९॥

śraddhāvāṁl labhate jñānaṁ tatparaḥ saṁyatendriyaḥ **।**
jñānaṁ labdhvā parāṁ śāntim acireṇādhigacchati **॥39॥**

The man of faith having knowledge as his supreme goal, having controlled the senses, obtains knowledge of ātmā, *and having obtained that, enjoys peace for ever.*

How does one get knowledge? What is the result (benefit) of such knowledge? Three essential necessities are mentioned to get this knowledge:

(1) Faith, (2) Devotion, (3) Self-control.

(1) **Faith**: Faith is the belief one has in any particular thing. The greater the belief, the greater the faith. Hindu philosophy does not advocate blind faith. "So and so said it, you must therefore do it", is not meant by faith.

The person who believes in the Self, who goes in search of it in a proper manner, will find at every step something or the other to prove the statement of the scriptures. As he experiences the value of faith, his progress becomes quick and easy. Faith never urges one to go against one's judgement.

Let us take the example of a child. Initially the child's mother warns the child not to go near the fire because it burns. Initially the child keeps away from the fire. Curiosity does make the child go and touch the fire and then he realises the truth of the mother's statement. He gets faith in his mother and knows that what she said was for his benefit. He will develop more faith in what she says in future.

Doubt never carries one towards progress. Doubts are to be cleared and faith established to make any progress.

(2) **By Devotion** (*tatparaḥ*): The person (*sādhaka*) should have the achievement of knowledge as his supreme goal.

There should be an aim in any work. If not, one cannot judge one's actions and reactions.

The more the devotion to the knowledge of *ātmā*, the more will be the efforts towards achieving it. Single-minded devotion gets the best results. If one wants to become a doctor, one must concentrate on studies towards it. If one gets divorced from that aim, and wants to have other pleasures as well, the end-result of becoming a doctor may fail or may take a long time.

If one has faith in oneself and wants to become a rich man, he does not get rich just by faith. By being a *tatparaḥ,* he works hard towards it and overcomes obstacles with determination. This determination is achieved by the third step "self-control".

(3) **Self-Control:** It means control of the senses. As we have discussed before, senses always find something in the outer world that pleases the mind. They let the mind run after such pleasures. Such a mind gets distracted easily. So, intellectual discrimination will subdue the mind in response to the stimuli from the outer world. If one has no control, no intellectual capacity to discriminate the right from the wrong, he will not make any spiritual progress.

What is the result of the above qualities?

Permanent peace, Bliss.

We have discussed before that in the physical world there is no such thing as eternal, pure happiness. All things at the physical plane are momentary (relatively speaking). They soon end and bring sorrow and pain. Physical happiness is not permanent.

But the knowledge of the Self brings a state of tranquillity that overcomes the temporary moments of happiness/sorrows of the physical world. Death, disease, loss of fame do not worry the person any more. One has to find peace in himself, because no one can take that 'peace' away.

Absolute joy is absolute peace. Our motivation should be to acquire that absolute joy by getting knowledge (*jñāna*) and performing desireless actions (*niṣkāma karma*). The latter leads one to the former and the former brings him the end-result *mokṣa*.

अज्ञश्चाश्रद्दधानश्च संशयात्मा विनश्यति ।
नायं लोकोऽस्ति न परो न सुखं संशयात्मनः ॥४०॥

ajñaścāśraddadhānaś ca saṁśayātmā vinaśyati |
nāyaṁ loko'sti na paro na sukhaṁ saṁśayātmanaḥ ||40||

The ignorant, faithless, doubting man goes to destruction. For the doubter, there is neither this world nor the other world nor the happiness.

By this negative statement Kṛṣṇa is emphasising on the truth. In contrast to the above verse, he talks of three types of men who do not progress and also talks of what they cannot achieve.

The ignorant are those who do not know about the Self. They are egotistic persons, who believe in the physical body and physical world alone.

They are like animals. They spend their time in getting sensual pleasures. They are ignorant of *dharma* and *adharma*, of sin and virtue.

Faithless: When there is no belief in God (divine), the actions become self-centred and do not result in welfare of the person or the society in which he lives. Faith takes one to higher levels of achievement. If one has no faith in the scriptures and the teachers, then he will lead himself to destruction by unrighteous means. There are some who say that they do not believe in God or scriptures but believe only in right action.

What is right action? If each one of us has his own idea of what is right and what is wrong, there will be millions of ideas of right and wrong actions. How then can our future generations know what is right and what is wrong?

The *śāstra*s are the consensus of opinion of learned men who have told us what is right and what is wrong. We must therefore follow the *śāstra*s.

Doubting person: Doubt is the seed of destruction. One can listen to what the scriptures say or the teachers teach, and then they can follow what they say. If they experience spirituality by such actions, they can proceed to the next step of reading/teaching. If one approaches with doubt instead of an open mind, one finds faults of some sort or the other and will not be able to develop the *śraddhā* needed.

By nature, a doubting person has doubts on everything and everybody. Because of it he cannot take any decisions. He doubts the value of *karma* and *jñāna-yoga*s and does not follow either. He doubts his wife, children etc. He constantly lives in uncertainty. Such a person surely cannot progress.

What happens to such persons?

They have no goal in life. They experience transitory happiness/sorrow and do not get satisfaction in life. They are failures in present life and their future life will also be no better. If they have not put in any efforts, they cannot expect any results.

Faith should be like that of a child's faith in its mother. The mother tells the child, ''He is your brother'' and the baby believes it. The Grace of the Lord comes with such faith (Sri Rama krishna).

योगसंन्यस्तकर्माणं ज्ञानसंछिन्नसंशयम् ।
आत्मवन्तं न कर्माणि निबध्नन्ति धनंजय ॥४१॥

***yogasaṁnyastakarmāṇaṁ jñānasaṁchinnasaṁśayam* I**
***ātmavantaṁ na karmāṇi nibadhnanti dhanañjaya* II41II**

O Arjuna, actions do not bind him who has renounced actions by yoga, whose doubts are cleared by knowledge and who is established in the Self.

Yoga-saṁnyasta-karmāṇam: It means to renounce all actions by the *yoga* of knowledge of the supreme. The aspirant performs all actions according to *śāstra*s but in the spirit of *kṛṣṇārpaṇam astu.*

Jñāna-saṁchinna-saṁśayam: After knowing that the Lord and the *ātman* are one, the person has no more doubts. He cuts asunder all his doubts.

In continuation of what has been said so far, Śrī Kṛṣṇa is putting the words in a different way, but the meaning is the same.

Practise *karma-yoga*—renounce the fruits of action—work with attachment to the Self and detachment with ego and its connections. Such work automatically becomes divine work. One is not working to enjoy the benefits, but working for the sake of work and fulfilling his worldly obligations.

In the last verse he condemned the doubting person. Here he says, "clear your doubts". How? By the knowledge of *ātmā*. How to get it? By the blessings of the *guru* and reading the scriptures. By asking the teacher to clear the doubts and not by having doubts about the teacher's ability.

Any desire leaves a *vāsanā* imprint. Actions follow the motive (desire). Because of the desire, actions bind the person with reactions and accumulate more *vāsanās*. By clearing (burning) of old *vāsanās*, one accumulates no more *vāsanās*.

Our present actions help us to burn old *vāsanās*. By not having desires from our present actions (*niṣkāma karma*) we will not add any more new *vāsanās* on our mind.

Niṣkāma karma does not bind the person to the wheel of *saṁsāra* (births and deaths).

तस्मादज्ञानसंभूतं हृत्स्थं ज्ञानासिनात्मनः ।
छित्त्वैनं संशयं योगमातिष्ठोत्तिष्ठ भारत ॥४२॥

tasmād ajñānasaṁbhūtaṁ hṛtsthaṁ jñānāsinātmanaḥ |
chittvainaṁ saṁśayam yogaṁ ātiṣṭhottiṣṭha bhārata ||42||

Therefore with the sword of knowledge, cut asunder the doubt born of ignorance about the Self, dwelling in the heart, and take refuge in yoga. Arise, O Arjuna.

This is the concluding verse of this chapter on knowledge.

Once, one has understood what the Self is, all his doubts will be cleared away. One has to cut all doubts which are deep-rooted in him. To cut them, one has to have a mighty sword. Kṛṣṇa is asking Arjuna, after teaching *jñāna*, to cut his doubts altogether.

Where are all the doubts? Why are all the doubts? What were Arjuna's doubts? Could one kill teachers and elders? Could one cause confusion in society by the death of a number of warriors? Is it not better to take *saṁnyāsa*?

Doubts are due to ignorance. Doubts are in the mind. The mind, normally has the intellectual capacity. Out of ignorance, this intellectual capacity is not used properly; sometimes it is used wrongly. But once the light of knowledge is lit, the darkness of ignorance (doubts) blocking the mind is lifted and the intellect can function normally. To put the intellect into proper use, one has to cut the knot of ignorance, which is binding the mind. The Lord says, the ignorance is in your heart. He means the ignorance is in you, it is deep-seated. It is in your mind. As soon as the lamp of knowledge is lit, the ignorance disappears.

Take refuge in *yoga*. Kṛṣṇa is reminding Arjuna of various types of *yajñas* mentioned in this chapter. By this, one should understand that when the light of the knowledge is lit, one would perform all actions for the welfare of the universe, i.e., *niṣkāma karma*.

If everybody who has become a *jñānī* decides to leave the material world and go to the forest for meditation, what would happen to the universe? One needs to carry the lamp and show the light to others. One need not look for any benefit in carrying the lamp and showing the way. Let the light in the purified man help to kindle the light of knowledge in others. Mahatma Gandhi, Buddha, Jesus, all did the same.

Uttiṣṭha: Arise. This is command for a *jñānī* to perform his actions.

Arjuna was in despair, kneeling at the feet of Kṛṣṇa. Kṛṣṇa asks him to get up and be a fit person to fight. He does not use the commanding word. "Get up and fight". He says "Get up" (cut the ignorance off and perform *niṣkāma karma*).

This is a call to the whole mankind. "You have got the intellect. Cut off your ignorance, be fit to fight the battle of life and attain liberation from sorrows and pains arising from the objective world", is the message by the Lord.

इति श्रीमद्भगवद्गीतासूपनिषत्सु ब्रह्मविद्यायां योगशास्त्रे
श्रीकृष्णार्जुनसंवादे ज्ञानयोगो नाम चतुर्थोऽध्यायः ॥

***iti śrīmadbhagavadgītāsūpaniṣatsu brahmavidyāyāṁ yogaśāstre
śrīkṛṣṇārjuna-saṁvāde jñānayogo nāma caturtho'dhyāyaḥ*** ॥

CHAPTER 5

KARMA-SAṀNYĀSA-YOGA

INTRODUCTION

After describing the *yoga* of action and knowledge, the Lord now takes up the theme of *karma-saṁnyāsa-yoga*.

Karma is action. *Saṁnyāsa* is renunciation. Arjuna's idea of *saṁnyāsa* was renunciation of his kingdom and retiring to jungles to meditate.

Karma-saṁnyāsa-yoga means renunciation of desire-prompted actions. How this will contribute to the inward development is discussed in this chapter. The Lord repeats the salient points of *karma* and *jñāna-yoga* and makes one realise how by understanding the Self, how action is possible to make the person highly developed in his spiritual progress.

The way of renunciation is explained in detail in this chapter. Also explained is the technique of controlling the mind against impulses from the outside world while engaged in activities. Two methods of renunciation are described: (*a*) renunciation of the sense of agency (ego) in activities, and (*b*) renunciation of desire and anxiety for the fruits of action.

अर्जुन उवाच
संन्यासं कर्मणां कृष्ण पुनर्योगं च शंससि ।
यच्छ्रेय एतयोरेकं तन्मे ब्रूहि सुनिश्चितम् ॥१॥

arjuna uvāca
***saṁnyāsaṁ karmaṇāṁ kṛṣṇa punar yogaṁ ca śaṁsasi* |**
***yac chreya etayor ekaṁ tan me brūhi suniścitam* ||1||**
Arjuna said

O Kṛṣṇa, you praise renunciation of actions and again yoga of action. Of these two which is better? Tell me conclusively.

Arjuna, who is in a state of utter despair has heard his teacher talking about *ātmā,* then about *karma* and *jñāna.*

He, from the teachings of the *Veda*s by his *guru*s, had come to know *karma* as in *karmakāṇḍa* of the *Veda*s, which involves rituals for fulfilment of desires. He had also learnt that great *ṛṣi*s of the past had gone to places like Himalayas to meditate. They had accepted renunciation of life, *saṁnyāsa*, as their path towards liberation.

Arjuna again requests clarification from his master. He is saying that he has heard that both the types of action will lead one to liberation. He now wants a definite answer as to which path he has to take. Which is better of the two?

Actually speaking, Kṛṣṇa has repeatedly stressed that both paths intermerge and one path automatically leads to another. We have to assume that, (*a*) Śrī Vyāsa is trying to tell us through this question what a majority of us have not understood before, or (*b*) Arjuna is still slightly confused after his hysterical outburst. As a student, his mind might have wandered off temporarily and he is sincerely asking for clarification of his doubts. We learnt in the last chapter, that clarification of doubts is an essential step towards understanding of what is taught.

श्रीभगवानुवाच
संन्यासः कर्मयोगश्च निःश्रेयसकरावुभौ ।
तयोस्तु कर्मसंन्यासात्कर्मयोगो विशिष्यते ॥२॥

śrī bhagavān uvāca
saṁnyāsaḥ karmayogaś ca niḥśreyasakarāv ubhau |
tayos tu karmasaṁnyāsāt karmayogo viśiṣyate ||2||
The Lord replied

Renunciation of action and yoga of action both lead to the highest bliss. But of these two, yoga *of action is superior to the renunciation of action.*

Kṛṣṇa accepting that both the paths lead towards attaining *mokṣa*, states that *yoga* of action is superior of the two. Why?

This discourse, through the medium of Arjuna, is meant for

millions of people in this world who were in the past, who are in the present and who will be in the future. We have all had some form of spiritual and moral teaching during our childhood by our parents and our elders. But unfortunately, we are ignorant of the *Vedas*. We cannot honestly renounce everything and think that we will attain *mokṣa* by such action.

The human mind, as such cannot stay quiet for any length of time. It will drag a person back to activity by a prompting for desire. Desire-fulfilment is a major part of our lives.

Śrī Rāmānujācārya says that the word *saṁnyāsa* in the context means *jñāna*, i.e., knowledge of the *ātman*. He considers that *karma-yoga* is the superior of the two. This is because it applies to a majority of us. We should be following it because it is easier of the two paths.

A *karmayogī*, while being part of the society performs *niṣkāma karma* and by that process attains *jñāna* of the *ātman*. If one takes to *saṁnyāsa*, before attaining the knowledge of *ātman*, he will lose this (present life) and that (liberation) [*ito bhraṣṭas tato naṣṭaḥ*] Hence Kṛṣṇa says that the *yoga* of action is superior.

One has to rise from idleness (*tamas*) to activity (*rajas*) and then to the quiet pure state (*sattva*, actionless state). Actionless actually means renunciation of fruits of action, which we have learnt earlier. This is a gradual process. One cannot drop all actions and go to meditate. Meditation is a difficult technique to develop and attain mastery.

ज्ञेयः स नित्यसंन्यासी यो न द्वेष्टि न काङ्क्षति ।
निर्द्वन्द्वोऽपि महाबाहो सुखं बन्धात्प्रमुच्यते ॥३॥

***jñeyaḥ sa nityasaṁnyāsī yo na dveṣṭi na kāṅkṣati* |**
***nirdvandvo'pi mahābāho sukhaṁ bandhāt pramucyate* ||3||**

O Arjuna, he who neither hates nor desires should be known as a man to eternal renunciation. He who is free from the pairs of opposites, is easily set free from bondage.

Kṛṣṇa has given a definitive meaning of the term *saṁnyāsī*. Many people in India consider that men who wear ochre robes are *saṁnyāsīs* and give reverence to them.

It is not the physical appearance that makes one a *saṁnyāsī*, but his mental attitude that makes him one.

Renouncing one's duty which one dislikes, or feeling happy because one escapes from duty, is not real *saṁnyāsa*. In such cases *saṁnyāsa* is only an external appearance due to selfishness. It is not self-denial. The external appearance of *saṁnyāsa* is not matched by the mind within, for their minds are full of agitations on account of various desires.

Desire and hatred are two essential wheels on which the mind rolls forward in the path of life. All our actions are prompted by these two emotions (*rāga* and *dveṣa*). We constantly have some desire or hatred directly or indirectly in our actions. So, the person who constantly frees himself from these two is a *saṁnyāsī* : *nitya saṁnyāsī*. He is a *karma-saṁnyāsī*.

Free from pairs of opposites: All our reactions to external stimuli are either the ones we like or the ones we do not like, e.g., heat and cold; happiness and sorrow; pain and pleasure. These are called *dvandvas*. One should develop a neutral attitude towards these stimuli from the outside world. The feeling one gets from them is only temporary, they do not last long. Our mind, if it likes them, would start asking for more and sends the organs of action out to find objects that give such feelings. Hence, the Lord states, "free from pairs of opposites".

Such persons are easily freed from bondage. That is the path to *mokṣa*. If one does not get bound to the world by attachment and aversion, if he gives up selfishness, he finds peace in all his actions. He can then be a householder and perform all the duties without getting attached to them and he will find eternal peace.

सांख्ययोगौ पृथग्बालाः प्रवदन्ति न पण्डिताः ।
एकमप्यास्थितः सम्यगुभयोर्विन्दते फलम् ॥४॥

***sāṁkhyayogau pṛthag bālāḥ pravadanti na paṇḍitāḥ* |**
***ekam apy āsthitaḥ samyag ubhayor vindate phalam* ||4||**

Children, not the wise, say that jñāna-yoga *and* karma-yoga *are distinct. He who is truly established in either of them obtains the fruits of both.*

A *jñānī* performs action with a state of renunciation of agency. It means that he has dropped his 'ego'. A *karmayogī* is one who has no desire for fruits of action. He does not prepare his mind for the fruits of his actions. He performs actions and knows the fruits will follow depending on his present efforts.

Both paths bring out the divinity of the follower. Both paths will give the person a "blissful state" in course of time. Both types of people attain *mokṣa.*

Those who argue that the two paths are different, are children, the Lord says. Children are not mature. They are still in the learning process. Similarly, a person who has not learnt the *śāstras* is like a child.

Śrī Kṛṣṇa is compassionate. He calls us children and ignorant. If we did not know the Self and the paths, then we would be ignorant like children.

Kṛṣṇa is asking all people to understand that all paths lead to the same goal. One should not hate others who do not follow the same path. Indirectly, he is advocating religious tolerance to mankind.

यत्साङ्ख्यैः प्राप्यते स्थानं तद्योगैरपि गम्यते ।
एकं साङ्ख्यं च योगं च यः पश्यति स पश्यति ॥५॥

***yat sāṁkhyaiḥ prāpyate sthānaṁ tad yogair api gamyate* ।**
***ekaṁ sāṁkhyaṁ ca yogaṁ ca yaḥ paśyati sa paśyati* ॥5॥**

That state which is reached by śāṁkhyas *is also reached by* yogīs. *He who sees the oneness of* śāṁkhya *and* yoga *really sees.*

Sāṁkhya, as we have learnt in chapter two, deals with *ātman.* The one who has understood the *ātman* is a *jñānī*. So, *sāṁkhyas* here means *jñānīs*. Similarly, the word *yogīs*, is used to describe men of action, i.e., *karmayogī*. As we have discussed before, the final goal is one and the same, i.e., *mokṣa* (liberation).

He who sees: Not in its literal meaning of seeing. It means, he who has understood. The man who has understood the aims and objectives of both the paths, also, knows that both paths meet at the end. A real *karmayogī* is a *jñānī* and a real *jñānī* is a *karmayogī*. He does not see them as two different paths.

The *Vedas* say the knower of *Brahman* becomes *Brahman*. There are two words one should note here. They are 'Knower' and 'Becomes.' The knowing aspect of the knower is *sāṁkhya* (*jñāna*) and the becoming aspect is *yoga* (*karma*).

संन्यासस्तु महाबाहो दुःखमाप्तुमयोगतः ।
योगयुक्तो मुनिर्ब्रह्म नचिरेणाधिगच्छति ॥६॥

saṁnyāsas tu mahābāho duḥkham āptum ayogataḥ I
yogayukto munir brahma nacireṇādhigacchati II6II

O Arjuna, but renunciation is hard to attain without the yoga *of action. The sage who is harmonised in* yoga *quickly goes to* Brahman.

Saṁnyāsa literally means renunciation of possessions. The real meaning of *saṁnyāsa* is different. It means renunciation of ego in relation to attachments to the objects of the world. Living the life of a householder without the sense of attachment is *saṁnyāsa*.

One should be a householder and perform all the duties prescribed by the *śāstras*. He should not be bound mentally to any member of the family. He should be prepared to part with his possessions at any time.

In life's journey, we are really on our own. Our only companion is our *ātman*. Everything else has to part company sooner or later. The one who keeps his sense of balance on parting with his possessions in a real *saṁnyāsī*. *Saṁnyāsa* is a mental/intellectual renunciation of attachment.

The *yoga* of action is therefore the first step in the ladder of evolution. One can even make a categorical statement that it is the foundation for evolution.

A man of *yoga* of proper action as described in the scriptures, quickly attains *mokṣa*, is the Lord's definite declaration. We can understand this better by looking at an example. Mangoes when unripe are not sweet. They grow sweet when they are ripe. How do they get ripe? They stay on the tree, they get exposed to the weather and are nourished by the tree and then only ripen. They stayed in their own environment, faced all weather conditions and then ripened. When it is ripe it severs its connection with the tree and falls off.

A *karmayogī*, similarly gets nourished by various modifications of nature, becomes a *jñānī* and attains *mokṣa*. He is one who puts principle (*śāstras*) into practice. He lives for others and not for himself. Such self-denial by a *karmayogī* is *karma-saṁnyāsa*.

The sage who is harmonised in yoga: A *muni* is one who contemplates on the Supreme. It means that action makes the *yogī* fit for the state of *muni* and a man who has attained the state of *muni*, soon attains *Brahman*. The Lord says "*na cireṇa*" which means, not so long afterwards.

There are very rare people who could be said to have become *jñānīs* directly. Śrī Śaṅkarācārya is one such person. Such persons are extremely rare. One should not follow the physical act like Śaṅkarācārya, but one should develop purity of mind like him. By Lord's grace Śaṅkarācārya was born with no impurities and became a *jñānī* quickly. The *Gitā* is meant for ordinary millions like us.

योगयुक्तो विशुद्धात्मा विजितात्मा जितेन्द्रियः ।
सर्वभूतात्मभूतात्मा कुर्वन्नपि न लिप्यते ॥७॥

***yogayukto viśuddhātmā vijitātmā jitendriyaḥ* |**
***sarvabhūtātma-bhūtātmā kurvann api na lipyate* ||7||**

He who is devoted to the yoga *of action, with heart purified, with mind controlled and senses subdued, who realises his 'Self' as the Self in all beings, though acting, is not tainted.*

Every word is important in this verse.

He who is devoted to the yoga of action: The word 'devoted' is emphasised. Devotion brings unselfish actions automatically. *Yoga* of action in its full sense means 'no ego-centric actions and no desire for the fruits of actions'. He is sincerely following the proper meaning of '*yoga* of action'.

Heart purified: The word heart is used to signify intellect. After the Self, its covering would be intellect, mind, senses and outer world, in that order.

The first step is purity of intellect. If the intellect is pure, it can discriminate between right and wrong. A pure intellect can easily control the mind. The one who is devoted to *yoga* of action exhausts his existing *vāsanās* and that purifies his intellect. He does not get disturbed by desires.

Mind controlled: A purer intellect easily controls the mind. It does not let the mind wander away. It provides the mind a balanced medium to react to the stimuli that bring in desires.

Senses subdued: Such an intellect, through the medium of mind holds the reins of the senses and pulls them back from wandering away.

He who realises his 'Self' as the Self in all: It is no use just controlling one's body, mind and intellect and realising the Self in oneself. He can act divinely by seeing the all-prevading Self as the being in all. One should not hate others and should not look for personal rewards.

In this verse, *viśuddhātmā* means "purified intellect". *Vijitātmā* means purified mind and *jitendriya* means purified senses. It is known as *trikaraṇa-śuddhi* of *mana, vāk* and *kāya* (i.e. the three types of purity, of mind, body, and speech). *Sarvabhūtātma-bhūtātmā* means *antaḥkaraṇa-śuddhi* (purity by being compassionate to all). If the seeker has all these qualities, then he cannot get any new *vāsanās* by his continued actions.

नैव किंचित्करोमीति युक्तो मन्येत तत्त्ववित् ।
पश्यञ्शृण्वन्स्पृशञ्जिघ्रन्नश्नन्गच्छन्स्वपन्श्वसन् ॥८॥

***naiva kiṁcit karomīti yukto manyeta tattvavit* |**
***paśyañ śṛṇvan spṛśañ jighrann aśnan gacchan svapan śvasan* ||8||**

प्रलपन्विसृजन्गृह्णन्नुन्मिषन्निमिषन्नपि ।
इन्द्रियाणीन्द्रियार्थेषु वर्तन्त इति धारयन् ॥९॥

***pralapan visṛjan gṛhṇann unmiṣan nimiṣann api* |**
***indriyāṇīndriyārtheṣu vartanta iti dhārayan* ||9||**

> *The harmonised* yogī, *who knows the Truth, thinks 'I do nothing at all' on seeing, thinking, hearing, touching, smelling, eating, moving, sleeping, breathing, speaking, giving, grasping, opening and closing eyelids. He is convinced that the senses move among the sense-objects.*

Here is a total enumeration of voluntary and involuntary actions which we all do sometime or other in our daily life. Some of those are essential for our survival and some are our reactions to impulses from sense-organs. Our *ātmā* (Self) is witnessing these actions constantly. It is *sākṣī.*

A harmonised *yogī* is one who realises his identity with *ātmā.* He is a man of perfect knowledge. Such a *yogī,* who is observing the five elements in him getting active in thousands of ways remains unconcerned and unperturbed. He stays back and has no feeling of his identity with such actions. He knows that it is interplay between the five elements through the medium of his senses.

Our eyes see innumerable things everyday. We cannot remember them all. Why? Because our mind did not register all of what we saw. It does register what it likes. If it sees something that gives satisfaction, it registers it and it may even act to get hold of it. A *yogī* is one who has no such desires. The desire-prompting messages do not register in him. His senses will still work to perform *nitya* and *naimittika karma*s. He does not attribute 'I'-ness to such actions.

Let us take an example. When sleeping we breathe, but are not conscious of it. When awake, we are conscious of our breathing if we concentrate on it. Also, during sleeping and awakened state, we are not conscious of our heart beats or food getting digested. All these actions continue because the Self propels them to all these activities.

"I do nothing. They just act because of their survival", is the attitude of a man perfect in detachment. He does not get frightened that he dies if they stop acting. He is not perturbed at the thought of death of the physical body.

ब्रह्मण्याधाय कर्माणि सङ्गं त्यक्त्वा करोति यः ।
लिप्यते न स पापेन पद्मपत्रमिवाम्भसा ॥१०॥

***brahmaṇy ādhāya karmāṇi saṅgaṁ tyaktvā karoti yaḥ* I**
***lipyate na sa pāpena padmapatram ivāmbhasā* II10II**

He who acts, offering them to Brahman, *giving up attachment, is unaffected by sin like a lotus-leaf by water.*

This is a reiteration of the doctrine of *karma-yoga* with another example.

We all know that the ego normally gets attached to the pluralistic world through the medium of the sense-organs. We also know that it is impossible to keep the mind quiet. It has millions of thought-waves erupting from it. Not to get attached to the worldly objects and keeping quiet is therefore impossible. Hence, if one wants to go on in the spiritual path, then he must divert his mind away from the worldly objects. This can be done by thoughts on *Brahman* and acting divinely. This is what is meant by, 'offering them to *Brahman*'.

In continuation and in conjunction with it, one has to act in the world without any sense of egotistic attachment.

What are the *karmas* we have to do? What does *karmāṇi* mean in this verse? The *karmas* one has to do include—

(a) devotion to the Lord,
(b) prayers to the Lord,
(c) service to parents and elders and *guru*,
(d) *yajña*,
(e) *dāna*,
(f) *tapas*,
(g) respect to guests, etc.

These are prescribed in the *śāstras*. One should do these acts without a sense of attachment. One may ask, "How can one leave attachment to God?" True, it is not possible in the earlier stages, but in later stages of development, one should not work with a desire to attain even *mokṣa*. One should work only as God's servant.

Later on, Śrī Kṛṣṇa says that all actions have some impurities inherent in them like fire with smoke (*sarvārambhā hi doṣeṇa dhūmenāgnirivāvṛtāḥ*). The *śāstras* therefore ask the person to utter here names of God at the end of each action (and ritual) with a prayer requesting the Lord to excuse him for faults done inadvertently. The names we utter are—*acyutāya namaḥ, anantāya namaḥ, govindāya namaḥ*. While walking, we do kill many small insects which we do not see and these three names are expiators.

Such a person, who is only burning the *vāsanās* is not going to get new *vāsanās*. Hence it is said that he is not tainted by sin.

Lotus flowers and leaves emerge from the water, remain in water and wither away in water. But one does not see a drop of water sticking to the leaf or the flower.

This therefore is a very good example. One must be born in this world, live in this world and die away in this world but should not get attached to the world. We are born with *karma* and sustained by *karmas* but we should not be affected by *karmas*.

कायेन मनसा बुद्ध्या केवलैरिन्द्रियैरपि ।
योगिनः कर्म कुर्वन्ति सङ्गं त्यक्त्वात्मशुद्धये ॥११॥

kāyena manasā buddhyā kevalair indriyair api |
yoginaḥ karma kurvanti saṅgaṁ tyaktvātmaśuddhaye ||11||

Yogīs, *abandoning all attachment, act for self-purification with body, mind, intellect and also senses.*

The Self (*ātman*) has an outer covering called the mind and physical body. The intellect is in between the *ātman* and the mind. Due to contact with the outer world via the sense-organs, the mind has thought-waves arising in it. Some thought-waves come repeatedly and they become desires. The thought-waves leave an imprint on the mind. These imprint are called *vāsanās*. Spiritually speaking, the *vāsanās* are called dirt on the mind. We are born with thousands of *vāsanās*. We have to wash them off. This happens when we fulfil the previous thought (which left an imprint on the mind).

While acting, to fulfil a previous *vāsanā*, one tends to accumulate more new *vāsanās*. Action and reaction lead to new *vāsanās*. This can be avoided if one performs *niṣkāma karma* and *karma-phala-tyāga*.

A real student of *karma-yoga*, is striving to wash off the dirt and trying not to accumulate more dirt and this is termed as purification. He therefore continues to act without attachment at all levels of action.

The real *yogī* performs actions at all levels without any sense of attachment. What are the different levels?

Kāya karma: Actions at the level of the body. The *yogī* performs these actions with no desires. It is comparable to the actions of a baby. The baby does not have the capacity to think at mental and intellectual level.

Mānasika karma: These are actions due to thoughts at mental level with no involvement of the senses. This is comparable to our dreams. Our mind dreams but our senses have no knowledge of such dreams. The *yogī*'s thoughts are constantly on the *ātman* with no involvement of the senses.

Indriya karmas: These are actions due to sense-organs coming in contact with the world. A drunken man who is inebriated does not know what he is doing. He has no sense of agency in his actions.

युक्तः कर्मफलं त्यक्त्वा शान्तिमाप्नोति नैष्ठिकीम् ।
अयुक्तः कामकारेण फले सक्तो निबध्यते ॥१२॥

***yuktaḥ karmaphalaṁ tyaktvā śāntim āpnoti naiṣṭhikīm* |**
***ayuktaḥ kāmakāreṇa phale sakto nibadhyate* ||12||**

The harmonised yogī, *having abandoned the fruits of action attains eternal peace. The non-harmonised, impelled by desire for the fruit of action, is bound.*

One can see that both *yogīs* and non-*yogīs* have to perform actions. The way they act is different and that difference is brought out in this verse.

Harmony means, in unity. In unity of what? Who is a *yogī*? How does he act? A *yogī* is one who is trying to unite his ego with the *ātmā*. A harmonised *yogī* is one who has dropped his sense of ego (doership) and merged himself with the Self. He is in tune with his 'Self'. In him the song of divinity comes out with a beautiful melody and is pleasing to the ears of others (listeners and observers).

Such a person, because life is still there in him, works without expecting any rewards. He is contented with his work, gets the reward for the work, in course of time. He does not dream or think of the results of his work. He does not look for rewards for his work.

Is there any doubt that such person who is living in peace with the outer world and in unity with the music of the Self gets as a reward nothing less than eternal peace?

In contrast, a non-harmonised person is one who is not in tune with the Self. In him the divinity does not express itself. Through his body and senses compelled by the desires of the mind and the intellect not using its discriminatory capacity, he works for the fulfilment of his desires. He works for getting a set of rewards for his work. He is dreaming for the end result.

Such a person is said to be a bound person. He is ever-bound to the outer world and so keeps on getting into the cycle of *saṁsāra* of births and deaths. He is born because of desires and dies with desires.

सर्वकर्माणि मनसा संन्यस्यास्ते सुखं वशी ।
नवद्वारे पुरे देही नैव कुर्वन्न कारयन् ॥१३॥

sarvakarmāṇi manasā saṁnyasyāste sukhaṁ vaśī |
navadvāre pure dehī naiva kurvan na kārayan ||13||

Mentally renouncing all actions and self-controlled, the embodied rests happily in the nine-gated city neither acting nor causing others to act.

It is another beautiful verse explaining the principle of happiness for all.

The mind is the first source for actions. Actions start because of desires. Desires develop because the senses send the message to the mind. The mind sends orders through the organs of action to get the desired object. Two states of mind are described here:

(1) Do not let desires crop up in your mind. If they come, do not let them grow. Kill them before they start spreading their roots and establishing themselves strongly.

(2) **Vaśī:** Self-controlled. He should control his bodily actions and thereby control the organs of action which are on the look out to get objects of desire of the mind.

The embodied: It is the king (the Soul—the *ātmā*) inside us.

The embodied rests happily: The Self is peaceful. The Self is always the *dṛk,* the seer. It is seeing the physical actions and mental thoughts. If the physical actions and mental thoughts are pure, it is described as the Self resting happily.

In point of fact, the Self is not bothered about what the body does. But it is the body that either wants to merge in Self and live in peace or bound to the world and live in agitation.

To make this point clear, the idea is expanded in the last half of the verse.

The Self-dwelling in the city of nine gates: In olden days the king who ruled stayed in the royal palace. This was inside a city and the city had fortresses. Fortresses were needed for people to go out and get their food/water etc. as also to prevent the enemy from entering. The king was safe in his haven and rested happily inside his palace, if all the fortresses were secure.

The Self inside the physical body is compared to the king. The physical body is compared to the fort which has nine gates to the city. The nine gates are; two eyes, two ears, two nostrils, one mouth, urethra and anus. These are the gates of the fortress. If one can control these apertures, one will not get impulses to agitate the mind.

The Self is really not acting and not causing others to act. The minister and subjects in the city are acting for the king who is inside. The simple fact that the king is there gives them an immense sense of security. The king does not come out and watch individual actions of all, at all times.

The soul is watching all actions. He is aware that because of him the body is acting. He is there inside as a watcher/witness.

He does not interfere with the body. It is up to the body to purify or destroy itself. The body which remembers the king inside and therefore acts for the king, will live peacefully. The body that forgets the king and lives for pleasures has no such peace.

न कर्तृत्वं न कर्माणि लोकस्य सृजति प्रभुः ।
न कर्मफलसंयोगं स्वभावस्तु प्रवर्तते ॥१४॥

***na kartṛtvaṁ na karmāṇi lokasya sṛjati prabhuḥ* I**
***na karmaphalasaṁyogaṁ svabhāvas tu pravartate* II14II**

The Lord does not create agency, nor action, nor union with the fruits of action. But nature leads to action.

The term Lord means *ātmā* or the Self in each of us. *Ātmā,* when it reflects out to the pluralistic world, becomes ego. It is only a reflection.

Nature is *māyā*, made up of three *guṇa*s. The power of the three *guṇas*, inherent in each of us in varying proportions, makes us do what we are doing. We call it '*prakṛti-māyā*'.

The Self is above the ego. The Self is separated from the ego by the veil of *māyā*. Once the reflection of ego has been produced, the reflector becomes only a witness looking at what is happening. It does not order the ego to do this or not to do that.

The Lord does not create and assign duties to us. He has given us a chance to perform actions. How we do, what we do, is all up to us and this depends upon our past *vāsanā*s. The ego takes over and it is controlled by nature, i.e., the three *guṇa*s. The *guṇa*s are the result of our past actions and are expressed as our *vāsanā*s. If we had a lot of lazy actions in the past, we will have the *vāsanā*s which predominantly reflect our continuation of that lazy nature.

For some good we have done in the past, we have been given the life of human beings with the power of intellect. This is the only saviour that can lift us out of the ocean of *saṁsāra*.

By the power of *vāsanā*s one gets attached to actions and that creates the sense of agency in that person. He thinks he is acting and he is the doer. He forgets he is only a reflection and the real one is *ātmā*. When one does good it is not the *ātmā* that does good. When one does evil it is not the *ātmā* that does it. Both are done according to *vāsanā*s one is born with.

Can we escape from this? Yes, we can. Through the intellect, let us realise the presence of *ātmā*—then identify ourselves with the Self, and let ego perform its actions and if we do not look for fruits of action, then we will escape.

People have a belief that God will punish us for this act and will bless us for that act. They think that the 'God is *karma-phala-dātā*': (i.e., if you do this, God will give you that). This is wrong interpretation of the Vedic teaching.

The ego or self is created by the Lord as his reflection. The ego then accumulates results of any action. If one does good, he retains benefits of such good actions. This is reflected in future reactions, which will be good.

Once the ego is created, the reflected *ātmā* becomes the one to give the results of actions of the physical body. By giving the intellect the power, we can burn the ego and we should not expect any results for our actions. Our aim is really to know who we are and drop the false image of self (ego) and continue to act because we are still alive.

नादत्ते कस्यचित्पापं न चैव सुकृतं विभुः ।
अज्ञानेनावृतं ज्ञानं तेन मुह्यन्ति जन्तवः ॥१५॥

nādatte kasyacit pāpaṁ na caiva sukṛtaṁ vibhuḥ |
ajñānenāvṛtaṁ jñānaṁ tena muhyanti jantavaḥ ||15||

The Lord does not receive either the bad or good of any one. Knowledge is enveloped by ignorance and by it beings are deluded.

This is continuation of the last verse, which proves that the Self is only a witness, and that it does not get tainted by any actions. Whatever we do, it falls on the ego, the reflection.

Let us take the example of a person standing in front of a mirror. You in front, is the Self and the reflection in the mirror is ego. The mirror becomes the *vāsanā*s or *māya*. The dust on the surface of the mirror gives a distorted reflection. The nature of distortion depends upon the nature of the dust on the surface.

Whatever we do, it never touches the *ātmā*. If we clean the mirror, the reflection is clear. If we polish it, the reflection is brighter. At all times, there was no change in you, the real Self, but it was only in the reflection.

Bad reflection is there because of the dust and one gets deluded. A small spot on the mirror, reflects a spot on your cheek. However much you wipe your cheek, it does not alter the image in the mirror. One has to wipe the spot on the mirror.

Similarly, knowledge of the true Self is enveloped by ignorance due to the three *guṇa*s inherent in all of us. Using the duster of good actions, the ignorance can be wiped eventually. When the knowledge dawns, ignorance ends.

The sun provides us light, we perform different acts in the daytime. One can meditate, one can go to a temple, one can do business or one can steal, commit a murder or rape someone. The sunlight is there for all. It does not take on the merits or sins of anyone's actions. Similarly, the pure *ātmā* inside us does not get affected by our good or bad actions.

ज्ञानेन तु तदज्ञानं येषां नाशितमात्मनः ।
तेषामादित्यवज्ज्ञानं प्रकाशयति तत्परम् ॥१६॥

***jñānena tu tad ajñānaṁ yeṣāṁ nāśitam ātmanaḥ* I**
***teṣām ādityavaj jñānaṁ prakāśayati tat param* II16II**

But to those whose ignorance is destroyed by the knowledge of ātmā, *shining like the Sun, knowledge reveals the Supreme to them.*

When we are dreaming, we consider ourselves as millionaires and enjoy the dream of a millionaire's luxury. We know the fact that we are not millionaires, but live in that world in our dream. As soon as the dream is ended, as soon as we wake up, we immediately know what we are and realise we are not millionaires. The ignorance gets lifted.

The sun gets hidden by the clouds. The sun is ever luminous.

But still we cannot feel or see it in the midst of clouds. A small cloud can completely block the sun even though it is far from it. Similarly, the ignorance in us is our *jīvabuddhi,* i.e., imagining that we are the self. We attach ourselves to the physical body.

The Light, the glorious Sun in us, is the *ātman* in us. Our inherent *vāsanā*s, or *māyā* puts a veil of ignorance and blocks the divine light in us. The ignorance we are talking of, is only ignorance of the self. It is not ignorance in actions pertaining to the world. It is not knowing the difference between *ātman* and *anātma.* As soon as the ignorance is lifted, the divinity shines in all its splendour.

The idol of the Lord, in the inner sanctum of the temple with all its fine carvings and decorations is closed by walls that surround the inner sanctum. Similarly, our *ātman* is enveloped by the ignorant body. As soon as the priest opens the door of the temple and lights the lamp, the splendour of the Lord is self-evident. Similarly, if we open up and light our knowledge, our divinity shines forth immediately. We do not have to light the *ātmā. Ātmā* is not lit by knowledge. By the light of knowledge, *ātmā* only shines forth. The *ātmā* is self-luminous.

The Lord says, that *ātmā* reveals itself with the light of knowledge. We can keep a lamp inside a pot and close the lid. The light is not seen from outside. Let us then break the pot. The Light shatters the darkness and reveals itself.

This knowledge can be had from the scriptures, teachers, meditation, by selfless acts, etc. and it will help us to overcome the sorrows of human life. We should all remember that there is a sun of divinity in all of us.

तद्बुद्धयस्तदात्मानस्तन्निष्ठास्तत्परायणाः ।
गच्छन्त्यपुनरावृत्तिं ज्ञाननिर्धूतकल्मषाः ॥१७॥

***tadbuddhayas tadātmānas tanniṣṭhās tatparāyaṇāḥ* I**
***gacchanty apunarāvṛttiṁ jñānanirdhūtakalmaṣāḥ* II17II**

Intellect absorbed in 'That', Self being 'That', established in 'That', 'That' being the Supreme goal, they go whence there is no return, their sins dispelled by knowledge.

Several questions we ask about spiritual knowledge. Some of them have their answers here.

One must have a goal in life. The *śāstra*s insist on "That being their goal". One should have God-realisation as one's prime goal in life. What is the next step?

When we have a main goal to achieve, we will then concentrate on that. Similarly in our human body, our minds are exposed to the outside world of pleasures constantly. By getting our intellect to think of *ātmā* all the time, one can control the mind. Intellect is the one that can discriminate between right and wrong in our thoughts and actions. If the intellect gets absorbed in the thought of divine in us, automatically, in course of time our physical body also gets absorbed in the thought and actions of divine in us. We can totally get established in that state. The outside world does not create waves in our mind. This is what is meant by the first half of the verse, "intellect . . . established in That." This is like a mariner's compass in which the needle is always directed to the North.

What happens immediately to such persons?

We all have accumulated *vāsanā*s from our past. As soon as we realise our goal in life, i.e., *mokṣa* (liberation), it does not mean we get *mokṣa* immediately. We need to burn the existing *vāsanā*s. By the knowledge we have obtained after realising what our goal in life is, and establishing our intellect in 'That', we will not accumulate any new *vāsanā*s. We will then be burning all past *saṁskāra*s.

What will we achieve by all this? We achieve a state of "no return", a state where there is no birth and death, i.e., *apunar āvṛtti*. The mariner's compass leads the sailor in the right direction.

We all put a lot of efforts to get what we want. To get it, to safeguard it when we have got it, we struggle hard. Still that thing which we get is not permanent. We get agitated for its safety. We get depressed on losing it. Nothing in the material world is permanent. Pleasures bring sorrows with them. Birth brings death, and death brings birth again and that is an ongoing cycle called *saṁsāra*.

If we stop in our path for a moment, think where we are going, why we are going, what will happen etc., we will be able to change our track and go on to the right path towards liberation.

विद्याविनयसंपन्ने ब्राह्मणे गवि हस्तिनि ।
शुनि चैव श्वपाके च पण्डिताः समदर्शिनः ॥१८॥

vidyāvinayasaṁpanne brāhmaṇe gavi hastini I
śuni caiva śvapāke ca paṇḍitāḥ samadarśinaḥ II18II

The sage look with equal eye on a brāhmaṇa endowed with knowledge and humility, a cow, an elephant, a dog and an outcaste who feeds on dog's flesh.

Universal love is the doctrine represented in this verse. We all have different levels for looking at any object.

(a) We look at the physical level (*dehadṛṣṭi*). We look at colour, shape, race etc.
(b) We look at the mental plane (*manodṛṣṭi*). We consider the character of a person, his status, his power.
(c) We look at the spiritual plane (*ātmadṛṣṭi*). We find the one God in all. We look through the person and realise the presence of God in him.

Let us take an example. On looking at a woman :

(a) One can look at the physical attributes of a woman and look at her physical beauty. We look at her as an object of sex (*dehadṛṣṭi*).
(b) We can look at her character and see the same woman as a mother, sister, wife of another person, i.e., respect the status of that person (*manodṛṣṭi*).
(c) We can see through the woman and realise the presence of god in her (*ātmadṛṣṭi*).

We all have five attributes:

sat	—	reality (*ātman* in us)
cit	—	light (knowledge)
ānanda	—	bliss

nāma — name
rūpa — form

We generally give importance to the last two attributes and forget the first three.

When we go to the jeweller to sell a gold ornament, he looks only for the gold content and not at its external beauty of skilful workmanship and he assesses its worth only on its gold content.

Who is a sage? A sage is one who has acquired the knowledge of *Brahman* (brahmajñāna). He has developed the essential quality of equal vision and universal love. To elaborate on this the Lord has given examples in this verse.

A brāhmaṇa is one who is pure in his thoughts. He tries to acquire the knowledge of *ātmā*. Among human beings a brāhmaṇa is of the highest order. The lowest order of man is one who is an outcaste. An outcaste is one with filthy habits. The example given is of that person who eats dog's flesh. To include all other creatures, examples of cow, elephant and dog are given. For the sage, the common ingredient in all living beings is the *ātmā* just as it is mere gold in all jewels for the jeweller. He sees divinity in all. He sees the same life in all.

इहैव तैर्जितः सर्गो येषां साम्ये स्थितं मनः ।
निर्दोषं हि समं ब्रह्म तस्माद् ब्रह्मणि ते स्थिताः ॥१९॥

***ihaiva tair jitaḥ sargo yeṣāṁ sāmye sthitaṁ manaḥ* I**
***nirdoṣaṁ hi samaṁ brahma tasmād brahmaṇi te sthitāḥ* II9II**

Even here, birth and death is overcome by those whose mind is established in equality. Brahman *is free from evil and is balanced and therefore they are established in* Brahman.

Saṁsāra is a state of birth and death. We all go through constant states of births and deaths. One goes through pains and pleasures throughout life. These are registered at our mental level. By our constant association with our ego, we associate these opposites (*dvandvas*) to ourselves.

Most of us believe that there is another world to go to after death. It is not really true. Heaven and hell are here in this world. It is what we experience in consequence of our actions. When our actions die, the result we get is heaven or hell. The results being of a temporary nature, we are born again, i.e., we act again. The constant cycle of actions-results-actions in this life is births-deaths-heaven-hell for us.

So, the Lord emphasises this point by stressing 'even here'. *Saṁsāra* is overcome by those whose mind is established in 'equality'. That means a person, who does not get elated on obtaining pleasures, or get depressed on obtaining the unpleasant. To him there is no cycle of birth and deaths (*saṁsāra*), of pains and pleasures.

The second half of this verse, mentions that *Brahman* is all-pervading. He is just a Witness to bodily (or worldly) actions. An individual (or universe) in his identification with *nāma* and *rūpa*, becomes a changing factor; but the substratum of *sat, cit, ānanda* for all is the same.

The Mind of a *jñānī*, established in the knowledge of *Brahman,* is therefore free from evil and is in a state of balance in reactions to opposites in life. He sees the Self in all has no disturbances at the mental level.

All this is achieved while living here in this world. Freedom does not come after death. To think of freedom after death is silly. By a pure and balanced mind one gets to be free in this life and attains the state of *Brahman* who is described as sinless and balanced.

न प्रहृष्येत्प्रियं प्राप्य नोद्विजेत्प्राप्य चाप्रियम् ।
स्थिरबुद्धिरसंमूढो ब्रह्मविद्ब्रह्मणि स्थितः ॥२०॥

***na prahṛṣyet priyaṁ prāpya nodvijet prāpya cāpriyam* |**
***sthirabuddhir asaṁmūḍho brahmavid brahmaṇi sthitaḥ* ||20||**

The man of steady intellect (sthirabuddhi) *undeluded* (asaṁmūḍhaḥ), *knower of* Brahman, *should not be elated having obtained the pleasant and should not be troubled having got the unpleasant.*

The Lord keeps on explaining the same point from different angles and repeats the theme here. He is answering the question—who is a *jñānī* and how will he act in relation to the reactions from his surroundings? A man of steady intellect is one who is unaffected by good or bad around him.

Ordinarily our reactions to the outer world are due to our mental contact with any particular event. We see and hear of a number of people who are ill and suffer innumerable varieties of illness. We do not react the same way to all of them. About some we get depressed, about others we show sympathy and about the majority we do not even think and react. Why ? Because we have no contact with them mentally.

Similarly, we know of a number of events that bring pleasure to many, if it happens to us we get happy. If it happens to our close associates we may feel happy; but we do not react if it happens to anybody else.

100,000 students sit for 'O' levels. We are concerned with none or only a handful depending upon our circumstances. We do not cry for those who failed nor feel happy for those who have passed unless we know them personally.

A *jñānī* is one with steady intellect. He is free from joy on receiving pleasant things and free from sorrow even on receiving unpleasant things. These events do not agitate his mind. He will continue to do his duty under all circumstances.

He is not deluded. He is *asaṁmūḍhaḥ*. The man of steady intellect has no delusions. As all reactions (pain-pleasure) are temporary, he looks upon them as delusion and does not hold on to these reactions.

Such a *jñānī* knows the Truth. He does not let his ego get attached to the world. He gets himself established in 'THAT'. Such a *jñānī,* the Lord repeats, should not be elated on getting the pleasant or depressed on getting the unpleasant.

बाह्यस्पर्शेष्वसक्तात्मा विन्दत्यात्मनि यत्सुखम् ।
स ब्रह्मयोगयुक्तात्मा सुखमक्षयमश्नुते ॥२१॥

***bāhyasparśeṣv asaktātmā vindaty ātmani yat sukham* I**
***sa brahmayoga-yuktātmā sukham akṣayam aśnute* II21II**

With the Self unattached to external objects, he finds happiness in the Self. With the Self united with Brahman *in meditation, he enjoys imperishable happiness.*

This verse is meant for those people who ask the question, "I do get happiness with the outside world. I know I do get sorrow as well. Even that happiness is worth getting it and enjoying it when I get it. Why should I engage in equanimity and not enjoy happiness? After all what should I gain by being like a stone, not feeling anything. I would be happy to have myself united with external objects", they say.

The Lord says that the nature of the Self itself is happiness. Much more so is the happiness when the Self unites with *Brahman*—because it is eternal bliss.

One cannot express that happiness in words. One cannot describe *Brahman*, because He is indescribable. The bliss of attaining *Brahman* is matter of experience only. This has been realised and experienced by very few and they have tried to express it to us as best as they can.

To realise what is the happiness in the Self one has to divert his mind and ego from the external world and concentrate on the divine with *bhakti*. This is a process of self-development. One has to do it oneself, no one can do it for him.

ये हि संस्पर्शजा भोगा दुःखयोनय एव ते ।
आद्यन्तवन्तः कौन्तेय न तेषु रमते बुधः ॥२२॥

***ye hi saṁsparśajā bhogā duḥkhayonaya eva te* I**
***ādyantavantaḥ kaunteya na teṣu ramate budhaḥ* II22II**

The enjoyments born of contact with external objects are themselves indeed the source of pain only. They have a beginning and an end. The wise do not rejoice in them, O Arjuna.

After having described the nature of *Brahman*, i.e., eternal bliss, the Lord goes back again to restate the fact to Arjuna that the pleasures of the outside world have two characteristics :

(a) They have in them a number of seeds that bring pain later.
(b) They are short-lived.

Bhoga: What does it mean? One goes to the jeweller's shop where there are a number of jewellery items on display. We like one necklace. The necklace is only an external object. The desire to get it is *bhoga*. When we pay for it and wear it, it gives us pleasure. This is short-lived. We try to keep it safe, we try to insure it. Why? Thieves are on the prowl. If we lose it, we get distressed.

Anyway, after sometime, we do not have the same excitement on wearing that particular jewellery. We want more varieties to wear on different occasions. We want to buy something else to match with the jewellery. The question of expenses might bring unhappiness between husband and wife. One way or the other, *bhoga* in its turn has a seed of sorrow or pain in it. If we analyse it with our own experiences, we cannot deny the fact.

Let us take the example of an alcoholic. He finds that it gives a sense of euphoria and he likes it. He starts boasting he can drink so many pints without losing control of himself. He even puts bets on that fact and tries to prove it. We know what the consequences of such actions are.

(a) He gets to a state where he cannot control the temptation and starts drinking at all times.
(b) He neglects his work and family.
(c) Loses a lot of money.
(d) His health is affected seriously.
(e) His own children may copy him and become alcoholics.
(f) He might get accidentally knocked over on the road.

We can say the same about gamblers, or those who go for sensual pleasures. Even a person who goes after wealth will find that his peace is short-lived and he has to live restlessly most of the time. He may gain external fame due to his wealth, but his mind is not at peace.

The Lord states that a *jñānī* is one who knows this truth and does not rejoice in momentary, external pleasures, i.e., he finds peace in equanimity.

शक्नोतीहैव यः सोढुं प्राक्शरीरविमोक्षणात् ।
कामक्रोधोद्भवं वेगं स युक्तः स सुखी नरः ॥२३॥

śaknotīhaiva yaḥ soḍhuṁ prāk śarīravimokṣaṇāt |
kāmakrodhodbhavaṁ vegaṁ sa yuktaḥ sa sukhī naraḥ ||23||

He who is able to resist the impulse of desire and anger, even in this world before the fall of the body he is a harmonised man and is happy.

The Lord has brought the idea of *kāma* and *krodha* as being our deadliest enemies a number of times already in his discourse. He is reiterating that here.

The *yogī* is a happy man. He is ever content. He is united with the Self and *Brahman.* He could not be expected to have reached that state overnight. He must have practised spiritual discipline and must have performed *sādhanā* to achieve the result (*sādhya*) which is happiness is equanimity.

How can one achieve this? Why not enjoy ourselves while we can and practise *sādhanā* at a later stage?

We do not know what happens next. We do not know when we may die or go insane. We have been blessed with the power of intellect. One cannot expect an animal like tiger, cow, etc. to change its way of life. They go after their natural instinct. But, we humans have intellect. So before we die or suffer from serious diseases, we must practice spiritual *sādhanā.*

As our body is not eternal, as what we enjoy in early days stays in memory, which can disturb us at any time including in old age, we should control the forces of desire and anger as early as possible in our life. We must instil that habit in our children also while we must practise it constantly.

We should practise to kill anger by knowledge just like putting out the fire with water. We all know the destructive power of fire. It can even engulf the forest.

We have learnt that desire is the root cause of all problems. The more we desire an object (to get it or to safekeep it once we get), the more attachment we develop towards it, and the greater will be our anger for any obstacle that comes in the way of achieving the desired object.

A *yogī*, can live happily even in this life (*ihaiva*).

योऽन्तःसुखोऽन्तरारामस्तथान्तर्ज्योतिरेव यः ।
स योगी ब्रह्मनिर्वाणं ब्रह्मभूतोऽधिगच्छति ॥२४॥

***yo'ntaḥ sukho'ntarārāmas tathāntarjyotir eva yaḥ* I**
***sa yogī brahmanirvāṇaṁ brahmabhūto'dhigacchati* II24II**

He who is happy within, who delights within, who is illuminated within, that yogī *becoming* Brahman *attains* mokṣa *(absolute liberation).*

In the last few verses the Lord tried to emphasise the temporary state of happiness one can achieve from the outer world via his physical body, senses, mind and intellect. He has also mentioned about total happiness one gets on realising the Self within. He is emphasising again, the state of *brahmānubhūti* and *mokṣa.*

What is *brahmānubhūti*? *Anubhūti* is an experience. The experience of *Brahman* is *brahmānubhūti.* This can be achieved by that person who has no joy from the physical body and who does not think of joy of the outer world at his mental level because he has succeeded in controlling the sense-organs. He is said to have learnt the art of seeing the Self within and living in it. Such a person is living in *Brahman.*

He has attained liberation or *mokṣa* even while living in this world. He is illuminated within. (Normally one gets illumination from the sun.) He is *antaḥsukhī* and *antarjyotiḥ.*

What are we? We delight in pleasures of the world. We are *bahir-sukhīs.* We have to develop *vyvavasāyātmikā buddhi* (single-pointed effort) to experience *antaḥsukha*, or internal happiness.

The Lord uses the word *antarārāmaḥ. Ārāma* is relaxation. Walking, sleeping, going to the garden, picnics, etc., are methods of relaxation for our physical body. Our mind can still be active during such times. So, one should learn to experience this relaxation by meditation on *ātmā*. Such a state of relaxation is *antarārāmaḥ*.

But, the *yogī* who has attained *brahmānubhūi*, who finds happiness in the Self, shines by the sheer light of his *ātmā*, i.e., divinity. One can see the divinity in him illumining the whole world. For example, Mahatma Gandhi and Vivekānanda shone brilliantly because of their *ātmajñāna*.

लभन्ते ब्रह्मनिर्वाणमृषयः क्षीणकल्मषाः ।
छिन्नद्वैधा यतात्मानः सर्वभूतहिते रताः ॥२५॥

***labhante brahmanirvāṇaṁ ṛṣayaḥ kṣīṇakalmaṣāḥ* I**
***chinnadvaidhā yatātmānaḥ sarvabhūtahite ratāḥ* II25II**

Ṛṣis, *whose sins are destroyed, whose dualities are torn asunder, who are self-controlled and who rejoice in the well-being of others, attain union with* Brahman.

Again, the Lord re-emphasises the way to attain *mokṣa.* He is using the term *ṛṣi.* He has defined his characteristics and he has also defined the duties of such a *ṛṣi* in his verse. He confirms that a *ṛṣi* who fulfils all the points mentioned here will attain *mokṣa.*

(1) **Kṣiṇakalmaṣāḥ:** *Kalmaṣa* is dirt. It means sins in our mind. It is the *vāsanā*s we have accumulated from past births which give us pain and sorrow in this worldly life. A *ṛṣi* is one who has viewed these pains and sorrows as God's blessings on him. He thinks that God is merciful to him because he has punished him for his past sins. By punishing, God has cleared the way for his *mokṣa*. He therefore accepts all sorrows and pains of the physical body and mind as God's grace on him.

(2) **Chinnadvaidhā***:* Whose dualities are torn. He does not react to either of the pairs of opposite reactions, such as happiness-sorrow, cold-warmth, pains-pleasures of any sort. Just as he does not react to pain, he also does not get elated on obtaining pleasures. He knows that it will bring sorrow and also that it will add new *vāsanā*s and that he would be delayed in his path to liberation.

Dvaidha also means uncertainty, i.e., when one has doubt whether what he is doing is right or wrong. *Chinnadvaidha* also means the person who has no doubt about *ātman* and living in *ātman*.

He, therefore, is self-controlled. He has mastered his senses and mind so that they do not produce any reaction that will lead to attachment.

So, a *ṛṣi* is not the one who lives in forests and performs *tapas* all the time. He is living in this world amongst us and carries on his normal obligatory duties.

So, what should he do? The man of knowledge shows that knowledge in action. This is showing "universal love". We should develop and practise the Vedic Doctrine—*lokāḥ samastāḥ sukhino bhavantu* (let all this world live peacefully). For him, the 'others' do not exist; he sees 'one' in all and does not hate or injure others. He is engaged in the good of all beings. In what manner he reacts to wicked people, one may ask?

He does not go and praise them. Actually, he is showing his divinity to others by his actions. Others will follow his path and will try to purify themselves. No one can wash others internally, it is up to each of us to purify ourselves. One should leave wicked people alone till they realise their wickedness and come to repent it. It is no good preaching to a person who does not want it. His mind will not register the teaching. Kṛṣṇa did not go to Duryodhana and preach because he did not ask for help.

कामक्रोधवियुक्तानां यतीनां यतचेतसाम् ।
अभितो ब्रह्मनिर्वाणं वर्तते विदितात्मनाम् ॥२६॥

kāma-krodha-viyuktānāṁ yatīnāṁ yatacetasām |
abhito brahmanirvāṇaṁ vartate viditātmanām ||26||

To the self-controlled sages who are free from desire and wrath, who have controlled their thoughts and who have realised the Self, absolute freedom exists on all sides.

A few more characteristics of a *ṛṣi* are mentioned here. The Lord uses the word *yati*, here. *Yati* is one who sacrifices everything for a great ideal. What does a *yati* sacrifice?

Kāma-krodha-viyuktānām: He sacrifices both desire and anger under all circumstances. We know how these two are great enemies of man. By this sacrifice he will learn to live in the world not for any pleasures but for doing good to one and all. He will then be able to burn the existing *vāsanās* and not accumulate new *vāsanās*. This is called *vāsanā-kṣaya.*

Yatacetasām: Controlling the thought. Thoughts come from the mind. If one can use the intellect, he can control the mind. This will lead to a calm state of mind. Otherwise one will have an agitated mind with millions of thoughts. This state is *manonāśa.*

Viditātmanām: Who has acquired the knowledge of *ātmā*. This is *tattvajñānam.* This can be obtained by the grace of *gurus*, reading scriptures and through self-discipline.

Such a person attains absolute freedom. The word used is *brahmanirvāṇam.*

Abhitaḥ Vartate: On all sides it exists. The state of *brahmanirvāṇam* exists on all sides. It means that he is liberated in the present state as well as after death. Freedom and bliss in all places, at all times and under all circumstances.

स्पर्शान्कृत्वा बहिर्बाह्यांश्चक्षुश्चैवान्तरे भ्रुवोः ।
प्राणापानौ समौ कृत्वा नासाभ्यन्तरचारिणौ ॥२७॥

***sparśān kṛtvā bahir bāhyāṁś cakṣuś caivāntare bhruvoḥ* |**
***prāṇāpānau samau kṛtvā nāsābhyantaracāriṇau* ||27||**

यतेन्द्रियमनोबुद्धिर्मुनिर्मोक्षपरायणः ।
विगतेच्छाभयक्रोधो यः सदा मुक्त एव सः ॥२८॥

***yatendriyamanobuddhir munir mokṣaparāyaṇaḥ* |**
***vigatecchā-bhaya-krodho yaḥ sadā mukta eva saḥ* ||28||**

The sage who has shut out all external contacts, fixing his gaze in the centre of the eye-brows, controlling incoming and outgoing breaths, with senses, mind and intellect controlled, free from desire, fear and hatred, having liberation as his goal, he enjoys freedom always.

Here is a technique of *dhyāna-yoga* and it is a prelude to the next chapter.

The first requirement for liberation is, having the goal decided. One has to believe in the Self and understand what the pluralistic world is. One should decide which one to follow. Once the decision is made, practice comes next.

The first practice is to shut out external contacts. In the process of meditation, eyes, ears and nose have to be kept under constant control.

One can imagine a deaf person sitting in front of a group of people who are shouting abuses at him. Or imagine a person who has lost the sense of smell and is in a restaurant with the scent of all delicious dishes. In both the situations there is no reaction from such handicapped persons. Similarly, for meditation, one must shut out all the stimuli from entering the mind. One should be deaf and blind to sensual distractions.

To help in this technique, textbooks on *yoga* ask the person to fix his gaze in the centre of the brows. It is *khecarī mudrā*. If one keeps his eyes open, in the early stages, one cannot avoid seeing things and therefore he would get distracted. If then one decides to close the eyes, it is easy to fall asleep. To avoid both these two situations, one is asked to concentrate his gaze on the middle of the brows. This spot is called *ājñācakra*. Some people concentrate on the tip of their nose. Any method can be followed.

Controlling the breathing: It is a known fact that breathing becomes irregular when one gets agitated. One can look at an angry or hysterical man to realise this. So, in *prāṇāyāma*, they give great importance to controlling the flow of breath. This in turn regulates one's blood circulation and that will have an effect of calming the mind.

After controlling the physical side and making it ready for meditation, the Lord describes the method for controlling the mind and intellect in the second *śloka*.

One's mind, having experienced the sense-pleasures, keeps a record of that event. During quiet period it tends to dwell on those pleasures. Desires breed more desires. For the person on the spiritual path, this can be controlled if he uses his intellectual powers to control the mind and senses, so that he can concentrate on the higher Self.

Of course, it is very important that such a person should be free from desire, fear and anger. These have been described in detail before and we know how desire leads to fear, fear to anger and that eventually destroys the person. If one can cultivate these qualities, his path to liberation is free and easy and he can meditate easily.

भोक्तारं यज्ञतपसां सर्वलोकमहेश्वरम् ।
सुहृदं सर्वभूतानां ज्ञात्वा मां शान्तिमृच्छति ॥२९॥

***bhoktāraṁ yajñatapasāṁ sarvaloka-maheśvaram* I**
***suhṛdaṁ sarvabhūtānāṁ jñātvā māṁ śāntim ṛcchati* II29II**

Knowing Me as the enjoyer of all sacrifices and austerities, the Lord and controller of all the worlds, and friend of all beings, man attains peace.

If one has to have faith in any person, he must know the qualities of that person. He must understand what sort of person he is. The Lord therefore enumerates some of His qualities. He is not boasting about it himself. As the student has come crying for help to Him, He out of great compassion to mankind, is simply enumerating His qualities.

Bhoktāraṁ yajñatapasām: Enjoyer of sacrifices and austerities. *Yajña* is self-dedicated work in any field of activity. *Tapas* is any form of austerity to purify oneself and drop the ego. Both these acts give peace. It is the *ātman* who enjoys the peace.

The foundation for all of us is the Lord (*ātmā*) in ourselves. *Ātmā* is a witness for all actions. God does not sit on the top of a mountain somewhere, receiving your offering and enjoying them. If one drops/kills his ego and merges into the Self, that Self is said to enjoy the Selfhood he has attained. As He is all-pervading, He is a Witness for all actions. The one who finds peace in himself is a *santuṣṭa*, he enjoys peace.

Sarvalokamaheśvara: *Loka,* as we have discussed before, is the world we create from our sense-organs. For example, a child playing absorbedly is said to live in its own world at that time. Nothing else exists for that child at that time.

The Lord for each sense-organ is called *deva. Deva* for the eyes is the sun. *Deva* for the ear is space and so on. The Lord for all the senses together is called Maheśvara. This is the mind as it controls all sense-organs. Without the mind the eyes cannot see and ears cannot hear. It is the mind that sees, hears, touches, smells or tastes.

The Lord is called *sarvalokamaheśvara.* It means "The Lord of all minds of all of us put together in this world which we created with our sense-organs."

Suhṛdam: The Lord stresses that even though He is Maheśvara, He is also friend of all. He has no particular affinity for any individual. Any person can sow the seeds. As long as he does it properly, he will get the crops. It does not matter if he is a murderer or a saint. Proper actions bring proper rewards.

He brings rain not for the benefit of any particular person in any one place. The sun shines equally on all. If one can depend on someone for help, one should have confidence in him. The child has confidence in her mother. She goes to her immediately for help. It is because the child knows that the mother is her friend and she loves her.

So, we should believe that the Lord is really our friend. We should believe in our own divinity and express it outwards in our actions.

Having known him, he attains peace. Knowing the Lord means, having heard or read about God. By practice (*sādhanā*) one can realise the Lord in oneself. One gets united with the Lord. The Lord in him, comes out. It is not like getting to see the Lord in front of him. It is not *darśana.* One will attain the state of oneness with *Brahman.*

इति श्रीमद्भगवद्गीतासूपनिषत्सु ब्रह्मविद्यायां योगशास्त्रे
श्रीकृष्णार्जुनसंवादे कर्मसंन्यासयोगो नाम पञ्चमोऽध्यायः ॥

***iti śrīmadbhagavadgītāsūpaniṣatsu brahmavidyāyāṁ yogaśāstre śrīkṛṣṇārjuna-saṁvāde karma-saṁnyāsa-yogo nāma pañcamo'dhyāyaḥ* II**

CHAPTER 6

ĀTMASAṀYAMA-YOGA

This is *yoga* of meditation and self-control. This chapter is also commonly known as *Dhyāna-yoga*. How one has to control his body consisting of senses, mind and intellect and concentrate on the Self during meditation has been described in detail.

After explaining about *ātmā* or Self in chapter 2, and of the proper mode of action in chapter 3, knowledge of the Self in chapter 4, and method of proper renunciation in chapter 5, the Lord has prepared Arjuna for the higher level of spiritual development in the form of meditation. He has trained his disciple towards attaining self-unfoldment by Self-contemplation.

श्रीभगवानुवाच
अनाश्रितः कर्मफलं कार्यं कर्म करोति यः ।
स संन्यासी च योगी च न निरग्निर्न चाक्रियः ॥१॥

śrī bhagavān uvāca
anāśritaḥ karmaphalaṁ kāryaṁ karma karoti yaḥ I
sa saṁnyāsī ca yogī ca na niragnir na cākriyaḥ II1II

The Lord said

He who performs his prescribed duties without depending on the fruits of action is a saṁnyāsī *and* yogī; *not he who gives up worship of the fire and who remains without action.*

Saṁnyāsī and *yogī* are not to be recognised by their physical appearance and their place of residence. By wearing ochre robes one does not become a *saṁnyāsī* and by running away to the jungles one does not become a *yogī*. The Lord gives a definition of a *saṁnyāsī* and of a *yogī*. According to the Lord, nobody can escape action, everyone of us has a duty to perform. We must all work for the sake of duty and renounce attachment to fruits of action. Working for the sake of duty (*niṣkāma karma*) makes one a *yogī* and working with no attachment to the fruit of action (*karma-phala-tyāga*) makes one a *saṁnyāsī*.

The scriptures have described in detail the duties for all of us. They clearly say that everyone of us has to purify himself first and to do this, one must drop his ego and not be anxious for fruits of his action. External renunciation comes after inner purification of oneself.

Some people consider that there is a contradictory statement by Lord Kṛṣṇa in this verse. In the second half of the verse, the Lord says he is not a *yogī* or a *saṁnyāsī* who is without sacred fire or without sacred rites (*na niragnir na cākriyaḥ*). *Śruti, smṛti, śāstra*s and *dharma-śāstra* clearly state that a *saṁnyāsī* has to give up worship of fire.

What is worship of fire?

*Yajña*s are performed by offering oblations to the sacred fire to fulfil the desires. As we have discussed before, *yajña* means action and the sacred fire represents knowledge. By dropping the ego and by dropping all actions that are against *śāstra*s in the Fire of Knowledge, one performs *niṣkāma karma* and *karma-phala-tyāga*. So, according to the *sāstra*s, a married man cannot be *saṁnyāsī*.

Śrī Kṛṣṇa says that he is a *saṁnyāsī* who renounces fruits of action. That means, he has to perform *yajña*. That means he has to be a *gṛhastha* man. (This is against what *śāstra*s say of a *saṁnyāsī*). Does it mean that a *yogī* cannot attain knowledge? A *yogī*, according to the Lord in this verse, is one who performs prescribed duties (*niṣkāma karma*).

We should understand that the Lord is saying that a *gṛhastha* or a married man can be called *saṁnyāsī* if he is performing actions with renunciation of the fruits of action. He is also a *yogī* because he is performing *niṣkāma karma*.

Pravṛtti-mārga is the path in relation to and in contact with the outer world. Action that bind us to the world (actions for fruits of action) are considered as *pravṛtti karma*s.

Nivṛtti-mārga is the path towards *ātman*. In other words, it is retreat. By *niṣkāma karma*, the *sādhaka* is said to be going in *nivṛtti-mārga* to attain *mokṣa*. Not performing one's duty, and taking up *saṁnyāsa,* is not really the character of a *saṁnyāsī*, is the Lord's ruling.

In olden days, the *sādhaka*s first performed *niṣkāma karma* and attained the status of *muni*s. Then, they decided to take up *saṁnyāsa*. Only on attaining *jñāna*, they took up *saṁnyāsa* and not before. But famous men like King Janaka, did not take up *saṁnyāsa* but still worked without looking for fruits of action. People like Janaka can be called *saṁnyāsī*s also.

In other words, a person can remain an active member of society, have a family and children and can still be called a *saṁnyāsī* if he does *karma-phala-tyāga*; or the person can, after attaining knowledge, renounce his family and become a *saṁnyāsī*. The common factor in both the persons is "knowledge of the *ātman*". Without knowledge of the *ātman* a person is not a *saṁnyāsī*. This is what we have to understand from this verse.

यं संन्यासमिति प्राहुर्योगं तं विद्धि पाण्डव ।
न ह्यसंन्यस्तसङ्कल्पो योगी भवति कश्चन ॥२॥

yaṁ saṁnyāsam iti prāhur yogaṁ taṁ viddhi pāṇḍava ǀ
na hy asaṁnyastasaṁkalpo yogī bhavati kaścana ǀǀ2ǀǀ

O Arjuna, that which is called saṁnyāsa, *know that to be* yoga *also. No one becomes a* yogī *without giving up desires.*

Yoga means union of the body with the Soul. The method of union is also called *yoga.* The *bādhaka* is called a *yogī.*

The Lord uses the word *saṁkalpa.* What does it mean? It means "selfish motives behind an action" (it could be a good motive like wanting to go to heaven, but it is still a *saṁkalpa*). In simple words, it means desire.

Śaṅkarācārya says that *saṁnyāsa* means actions and thoughts at the level of body, mind and senses, wherein all desires for fruits of actions are renounced and the mind is directed towards the Lord. *Yoga* is the acts without desires for the worldly objects and performed only to please the Lord. *Tyāga* or renunciation is implied in both *saṁnyāsa* and *yoga.*

By desireless performance of actions (*yoga*) one can develop the faculty to renounce the desires for fruits of action (*saṁnyāsa*). Through *yoga* one attains *saṁnyāsa*. The hallmark of a *yogī* is not to have any desires in his actions.

We all have to work to exist. If we get desires, our actions are directed towards the desired objects, and we deviate from our path to *mokṣa*. Automatically, one learns to look forward to fruits of action.

Our minds are full of thoughts and desires. Some desires are strong and some are weak. We keep on adding new thoughts and desires because of our contact with the external world through our sense-organs. It would be easier if we had a one-track mind to achieve a single goal. But the mind being one and the tracks planned being many, we get confused on which track to go and which desire to fulfil.

Asaṁnyastasaṁkalpa: It means not renouncing desires. If one does not drop desires, he cannot be called a *yogī*. A *saṁnyāsī* cannot therefore be a *yogī* if he does not renounce desires.

So, giving up desires would obviously make the way clear for anyone on his pilgrimage in life to *mokṣa.* No progress is possible without giving up desires. One has to learn to become a *yogī*, who has one desire only and that is "to unite with the Self". *Yoga* is union with the Self.

In other words, *saṁnyāsa* includes *yoga* and *yoga* includes *saṁnyāsa*. We all have to perform *niṣkāma karma* and *karma-phala-tyāga.*

आरुरुक्षोर्मुनेर्योगं कर्म कारणमुच्यते ।
योगारूढस्य तस्यैव शमः कारणमुच्यते ॥३॥

***āruruksor muner yogaṁ karma kāraṇam ucyate* I**
***yogārūḍhasya tasyaiva śamaḥ kāraṇam ucyate* II3II**

For a muni, *who wishes to attain* yoga, *action is said to be the means. For the same sage who has "attained to* yoga" *inaction is said to be the means.*

Yoga here is to be understood as *dhyāna-yoga*. *Dhyāna-yoga* is another path to attain *mokṣa*. The Lord, before describing the technique, is warning those who are contemplating to follow this path, that they should not start on this path before preparing themselves for the technique. It is impossible to suddenly go and sit in a jungle, close one's eyes and meditate.

A child has to learn his alphabets, go through kindergarten, primary school, etc. to reach P.G. course. One cannot suddenly go into Ph.D. course classes, sit there and think he can achieve the Ph.D. degree.

The first step is *yoga* of action (*karma-yoga*). By following what is taught in chapters 3, 4 and 5, one can drop the ego of 'I' and mine in one's actions and then develop renunciation of the desire for fruits of action. This is like getting a degree in colleges. He is then a *yogī*.

The next step towards meditation (after attaining purity) is to reduce actions. This is *dhyāna-yoga*. He should work at transferring his field of activity from the realm of external objects to his *ātmā*. He should hear, think and meditate (*śravaṇa, manana, nididhyāsana*) on *ātmā*. He would then develop supreme satisfaction in his self and get absorbed in *ātmā*. He should drop all his thoughts of the outer world and realise the Self.

Ārurukṣu: Aspiring to ascend. One has to learn to ascend and ride over one's mind. The mind is like a horse, running away, carried by impulses. By using the intellect one can control the mind. One has to drop the ego and the desire for fruits of action by riding over one's mind. This is achieved by *niṣkāma karma*.

Yōgārūḍha: One who has ridden over his mind, one who has become a *yogī* and controlled the agitations of the mind by dropping all desire-prompted actions, is a *yogārūḍha*.

Śama (Quiescence): Serenity (for a *yogī*) is needed to achieve higher perfection. If one wants to concentrate on the *ātman,* one should not be distracted towards external objects. The mind which is not distracted is said to be in a serene state. This control of the mind and its ability to stay in quiescence, is *śama*. *Karma-saṁnyāsa* is *śama*. This state which is needed for *dhyāna* should fulfill the above two conditions.

यदा हि नेन्द्रियार्थेषु न कर्मस्वनुषज्जते ।
सर्वसङ्कल्पसंन्यासी योगारूढस्तदोच्यते ॥४॥

yadā hi nendriyārtheṣu na karmasvanuṣajjate |
sarvasaṁkalpasaṁnyāsī yogārūḍhas tadocyate ||4||

When a man is not attached to sense-objects and actions, having renounced all thoughts, he is said to have attained to yoga.

Yoga is union of the ego with *ātmā* and union of the *ātmā* with *Paramātmā*. To unite with the *ātmā* one should renounce the contact with the outer world. A *yogī* cannot meditate on *ātmā* unless he can draw his mind away from averything concerning the external world.

There are innumerable objects in the world one would like to get because of the pleasures they give. The first step to become a *yogārūḍha* (riding over one's mind) is to develop non-attachment to these objects. One should always think of the consequences, i.e., that happiness brings pain in course of time. The mind should be trained not to derive any sense of pleasure on seeing the sense-objects.

The second step would be to renounce the attachment to actions. Actions, as we know, bring results. By desiring the fruits of action, actions become binding. Actions should be carried out to burn the existing *vāsanās* and not accumulate new *vāsanās*. So, the second stage is *niṣkāma karma*.

The term *anuṣajjate* is used to emphasise non-attachment to sense-objects and actions. It means not even a trace of attachment.

The third stage is when the mind is trained not even to have any thoughts. To develop this, the first step is to give up bad thoughts. The second step is to give up good thoughts also. The third step is to give up all thoughts. The word used is *sarva-saṁkalpa-saṁnyāsī*. By not having any thoughts, no more *vāsanā* disturbances can occur. *Saṁkalpa* (*vāsanās*) are imprints on our mind. The mind should not have any imprints (thought-processes of the past) and should not add any new imprints (new thoughts).

By these three steps no new *vāsanā*s will come in. Bad thoughts are given up by cultivating noble ideas and selfless acts of welfare. Good thoughts should also be given up in course of time by study of the *śāstra*s in the company of learned men (*guru*s). Divine thoughts should become a way of life rather than mere thinking only.

Manusmṛti says that desires are born of *saṁkalpa*. *Yajña*s are born of *saṁkalpa*. If one does not have any *saṁkalpa*s, then he will not have any trace of desire in him. Once this state is achieved, one can go into intense meditation and withdraw from all activities (voluntary actions). This will help one to unite with the *ātmā* and experience pure, undisturbed bliss.

Such a sage is said to have reached the stage of *yogārūḍha* (ascending over one's mind). It is thought-free state. It does not mean such a person is sleeping. He is fully awake but is in the state of super-consciousness (knowledge). When the rest of the world is awake and yet is in a sleeping state (because of not being aware of knowledge), the *muni* is said to be awake (he is aware of the knowledge and is merged in it. For others he may appear to be in a state of sleep.)

उद्धरेदात्मनात्मानं नात्मानमवसादयेत्।
आत्मैव ह्यात्मनो बन्धुरात्मैव रिपुरात्मनः ॥५॥

uddhared ātmanātmānaṁ nātmānam avasādayet |
ātmaiva hy ātmano bandhur ātmaiva ripur ātmanaḥ ||5||

Let a man raise himself by the self, not let the self go down. For this Self is the friend of the self and Self is the enemy of the self.

It is a very beautiful verse, with great meaning in it. We all have dual personalities like Dr. Jekyll and Mr. Hyde in us. Our mind is full of thoughts and thought-imprints. Some are good thoughts and some are bad thoughts. The proportion varies.

One fine day, when we realise that we want to get better and we want to travel on the spiritual path to liberation, we use our intellect and think of what we have been doing and where we are going. We should see the bad (Hyde) in us and try to get away from that.

The starting point is in the ocean called the mind. At the bottom of the ocean, think you have found a thought that you are the Self and not the ego. Now, you will have to lift it up to the top. You have to do it yourself, no one can do it for you.

Of course it does not mean you do not get help. A person wanting to get the treasure from out of the bottom of the sea, has first of all to be a good deep-sea diver, and should have learnt the technique of deep-sea diving. Without that technique he cannot dive down. Likewise, to get the treasure of our own *ātmā* out, we must know the technique. This has to be learnt by study of scriptures, learning under learned people and by developing a sense of humbleness. If one has to drop his ego, he should not develop another form of ego in thinking "I am the master and I will do it myself without anybody's help."

One has to learn to wash himself not only physically, but also mentally. He should get the soap and water (learn from elders and *śāstras*) and cleanse himself.

Man is the architect of his own destiny. God helps those who help themselves. One has to pay the price for what one gets. The price we pay to purify ourselves is our total effort. If a sick man has to get better, he has to realise that he is sick in the first instance. He should then go to the physician and get examined. He should take the medication himself to get better.

We are all mentally sick, but unfortunately we do not realise it. We must go to our doctor (*śāstras*, *gurus*) and get medicine. We should purify ourselves. What we want to be intellectually, we should make our minds to be the same. The intellect is the Jekyll and the mind is the Hyde. Let the mind die away (*manonāśa*) and intellect brighten up.

By spiritual technique let us bring our lower mind under the command of the higher intellect. This is what is meant by "let one raise the 'self' by the Self".

Not let the self go down: We all know how easy it is to go down the stairs. One can go down 50 steps in may be 2 minutes.

But climbing up 50 steps may take 10-20 minutes. One gets breathless on climbing up but feels no tiredness on going down.

While we are lifting ourselves up, as it is a hard (mentally) job, we get tired and we may easily drop down. How? Our senses are very strong. It needs a very strong will-power to control our senses. A momentary lapse makes us lose our track (the story of Viśvāmitra and Menakā makes one understand it easily). The sensual desires pull us down from our upward path.

Self is the friend and the foe: Our mind has both good thoughts and bad thoughts. Once we decide to go on the spiritual path, it means we have gone to war. We are in the battlefield in our own minds. The forces are in two camps. They are *dharma* and *adharma* (righteousness and unrighteousness). Hence the self is the friend and the foe. We have both of them in us. If we follow bad thoughts we will ruin ourselves. If we follow good thoughts we will lift ourselves up. Our army will be as strong as our thoughts are.

Bandhu means one that binds. Family, friends, wealth bind us to *saṁsāra* (*pravṛtti*). The thought of *ātman* will help us to bind ourselves to the *ātman* (*nivṛtti*). So, the Lord says, "*ātmaiva hyātmano bandhur āmaiva ripurātmanaḥ.*"

An impure mind is our enemy and a pure mind is our friend. Holding on to pure thoughts in all circumstances is called *japa* and it helps us to win the war.

बन्धुरात्मात्मनस्तस्य येनात्मैवात्मना जितः ।
अनात्मनस्तु शत्रुत्वे वर्तेतात्मैव शत्रुवत् ॥६॥

bandhur ātmātmanas tasya yenātmaivātmanā jitaḥ I
anātmanas tu śatrutve vartetātmaiva śatruvat II6II

The Self is the friend of the self for him who has conquered himself by the Self. But to him who has not conquered the self, the self itself acts like an enemy.

This verse is an elaboration of the previous verse. In this verse self is used several times which might cause confusion if not understood properly. Two "selfs" are used here. Higher Self is the real *ātmā* inside us and the lower self is the ego in us. Ego is the reflection of the real Self and has the advantage (or disadvantage, depending on the way one looks at it) of the mind, intellect and senses as its components. It, therefore, has constant contact with the pluralistic world.

Friends and foes are in plenty in our contact with the external world. These can change their colours any time under circumstances that suit them. Friends can become foes and *vice-versa.*

Friends and foes are inside us also. We have discussed it in the previous verse. We have noble (divine) and satanic thoughts in our own mind. They will lead the ego either to merge with *ātmā* or they will lead him to the cycle of births and deaths with their associated sufferings.

Dhyāna-yoga is meant to help to subdue the mind and keep it under constant control of the intellect. This will lead one to achieve the *ānanda* which is our inherent right.

जितात्मनः प्रशान्तस्य परमात्मा समाहितः ।
शीतोष्णसुखदुःखेषु तथा मानापमानयोः ॥७॥

***jitātmanaḥ praśāntasya paramātmā samāhitaḥ* |**
***śītoṣṇasukhaduḥkheṣu tathā mānāpamānayoḥ* ||7||**

The man who has subdued the mind is full of peace. He experiences the Supreme Self under all conditions in heat and cold, pleasure and pain, honour and dishonour.

The mind reacts by going through different moods and passions constantly. As the ego is exposed to the outer world, there is constant input of impulses from the outer world into our mind.

If we analyse our ego as intellect, mind and the physical body, our reactions to the external world can be classified at these three levels. The Lord gives one example for each level.

At the physical level, we can feel heat or cold; at the mental level, we experience pleasure and pain (hatred and love, kindness and cruelty, etc.) which are our emotions. At the intellectual level it is honour and dishonour (pride when we get praise and sorrow when we are disgraced).

If one has conquered his mind by intellect (*yogārūḍha*). He is in a state of constant peace and bliss. He is united with the higher Self in him and the above-mentioned *dvandvas* do not disturb his peace. For a *dhyāna-yogī* this method of *sādhanā* is advocated.

ज्ञानविज्ञानतृप्तात्मा कूटस्थो विजितेन्द्रियः ।
युक्त इत्युच्यते योगी समलोष्टाश्मकाञ्चनः ॥८॥

***jñāna-vijñāna-tṛptātmā kūṭastho vijitendriyaḥ* I**
***yukta ity ucyate yogī sama-loṣṭāśma-kāñcanaḥ* II8II**

The yogī *who is satisfied with knowledge and wisdom, who remains immovable, who has conquered his senses, who looks equally on mud, stone and gold, is said to be harmonised.*

Jñāna-vijñāna-tṛptātmā: *Jñāna* is knowledge and *vijñāna* is wisdom. One gets knowledge by the study of books and the teaching by scholars. This is theoretical knowledge. One gets wisdom by direct Self-realisation. This is practical knowledge.

In a physics lecture class the teacher gives different theories on how the rays of light go through different media. By remembering the words used, one can understand what is taught. This is *jñāna*. He can pass his theory exams. He will find it hard to explain the same at a later date to his students if he has gained only theoretical knowledge.

In a physics laboratory, the teacher makes each student perform practical work. The students make mistakes initially but later on they do it properly. It makes them understand the theory better. They are then said to have wisdom (*vijñāna*).

Similarly, experiences in life make one a *vijñānī*. *Śāstras* can say a lot of things but experience makes one a better person. Mum says to a child that the fire is hot. The child who touches the fire and gets burnt is all the wiser. One knows by experience that happiness of winning a million pounds in its turn brings a number of pains.

Kūṭastha: Immovable *Kūṭa* is the iron block used by jewellers to shape the ornaments. The jeweller shapes his jewels by hitting the piece of gold/silver on the block. The block remains firm and immovable always.

Similarly, for a *yogī*, all the external changes of the outside world hammer him, yet the Self remains steady.

Vijitendriyaḥ: (Who has conquered the senses.) *Jaya* means conquer. *Vijaya* means perfect victory. One should be perfectly victorious in ruling over all senses at all times. Perfect self-control is a must for spiritual realisation.

Samaloṣṭāśmakāñcanaḥ: Looks equally on mud, stone and gold.

We value any objects according to their availability or non-availability and our mind decides the value of the objects. Anything that is available easily is not valued high.

Water and petrol are examples for this. In U.K., for example, water is freely available most of the times. Petrol is not as freely available. In the Middle-East, one buys water but gets petrol at almost no cost. In a desert, a millionaire is willing to give all his wealth away if he gets water when he is thirsty.

All objects in the world are a combination of five elements in varying proportions. For a *jñānī*, therefore, mud, stone and gold are nothing but the five elements.

Yogārūḍha, or a man of self-realisation, sees the substratum of Self in all. He does not look upon him as brāhmaṇa, śūdra, Hindu, Christian, etc. The Lord uses the expression *yukta ity ucyate yogī*.

Yoga is union of the ego with the Self and union of *ātmā* with *Paramātmā*. The one who has attained it, is a *yogī*.

सुहृन्मित्रार्युदासीनमध्यस्थद्वेष्यबन्धुषु ।
साधुष्वपि च पापेषु समबुद्धिर्विशिष्यते ॥९॥

***suhṛnmitrāryudāsīna-madhyastha-dveṣya-bandhuṣu* I**
***sādhuṣv api ca pāpeṣu samabuddhir viśiṣyate* II9II**

He who is equal-minded towards good-hearted friends and enemies, the indifferent, the neutrals, the hatefuls, relatives, the righteous and unrighteous, he excels.

In the last verse, the Lord gave us the idea of how to react to the outer world of objects.

In this verse, he gives us the method of reacting to the world of men. We all need to survive and in that process of survival, we should not become self-centred and egotistic. We should be able not only to receive the benefit (freely) from the outer world but we should be giving something in return.

We should be able to give others what we have in plenty. We all have plenty of love in us. We can give our love to others and still multiply the love we have inside us. We should show compassion in our actions. *Suhṛt* is that person who gives help in need without expecting any returns of favour at any time.

We have read before that we can look at different objects at different angles and get a different meaning.

ariḥ	—	enemy
udāsīnaḥ	—	not a friend, not an enemy
madhyastha	—	meditator between two parties in dispute
dveṣyaḥ	—	getting to envy somebody for no apparent reason
bandhuḥ	—	family and friends who are there when one is in need of help
sādhuḥ	—	gentle-natured person
pāpāḥ	—	sinners

A *yogārūḍha* is that person who sees all the above classes of people equally.

If we look at the world from the physical and the mental plane, the world of men and women appears as the variety of people enumerated above. It is *dehadṛṣṭi* and *manodṛṣṭi*. If we develop *ātmadṛṣṭi* we can see the same *ātmā* in all. The Lord is advocating equal-minded approach to all classes of people.

One has to interpret the statement in more depth. A sinner may come to you for help. As long as he wishes to come to you, you should not say 'no' to him. Listen to him and see what he wants. If you consider it proper, give him what he wants.

Similarly, if one is **asked** to go to such a man, he should go. You should not punish the person for his sins. That person is bound to be punished for his sins. (We are no God to punish so and so. He will be punished for his actions in due course.) If asked to help, one should not refuse to give help because he is a sinner.

Also, one should realise that the Lord is not suggesting that you should go and preach to a sinner to become a saint. If the sinner requests help, one should give it. Give what one asks for and it is proper *dāna*. Do not give what one does not ask for.

The Lord also mentions 'the indifferent and neutrals'. What does this mean?

There are millions in the world we do not know of. For example, when there is an earthquake or a similar natural disaster, you may not know the victims, but it is your duty to contribute to help them. You must be equal-minded to show your love to such people.

This verse is best understood if we take our own body as an example. If I burn my finger or hurt my toe, my mind reacts equally to both and reacts properly in both situations. My leg is the same to me as my arm. It is all part of me.

योगी युञ्जीत सततमात्मानं रहसि स्थितः ।
एकाकी यतचित्तात्मा निराशीरपरिग्रहः ॥१०॥

yogī yuñjīta satatam ātmānaṁ rahasi sthitaḥ I
ekākī yatacittātmā nirāśīr aparigrahaḥ II10II

The yogī *sitting in a solitary place, alone, self-controlled, without desire, without receiving anything from others, should unite the self with the* ātmā.

The practice of uniting the lower self (ego) in us with the higher Self is explained in this and the following verses. This is practical teaching of *dhyāna-yoga*.

A *yogī* is, in this context, a practical student practising to unite his ego with the *ātmā*.

Rahasi sthitaḥ: Sits in a solitary place in the early stages of meditation. The 'will' should be there to achieve *mokṣa*, but it will not be strong compared to the temptations of the outer world. Our senses will throw in so many desires onto our minds.

It does not mean one should go to a jungle. Any serene, calm place would do. Of course going to riverbanks or a forest would bring natural peace because nature is beautiful. In the present world this is not easy. It is possible to allocate a part of the house for this purpose. This, our ancestors called a prayer-room and used to put idols of gods in that room.

No amount of space is ever enough for anybody. Do we not have the necessity to purify our minds? Can we not have proper space for meditation and prayers? We just need a quiet place for mental withdrawal from the outside world.

One should not make a show of meditation just to impress others. One must secretly practise it in his own heart. Hence, a place of solitude is advocated.

Ekākī: Alone. In *bhakti-yoga*, *bhajan*s can be carried on in a group by like-minded people. But in *dhyāna-yoga*, in the early stages, group activity is not advocated because one might be tempted to see how the other one is doing *dhyāna*.

Nirāśiḥ, yatacittātmā: Desirelessness and self-control are advocated so often in the *Gītā*. This is an essential quality for *dhyāna-yoga* also. The mind has to be quite for *dhyāna*. Normally the mind has thousands of thoughts at any time and some of them may be desires (small or great). Self-control (controlling senses), and desirelessness help to quieten the mind and prepare one towards contemplation of the *ātmā*.

Aprigrahaḥ: One should not receive anything from others apart from bare necessities and simple food and even that for survival only. If one does, then the meditation will lose its concentration. One may start hoarding and protecting what he gets and lose the power of concentration. The body starts getting likes and dislikes instead of being in *dhyāna*. The mind will wander and begin to think what food one will get that day and how tasty it will be and so on. One should wear simple clothes.

This is symbolised in our culture by sages wearing simple ochre robes (of course it is not a *sine qua non* that wearing ochre robes makes one a sage).

Lastly, the Lord states that the *dhyāna* should be continuous and undisturbed. The light of *sattva* should keep away the darkness of *rajas* and *tamas* from entering the mind.

शुचौ देशे प्रतिष्ठाप्य स्थिरमासनमात्मनः ।
नात्युच्छ्रितं नातिनीचं चैलाजिनकुशोत्तरम् ॥११॥
***śucau deśe pratiṣṭhāpya sthiram āsanam ātmanaḥ* |**
***nātyucchritaṁ nātinīcaṁ cailājinakuśottaram* ||11||**

तत्रैकाग्रं मनः कृत्वा यतचित्तेन्द्रियक्रियः ।
उपविश्यासने युञ्ज्याद्योगमात्मविशुद्धये ॥१२॥
***tatraikāgraṁ manaḥ kṛtvā yatacittendriyakriyaḥ* |**
***upaviśyāsane yuñjyād yogam ātmaviśuddhaye* ||12||**

Having established on a clean spot, a firm seat, which is neither too high nor too low, covered by cloths, skin and holy grass one over the other;

There, having made the mind one-pointed, with the action of mind and senses controlled, let him practice yoga *for self-purification.*

The step by step guidance, towards *dhyāna* is given in these two verses.

Yoga, here means *dhyāna* (meditation). This is to be done for self-purification, which is a pre-requisite towards achieving the status of a *yogī*.

It is not only important to control the mind, but it is also important where one sits and how one sits.

Śucau deśe: At a clean spot. If the spot is not clean, it will be either smelly or breed germs like flies, mosquitoes, etc. These will disturb one's concentration. It is necessary for the *dhyānī* to have a clean spot, clean body and pure mind. Initially, for this *yoga,* it is a necessary condition to be fulfilled. When one gets mastery over the control of himself he can meditate in any place because he would be a *yogārūḍha.*

Nātyucchṛitam, nātinīcam: The seat should not be too high or too low. If the seat is too high, during meditation if one nods off to sleep, he will injure himself. Similarly, if the seat is too low, it is possible that insects start crawling over. Also dampness would cause health problems.

Sthiram: The seat has to be firm, not wobbly and one should also sit firmly on that seat. Physical movements disturb the concentration. (One can try for how long one can sit without rubbing the nose or scratching or shifting the position of sitting.)

Cailajinakuśottaram: The seat should have *kuśa* grass, deer-skin and cloth one over the other. *Kuśa* grass keeps the seat warm in winter months. This would help in providing comfort to sit for long periods.

This is covered by deer skin, because it will be hard to sit directly on grass. A layer of cloth is put on top. This is to avoid sweating when one sits directly on animal skin. This will give a comfortable *āsana* (seat) to sit on. One can sit in any position (*āsana*) he feels comfortable. This is only a physical requisite.

Our sense-organs and mind should be controlled. Senses as we know draw one away very easily, even when they are controlled. We also know that our mind can dwell on memories and imaginations of pleasures of the outer world. So, these two need constant control.

The mind should be one-pointed. Again, we know that, to take the mind away from the outer world a point of concentration to concentrate upon is needed. Mind cannot be blank. It needs thoughts. So, instead of a multitude of thoughts which give a multitude of temporary benefits or pains, one should concentrate on the *ātmā*.

Why should one do this at all? If one has to attain liberation, one must purify oneself. This method of *dhyāna* helps in self-purification. There will not be any agitations of the mind which will bring in new *vāsanā*s.

One should remember that this is not the only method of self-purification to achieve *mokṣa.*

समं कायशिरोग्रीवं धारयन्नचलं स्थिरः ।
संप्रेक्ष्य नासिकाग्रं स्वं दिशश्चानवलोकयन् ॥१३॥

samaṁ kāyaśirogrīvaṁ dhārayann acalaṁ sthiraḥ I
saṁprekṣya nāsikāgraṁ svaṁ diśaś cānavalokayan II13II

प्रशान्तात्मा विगतभीर्ब्रह्मचारिव्रते स्थितः ।
मनः संयम्य मच्चित्तो युक्त आसीत मत्परः ॥१४॥

praśāntātmā vigatabhīr brahmacārivrate sthitaḥ I
manaḥ saṁyamya maccitto yukta āsīta matparaḥ II14II

Let him firmly hold the body, head and neck erect, gazing at the tip of his nose, without looking around;

Let him sit serene-minded, fearless, firm in the vow of celibacy, self-controlled and balanced, thinking of Me as the supreme goal.

The physical position and mental composure for meditation are described in these two verses.

Firmly hold the body and keep the neck erect: 'Firmly' should not be understood as sitting in a state of tension. One should be relaxed and at the same time keep a posture in which his vertebral column is erect. The back should be at a right angle to the seat. It is believed that the current will flow freely upwards from the spinal column to the brain centre called *sahasrāra*. They say that this will enable one to generate spiritual experiences in oneself.

One should also realise that this is meant to let the person develop a method of sitting. There are those who may not be able to sit like this because of physical illness or deformities. They can develop their own methods to relax and concentrate. If one can sit in one posture constantly for three hours, he is said to have achieved *āsanajaya* (victory over posture).

Fixing the gaze on the tip of his nose, and not looking around: 'Fixing the eye-ball in such a way that it is looking at the tip of the nose' is what is meant here. This is only to help in developing concentration and also suggesting that one should not close his eyes totally in *dhyāna*. One can also try other methods like concentrating on the inner ends of the eye-brows which is more difficult.

He should not look around. If one starts looking around it negates the whole point of meditation, as one gets distracted easily.

Four basic virtues are necessary for the aspirant. Peace, fearlessness, celibacy and self-control.

Peace: It is an inward state of joy. The pleasure one gets on contentment is peace. By assuming the above posture and relaxing, one experiences a state of peace in himself. It is something one has to experience and not easy to describe.

Fearlessness: Fear of what? Fear in the progress in the path of meditation! Why? Daily in the multitude of actions one pursues, one's mind is occupied one way or other. When suddenly one decides to drop it all and go into meditation, there is "nothingness" around. This can be overcome by first of all trying to know what one is trying to achieve by *dhyāna-yoga*. One wants to achieve union with the Self inside. For this, one must know what is the Self, and one must believe in the Self. Then only he should start his practice. There will not be any fear for such a person.

One should not be frightened to follow the path of liberation. One should first of all study the various paths, analyse and find out that which suits him. Having decided that there should not be any fear. One should also not worry or fear about others' opinions. (There will be some ignorant people who would laugh at the *sādhaka*.)

Brahmacarya and saṁnyāsa: Celibacy and self-control.

Brahamacarya is ordinarily understood as not having sex. It is not really so. It really means *brahma-vicāra* or actual enquiry into *Brahman* and engaging one's mind in *Brahman*. This is not possible if our sense-organs agitate the mind with thoughts of the outer world and its pleasures. One should cultivate control of all sense-organs and the impulses they bring. Total self-control is *brahmacarya*. Total celibacy helps in single-pointed concentration on *Brahman*.

The mind of a person in *dhyāna-yoga* should also not indulge in sense-thoughts which flow in from all sense-organs. By outward shutting of the sense-organs, one does not achieve total celibacy. His mind should be pure as well. A person whose mind is pure, whose sense-organs do not wander around for pleasures is a *brahmacārī*.

Lastly, the Lord says "Think of Me as the supreme goal". This is essential. Unless one has faith in what one is doing, total effort is impossible. Without it, one will not achieve success.

युञ्जन्नेवं सदात्मानं योगी नियतमानसः ।
शान्तिं निर्वाणपरमां मत्संस्थामधिगच्छति ॥१५॥

***yuñjann evaṁ sadātmānaṁ yogī niyatamānasaḥ* I**
***śāntiṁ nirvāṇaparamāṁ matsaṁsthām adhigacchati* II15II**

Thus, the self-controlled yogī, *always keeping the mind balanced, attains peace abiding in Me which culminates in the highest bliss of liberation.*

What will one achieve by practising *dhyāna-yoga*? What is the end-result?

Peace abiding in Me: Who is Me? "Me" is the 'Inner Self' in external 'me'. There is total peace in the 'Self' (*ātmā*). This has to be experienced.

By getting to experience the peace in oneself, one is freed from the cycle of *saṁsāra* (births and deaths, of joys and sorrows of life). This is the highest bliss and is termed in spiritual terms as *mokṣa*. In this verse the word used is *nirvāṇa-paramām* (supreme liberation, or the highest bliss of *mokṣa*).

The *dhyāna-yogī*, finally experiences the Self within and unites with Him. This is a state of *advaita* (non-dualism).

नात्यश्नतस्तु योगोऽस्ति न चैकान्तमनश्नतः ।
न चातिस्वप्नशीलस्य जाग्रतो नैव चार्जुन ॥१६॥

***nātyaśnatas tu yogo'sti na caikāntam anaśnataḥ* I**
***na cātisvapnaśīlasya jāgrato naiva cā'rjuna* II16II**

O Arjuna, yoga *is not possible for him who eats too much or who does not eat at all. Nor for him who sleeps too much or who does not sleep at all.*

When one is planning to practise *dhyāna-yoga*, he is bound to think "what about my eating and sleeping? How should I eat? Should I not eat at all? Should I not be going to sleep at all?" Thinking thus, he gets frightened and does not want to do *dhyāna.*

The answer is given in this verse. Of course one has to eat and one has to sleep. These are necessary needs of the bodily organs, and food and sleep are essential for the functions of the body. Moderation in both, is the answer.

By not eating, hunger will be the first result. The next effect of not eating is weakness (physical weakness). A weak body will result in a weak mind. A strong healthy body is needed for the *yogī.*

By overeating, one becomes unhealthy and gets diseases. An unhealthy body will have no power to concentrate. Also, one gets pleasures of eating (not satisfaction, but pleasure) and these pleasures distract the mind away from meditation. One will always think of food. "Where is it coming from? What is it like? When is it coming? Should I keep stock of the food?" etc.

Sleep is a normal requisite for the body and mind. A good sleep at the right time for a proper length of time would refresh the person. He can meditate better.

By not sleeping, physical exhaustion develops. One eventually drops down for sheer lack of energy. By oversleeping, dullness develops. Sleep is tāmasic (lazy) in character. Laziness is not helpful in the spiritual path or in any form of *yoga* and specially so in *dhyāna-yoga.*

One can give a different interpretation to this verse. One can say : be moderate in sense-pleasures (at physical, mental and intellectual levels). Do not punish your physical body and do not be lazy as well.

युक्ताहारविहारस्य युक्तचेष्टस्य कर्मसु ।
युक्तस्वप्नावबोधस्य योगो भवति दुःखहा ॥१७॥

yuktāhāra vihārasya yuktaceṣṭasya karmasu I
yuktasvapnāvabodhasya yogo bhavati duḥkhahā II17II

For him who is moderate in food and recreation, moderate in exertion in all actions, moderate in sleep and wakefulness, yoga *destroys all pain and suffering.*

By this, one has to understand that *dhyāna-yoga* is a slow and steady process. It cannot be shutting oneself away suddenly and sitting in meditation.

Yuktāhāra means moderation in food. One should eat *sāttvic* food (verse 8, 9, 10 chap. 17). What one eats should be earned by righteous means. It should be offered to God first. Pure food has to fulfil these conditions and in turn it gives a pure mind.

Yuktavihāra: *Vihāra* is movement of limbs. One should control the movements of the limbs at the time of *dhyāna.* To keep the proper circulation of blood, one needs to stroll ever so often.

Yuktaceṣṭasya karmasu: *Ceṣṭā* is *karma.* It means among the *karmas*, only proper *karmas* (*nitya, namittika*) should be performed.

Yuktasvapnāvabodhasya: *Svapna* in this context refers to sleep. Moderation in sleep is essential for *dhyāna.* It also means that one should have a proper habit of going to bed early in the night and get up at dawn. Five to seven hours of sleep is said to be sufficient for the body of an average person. *Śāstras* say that 4.45 O'clock in the morning is an auspicious time for *dhyāna.* It is known as *brāhma-muhūrta.*

One has to think of the actions. Think what you want to achieve. Think of what you believe. Think of your position in life. Then only start practising. Slow but steady is the rule to follow.

In course of time one develops the technique properly and will realise the Self within. This is what is meant by "*yoga* destroys all pain and suffering".

Overindulgence in the activities of life in the process of meditation is harmful. Let us take the example of a student. Overzealous studying in the early stages makes him tired and later on he loses concentration in study. Overindulgence in *sādhanā* similarly gets a person tired easily. Over-exertion defeats its purpose.

Avabodha means absolute knowledge.

यदा विनियतं चित्तमात्मन्येवावतिष्ठते ।
निःस्पृहः सर्वकामेभ्यो युक्त इत्युच्यते तदा ॥१८॥

yadā viniyataṁ cittam ātmany evāvatiṣṭhate ।
niḥspṛhaḥ sarvakāmebhyo yukta ity ucyate tadā ॥18॥

When the perfectly-controlled mind rests in the Self, free from longing for all enjoyments, then it is said that the yogī *is united.*

Three conditions to attain *mokṣa* are enumerated again in this verse.

niḥspṛhaḥ	:	Free from longing for desires.
cittaṁ viniyatam	:	Mind perfectly controlled.
ātmany evāvatiṣṭhate	:	Rest in the *ātmā* only.

Niḥspṛha: It means free from longing for desires. One can note a subtle difference in the word used. The Lord does not say free from desires. One should not cling to his desires.

For example, desire to become a doctor is not wrong, as long as the true purpose of becoming a doctor is kept in mind, i.e., to help the sick. But to cling to the desire of benefits one gets on becoming a doctor is not right.

This *niḥspṛha* automatically leads one later on to lose all desires. One has to burn the existing *vāsanā*s and this is done by *niṣkāma karma* and *karma-phala-tyāga.*

The first condition can therefore be termed as *vāsanā-kṣaya,* destruction of *vāsanā*s. The second condition is to train the mind to know who is the boss.

The mind should rest in the *ātmā*. The mind could rest in the Self only when it realises what the Self is. In other words such a person becomes a true *jñānī*. True *jñāna* is *tattvajñāna.* Automatically, such a person has attained *mokṣa*. It is the end-result to a perfect *dhyānī,* who fulfils the above three conditions.

The mind should be under the control of the intellect. The Lord states that it has to be perfectly controlled (*viniyatam*). This state of mind is called *manonāśa* (destruction of the mind).

The Lord says: "*niḥspṛhaḥ sarvakāmebhyo*". *Sarvakāma* includes desires for pleasures in this and the other world.

यथा दीपो निवातस्थो नेङ्गते सोपमा स्मृता ।
योगिनो यतचित्तस्य युञ्जतो योगमात्मनः ॥१९॥

***yathā dīpo nivātastho neṅgate sopamā smṛtā* I**
***yogino yatacittasya yuñjato yogam ātmanaḥ* II19II**

'As a lamp in a windless place does not flicker' is the comparison of the yogī *of controlled mind practising the* yoga *of the Self.*

For the *yogī* who has been practising *dhyāna-yoga,* and has reached the stage where he has become a *yogārūḍha*, his mind has only one constant thought. That is his lamp of knowledge and this lamp is steady. This has been compared to that of a lamp which is lit and is kept in a windless state.

Any student of physics knows that the flame actually consists of fast continuous flickering (as the matter that is being burnt particle by particle). As the frequency of flickering is so fast, it gives the appearance of a steady flame.

Similarly, the mind of a *yogārūḍha* produces sparks of *Brahman* so fast that his lamp of knowledge is steady and non-flickering. His knowledge, *jñāna*, is perfect and he is absorbed constantly in the self. The windows which bring in the wind to disturb the flame in a *yogārūḍha* are the five senses. All senses are so perfectly controlled that the mind does not get the wind of desires which will extinguish or disturb the flame of knowledge in that person.

यत्रोपरमते चित्तं निरुद्धं योगसेवया ।
यत्र चैवात्मनात्मानं पश्यन्नात्मनि तुष्यति ॥२०॥

yatroparamate cittaṁ niruddhaṁ yogasevayā |
yatra caivātmanātmānaṁ paśyann ātmani tuṣyati ||20||

When the mind rests, restrained by the practice of yoga *and when seeing the Self by the Self is delighted in Self.*

सुखमात्यन्तिकं यत्तद् बुद्धिग्राह्यमतीन्द्रियम् ।
वेत्ति यत्र न चैवायं स्थितश्चलति तत्त्वतः ॥२१॥

sukham ātyantikaṁ yat tad buddhigrāhyam atīndriyam |
vetti yatra na caivāyam sthitaś calati tattvataḥ ||21||

Where established, the yogī *knows that bliss which transcends the senses, which is understandable by the purified intellect only and from the experience of the Self does not even move from the reality.*

यं लब्ध्वा चापरं लाभं मन्यते नाधिकं ततः ।
यस्मिन्स्थितो न दुःखेन गुरुणापि विचाल्यते ॥२२॥

yaṁ labdhvā cāparaṁ lābhaṁ manyate nādhikaṁ tataḥ |
yasmin sthito na duḥkhena guruṇāpi vicālyate ||22||

Which having obtained, he does not think any other gain superior to it; wherein established, he is not moved even by great sorrow.

तं विद्याद्दुःखसंयोगवियोगं योगसंज्ञितम् ।
स निश्चयेन योक्तव्यो योगाऽनिर्विण्णचेतसा ॥२३॥

taṁ vidyād duḥkhasaṁyogaviyogaṁ yogasaṁjñitam |
sa niścayena yoktavyo yogonirviṇṇa-cetasā ||23||

Let it be known, as yoga, *and that* yoga *which is free from sorrow should be attained by the undespairing and determined mind.*

What has been described so far, has been put together in these four verses and in the last verse the Lord gives the specific definition of 'true *yoga*'.

We have our sense-organs which bring in impulses from the

outer world to the mind and they disturb the mind. The mind which is full of thoughts, analyses what it likes and what it does not like. If the intellect is not brought into use to analyse these reactions, one tends to be always looking for something which gives happiness always. We know that permanent happiness cannot be obtained from any material objects of the outer world.

Happiness and sorrow are only states of the mind. What is happiness to one is not happiness to others. The amount of pain one suffers from the pain-stimulus varies from person to person. So, one can definitely say that all these reactions are only in the mind.

Training the mind to understand the temporary nature of the impulses from the outer world is the first step in *dhyāna-yoga.* One has to know what he has to do and why he has to do anything. (Wind coming in through the windows, scatters the papers in the room. One must know that the wind is actually the reason for the disturbance, then find out where it is coming from and then go and shut the window.)

The next step is to find out where one gets peace and happiness which is not temporary. This is realised only by understanding one's real nature. ('The True Self' which is in all of us.)

The first verse states this fact by saying "when the mind rests, restrained by the practice of *yoga,* when seeing the Self, by the Self, is delighted in the Self". The inner Self should be seen by the outer unreal self which is ego.

When one realises the delight one gets by seeing the Self and understands that such bliss is permanent and well beyond the pleasures one gets from the senses, he will then try to shut away the senses and transcend them. He will go deeper and deeper to realise the Self and get established in that state.

We humans have intellect which is a powerful weapon. We have somehow kept it in a dark place and not sharpened it. Hence our intellect has gone dull and blunt.

If one can analyse all reactions which the mind makes or takes, one can stop the mind from running away. The ocean of the mind does not get waves of disturbances if intellectual capacity is used at all times. One should learn to remove the *tāmasika* and *rājasika* tendencies in his actions. To that extent his intellect will become *sāttvika* (pure). Only a *sāttvika* (purified) intellect knows and understands the "real nature" of all of us, i.e., "The *ātmā* or Self" in us.

When one knows the reality of oneself, that he is not the ego and that the "ego is false", (*jagat* is *mithyā* and *ātmā* is *satya*) by his purified intellect, he will not move away from this thought any time. This is the meaning of the second verse here.

The mind has now realised the two opposite types of happiness: one state where happiness is temporary and followed by sorrow; another state where happiness is pure bliss and is not followed by sorrow.

A *sāttvika* intellect can analyse and come to the conclusion that the bliss of *ātmā* is absolute bliss. For such a person, no great sorrow on earth can cause any disturbances. He takes every sorrow as a punishment for his past deeds. He also knows that by that sorrow a number of past *vāsanās* are burnt. He gets delight at the thought that the Lord is merciful and is burning his *vāsanā*s away. For example, think of a thief who is living in fear of being caught and sent to prison (our present life with past sins), caught by the police and taken to court and sent to prison (the sorrows we experience); then he comes out of the prison (our *vāsanā*s burnt) as a free man as far as that crime is concerned (free from that *vāsanā*). We should strive for pure work (not steal again).

Yaṁ labdhvā . . . vicālyate: The *yogī* at the end achieves that state when he realises that there is nothing greater than what he has achieved. This is the state of absolute bliss. No amount of sorrow from his contact with the outer world can disturb such a *yogī*. This is the meaning of the third verse.

The last verse defines that state as *yoga*. The Lord asks mankind to try to achieve that state. He does not want people to go into states of despair. He wants people to be determined in their efforts.

What is to be known by us? We are really "the Self". The

experience one gets on knowing the Self is *yoga*. The means to experience this is also *yoga*. The practice and result are both termed *yoga*. In other words, *yoga* is contact of ego with the Self. *Yoga* in ordinary terms can be interpreted as contact. The Lord uses the word *duḥkha-saṁyoga-viyoga*.

What does it mean? The contact of ego with the outer world bring sorrow, i.e., *duḥkha-saṁyoga*. *Viyoga* is detachment. *Saṁyoga* is attachment. To detach from attachment that produces pain and sorrow is *duḥkha-saṁyoga-viyoga*. This has to be total detachment at physical, mental and intellectual levels. This is possible by total contact with the *ātmā* or the pure blissful state. Attach yourself to the Real and bear with the unreal.

The Lord asks all *sādhaka*s to be determined in *yoga*-practice and not to despair because of temporary upsets in the path of spiritual progress by *dhyāna-yoga*.

संङ्कल्पप्रभवान्कामांस्त्यक्त्वा सर्वानशेषतः ।
मनसैवेन्द्रियग्रामं विनियम्य समन्ततः ॥२४॥

saṁkalpaprabhavān kāmāṁs tyaktvā sarvān aśeṣataḥ ।
manasaive'ndriyagrāmaṁ viniyamya samantataḥ ॥24॥

शनैः शनैरुपरमेद्बुद्ध्या धृतिगृहीतया ।
आत्मसंस्थं मनः कृत्वा न किञ्चिदपि चिन्तयेत् ॥२५॥

śanaiḥśanair uparamed buddhyā dhṛtigṛhītayā ।
ātmasaṁsthaṁ manaḥ kṛtvā na kiñcid api cintayet ॥25॥

Abandoning all desires born of saṁkalpa, *completely restraining the entire group of senses with the mind from all sides slowly and steadily, let him attain quietude by his intellect held firmly, and fixing the mind in* ātmā, *he should not think of anything else.*

Here again, the same technique has been described to emphasise its importance. In these two verses, the Lord has given a step by step process to be followed in *dhyāna-yoga*.

Saṁkalpaprabhavān kāmān tyaktvā: Desires born of *saṁkalpa* should be abandoned.

We all perform acts all the time voluntarily and involuntarily. Involuntary actions (like breathing) are necessary for survival. Voluntary actions are those that we decide to do. When we want something only then we act. We even keep quiet sometimes because we want to be quiet. To achieve something we act. We get a desire to achieve it and enjoy the benefit of the work.

Our nature (due to our *vāsanā*s) makes us act the way we do. We should not act because of desires for fruit of action.

Saṁkalpa means the resolve to do something. When there is no thought or resolve there will be no desire. The Lord commands that these desires born of *saṁkalpa* should be abandoned totally, without any trace (*sarvān aśeṣataḥ*).

There are three things in relation to one's contact with the outer world that should not have any trace left. They are disease, enemy and fire. Any trace of disease left will give a chance for the disease to get worse. Any part of the enemy force allowed to survive gives the chance for the enemy to get strong and fight back. A spark of fire allowed to remain can turn into a great fire and burn the forest. Similarly, all desires must be rooted out without any trace.

For example, there is a saying *kaupīna-saṁrakṣaṇārtham*. Once there was a *saṁnyāsī* who lived with bare necessities. He had only a loincloth to wear which he washed daily. Mice entered his hut and started chewing the cloth. To protect the cloth from mice, he got a cat. He needed to feed the cat. So he got a cow. To milk the cow, he married and asked the wife to milk the cow. Thus his desires multiplied.

We have learnt that desires cause agitations in the mind. By rooting out all desires one can get the mind to be quiet and calm.

All desires: This means both good and bad desires; even the desire to attain liberation should be given up.

It is the ego that binds us to our actions. If we can renounce our ego then actions do not bind us.

When we perform some *vrata*s like Satyanārāyaṇa *vrata*, we are asked by the priests to say "I do this *pūjā*" (*saṁkalpam*). Even this is wrong. "I" ness should not be there. You are performing the *pūjā* really to purify yourself and not to desire to achieve something. Even achieving purity should not be desired. The belief in the scriptures should be so strong that you perform the *pūjā/vrata* sincerely and drop the sense of 'I do this to get this'.

All senses must be restrained from all sides. This is the second step. Unless one has controlled his mind to give up all desires, sense-control will not work on its own. Giving up all desires automatically stengthens the mind. The strong mind will easily control the wild senses.

Controlling the mind and senses has to be a slow process (*śanaiḥ śanaiḥ*). There should not be force. Force will cause a jerk and by jerking one injures himself.

The next step is to use the intellect to hold the mind and senses firmly. This will bring a total sense of calmness of the mind. The intellect is higher than the mind and the mind is higher than the senses. The capacity to hold the mind firmly is *dhṛti*. It is a virtue one can develop by living a disciplined life.

If we now compare this to a chariot drawn by horses, we will understand this better. The horses of the chariot are the senses. They are wild. If not controlled, they pull the chariot in all directions and the chariot will not go on the straight path steadily. The reins must be strong to hold the horses. The mind should be like strong reins. The reins have to be controlled by the charioteer. The mind should be controlled by the intellect. The charioteer does not hold the reins very tight. He controls the reins so that the horses stop slowly.

So, in the path of *dhyāna-yoga* the intellect should control the mind always. If the mind is pure and godly the senses will not cause any disturbance. By constant thinking and discrimination (by intellect) the mind will be brought under control.

As the mind is a stream of flowing thoughts, thoughts of divinity only should be made to flow in it always. There should be oneness with the object of meditation. Constant thinking of *ātmā* (in *dhyāna*) without interruption is essential. To attain this highest state of *dhyāna*, to avoid any entry for thoughts other than the Self, the senses should be controlled totally from all sides.

In simple terms, one can say, "establish the mind in the self and do no think of anything else".

यतो यतो निश्चरति मनश्चञ्चलमस्थिरम् ।
ततस्ततो नियम्यैतदात्मन्येव वशं नयेत् ॥२६॥

yato yato niścarati manaś cañcalam asthiram |
tatas-tato niyamyaitad ātmany eva vaśaṁ nayet ||26||

Towards whatsoever sense-objects the moving and unsteady mind wanders away, from them all it should be withdrawn and fixed in ātmā.

This is a simple but firm statement. It just asks all to develop the habit of constantly reminding themselves not to relax even for a second. Stop the senses before they start pulling you away.

In a class-room, one is expected to concentrate on the lessons taught by the teacher. The student's mind tends to wander away from time to time to something other than the lessons. The teacher who knows this, shouts at that student and asks him to pay 'attention to lessons'. The teacher is the intellect and the student is the mind and lessons are the *ātmā*. One can understand the meaning of this verse better by this example.

Also, in the first term of the class, the teacher insists more on attention. But as the year comes to an end the true student knows the importance of the lessons and does not allow his mind to wander off easily from the lessons.

Similarly, in the early stages of *dhyāna-yoga*, the mind wanders but in the later stages the mind is able to fix itself on *ātmā*. By making the mind understand the painful nature of pleasures from worldly objects one purifies the mind. The purified mind can rest in *ātmā* by knowing that the bliss of *ātmā* is not followed by painful sorrow. It means from whatsoever objects and it does not mean from whatever reason. When someone is in *dhyāna,* he would then have selected a suitable, solitary place where there are no external disturbances. So, the senses have no reason in bringing in impulses that disturb the *sādhaka.*

But the *sādhaka*'s mind can think of objects, the memory of which is stored in it. The *sādhaka* must control the mind from opening its Pandora's box.

In the early stages the mind is *cañcala* (restless) and *asthira* (unsteady). The Lord asks the mind to be brought under the control of the Self alone (concentrate on *ātmā* always).

प्रशान्तमनसं ह्येनं योगिनं सुखमुत्तमम् ।
उपैति शान्तरजसं ब्रह्मभूतमकल्मषम् ॥२७॥

praśāntamanasaṁ hy enaṁ yoginaṁ sukham uttamam |
upaiti śāntarajasaṁ brahmabhūtam akalmaṣam ||27||

To this yogī, *whose mind is quiet and peaceful, of subdued* rajas, *who has become* Brahman, *free from evil, comes supreme bliss.*

We know that worldly pleasures do bring pains. Here the Lord is saying that by *dhyāna-yoga* one attains supreme bliss. A *dhyāna-yogī* will have to subdue his *rājasika* qualities. What are they? *Kāma-krodha,* etc. By giving up desires his mind is calm and by controlling *rajas*, he will not whip up any new desires. There is no use of looking for desires only.

Another important quality essential is *akalmaṣam.* One should root out the evil in oneself. For example, if we move into a house, we open all windows to let light in, to let fresh air in, and then clean the house of all dirt that has accumulated in the house. Similarly, we have accumulated *vāsanās* from previous births which are impurities. We must wash out all *vāsanās* and that is *akalmaṣam.*

We must also not bring in any new *vāsanās*. This is achieved by attaining the state of *sattva*. One can reach *sattva* by climbing over *rajas.* This is by purifying the mind from dirt of *kāma-krodha, lobha-moha,* etc. By this process, the new house will be so nice to look at and live in. Similarly, we find that this process gives us calm and peace.

One can only experience this state by cleaning the dirt out. The state of *Brahman* or pure bliss is only to be realised by experience. Slowly and steadily one can achieve this state of bliss. The person realises that he is none other than Him. *Dvaita* becomes *advaita*. *Brahma-bhūtam* is Self-realisation. There is no more duality in you. You are *ātmā* and nothing else. Ego rediscovers its true nature and drops off totally.

युञ्जन्नेवं सदात्मानं योगी विगतकल्मषः ।
सुखेन ब्रह्मसंस्पर्शमत्यन्तं सुखमश्नुते ॥२८॥

yuñjann evaṁ sadātmānaṁ yogī vigata-kalmaṣaḥ I
sukhena brahma-saṁsparśam atyantaṁ sukham aśnute II28II

The yogī *free from evil, practising* yoga, *easily enjoys the highest bliss resulting from contact with* Brahman.

A *yogī* is one who practises union with the Self. He is free from evil means, free from all existing *vāsanās*, his mind is pure, his mind is not agitated by the impulses from sense-organs and he does not dwell on memories of past pleasures.

Practising *yoga* means practising *dhyāna-yoga*. What does such *yogī* achieve? *Sukhena brahma-saṁsparśam.* He easily realises *Brahman*. What is *Brahman?* Infinite happiness—*atyantam sukham.* The Lord insists on *sadā* in this verse. The *yogī* must constantly follow the steps of procedure, i.e., he should be free from evil and totally absorbed in *dhyāna* on *ātmā*.

सर्वभूतस्थमात्मानं सर्वभूतानि चात्मनि ।
ईक्षते योगयुक्तात्मा सर्वत्र समदर्शनः ॥२९॥

sarvabhūtastham ātmānaṁ sarvabhūtāni cātmani I
īkṣate yogayuktātmā sarvatra samadarśanaḥ II29II

The yogī *harmonised in* yoga *sees the Self in all beings, and all beings in the Self. He sees the same everywhere.*

The Yogī Harmonised in Yoga

He is a *yogī* (sage) who has achieved union with the Self. This can be achieved by following any path like *karma, bhakti, jñāna* or *dhyāna*. The one who has dropped his ego and merged in *ātmā* automatically sees the pluralistic world as only a projection (reflection) of the Self. He sees no difference in the objects around him. For him, what he sees is 'Truth' everywhere.

Nāma-rūpa has no meaning for him. He sees *sat, cit, ānanda* everywhere around him. He has developed *ātmadṛṣṭi* in contrast to what we normally have, i.e., *dehadṛṣṭi* and *manodṛṣṭi.*

The final proof of God-realisation is experiencing the divinity inherent in all. The gold inherent in all gold jewellery is the same. Name and forms of jewellery are different. This is understood by the man of knowledge of the jewellery, i.e., the jeweller. He values jewellery on the amount of gold in it and not on its shape and external beauty.

If I love my wife and children, I do so because I get a feeling of oneness with my wife and children. By extending this attitude, love for all can be developed by realising the 'oneness' of all.

यो मां पश्यति सर्वत्र सर्वं च मयि पश्यति ।
तस्याहं न प्रणश्यामि स च मे न प्रणश्यति ॥३०॥

yo māṁ paśyati sarvatra sarvaṁ ca mayi paśyati |
tasyāhaṁ na praṇaśyāmi sa ca me na praṇaśyati ||30||

He who sees Me everywhere, and who sees everything in Me, he never gets separated from Me and I do not get separated from him.

The realised *yogī* has transcended the mind and intellect, and has dropped his ego and united with the Self. His ego does not project out analysing the pluralistic world. Here *paśyati* does not mean that he actually sees. If he did so, he drops down from the ladder of achievement and become ego once again.

Paśyati means realises. We, the ignorant are really misguided. The God in us has been forgotten and we consider the 'ego' as our masters. We are master over ourselves and our ego becomes strong. The actor, who is acting the part of a king on the stage, cannot continue acting like a king when he comes off the stage. If he does so, people would call him a fool.

Man should become God. When man becomes God (divine) he never gets separated from such a state because he is divinity himself (no taint of impurity of any sort, all the time).

"I do not get separated from him" (*na praṇaśyati*); My divinity will remain and the ego is united with it. That is the meaning of this statement. That person has no more ego.

The aim of a *yogī* is to develop the theme "To see the Lord in all and all in the Lord". In Vedāntic terms it is called *sarva-ātma-dṛṣti. Sarvaṁ viṣṇumayaṁ jagat,* is also a common saying. *Īśāvāsyam idaṁ sarvam,* says *Īśāvāsya Upaniṣad.* The meaning is the same in all these.

सर्वभूतस्थितं यो मां भजत्येकत्वमास्थितः ।
सर्वथा वर्तमानोऽपि स योगी मयि वर्तते ॥३१॥

***sarvabhūtasthitaṁ yo māṁ bhajaty ekatvam āsthitaḥ* I**
***sarvathā vartamāno'pi sa yogī mayi vartate* II31II**

He who worships Me abiding in all beings and who is established in unity, that yogī abides in Me whatever be his mode of action.

sarvabhūtasthitam	:	abiding in all beings.
māṁ bhajati	:	worships me
ekatvam āsthitaḥ	:	established in unity.

The one who has become a *yogī* attains that state by dropping his ego. He has established his unity with the Lord. He has also realised that the Self is the same everywhere. He sees the Lord in all beings. How should he act? He should worship him, who is in all. He knows that God is everywhere in and around him.

How should one worship? By not harming others. Love all; be kind and friendly to all. Do your best and help others in whatever way you can. Do your job well and selflessly. Dedicated, selfless act by all is the way for continuation of the Universe. "That *yogī* abides in Me, whatever be his mode of action", the Lord says.

This line states that actually one attaining the yogic state, should not always remain in meditation. He should work. Working and at the same time meditating on *ātmā* becomes his way of life.

Sarvathā vartamāno'pi sa yogī mayi vartate

"Whatever way he remains, whatever way he acts, he will abide in Me." The second half of the verse applies to the *yogī* who sees God in all and worships Him as such. He may be meditating, performing his obligatory duties or resting but his mind is fixed on the *Brahman*. One can ask, "what about a murderer?" If one is a *yogī*, he will not perform any sinful acts at all. A murderer can not therefore be a *yogī*.

आत्मौपम्येन सर्वत्र समं पश्यति योऽर्जुन ।
सुखं वा यदि वा दुःखं स योगी परमो मतः ॥३२॥

ātmaupamyena sarvatra samaṁ paśyati yo'rjuna |
sukhaṁ vā yadi vā duḥkhaṁ sa yogī paramo mataḥ ||32||

He who judges pleasure or pain everywhere by the same standard as he applies to himself, that yogī is considered to be the highest.

The highest *yogī* is one who sees the Self everywhere and acts accordingly. He has dropped his ego totally and finds satisfaction in the bliss of *ātmā*. He is an *ātmānanda* and as *ātmā* is the same everywhere, he is *jagat-paramātmānanda*.

How will he show it in his actions? This is explained in this verse. Whatever reaction he shows for pains and pleasures, whatever actions he takes in return for the results of pains and pleasures, he would apply it similarly to all living creatures. The theory of universal love and compassion is the theme of this verse. Such a person is kind to all, does not hate others, does not get jealous. He feels the pangs of hunger and bereavement of others similar to what he himself would feel in a similar situation. He also shares the happiness of others.

Just as we treat all parts of the body equally, we should treat all others in the world similarly. This includes animals as well. In our human body all parts and organs work for the mutual welfare of each other. Similarly we should work for the welfare of the Universe.

If a person is very happy because he has won a prize in the lottery, a *yogī* would not get jealous. If another person gets famous and is praised by the media, he does not get jealous. He feels sincerely happy for that person. Similarly, if he sees the suffering of others, it will hurt him. He will do his best to help that person to overcome his suffering.

It does not mean that he will give away all his wealth in one day to the sufferers and become penniless the next day. He will act in such a way that 'to the best of his capacity he will help'. He will not allow a beggar to be hit and thrown out of his house while he is enjoying a special meal. On the other hand, he will not overindulge in his personal luxuries. He thinks of others all the time.

अर्जुन उवाच

योऽयं योगस्त्वया प्रोक्तः साम्येन मधुसूदन ।
एतस्याहं न पश्यामि चञ्चलत्वात्स्थितिं स्थिराम् ॥३३॥

arjuna uvāca

***yo'yaṁ yogas tvayā proktaḥ sāmyena madhusūdana* |**
***etasyāhaṁ na paśyāmi cañcalatvāt sthitiṁ sthirām* ||33||**

Arjuna said

O Madhusūdana, this dhyāna-yoga *taught by you and attainable by equanimity, I am not able to see any stability for it on account of unsteadiness of mind.*

This state of Arjuna, where he admits his own personal inadequacies in power of concentration of the mind, is not special only to Arjuna. The sage-poet, Veda Vyāsa, has evidently put the statement into Arjuna's mouth and it is true of millions of us.

Sāmyena: Equanimity. Śrī Kṛṣṇa has asked Arjuna to see the Lord in all. This is not easy because the mind by its own nature is restless.

The mind is very active and it is difficult to concentrate on one point only. Even after years of practice, it is possible for the mind to fall away from the *ātmā*. One can imagine how Arjuna would have managed if he ran away from the battle. Arjuna thought the path (namely, *saṁnyāsa*) on the other side is beautiful. He had not really looked into what *dhyāna-yoga* was about. He was rather reckless when he said that he would rather be a *saṁnyāsī*.

Another subtle point to note in this verse is, how Arjuna is talking to Lord Kṛṣṇa. He has no hesitation in putting forward his own doubts. He is not, on the other hand, making fun of his teacher. He is sincerely expressing his inadequacies and nothing else. This should be the attitude of all while learning.

चञ्चलं हि मनः कृष्ण प्रमाथि बलवद्दृढम् ।
तस्याहं निग्रहं मन्ये वायोरिव सुदुष्करम् ॥३४॥

cañcalaṁ hi manaḥ kṛṣṇa pramāthi balavad dṛḍham |
tasyāhaṁ nigrahaṁ manye vāyor iva suduṣkaram ||34||

O Kṛṣṇa, the mind verily is restless, turbulent, strong and unyielding. I think it is as difficult to control as the wind.

Arjuna continues to express his fears and gives an example to support his views. The mind has four attributes:

It is restless: Thoughts flow in thousands and cause restlesness. It is difficult to suddenly drop all thoughts.

It is turbulent: The thoughts cause agitations in our mind. "What should I do for this, what should I get, how should I get" etc. are questions that flow in. The mind is so turbulent and hence the saying: 'A lazy mind is the devil's workshop'.

It is strong: If the mind comes across an object through its senses, and it likes it much and it gets attached to that object so strongly that it is very difficult to draw it away. (A thief's mind is always thinking of the next place where he is going to steal.)

Unyielding (dṛḍha): The temptation is so strong, and so deep-rooted that it is difficult to take the mind away from the temptation. Unless one puts the blinkers on the horse, and constantly holds on to the reins, it will not take the rider in a straight path.

This is like the wind. A gale-force wind has all these characteristics.

One has to burn the existing *vāsanās* and stop acquiring new ones. This is a slow process. It is achieved by first realising the truth that there is a divine power in us and then trying to bring it out slowly.

श्री भगवानुवाच
असंशयं महाबाहो मनो दुर्निग्रहं चलम् ।
अभ्यासेन तु कौन्तेय वैराग्येण च गृह्यते ॥३५॥

śrī bhagavān uvāca
asaṁśayaṁ mahābāho mano durnigrahaṁ calam I
abhyāsena tu kaunteya vairāgyeṇa ca gṛhyate II35II

The Lord said

O Mahābāhu, doubtless the mind is restless and difficult to control, but by practice, O son of Kunti, and by dispassion, it is controlled.

In reply to Arjuna's statement, the Lord, like a true teacher, agrees with his student. He does not get angry. He does not say, "What have you heard so far? Have I wasted my breath?"

While accepting the fact that it is difficult to control the mind which is restless due to agitation, Lord Kṛṣṇa gives in a nutshell the means to control it.

In the battlefield, there will be a lot of agitations and restless activity going on around every soldier. From all corners, soldiers may be overpowered by a strong warrior of the enemy force. But Arjuna was a highly skilled soldier. He was 'Mahābāhu', he had strong arms. He could send a number of arrows in one single action and wound a number of enemies at one go. He also had special weapons to kill strong soldiers. Hence Arjuna was 'Mahābāhu'. How did he become one? He was born in a kṣatriya family and trained to be a warrior.

Before the war, he did penance and obtained powerful weapons. He left his family under the care of elders, performed penance and came back. He did care for his family but at that time he practised *vairāgya* (dispassion). This was to achieve greater powers.

Why? He wanted to win the throne, which was a birthright for him and his brothers. Now, the Lord uses the same logic and tells Arjuna that practice and dispassion are needed to achieve liberation.

How to do this? One must be mighty-armed. The mind has to be single-pointed. One must possess strong will and kill the agitations before they start getting their roots in. The agitations are both from existing *vāsānas* and also new impulses coming in from the outer world. By constant practice one can achieve this. *Abhyāsa* is the first step.

Let us take the example of an Olympic runner. For this he has to be a runner first. He must have practised running daily. For the Olympic run, he must have been trained by a coach and won a few medals before. He then puts more effort for the run. 'Practice makes one perfect' is the saying of scholars; once practised, it becomes a way of life.

Similarly, we should develop this divine worship from childhood. We should get our children to get up early, wash and go to the prayer-room and pray for a while. We should let the children develop the habit of praying to God. Later on, it becomes a way of life for that child. Do we not clean our teeth as a way of life? Why? Because we do not want dental decay and we were taught to do it from childhood. We feel that something is not right on the days we do not clean our teeth.

The second step is *vairāgya*. *Vairāgya* means disinterest. It is opposite to *rāga*. *Rāga* is attachment to the objects we like. *Vairāgya* is not running away to a mountain resort to escape from attachment. *Vairāgya* is disinterest in:

(a) attachment to the objects around, and
(b) to the fruits of action.

We have discussed it before in *karma-yoga*. The attachment to the objects with a sense of detachment is *vairāgya*. You need to be attached to objects as part of society. But you should not hold on strongly to that object because that object is not eternal.

Someone or other has to be separated by death. Death is a fact of life. Death, disease, parting from someone should not cause depression. Similarly, not clinging to and living for fruits of action is *vairāgya*.

Your child's education is an example. You provide your child all the means to achieve the stipulated goal. If the child cannot achieve what you want it to, you should not be disappointed. You can do your best to help your child but do not live in the hope that the child will do what you want. That is *vairāgya*.

Vairāgya is difficult. Hence the Lord puts *abhyāsa* first. The Lord says, O Man, realise the Self in you. Practise spiritual exercise, make it a part of your life and develop dispassion. You will achieve liberation. Good habits will save you. Bad habits will ruin you.

असंयतात्मना योगो दुष्प्राप इति मे मतिः ।
वश्यात्मना तु यतता शक्योऽवाप्तुमुपायतः ॥३६॥

asaṁyatātmanā yogo duṣprāpa iti me matiḥ ।
vaśyātmanā tu yatatā śakyo'vāptum upāyataḥ ॥36॥

It is my idea that yoga *is not attainable by one whose mind is not controlled. But the self-controlled, striving, can obtain it by proper means.*

The Lord in this verse is expanding on what is *abhyāsa* in spiritual practice. Self-control is the *abhyāsa* one has to practise. There are two aspects in self-control. One is, controlling the mind from the outer world, and the other is, directing the mind towards the divine (*ātmā*).

The mind, as we know, receives impulses, makes impressions, keeps them in memory and brings out actions. It has sense-organs and organs of action for this purpose. In the younger days of learning, it is the elders who should give us ideas of what is wrong and what is right, divine, not divine, etc. They should train child to understand what is stealing, what are lies, what are morals, etc. This foundation, as the child grows, will help the child to have a stronger moral base. The temptations for the pleasure of the world is more in the teens and younger days. By the habit one develops from childhood one can control the mind in two ways: by not letting sense-organs bringing impulses to distract the mind, and by not letting the mind dwell on its memories of worldly pleasures. If one has not got these, he cannot attain *yoga* (Union with Self).

If, one has the practice of self-control, he can achieve *yoga*. The Lord uses the word *yatata*, which means 'striving'. Not only that, but Lord also says *upāyataḥ*, i.e., skilfully. The practice must be constant and skilful. The skills must be used properly. To control a powerful enemy, to convert him to be your friend, requires skill.

A student who is appearing for degree exams, must use his skills. He should not overload his mind but should give it rest whenever necessary. Skilfully, he spends his time in the college. He studies, rests and relaxes. He does not, suddenly, a month before, sit and burn the midnight oil and sleep only for a few hours a day. If he does so, his efforts will not yield the best results. Similarly, reading all the night before the exams, he will fall asleep on the examination table. A skilful student is ready for exams any day.

Similarly, spiritual progress is not merely through strict discipline, self-denial and self-punishment. "Striving rightly, control the mind", is the Lord's advice.

अर्जुन उवाच

अयतिः श्रद्धयोपेतो योगाच्चलितमानसः ।
अप्राप्य योगसंसिद्धिं कां गतिं कृष्ण गच्छति ॥३७॥

arjuna uvāca

ayatiḥ śraddhayopeto yogāc calitamānasaḥ |
aprāpya yogasaṁsiddhiṁ kāṁ gatiṁ kṛṣṇa gacchati ||37||

Arjuna said

Though possessing faith, yet uncontrolled, what end does the yogī *whose mind falls from* yoga, *meet if he departs without attaining perfoection in* yoga?

This is a very interesting question. Arjuna is saying to Kṛṣṇa:

> "Yes, I agree I have developed faith in the Self and I am moving in the spiritual path to liberation. Yes, I agree that I am still on the road to perfection. I have not attained liberation yet. But, if I die now, what happens?"

He wanted to get *brahmānanda.* He denied *dehānanda.* Suppose he die without getting both.

"If I do not know, when death is coming, should I at least get some form of *ānanda?"* It is a valid question. The answer will be simple if one understands philosophy.

Death is just another event in one's life-cycle of births and deaths. Yesterday is dead; tomorrow is not yet born. Every second gone is dead and we are reborn every second. They are all links in a chain. **Tomorrow is nothing but the continuation of yesterday but modified by thoughts of yesterday and actions of yesterday.**

Evidently, Arjuna has not understood this. The Lord will answer this question later.

कच्चिन्नोभयविभ्रष्टश्छिन्नाभ्रमिव नश्यति ।
अप्रतिष्ठो महाबाहो विमूढो ब्राह्मणः पथि ॥३८॥

kaccin nobhayavibhraṣṭaś chinnābhram iva naśyati |
apratiṣṭho mahābāho vimūḍho brahmaṇaḥ pathi ||38||

O Mahābāhu, not established in yoga, *and deluded in the path of* Brahman, *fallen from both does he not perish like a rent cloud?*

Chinnābhramiva: Like a rent cloud.

A mass of clouds sometimes get separated and some small cloudlets come out of the mass. These are called rent clouds. They are of no use to anybody. They get tossed hither and either by the winds and do not serve any useful purpose.

Likewise, Arjuna says, if one dies before achieving liberation, he has fallen from both. What is 'both'?

svarga	—	heavenly pleasures of this world.
mokṣa	—	eternal bliss.

Because he performed *niṣkāma karma* to attain liberation, the person did not enjoy the pleasures of the world. As he died before attaining liberation, he missed experiencing that eternal bliss. He lost both the types of pleasures.

एतन्मे संशयं कृष्ण छेत्तुमर्हस्यशेषतः ।
त्वदन्यः संशयस्यास्य छेत्ता न ह्युपपद्यते ॥३९॥

etan me saṁśayaṁ kṛṣṇa chettum arhasy aśeṣataḥ I
tvadanyaḥ saṁśayasyāsya chettā na hy upapadyate II39II

O Kṛṣṇa, you ought to dispel my doubt completely. I cannot indeed get another like you fit enough to clear it.

This verse confirms that Arjuna had faith and devotion in his teacher, Kṛṣṇa. One should not be arrogant in learning, from parents, elders or *guru.*

श्रीभगवानुवाच
पार्थ नैवेह नामुत्र विनाशस्तस्य विद्यते ।
न हि कल्याणकृत्कश्चिद्दुर्गतिं तात गच्छति ॥४०॥

śrī bhagavān uvāca
pārtha naiveha nāmutra vināśas tasya vidyate I
na hi kalyāṇakṛt kaścid durgatiṁ tāta gacchati II40II

The Lord said

O Pārtha, neither in this world, nor in the next world, is there destruction for him? O my son, never indeed anyone who does good ever comes to grief.

Kṛṣṇa, addressing Arjuna in a paternal way (O my son) is assuring him that good action brings good results.

As we discussed before, tomorrow is nothing but a continuation of yesterday. By our thoughts of yesterday and today, we are building our tomorrow. It is what we do now that gets proper results later. Whatever is done sincerely, with total commitment, will bring the best results.

By saying 'neither in this world, nor in the next', the Lord is asserting the theory of re-incarnation for all. Births and deaths are but incidents in our existence in the cycle of life.

For example, a student who sincerely studies and gets his degree will get his benefit in course of time. A farmer, who sows the seeds properly and looks after them at every stage of growth, will reap a good harvest later. He may have accidental mishaps (cyclones, locusts, etc.) in years but in his course of farming years, accidents do not happen every year.

Some might argue, "what about unemployment for degree graduates?" Yes, it is there. One way of looking at it is, you are probably looking at yesterday's work and its results. What about the days gone by? You do not know. You have to pay for actions/ thoughts of those days also.

प्राप्य पुण्यकृतांल्लोकानुषित्वा शाश्वतीः समाः ।
शुचीनां श्रीमतां गेहे योगभ्रष्टोऽभिजायते ॥४१॥

***prāpya puṇyakṛtāṁ lokān uṣitvā śāśvatīḥ samāḥ* |**
***śucīnāṁ śrīmatāṁ gehe yogabhraṣṭo'bhijāyate* ||41||**

The yogī *who has fallen from* yoga, *attains the worlds of the good, and having lived there for many years, is born in the house of the pure and prosperous.*

Yogabhraṣta: A *yogī* who dies without attaining perfection.

For having attempted to purify himself, for having realised the existence of divinity, the *yogī* who dies prematurely will get just rewards.

First of all he will go to the plane of consciousness, that fulfils his desires of the past. Having enjoyed the fruits of actions (desires), the Lord says, he will be given a proper environment to be born again. This will be a place which is pure and prosperous. The Lord mentions pure first and prosperous next.

By pure, he means that his family members will provide proper moral upbringing. It will be like a spiritual home. Prosperous does not mean full of richness in terms of money only. It means, the home would be a place where there is no poverty, where daily physical needs are sufficient for a simple life. If one has to live in poverty where one does not know where his next meal is coming from, the discipline for spiritual work will not be adequate.

"Prosperous" does not apply only to material wealth. It could mean prosperity in health, food, etc.

A pure and prosperous home will act as a good foundation in the next birth for the *yogī* to continue his discipline. He will reach better heights in course of time.

अथवा योगिनामेव कुले भवति धीमताम् ।
एतद्धि दुर्लभतरं लोके जन्म यदीदृशम् ॥४२॥

athavā yogināṁ eva kule bhavati dhīmatām |
etaddhi durlabhataraṁ loke janma yad īdṛśam ||42||

Or, he is even born in the family of the wise yogīs. *This kind of birth is indeed very difficult to attain.*

Or the *yogī*, who has attained higher levels in the present, will get best results in future. He will be born in the family of *yogīs*.

By having been born in such a household, the *yogī* has a chance to carry on his spiritual *sādhanā* from a very early age. He will be seeing the work of his *yogī* parents from childhood, he will be taught by such *yogī* parents. It is a great boon but very few people attain this state.

Here, the Lord does not say that he will attain the worlds of the good. The *yogī* will immediately be born in the household of *yogīs*. For this, he must have reached high levels of purity.

This principle applies to followers of any of the four paths of liberation.

तत्र तं बुद्धिसंयोगं लभते पौर्वदेहिकम् ।
यतते च ततो भूयः संसिद्धौ कुरुनन्दन ॥४३॥

tatra taṁ buddhi-saṁyogaṁ labhate paurvadehikam |
yatate ca tato bhūyaḥ saṁsiddhau kurunandana ||43||

O Arjuna, being born in the family of yogīs, *he comes to be united with the knowledge acquired in his previous birth, and again strives for perfection in* yoga.

If one can read between the lines here, it will be possible to grasp the theory of re-incarnation.

The knowledge one acquires will be what is stored in one's memory, in his mind. The mind is the subtle body. The physical body is our gross body made up of the five gross elements.

For the *yogabhraṣṭa*, who has attained higher levels of progress in *yoga* before his death, his subtle body will be carrying all the good *vāsanās*. As soon as it acquires a new body, it will express the good *vāsanās* in actions and thoughts. He will immediately strive to attain liberation.

In a negative way, one should understand the same principle for bad actions/thoughts. The mind with such bad *vāsanās* will go to the next birth with impure *vāsanās* to be born with. If we can realise this, it will be the first step in purifying ourselves.

Man is the maker of his own destiny. He get results of what he has sown in the past. Our bank balance is either healthy or overdrawn depending on what we have used.

पूर्वाभ्यासेन तेनैव ह्रियते ह्यवशोऽपि सः ।
जिज्ञासुरपि योगस्य शब्दब्रह्मातिवर्तते ॥४४॥

pūrvābhyāsena tenaiva hriyate hy avaśo'pi saḥ |
jijñāsur api yogasya śabdabrahmātivartate ||44||

By the force of practice in the past birth, he is drawn to yoga *without volition. Though, desirous only of the knowledge of* yoga, *he transcends beyond* śabdabrahma.

The *yogī* who really reached higher levels of achievement but died before achieving liberation, is immediately drawn to *yoga.* He will be like a fish left in water. Fish takes to water and need not be taught to swim. It will be easy for the new born to follow any of the spiritual paths.

In the second half of the verse, the Lord declares some benefits of knowledge.

The first part of the *Vedas* is *karma-kāṇḍa.* The Second part is *upāsanā-kāṇḍa* and the third part is *jñāna-kāṇḍa.*

Karma-kāṇḍa describes rituals and benefits from rituals. If one desirous of a particular benefit performs the proper ritual, he will get it, it says. But, if one wants to know the Supreme, the knowledge, it means he is not desirous of material benefits. "Even a desire to know the Supreme", the Lord says, "is beneficial".

Śabda-brahman: What does it mean? *Brahman,* The Creator first produced the knowledge, that is the *Vedas*. *Śabda* that came from *Brahman* means the *Vedas*. 'Beyond *śabda-brahman'* means 'beyond *Vedas*'. Such a person achieves "supreme knowledge". It means one attains *mokṣa*. It does not mean that the immediate result is *mokṣa*. Wanting to know is the first step towards the goal to achieve.

प्रयत्नाद्यतमानस्तु योगी संशुद्धकिल्बिषः ।
अनेकजन्मसंसिद्धस्ततो याति परां गतिम् ॥४५॥

***prayatnād yatamānas tu yogī saṁśuddhakilbiṣaḥ* |**
***anekajanmasaṁsiddhas tato yāti parāṁ gatim* ||45||**

The yogī *who is practising sincerely and hard, having acquired perfection through many births attains the supreme state purified of all sins.*

pryatnāt	:	trying
yatamānaḥ	:	striving

What is the *yogī* striving to achieve? He is trying to achieve liberation. How does he achieve it? By practice. By practising any of the four paths to liberation, one can achieve the state of a pure *yogī*. He is trying to purify himself of all sins.

How is purity achieved? By using the intellect. By analysing right and wrong. By realising the true nature of the *ātmā*. Afterwards, performance of *niṣkāma karma* will burn the existing *vāsanās*. What about acquiring new *vāsanās*?

By *karma-phala-tyāga* and meditating on the *ātmā*, no new *vāsanās* come in. One is achieving a *vāsanā*-less state of mind which is the only way towards final liberation.

How long does it take? It depends on your existing *vāsanās*. It may take several births to achieve perfection and purity. Once the mind starts to clear impurities, it will be possible to achieve *mokṣa* even in this birth. When the Lord says it takes several births, nobody should be disheartened. There is no quick and easy way to success. Success needs planning and determination. These two take a long time. Once they are acquired, success is very easy.

Similarly, clearing *vāsanās* and fixing the mind totally on *ātmā* by totally dropping the ego, takes a long time. Afterwards it is very quick indeed.

तपस्विभ्योऽधिको योगी ज्ञानिभ्योऽपि मतोऽधिकः ।
कर्मिभ्यश्चाधिको योगी तस्माद्योगी भवार्जुन ॥४६॥

tapasvibhyo'dhiko yogī jñānibhyo'pi mato'dhikaḥ I
karmibhyaś cādhiko yogī tasmād yogī bhavārjuna II46II

The yogī *is thought to be greater than the ascetic, even superior to men of knowledge. He is also superior to men of action. Therefore, strive to be a* yogī. *O Arjuna.*

Śrī Kṛṣṇa is saying that *dhyāna-yoga* is superior to all other types of *yoga*, i.e., *bhakti*, *jñāna, karma.*

One should not misunderstand this statement and say that the best way to achieve the best is by following the best path viz., *dhyāna-yoga.* This is wrong. If one has understood the Lord's teaching so far, one can understand that the four paths are intermingled and the final goal achieved is the same. Also, the true state of *dhyāna-yoga* is at a higher level on the path to liberation.

One has to climb many, many steps to achieve *mokṣa*. *Dhyāna-*

yoga's rung in the ladder is nearer to the top. One has to perform work (*karma*), have love in divinity (*bhakti*), acquire knowledge (*jñāna*) and then meditate on *ātmā* by dropping the ego (*dhyāna*). After several births of *karma, bhakti* and *jñāna* to purify the mind, one can come to a state where he becomes a *dhyānī*. Once he becomes a true *dhyana-yogī*, he will attain *mokṣa* quickly.

The Lord now states whom he considers the best of *yogīs*.

योगिनामपि सर्वेषां मद्गतेनान्तरात्मना ।
श्रद्धावान्भजते यो मां स मे युक्ततमो मतः ॥४७॥

yoginām api sarveṣāṁ madgatenāntarātmanā |
śraddhāvān bhajate yo māṁ sa me yuktatamo mataḥ ||47||

Even among all the yogīs, *he who worships Me with mind fixed in Me, full of faith, is deemed to be the most devout* (yogī).

The concluding statement in this chapter by Lord Kṛṣṇa is that love of the Self, and dedication to what one loves is the best path.

There are different types of *yogīs*. Some may be trying for fulfilment of some worldly pleasures and pray to minor detieis and *devas*. It is then *sakāma yoga*. If one performs *yoga* not for worldly pleasures but to attain liberation, such a *yogī* is the best.

The purpose of *dhyāna* is of course to unite with the Self totally. But the world of plurality the ego enjoys, is so vast and apparently beautiful, that one will find it difficult to drop it and go to the Self. By knowing about the Self, by believing about the Self, by worshipping the divine Self, one can attempt to drop the ego. To do this, one must learn the art of worship. One must have faith in what one is doing. Faith and dedication are essential pre-requisites to achieve success in any field of activity.

In the practical world, in any course of higher studies, we find a variety of students. The majority would have come only to pass the exams. A few would have come to enjoy and to know what university life is about. Among those who want to pass, there are those who do not really know what actually they get and achieve in the end. "I want to be a nurse, I want to be a doctor,

I want to be a vet", is all they care about. What actually the nurse does and achieve, what actually a doctor does and achieve is not known by the majority of students.

The best of the students are those who know completely what the professionals in any profession can achieve. Such students develop a sense of love for that profession, they put all their faith in it and put their best efforts to achieve it. It is but natural that they will become best in that profession and do well in their exams.

Similalry, the one who loves the inner Self, who has merged his mind and intellect in the Self, who has faith in the Self, is the best of those *yogīs* who have taken up the path of *dhyāna.*

The *Gītā,* consisting of 18 chapters, aims at explaining the fundamental principle underlying the *mahāvākya, tat tvam asi,* Thou Art That.

TAT: That	
TVAM: Thou	What art thou?
ASI: Art	Thou Art The Self.

This is the fundamental truth. It is *advaita* philosophy. There are no two entities such as you and God. There are only two entities, viz., Self and ego (true and false). There is only one truth and that is, "You are the Self".

In this explanation of the fundamental principle the first six chapters have dwelt on the 'Thou' (*tvam*) aspect of it. Arjuna's question in the first chapter was to show the false 'I' in us. *Sāṁkhya-yoga* described about the true 'I' in us. *Karma, jñāna, dhyāna* and *karma-saṁnyāsa yoga*s explained the methods in dropping the false 'I'. Hence the first six chapters make one-third of the *Gītā*'s doctrine "*TAT TVAM ASI*". Scholars say that the first six chapters deal with the '*tvam*' aspect of *tat tvam asi,* the second six chapters with the '*tat*' aspect and the last six chapters with the '*asi*' aspect. From the next chapter onwards we shall see the second section of this three-section discourse.

इति श्रीमद्भगवद्गीतासूपनिषत्सु ब्रह्मविद्यायां योगशास्त्रे
श्रीकृष्णार्जुनसंवादे आत्मसंयमयोगो नाम षष्ठोऽध्यायः ॥

iti śrīmadbhagavadgītāsūpaniṣatsu brahmavidyāyāṁ yogaśāstre
śrīkṛṣṇārjuna-saṁvāde ātmasaṁyama-yogo
***nāma ṣaṣṭho'dhyāyaḥ* ॥**

CHAPTER 7

JÑĀNA-VIJÑĀNA-YOGA

Chapters 7-12 are considered as dealing with *TAT*, i.e., "THAT" aspect of *tat tvam asi.* This chapter deals with the excellence and significance of the Self.

Jñāna is knowledge. *Vijñāna* is wisdom. Knowledge can be had by learning theory, by reading scriptures, etc. One can impart knowledge to others.

When a person practically experiences the knowledge he has acquired, he becomes wiser. He will be called a man-of-wisdom. Wisdom makes one a better person. The purpose of religion is to make us men-of-wisdom. The Philosophy of religion gives knowledge. When people live that knowledge and experience practically what is said, they are considered as wise.

For example, a child is told by her mother repeatedly that fire burns and she is asked not to touch it. The same child like a parrot repeats to others who go near the fire that it burns and tells them not to touch it. That child is a *jñānī* as far as the theory of fire is concerned.

When the child, out of curiosity or by accident, touches it, she will experience the heat of fire and might even get hurt. The child is then said to be a *vijñānī* as far as the heat-property of fire is considered. The child becomes wiser.

Similarly, a real *vijñānī* is one who has experienced the philosophy of religion. *Tat* means 'That' and 'That' is *ātmā* or *Paramātmā* which pervades the whole universe and is in every individaul.

Experience of the knowledge that is to be known (i.e., *ātmā*) is *vijñāna*.

श्रीभगवानुवाच

मय्यासक्तमनाः पार्थ योगं युञ्जन्मदाश्रयः ।
असंशयं समग्रं मां यथा ज्ञास्यसि तच्छृणु ॥१॥

śrī bhagavān uvāca
mayy āsaktamanāḥ pārtha yogaṁ yuñjan madāśrayaḥ |
asaṁśayaṁ samagraṁ māṁ yathā jñāsyasi tacchṛṇu ||1||

The Lord said

O Pārtha, how with the mind intent on Me, practising yoga *and taking refuge in Me, you shall know Me fully, doubtlessly, thou hear.*

Many people would want to know the Lord. They can read scriptures, philosophical books and learn about the Lord. They are only theoretical people. There could even be some masters in theory. They actually have not lived the principles of life as laid down in the books and have no direct experience of the essence of religion.

The Lord therefore says that:

Know Me fully and doubtlessly: One should know about the Lord as fully as possible. Taking a step here, a step there, to know merely is not knowing it completely.

Also, one should not have doubt in the Lord. Only those people who have experience can say they have no doubt about the Lord. Theoretical masters will still have doubt on what they have learnt, but when they experience it, they will have no doubts.

The bliss one gets on attachment to the Lord is experienced individually. It can never be explained. Understanding the temporary nature of worldly pleasure also comes by experiencing and realising the sorrow that follows these pleasures.

How should one know the Lord then? The Lord puts three conditions:

(a) mind absorbed in Him,
(b) taking refuge in Him,
(c) practising *yoga.*

The mind as we know is like a revolving torch-light. It lights up only that on which the light is directed. If the light of the torch is directed outwards, one sees the world as it is. If it is directed inwards, it will show the *ātmā*. Keeping that torch constantly directed towards *ātmā* is what is meant by "Mind absorbed in

Me". See Him always, hear Him always, touch Him always, smell Him always, digest Him always. Whatever your senses do, see the God in that and eliminate the undivine in that impulse.

To take refuge in Him: One should consider the Lord as his sole saviour. Total faith in the Lord would help him overcome all the worldly pains. One should therefore be a total *bhakta* of the Lord. As a *bhakta* or devotee, he should practise the *yoga* of meditation. This was the teaching of the Lord in the last section of the last chapter. The Lord has taken up and eleborated on that theme in this chapter.

ज्ञानं तेऽहं सविज्ञानमिदं वक्ष्याम्यशेषतः ।
यज्ज्ञात्वा नेह भूयोऽन्यज्ज्ञातव्यमवशिष्यते ॥२॥

***jñānaṁ te'haṁ savijñānam idaṁ vakṣyāmy aśeṣataḥ* I**
***yaj jñātvā ne'ha bhūyo'nyaj jñātavyam avaśiṣyate* II2II**

Knowing which there shall not be any other to be known in this world, that knowledge combined with experience, I shall declare to you totally.

All the knowledge of different things in the world is of course good but it is not complete. There is still something more to be known. By knowing the basic principle behind the existence of this universe, there will not be anything more to know.

The Lord is telling Arjuna that he will teach him that knowledge, experiencing which, there would be nothing else to know.

मनुष्याणां सहस्रेषु कश्चिद्यतति सिद्धये ।
यततामपि सिद्धानां कश्चिन्मां वेत्ति तत्त्वतः ॥३॥

***manuṣyāṇāṁ sahasreṣu kaścid yatati siddhaye* I**
***yatatām api siddhānāṁ kaścin māṁ vetti tattvataḥ* II3II**

Among thousands of men, one strives for perfection, and even among those who strive and succeed, only some will know Me in essence.

This is not to be taken as discouraging statement to make the student run away before he starts his lessons. One must be made to understand how hard the 'path to perfection' is. Only to make the *sādhaka* put in his 'best efforts' in his path is the purpose of the Lord.

Let us take the example of sports. Generally, only a small percentage of people take up sports. The highest achievement in sports would be winning the Olympic gold medal. If one explains that only one athlete can win the gold medal in one event, it does not mean other athletes should drop off immediately. It is only to make that athlete fix his eye on the ultimate glory in that field and put in his best effort to achieve it. In this process only a few people succeed to a level where they become national champions. Among those national champions, only one will win the gold medal at the Olympics.

If this be so in sports, how hard it will be to achieve *mokṣa*, (realise *ātmā*)? Just as practising a field event makes the person a healthy man, practising philosophy makes one a better intellectual person. As the Lord has said before, one achieves success (by preserving) in the course of his births and deaths because he will be given the necessary environment always to pursue his path.

The Lord emphasises by using the word *tattvataḥ*. It means the need to know Him in essence totally. Superficial knowledge is not enough. Very few people would know Him fully by practically experiencing Him totally.

भूमिरापोऽनलो वायुः खं मनो बुद्धिरेव च ।
अहङ्कार इतीयं मे भिन्ना प्रकृतिरष्टधा ॥४॥

bhūmir āpo'nalo vāyuḥ khaṁ mano buddhir eva ca |
ahaṁkāra itīyaṁ me bhinnā prakṛtir aṣṭadhā ||4||

Earth, water, fire, air, ether, mind, reason and ego are the eight-fold division of my nature.

Hindu philosophy believes that the union of the spirit with the matter is responsible for life as we know. The spirit is the life-element and is known as *puruṣa*. Matter is insentient and gets vitalised by the spirit. Matter is known as *prakṛti*. The Lord explains as to what constitutes *prakṛti*.

The five great elements are represented microcosmically in each individual by the five sense-organs. Sense-organs are the medium through which an individual experiences and comes to live with the sense-objects in the world around.

The sense-organs with the organs of action form the physical body. The impulses that reach inside us and the focal point they reach and where analysis takes place is the mind. The mind sends necessary impulses to the organs of action to act specifically.

We humans have a reasoning capacity called intellect. This helps us to act properly if it is wisely made use of. It makes us not to act by impulse as animals do. These two (i.e., mind and the intellect) form the subtle body.

The Self within the *puruṣa* when He identifies Himself with the subtle and physical body becomes the ego or *jīva*. The ego has to rediscover itself to be nothing other than the Self and drop itself off. The 'I'-ness at physical, mental and intellectual level is ego. The merging of 'I'-ness with the Self is called liberation.

The Lord has enumerated the five great elements along with the mind, intellect and ego as his *prakṛti* (Nature). Without the *prakṛti*, the *puruṣa* cannot shine forth. *Prakṛti* is the medium for *puruṣa* to express Himself and somewhere in the middle, the real *puruṣa* is forgotten. The shadow or reflection in the mirror is believed to be real. The real behind the shadow or mirror, looks upon the foolishness of the false real and waits for it to realise the Truth. The drama of life lasts until this Truth is realised.

अपरेयमितस्त्वन्यां प्रकृतिं विद्धि मे पराम् ।
जीवभूतां महाबाहो ययेदं धार्यते जगत् ॥५॥

apareyam itas tv anyāṁ prakṛtiṁ viddhi me parām |
jīvabhūtāṁ mahābāho yayedaṁ dhāryate jagat ||5||

O Arjuna. This is lower prakṛti. *Know my other nature, the higher—*parāprakṛti, *the life-element by which the universe is upheld.*

In the last verse, the five gross elements, senses, mind and ego were put together as *prakṛti.* The Lord is saying that it is *aparā prakṛti* or lower, outwardly manifested nature of Himself.

The lower nature is controlled by what is called awareness of Conscious Principle. It is this spiritual entity that makes the body vibrate with life. This consciousness makes us aware of all our actions with the world outside. This can be called our personality state.

Parāprakṛti upholds the universe: We have learnt before that the universe is what we perceive through our sense-organs and what our mind interprets. Without our consciousness this opinion of what the universe is, cannot be sustained. Hence the statement that consciousness upholds the universe. The universe is there because we are aware of it. If we were not aware of it, as far as we are concerned, it does not exist. The senses send the impulses to the brain but if there is no awareness, the brain does not react. There is consciously or subconsciously a sense of awareness in all our actions and this is the higher nature of the Lord.

एतद्योनीनि भूतानि सर्वाणीत्युपधारय ।
अहं कृत्स्नस्य जगतः प्रभवः प्रलयस्तथा ॥६॥

etadyonīni bhūtāni sarvāṇīty upadhāraya |
ahaṁ kṛtsnasya jagataḥ prabhavaḥ pralayas tathā ||6||

Know this (prakṛti) *to be the womb of all beings. I am the source of creation and dissolution of the whole universe.*

This can be understood by the example of the fuel and the car. The fuel is the 'spirit' in us, 'the energy' in us. The *parā* and *aparā prakṛtis* will be the car, the inert matter, and the driver of the car.

Without the energy from the petrol, the car is like dead matter. When the ignition is turned on, the car moves, i.e., comes to life. When the ignition is turned off, the car comes to a halt. Similarly, without the Self or *ātmā* in us, the *prakṛti* elements in us are dead and with the Self in, they become a living being. Likewise, the whole universe comes out of *Brahman* and gets dissolved in *Brahman* (Primordial Energy).

Unfortunately, on coming to life, the Self identifying with the *prakṛti* forgets its divine nature and suffers. On rediscovery of its true nature, it drops off the *prakṛti*-identification and enjoys the bliss which is its true nature.

मत्तः परतरं नान्यत्किञ्चिदस्ति धनञ्जय ।
मयि सर्वमिदं प्रोतं सूत्रे मणिगणा इव ॥७॥

mattaḥ parataraṁ nānyat kiñcid asti dhanañjaya |
mayi sarvam idaṁ protaṁ sūtre maṇigaṇā iva ||7||

O Dhanañjaya, there is nothing whatsoever higher than Me. All this is strung in Me, as clusters of gems on a string.

The principle of God, the primordial energy holding the world together is brought out in this verse by the use of a beautiful simile. By using that simile, the idea that God is higher than all of us is also brought out.

There are a number of gems of different shapes, colours and sizes. They are all individual entities. When they are strung together, they form a necklace. They all become 'One', viz., the necklace. The person who looks at the necklace looks at the beauty of each gem. An intelligent man, while appreciating the gems in the necklace would be aware of the string that holds them together. Without the string the gems fall out loosely and lose their unity.

Similarly, the world is made up of gems of different living creatures (including men of different races, cultures, religions, etc.). The principle that sustains them together, without which they cannot exist, is the Divine Energy or God. This cannot be seen by the naked eye. This is something one has to get a knowledge of. The eye of knowledge can only realise the divinity behind the existence of the universe. The eye of an ignorant, egotistical person does not see and accept this principle. Spiritual knowledge opens the eyes of the ignorant to realise the principle that God is the sustaining force in the universe.

रसोऽहमप्सु कौन्तेय प्रभास्मि शशिसूर्ययोः ।
प्रणवः सर्ववेदेषु शब्दः खे पौरुषं नृषु ॥८॥

raso'ham apsu kaunteya prabhāsmi śaśisūryayoḥ |
praṇavaḥ sarvavedeṣu śabdaḥ khe pauruṣaṁ nṛṣu ||8||

I am the sapidity in water. I am the light in the moon and sun and I am the syllable OṀ in all Vedas. *I am sound in ether and virility in men, O Kaunteya.*

The basic principle of *dharma* or the Law of Being is the 'divine principle'. Without that principle, a being has no existence.

The principle of water is its taste. The principle of fire is brilliance like the Sun (light). The principle of ether is sound. The principle of earth is its fragrance and the principle of air is touch. The five elements and the five senses (touch, taste, sound, smell and vision) are brought out in these five examples.

"I am *OṀ* in all *Veda*s". What does this mean? A word is nothing but a form of expression to denote an object; e.g., 'apple' means the fruit (apple) we know of. Our *Vedic ṛṣi*s realised that *Brahman* is responsible for creating and sustaining the universe. As He has no form or shape, and He is beyond all, the word *OṀ* was brought to mean *Brahman.*

The entire *Veda*s are meant for one to realise *Brahman.* So, the essence of all *Veda*s is *Brahman,* expressed as *OṀ.*

I am virility in all beings: Virility is a divine quality. Virility is responsible for creation of new beings and sustaining the continuity. If there were no new births, the universe would have come to standstill.

पुण्यो गन्धः पृथिव्यां च तेजश्चास्मि विभावसौ ।
जीवनं सर्वभूतेषु तपश्चास्मि तपस्विषु ॥९॥

puṇyo gandhaḥ pṛthivyāṁ ca tejaś cāsmi vibhāvasau |
jīvanaṁ sarvabhūteṣu tapaś cāsmi tapasviṣu ||9||

I am the sweet fragrance in the earth, the brilliance in the fire, life in all beings and austerity in ascetics.

In essence, the principal character of everything is divinity of the Lord himself.

बीजं मां सर्वभूतानां विद्धि पार्थ सनातनम् ।
बुद्धिर्बुद्धिमतामस्मि तेजस्तेजस्विनामहम् ॥१०॥

***bījaṁ māṁ sarvabhūtānāṁ viddhi pārtha sanātanam* I**
***buddhir buddhimatām asmi tejas tejasvinām aham* II10II**

O Arjuna, know Me as the eternal seed of all beings. I am the intelligence of the wise and I am the splendour of the splendid.

Continuing to give examples of different objects, expressing the fundamental principle of existence, the Lord confirms that he is "that fundamental principle". Because of him an object has its existence and all the other features of that object cannot exist without it. (Fire has heat, colour, flame, sparks, etc. Of these brilliant heat is the principle. Other features do not exist if there is no brilliance.)

He says that He is the eternal seed of all beings (*mūla puruṣa*). There is no question of egg and chicken. He is the first seed and all beings come later. By this, He confirms that we are all carrying a part of Him in us because of the law of inheritance which is the scientific principle we know of. That part which we are carrying is "The Self" or *ātmā.*

The intelligence (conscious principle) of an intelligent man and splendour of the splendid is also the Lord.

बलं बलवतामस्मि कामरागविवर्जितम् ।
धर्माविरुद्धो भूतेषु कामोऽस्मि भरतर्षभ ॥११॥

***balaṁ balavatām asmi kāma-rāga-vivarjitam* I**
***dharmāviruddho bhūteṣu kāmo'smi bharatarṣabha* II11II**

O best amongst the Bharatas, I am the strength of the strong, devoid of desire and attachment; and in all beings I am desire not contrary to dharma.

This is a verse with great meaning. One should analyse it in great detail.

Balaṁ balavatāmasmi, kāmarāgavivarjitam: I am the strength of the strong, devoid of desire and attachment.

Śrī Śaṅkarācārya has given a clear distinction between *kāma* and *rāga*. *Kāma*, he says, is "desire for what is not with the person" and *rāga* is "affection for what the person already has".

To get what one has not got and not to lose that to which he is attached, one uses his strength. That strength of any person who is doing good work for the society, or divine worship, employing it for selfless work, will get divine power.

Dharmāviruddho bhūteṣu, kāmo'msi: "I am desire unopposed to *dharma*".

We all have lots of desires. Our mind is full of ideas to fulfil the desires. There are thousands of waves of thoughts that go through the ocean of the mind always.

Some desires are for the good of the family and society without any evil in them. Bad desires, contrary to *dharma* are those that involve running after gratification of sense-desires (lust and greed). For example, if one wants to be a professional only for the purpose of making money with which he will enjoy luxuries beyond his means, that desire is *adharma*. There is no divinity in it. Such a person will eventually ruin himself and will not go to spiritual heights.

Desires to relieve the suffering of others and those towards welfare of the family (according to scriptures) are said to be divine and the Lord is such desire behind that action.

All actions (physical), thoughts (mental) and ideas (intellectual level) entertained by the person sanctioned by the scriptures is *dharma*. They would not be opposed to his essential divine nature. Taking the same example as before, the person who wants to be a doctor, is said to have divinity in his desire if he has no selfish motive behind the desire. The first conscious thought to become a doctor should be to relieve the suffering of others. Of course getting the proper reward for such action is not wrong. Charging a fee is not wrong. (The fee has to be reasonable.)

The ultimate stage to be reached in spiritual progress, of course, is where there should be no desires at all. That stage is *nirviṣaya* state of mind. Be contented in the Self and do not even have a desire for *mokṣa,* is the Lord's advice to all in their spiritual path.

All desires according to the above explanation, which are contrary to the essential nature of the person, will then become unrighteous, i.e., *adharma.*

ये चैव सात्त्विका भावा राजसास्तामसाश्च ये ।
मत्त एवेति तान्विद्धि न त्वहं तेषु ते मयि ॥१२॥

***ye caiva sāttvikā bhāvā rājasās tāmasāśca ye* |**
***matta eveti tān viddhi na tv ahaṁ teṣu te mayi* ||12||**

Whatever beings that are pure, active or inert, know them to proceed from Me. But I am not in them, they are in Me.

Sattva, rajas and *tatmas* are the three *guṇa*s. They are moods of our subtle body. Actions by our physical body depend on these moods. All the thoughts and ideas that arise in us can be classified according to the three *guṇa*s. The three *guṇa*s give different impulses under which our minds act. They envelop our minds totally and veil it away from the Real Self behind the mind and intellect. This is called *māyā*. The three *guṇa*s are the result of our *vāsanā*s (thought-processes) from our past. They are discussed in detail in chapter 14.

The Lord states that the three *guṇa*s proceed from the Lord and the Lord is not in them. It is not a cause and effect relationship. (One can understand it better by observing the lotus leaf. The lotus flower emerges from the water, but its leaves do not get wet with the water.) It is simply a state of superimposition of matter upon the spirit. The waves that rise from the ocean can be said to be in the ocean. But the ocean cannot be said to be in the waves. The Lord is only a witness (*sākṣī*) to our subtle and physical body's actions and thoughts. As *guṇa*s are from subtle body, they are in no way affecting the divine. They are connected to the ego and ego is only a reflection of True Self.

त्रिभिर्गुणमयैर्भावैरेभिः सर्वमिदं जगत् ।
मोहितं नाभिजानाति मामेभ्यः परमव्ययम् ॥१३॥

***tribhir guṇamayair bhāvair ebhiḥ sarvam idaṁ jagat* I**
***mohitaṁ nābhijānāti mām ebhyaḥ param avyayam* II13II**

Deluded by these natures, composed of the three guṇas, *all the world does not know Me, the higher and imperishable.*

The real Self, *ātmā,* is transcendental. It is above the mind and intellect level. The three *guṇas*, which constitute *māyā,* envelop the *ātmā* and hide it from the physical body. By saying this, the Lord is giving the reason for the ignorance of the Self. We all have the divine *ātmā* in us. We cannot see it. Why then do we not know of its presence? We may not realise it, but why not know it?

It is because of *māyā,* composed of the three *guṇas*. Only a few exceptional people know the Truth and they are *jīvanmuktas*. There are a few who are aware of the *ātmā* and are trying to realise it. The majority, are ignorant and do not have time to contemplate on *ātmā*. They are immersed in their day-to-day activities by attachment to their ego.

The Lord now explains how to clear the ignorance (*māyā*) and reach Him.

दैवी ह्येषा गुणमयी मम माया दुरत्यया ।
मामेव ये प्रपद्यन्ते मायामेतां तरन्ति ते ॥१४॥

***daivī hy eṣā guṇamayī mama māyā duratyayā* I**
***mām eva ye prapadyante māyām etāṁ taranti te* II14II**

This divine illusion of Mine, made up of three guṇas, *is difficult to cross over. Those who take refuge in Me alone can cross over the illusion.*

The first half of the verse describes "What is *māyā*". The second half gives means to go beyond *māyā.*

(1) **Daivī:** It is divine. It can be won over by divine help only. The Lord has the infinite power to remove it from us. The Lord is the only one who is above *māyā.*

(2) **Guṇamayī:** The *māyā* is constituted of *guṇa*s. They are *sattva, rajas* and *tamas*. We know only the qualities. They have no form. If we can remove the qualities in us, *māyā* disappears.

(3) **Mama:** It is the Lord's. It is His power and is under his control. *Māyā* has no control over the Lord.

(4) **Duratyayā:** It is difficult to cross over. One should note that the Lord does not say it is impossible.

How to cross over *māyā*? One can cross over *māyā* by taking refuge in Him alone.

Only the Lord can get you across *māyā.* One should surrender to the Lord. If one has to surrender, one should have faith in Him. One should realise His presence in all. All bad qualities should be surrendered to good qualities. One should develop good qualities. Learning from elders and teachers is essential. God is in elders and teachers also. Surrendering to elders and teachers means, developing moral qualities taught by them and eschewing the immoral acts in our life. Performance of sacred, selfless work, meditation on Self and similar practices are the means of taking refuge in Him. All efforts have to be single-pointed to realise *ātman* ''in Him'' and ''in all''.

न मां दुष्कृतिनो मूढाः प्रपद्यन्ते नराधमाः ।
माययापहृतज्ञाना आसुरं भावमाश्रिताः ॥१५॥

na māṁ duṣkṛtino mūḍhāḥ prapadyante narādhamāḥ |
māyayā'pahṛtajñānā āsuraṁ bhāvam āśritāḥ ||15||

Evil-doers, the deluded, the lowest of men, deprived of knowledge by māyā, *having taken to demoniacal ways do not take refuge in Me.*

Having said how to cross over *māyā*, the Lord now explains what happens if one does not want to cross over *māyā*. Actually this theme is taken up in detail in chapter 16.

A person who does not take refuge in Me: It means those who know the existence of Self but do not believe in it and get carried away by the power of ignorance. These people get attached to worldly objects and go after sensual pleasures. They do not realise the temporary nature of the pleasure coming from sensual objects and do not realise that such a pleasure ends in sorrow. They therefore fall down to the lower level of the three *guṇas*, i.e., *rājasika* and *tāmasika*. Their actions are those of the lowest class of men who have lost the power of intellect and do evil to themselves and to society. The Lord calls such people *mūḍhāḥ*, i.e., deluded. Their way of life is *āsurabhāva*, i.e., of demoniacal nature.

चतुर्विधा भजन्ते मां जनाः सुकृतिनोऽर्जुन ।
आर्तो जिज्ञासुरर्थार्थी ज्ञानी च भरतर्षभ ॥१६॥

caturvidhā bhajante māṁ janāḥ sukṛtino'rjuna **I**
ārto jijñāsur arthārthī jñānī ca bharatarṣabha **II16II**

O best one amongst Bharatas, four kinds of virtuous men worship Me: a distressed, a seeker of knowledge, a seeker of wealth and wise one.

In the preceding verse the Lord spoke about *āsurika* type of men and how they reject the Lord. As opposed to them there are righteous people who worship the Lord. The reason for their offering worship can help us in classifying such people into four types. These people are all *sukṛtinaḥ* (righteous).

What is worship?

Spiritually it is a form of religious reverence. Those who worship have one thing in common. They have a belief in something higher than themselves. They either would want that higher being to help them, or they would want to know the higher one. Some may even want to become one with the higher being.

Ārta: People go through variety of distresses in life. Some may suffer illness which is of a serious nature and they may not be getting better. They may have a terminal illness. Some may see the suffering of their loved ones and cannot themselves help them . Some may be attacked by wicked people and cry for help. The majority of people are usually of this type. They remember the Lord and pray for His help when they are in distress.

Draupadī asked for Kṛṣṇa's help when Duḥśāsana was insulting her. Gajendra asked for help when attacked by a crocodile.

Jijñāsu: These are people who have heard about the Self and are sincerely trying to find all about the Self by reading scriptures, taking guidance of *gurus*, etc. They want to know *Brahman,* the Lord of Creation. King Parīkṣita is an example of this type.

Arthārthī: A seeker of wealth. Not all seekers of wealth can be termed righteous people. Only those who follow the rules of *Dharma* in pursuit of wealth are righteous.

Wealth can be of different varieties. Monetary wealth is to acquire more money for prosperity and possessions. It could also be the wealth of health. It could be in the form of children and again it could be wealth in food materials to overcome hunger. ''Please get me more money, children, food or health'', is what people ask the Lord.

Sugrīva asked Rāma to help him get his kingdom from his brother Vālī.

Jñānī: This type of people already know about the Self and *Brahman.* They do not worship Him for anything for themselves. They ask Him to help others to overcome their sorrows or they ask Him to accept them back into Him, to be made one with Him.

Nārada Muni and Prahlāda were *jñānī*s.

तेषां ज्ञानी नित्ययुक्त एकभक्तिर्विशिष्यते ।
प्रियो हि ज्ञानिनोऽत्यर्थमहं स च मम प्रियः ॥१७॥

teṣāṁ jñānī nityayukta ekabhaktir viśiṣyate |
priyo hi jñānino'tyartham ahaṁ sa ca mama priyaḥ ||17||

Of these, the wise, constantly harmonised and singularly devoted to Me, is the best. I am exceedingly dear to Him and He is dear to Me.

Nitya-yuktah: One constantly in contact with the *ātmā.*
Ekabhakti: One having single-pointed devotion.

The *jñānī* has these two attributes. Normally people think of the Lord only now and then.

Usually, people have different goals and ambitions. They pursue a number of them at any one given time. Their energies are diverted in various fields of desires. Whereas a *jñānī*, has only one desire, i.e., to unite with *ātmā*. His energies are directed to only one channel—the path of *mokṣa*. Hence the Lord says that the *jñānī* is the best among the four types of men.

It is but natural that such a *jñānī* dearly loves the Lord. If he did not love Him, he would not be thinking of Him always and would not be wanting to be one with Him. Love in the highest form involves total identification of oneself with the one he loves. In true love one gets united with the loved one and does not want separation at any time. Such a person would give all that he has to the loved one without expecting anything in return.

We should all be giving all our love towards the welfare of others without expecting anything in return. We will of course receive dividends for such acts but we should not give expecting great dividends.

Because the *jñānī* dearly loves the Lord, the love from the Lord flows back into the *jñānī*.

One must realise here that it does not mean that the Lord is partial to *jñānī*s. Everybody gets results for what and how he puts in, in any field of activity. As we have read before, each of us is responsible for one's own destiny. The Lord simply says that the *jñānī* is dear to Him. (He does not get any special favours. He has put his love in and gets love in return.)

उदाराः सर्व एवैते ज्ञानी त्वात्मैव मे मतम् ।
आस्थितः स हि युक्तात्मा मामेवानुत्तमां गतिम् ॥१८॥

***udārāḥ sarva evaite jñānī tv ātmaiva me matam* I**
***āsthitaḥ sa hi yuktātmā mām evānuttamāṁ gatim* II18II**

Noble are all these, but I hold the wise as my very Self, because he is Self-united, is established in Me alone as the supreme goal.

The Lord first asserts that these four types of men are noble. They all have one thing in common. They believe in the Lord.

But the similarity ends there. *Arthī* and *arthārthī* pray to the Lord for their selfish needs only. They worship the Lord only sometimes. *Jijñāsu* is trying to find the truth but has not found it yet.

A *jñānī* has found the truth and is established in it. He is *yuktātmā;* he is harmonised with the Self always. If someone asks, "Where is God? Can I see Him?" The answer is simple. God is everywhere. He is seen in a *jñānī* because the *jñānī* has dropped his ego, has united with the Self. He is showing his divine qualities outwardly and he is therefore 'God himself'.

The Lord says that He holds the *jñānī* as Himself. The knower becomes the one to be known. The Lord also states that the supreme goal of all *sādhaka*s is "union with the Lord".

बहूनां जन्मनामन्ते ज्ञानवान्मां प्रपद्यते ।
वासुदेवः सर्वमिति स महात्मा सुदुर्लभः ॥१९॥

***bahūnāṁ janmanām ante jñānavān māṁ prapadyate* |**
***vāsudevaḥ sarvam iti sa mahātmā sudurlabhaḥ* ||19||**

At the end of several births, the jñānī *realises Me knowing that all this is Vāsudeva. Such a* mahātmā *is very rare to find.*

This verse should not be misunderstood. *Sādhaka*s should not drop their aim and run away thinking that if it is so rare, why should they try hard and miss the benefits of the present life? On the contrary, the Lord is making the observation that it needs time to polish off the dirt from one's mind. This may take several births. It is not easy to drop off all worldly attachments. Only a few people can achieve the real *jñānī*-status.

Do we not see a number of athletes in any field of sport? Do all win the highest medal? The fact that we are all born as humans itself shows that we have already been blessed by our Lord. We have been blessed with having *buddhi* (intellect and the ability to think).

The fact that we have tried to read and understand the *śloka,* means that we are on the next step in spiritual progress and have acquired the title *sādhaka.*

Go on, you man, put your best *sādhanā* (efforts) in it, and attain *sādhya* (goal). We are nearly half way on our path because we have come to question ourselves. If we now have faith in Vāsudeva (the Lord) it is not impossible for us to become a true *jñānī*. We should not "aspire" to becoming *jñānīs*. It then becomes egotistic.

It is possible to achieve liberation, even in this birth. If we put forth our efforts, the rewards will come in due course.

कामैस्तैस्तैर्हृतज्ञानाः प्रपद्यन्तेऽन्यदेवताः ।
तं तं नियममास्थाय प्रकृत्या नियताः स्वया ॥२०॥

***kāmais tais tair hṛtajñānāḥ prapadyante'nyadevatāḥ* |**
***taṁ-taṁ niyamam āsthāya prakṛtyā niyatāḥ svayā* ||20||**

Those whose wisdom has been led astray by desires, go to other gods, following this or that rite, led by their own nature.

What is wisdom? True wisdom is realising the oneness of the outer with the inner Self. What should one do? One should develop a desire to know the Truth and concentrate on dropping attachment to worldly pleasures. One should try to get united with the Self by following any of the four spiritual paths to liberation.

Is it hard to concentrate on the Truth?

Yes, desires for worldly objects are numerous. One can follow one's thought-process and act (follow this ritual or other) to fulfil a particular desire. Once he achieves that he will do the same to get more of what he has got or to get something new.

Desires for sensual gratification demolish the desire to merge with the Self. The channel of action concentrates on gaining sense-gratification (go to other gods).

Why does this happen? Each of us is born with *vāsanās* from our past. They act as natural forces diverting the mind to the objects of desire of the past. The force of *vāsanās* is very strong because it becomes the nature of that person to follow his inbred *guṇas* (tendencies).

How can one overcome this?

By using *buddhi*, by doing selfless acts he will burn the existing *vāsanās*. By *niṣkāma karma* he will not acquire new *vāsanās*.

यो यो यां यां तनुं भक्तः श्रद्धयार्चितुमिच्छति ।
तस्य तस्याचलं श्रद्धां तामेव विदधाम्यहम् ॥२१॥

yo yo yāṁ yāṁ tanuṁ bhaktaḥ śraddhayārcitum icchati |
tasya tasyācalaṁ śraddhāṁ tām eva vidadhāmy ahaṁ ||21||

Whosoever desires to worship whatsoever form of devas *with faith, to such and such, I make his faith unswerving.*

The love of the Lord to all is very clear in this verse. It is very hard for all acquire the universal vision of Absolute Truth.

Hindu philosophy accepts that the thinking process of millions of people varies in trillions of ways. After all the God-principle is only a creation made by our ancestors. 'Man created God in his mind'.

If we trace our way back to the *Vedic* period, there is no mention of gods. Our *Vedic* ancestors sought for answers and found them in natural forces. They found that life came from primordial energy which does not have any form (takes the form of steam to move an engine, form of electricity to produce light, etc).

Only in the *Purāṇic* period, the concept of god came in. Just as we use steam, electricity, etc. for different purposes, different attributes of energy found their expression as different gods.

Later on, rare people with total divine qualities also were given divine status. So, different gods came into existence in Hindu religion. The choice to appeal to any god of their imagination has been given to our men. The only condition the Lord insists is that the worship of the desired god should be with faith, without back-tracking in the path. Depending on their efforts, they will be given their rewards. This is all that the Lord is promising. A faithful follower of the *Gītā* therefore should not be sectarian. After all, *Gītā* is the *advaita* (philosophy of non-dualism).

'As we think, so we become'. We are bound by our own habits and we get attached to our own type of thinking. The more sincere efforts we put in our thinking, the Lord gives us that much power in that field of thinking.

स तया श्रद्धया युक्तस्तस्याराधनमीहते ।
लभते च ततः कामान्मयैव विहितान्हि तान् ॥२२॥

***sa tayā śraddhayā yuktas tasyārādhanam īhate* |**
***labhate ca tataḥ kāmān mayaiva vihitān hi tān* ||22||**

Endowed with that faith, he engages in the worship of his chosen deity and from it he obtains his desire or fulfilments, which are being ordainded by Me, indeed.

To fulfil a desire, the person performs with full faith any sacrifice (activity) to invoke the *devatā* of his choice (i.e., Indra, Agni, Varuṇa, etc). That person will get his desire fulfilled. The performer would believe that his *devatā* has blessed him.

But the Lord says that it was indeed the Lord Himself who has blessed that person through the *devatā*. All elemental forces are under the control of the Lord. In return for the faithful activity, the Lord dispenses the exact result for each action.

One can invoke the *deva* of his choice. If that *deva* gives him the power to do the work with faith, he should do so.

If one is trying to achieve material benefits in this world, he would then do so by this method. On the other hand, if one is really trying for liberation, he would in the course of time, understand that the material benefits are not everlasting. He will concentrate on the Self and try to merge into the Self.

By invoking the *devas*, at least the person is aware that there is a higher power than him. For example, if one is trying to listen to a particular channel of his radio he would switch the power on first, and then tune to that channel. By tuning into the right wave-length he gets the station of his choice. He is blessed by that channel. This central power is the Lord through switched on electricity.

अन्तवत्तु फलं तेषां तद्भवत्यल्पमेधसाम् ।
देवान्देवयजो यान्ति मद्भक्ता यान्ति मामपि ॥२३॥

***antavattu phalaṁ teṣāṁ tad bhavaty alpamedhasām* |**
***devān devayajo yānti madbhaktā yānti māmapi* ||23||**

The fruits that accrues to these men of little wisdom is finite indeed. Those who worship the devas, *go to the* devas. *My devotees come to Me.*

By invoking the *devas* to fulfil a desire, the devotee will get the proper result of his action. But because of the material benefit which they are looking for, the resulting benefit does not last long. The happiness of fulfilment of the desire is short-lived and is followed by sorrow.

The devotee will go back to that *devatā* again to fulfil some more desires. He gets bound to the wheel of *saṁsāra*. Therefore, the Lord calls them *alpamedhas*, i.e., men of little wisdom.

Those who realise the Self in themselves, who strive hard to meditate on it, will get absorbed into the Self. They achieve liberation (from births and deaths, from happiness and sorrows of life) and it results in infinite bliss. There is no more sorrow to follow for such persons. The seekers of the Self discover that they are indeed the Self and become the Self. They drop their ego totally.

अव्यक्तं व्यक्तिमापन्नं मन्यन्ते मामबुद्धयः ।
परं भावमजानन्तो ममाव्ययमनुत्तमम् ॥२४॥

***avyaktaṁ vyaktim āpannaṁ manyante mām abuddhayaḥ* |**
***paraṁ bhāvam ajānanto mamāvyayam anuttamam* ||24||**

The ignorant think of Me, the unmanifested, as having name and form, not knowing My imperishable, supreme and transcendental nature.

The Lord says that mere idol-worship is not enough. The idol, as far as the devotee is concerned, is the Lord himself. This is partial knowledge. It is indeed foolish to have partial knowledge. The idol is only the means to achieve the end-result.

What one is looking for is happiness which does not end in sorrow. The idols of Lord Rāma, Kṛṣṇa, Jesus do not give one permanent happiness. One cannot actually go and sit in front of the idol and ask it to take away one's worries or miseries. That is why the Lord calls such people foolish.

The idols of names and forms, really speaking, are of great people of the past who did selfless work for the benefit of the universe. The Lord really is unmanifest. The idol is not really the God. It is meant to give you a point of concentration. The end-result is to see the Lord in yourself.

What is manifest? It is something one can see, feel or understand. The fire is said to be manifest because one can see and feel it. That which is beyond the perception at physical, mental and intellectual level of understanding is called unmanifest. Electricity is unmanifest. The light from the bulb that glows with electricity is manifest. One should not just look at the light. To understand the light, he should work till he realises the source of the light.

The Lord gives four attributes of His higher nature:

(1)	He is *avyakata*	:	Unmanifest
(2)	He is *para*	:	Transcendental
(3)	He is *avyaya*	:	Imperishable
(4)	He is *anuttama*	:	Supreme

He is not manifest and hence *avyakta*. One cannot know Him at the physical planes of body, mind and intellect. One cannot know Him by name and form of His incarnations (*avatāra*s). His *avatāra*s were meant to kill evil and show the proper way of life (*dharma*) for the people. We are expected to follow *dharma* by recollecting the great work done by the Lord through His *avatāra*s.

The Lord was not born or dead because of His *vāsanā*s. He is beyond *māyā* (*param*—transcendental) and imperishable (*avyayam*). The Lord is actually condemning those who attribute mortality to the Lord's incarnations.

Of course it is very important that one needs a point of concentration for worship. This is at the primary level of learning.

One should aim at getting a degree. One gets a spiritual degree when he drops his ego totally at the feet of the Lord.

Do not see Rāma or Kṛṣṇa or Jesus in the idol but see the divinity behind that and try to bring out the divinity in you. Kṛṣṇa uses the word *abuddhayaḥ* (the foolish) for those who consider Him as having name and form and not realising His supreme nature. *Abuddhi* is, "not intelligent".

नाहं प्रकाशः सर्वस्य योगमायासमावृतः ।
मूढोऽयं नाभिजानाति लोको मामजमव्ययम् ॥२५॥

***nāhaṁ prakāśaḥ sarvasya yogamāyāsamāvṛtaḥ* |**
***mūḍho'yaṁ nābhijānāti loko mām ajam avyayam* ||25||**

I am not manifest to all. Veiled by my Yogamāyā, this world deluded, knows Me not, the unborn, imperishable.

Vedas declare that the Lord is in each one of us and He is omnipresent. He is all-pervading. Why is it that we cannot see the Lord in and around us? Our inner eye has a cataract called ignorance *(māyā)*. The Lord says that *māyā* (illusion) acts like a cloud between the Lord and the individual. *Māyā,* as we have seen before, is composed of three qualities, viz., *sattva, rajas* and *tamas.*

The Lord calls this Yogamāyā or cosmic illusion. The Lord says He is unborn and imperishable. He is ever present and witnesses all our actions. *Māyā* has no power over Him. He is beyond *māyā* and *māyā* is His weapon.

Because of the mental temperament, consisting of the three *guṇa*s, the veil of ignorance clouds us, and we all get the ego dominating us. This ego gives us the feeling of 'I' and 'My' ness. It works so strongly that we become ignorant of the omnipresent nature of the Lord.

The Lord is always bright and glorious like the sun. The clouds that stand between us and the sun give a wrong notion that it is dark. Hence clouds can be used as a comparison to *māyā.* Clouds do not affect the sun at any time. They only affect the people who are under the clouds.

वेदाहं समतीतानि वर्तमानानि चाऽर्जुन ।
भविष्याणि च भूतानि मां तु वेद न कश्चन ॥२६॥

***vedāhaṁ samatītāni vartamānāni cā'rjuna* |**
***bhaviṣyāṇi ca bhūtāni māṁ tu veda na kaścana* ||26||**

O Arjuna. I know the past, present and future of all beings. But Me, no one knows.

samatītāni	:	The past
vartamānāni	:	The present
bhaviṣyāṇi	:	The future

The last verse brought out the omnipresent nature of the Lord. This verse brings out the nature of His omniscience. Omniscient means 'all-knowing'. For the imperishable Lord there is no time factor. Past, present and future are only in relation to something perishable.

For me, who is going to die sometime later, there is a past, present and future. If we take the example of the sun, we can understand it better. The sun, evershining and always present, has covered this universe from time immemorial. He was shining and did shine on our ancestors of the past. He is shining now, on us of the present time. He will shine on our progeny, later, in the future.

One can say that the sun knows the past, present and future of all of us. The men of perfect knowledge, as we have discussed before, have become one with the Self. There is no 'duality' in such people. So the rest of us who are ignorant and who live in dualism, do not know His real nature. Once we know and realise Him, we become one with Him, like salt dissolving in water.

As the Lord knows all, He is *sarvajña.* We, in comparison, are *kiñcijñas,* i.e., men of little knowledge.

इच्छाद्वेषसमुत्थेन द्वन्द्वमोहेन भारत ।
सर्वभूतानि संमोहं सर्गे यान्ति परंतप ॥२७॥

***icchā-dveṣa-samutthena dvandva-mohena bhārata* |**
***sarvabhūtāni saṁmohaṁ sarge yānti parantapa* ||27||**

O Bhārata, O Parantapa, by the delusion of the pairs of opposites arising from desire and aversion, all beings are subject to illusion at birth in the world.

Sarge: At birth.

This verse deals with the fundamental truth of life. What is birth? What is desire? What is aversion? What is *dvandva*? What is delusion?

Desire is an impulse flowing towards an object, which brings the feeling of pleasure (happiness) on obtaining that object. On obtaining it, there is a feeling of happiness. As all worldly objects are not eternal, they have to perish in course of time. The happiness from such objects is not going to last long.

Once we get the object, we get attached to it. Because of attachment, we get depressed on losing it. We also get depressed when someone else steals the object of our desire. All these reactions cause agitations in our mind. Our minds are an ocean of agitations. What is aversion? Dislike towards an unpleasant object is aversion. We all try to avoid unpleasant objects. Our mind is deluded with these pairs of opposites, of likes and dislikes.

As we have discussed earlier, imprints of thought-processes are *vāsanā*s. We are in the process of burning our existing *vāsanā*s and accumulating more *vāsanā*s. These *vāsanā*s create the temperament of three *guṇa*s in us. As we know, *māyā*, which comprises of the three *guṇa*s, is responsible for the ignorance in us.

If we do not burn all *vāsanā*s, we are born again and we are born with *vāsanā*s. It means, even at birth, we are ignorant. Hence the Lord says that all beings are subject to delusion at birth.

We should realise another important point here. Even though we are born with delusion at birth itself, during our childhood, our desires and aversions are not many, and not strong. It is easy to educate a child's mind. As the saying goes, 'one can direct a plant the way he wants when it is young'. One cannot do so when it becomes a tree. So it is important that spiritual teaching should start at an early age. It is the duty of parents, of the family and of society to introduce spirituality, morality and divinity into their children's lives from an early stage.

Arjuna is addressed as 'Parantapa', i.e., scorcher of enemies. He is advised to kill the enemies of desire and aversion inside him.

येषां त्वन्तगतं पापं जनानां पुण्यकर्मणाम् ।
ते द्वन्द्वमोहनिर्मुक्ता भजन्ते मां दृढव्रताः ॥२८॥

***yeṣāṁ tv antagataṁ pāpaṁ janānāṁ puṇyakarmaṇām* |**
***te dvandva-moha-nirmuktā bhajante māṁ dṛḍhavratāḥ* ||28||**

But those men of good deeds whose sins have come to an end, who are freed from delusion of the pairs of opposites and are steadfast in vows, worship Me.

Puṇyakarma: Good deeds, actions, thoughts. Feelings which are Godly and divine are considered as *puṇya karmas*. These include charitable work towards the disabled, chronically ill and the poor. It is self-sacrifice for the sake of others. It also includes scriptural reading, learning from *gurus*, and meditating on God.

Contrary to Good is Bad. Actions, thoughts and feelings which are egotistic, self-centred and are for sense-gratification, constitute sin. Sinful deeds leave an impression on our mind. We do not get liberation till we burn all existing *vāsanās*. To burn the sins is therefore possible by doing good deeds.

The first half of this verse deals with burning of sins by good deeds. Such people, who continue to do Godly work, do not get affected by pairs of opposite reactions of pains and pleasures.

The last quarter says "steadfast in vows". Vow is discipline practised for a purpose. In *Mahābhārata,* Bhīṣma vows that he will not marry and he will protect the throne of Hastināpura. He kept this vow until his death. Similarly, vows in spiritual practice are a discipline in talking, eating, celibacy, etc. These are all instruments for self-perfection.

Unfortunately, our vows are usually not strong and we break them easily. Steadfastness in vows is essential to progress. Such men, whose good works have burnt their sins, who are free from delusion of pairs of opposites, who have tuned their mind and intellect properly, can remain steadfast in vows and worship the Lord. Spiritual practice is easy for such a person.

जरामरणमोक्षाय मामाश्रित्य यतन्ति ये ।
ते ब्रह्म तद्विदुः कृत्स्नमध्यात्मं कर्म चाखिलम् ॥२९॥

jarāmaraṇamokṣāya mām āśritya yatanti ye |
te brahma tad viduḥ kṛtsnam adhyātmaṁ karma cākhilam ||29||

Those who strive for liberation from old age and death, taking refuge in Me, realise in full that Brahman, *the whole knowledge of the Self and all action.*

This verse brings out the '*tat*' aspect of *tat tvam asi*. The realised person understands that what exists is only *Brahman* and all actions originate from Him.

Those who strive for liberation from old age and death: One should not take the literal meaning of this sentence. It really means those who do not want to associate themselves with modifications or changes in manifestations from birth to death of individual beings. One cannot stop changes from baby to childhood, childhood to teenage life, teenager to adult, adult to old age and old age to death. This is the natural order. In every manifestation one has to suffer pains and agonies of that manifestation. Diseases and injuries are common to all ages. Those who understand that they are not the physical body, but really the Self inside, will overcome the problem. They will get liberated from old age and death modifications of the physical body.

To get liberated, they have to take refuge (*āśritya*) in the Lord. They have to believe in *Brahman* inside them and realise that *Brahman* is real and that the body is false. They have to strive (*yatanti*) to reach this state of understanding.

They must understand the truth *ahaṁ brahmāsmi*.

साधिभूताधिदैवं मां साधियज्ञं च ये विदुः ।
प्रयाणकालेऽपि च मां ते विदुर्युक्तचेतसः ॥३०॥

***sādhibhūtādhidaivaṁ māṁ sādhiyajñaṁ ca ye viduḥ* I**
***prayāṇakāle'pi ca māṁ te vidur yuktacetasaḥ* II30II**

Those who realise Me in the adhibhūta, adhidaiva *and the* adhiyajña, *know Me even at the time of death, having self-control.*

The verse is a preview of the next chapter. The main topic of the discussion in the next chapter is summarised here. The whole universe is *'Tat'* (That) i.e., Brahman, is the meaning hidden in this verse.

Adhibhūta: It is the principle that graces the whole world of objects.

Adhidaiva: It is the principle that graces all the gods (i.e., all sense-organs, mind and intellect and their activities).

Adhiyajña: It is the principle that graces all sacrifices (activities).

Those who know that it is *Brahman*, the Lord, that graces the above three, realise that all is *Brahman*. There is nothing that is 'not *Brahman*'.

One cannot get a sudden view of this mighty concept. It comes with continuous practice (*sādhanā*).

With steadfast mind (*yuktacetasā*), self-control they keep the idea constantly of *ahaṁ brahmāsmi*, and *idam lokaṁ sarvamaheśvaram*. By doing so, they will remember it even at the time of death. It is natural that what we have been thinking most, is what we will remember at the time of death or at the time of loss of memory (whichever comes first).

So, memory of the Lord, existence of the Lord in you and in all should be kept in mind from a very early age. For this, spiritual teaching as early as possible should be started and once started practised regularly till one achieves self-control.

Individual efforts is therefore the rule to achieve liberation. God will not come down to earth and bless you with liberation. God in you has to come out to liberate you.

इति श्रीमद्भगवद्गीतासूपनिषत्सु ब्रह्मविद्यायां योगशास्त्रे
श्रीकृष्णार्जुनसंवादे ज्ञानविज्ञानयोगो नाम सप्तमोऽध्यायः ॥

iti śrīmadbhagavadgītāsūpaniṣatsu brahmavidyāyām yogaśāstre śrīkṛṣṇārjunasaṁvāde jñāna-vijñāna-yogo nāma saptamo'dhyāyaḥ ||

CHAPTER 8

AKṢARA-PARABRAHMA-YOGA

Akṣara is letters in the alphabet. *Akṣara* also means that which does not perish.

The letters and words which we learn in early childhood do not perish. They will be with us till our death. The alphabet we learn and the words we make are the foundation for learning and expressing ourselves all our life. They will only die with the mental or physical death of the person.

The creator and sustainer of the universe is Brahmā, the Supreme. He is *Parabrahma*. *Parabrahma* does not perish, he is *akṣara*. This chapter deals with Him and describes how he is the master of all actions at physical, mental and intellectual levels. Our ancient *ṛṣi*s gave the word *OṀ* to represent this *akṣara parabrahma*.

अर्जुन उवाच

किं तद्ब्रह्म किमध्यात्मं किं कर्म पुरुषोत्तम ।
अधिभूतं च किं प्रोक्तमधिदैवं किमुच्यते ॥१॥

arjuna uvāca

***kiṁ tad brahma kim adhyātmaṁ kiṁ karma puruṣottama* I**
***adhibhūtaṁ ca kiṁ proktam adhidaivaṁ kim ucyate* II1II**

Arjuna said

What is Brahman? *What is* adhyātma? *What is action? What is declared to be* adhibhūta? *What is* adhidaiva *said to be? O, best among men.*

अधियज्ञः कथं कोऽत्र देहेऽस्मिन्मधुसूदन ।
प्रयाणकाले च कथं ज्ञेयोऽसि नियतात्मभिः ॥२॥

***adhiyajñaḥ kathaṁ ko'tra dehe'smin madhusūdana* I**
***prayāṇakāle ca kathaṁ jñeyo'si niyatātmabhiḥ* II2II**

O Madhusūdana, who and how is adhiyajña *here in this body? And how at the time of death are you to be known by the self-controlled?*

Arjuna really got perplexed on hearing the last stanza of the last chapter. He had not heard of *adhibhūta*, *adhidaiva* and *adhiyajña*. He is humbly requesting the Lord to define those words, He also wants to know how one can realise the Self at the time of death.

श्रीभगवानुवाच
अक्षरं ब्रह्म परमं स्वभावोऽध्यात्ममुच्यते ।
भूतभावोद्भवकरो विसर्गः कर्मसंज्ञितः ॥३॥

śrī bhagavān uvāca
akṣaraṁ brahma paramaṁ svabhāvo'dhyātmam ucyate ।
bhūtabhāvodbhavakaro visargaḥ karmasaṁjñitaḥ ॥3॥

The Lord said

Brahman *is supreme and imperishable. His essential nature is called Self-knowledge. The act of sacrifice that causes beings to be born into manifestation is called* 'karma'.

Brahman (*OṀ*), indicates that which is the essence behind the pluralistic world. It is the primordial energy. There is nothing superior to it. It has no physical form. Hence it is *param.*

It is *akṣara*: imperishable. It is only the material world and objects that perish. As He has no physical form, He is said to be deathless. Birth and death are the laws of nature, but the only one who is not born and dead is *Brahman.* He is above nature (*prakṛti*). *Brahman* is the conscious principle behind life's existence at all levels and in all forms.

Adhyātma is nature (*svabhāva*). What is really our nature? It is the Self in us, the Self which is the real man, the *Brahman*, the imperishable, He is divine and formless, and the all-knower. Our nature or *svabhāva* is divine. Divinity is our *dharma.* But due to the reflected ego and the superimposition by it, we forget our true nature. To rediscover our divinity is the teaching of the *Gītā.*

Karma is action. It is an act of sacrifice. In chapter 3, verse 14 (*annād bhavanti bhūtāni*) this aspect has been described in detail. An act of sacrifice is *yajña*. Rains, food and beings are produced out of the *yajñas*. The creative force behind every intellect that ends in creation (thoughts, beings) is *karma*. *Karma* is not just physical work.

Bhūtabhāvodbhavakaraḥ: Factors causing births of beings.

Visargaḥ: Act of sacrifice, or that which is given away in sacrifice. Action (*karma*) in the form of service to mankind is a form of sacrifice.

The second half of the verse says that the act of sacrifice that causes beings to be born into manifestation is called *karma*. It means the rituals in the *karma-kāṇḍa* of the *Vedas*. They are performed to obtain personal desires and cause beings to be born. We are born to fulfil all our desires. We are born to burn out our existing *vāsanās*.

अधिभूतं क्षरो भावः पुरुषश्चाधिदैवतम् ।
अधियज्ञोऽहमेवात्र देहे देहभृतां वर ॥४॥

adhibhūtaṁ kṣaro bhāvaḥ puruṣaś cādhidaivatam |
adhiyajño'ham evātra dehe dehabhṛtāṁ vara ||4||

O best of embodied beings, the perishable element is adhibhūta. *Creative energy is* adhidaiva *and is here, in this body. I, Myself, am* adhiyajña.

Dehabhṛtāṁ vara: Best of embodied beings.

Adhibhūta: *Bhūta* is the perishable element (*kṣara*). *Adhibhūta* is the principle behind the persihable. The entire *prakṛti* is perishable.

Adhidaiva: The *puruṣa* is *adhidaiva*. *Mūla puruṣa* is the creative enery (*hiraṇyagarbha, virāṭ*) responsible for the total creation. He is the supreme Lord. In the body, each of the five senses has one *devatā*,*e.g.*, *devatā* for the eye is the fire (sun), for the ear is the air, for the nose is the earth, etc. These represent the five great elements; one element is the *devatā* for one sense-organ. The mind presides over all sense-organs and is the creative force. The *deva* for the mind and intellect is the *puruṣa,* i.e., *adhidaiva.*

Adhiyajña: *Yajña* is sacrifice. In relation to the physical body it is sacrifice of acts of perception, feelings and thoughts at three levels of existence (physical, mental, intellectual). What is poured in the sacrifice is called oblations. In relation to our body, sense-objects are oblations.

Oblations are poured to invoke *devatās* who bless the person. By pouring sense-objects in relation to each sense-organ, that particular *devatā* is invoked. For example, the presiding faculty or deity for eyes is the fire. Sun is the hottest fire-ball. Through the medium of the light of the sun we see. By pouring into the sacrifice and burning away the bad things we do with our eyes, we invoke the *devatā* called fire. He will bless us, and we become pure as far as the faculty of vision is concerned.

By offering oblations of all objects at all the three levels of existence, we are blessed with the Light of Knowledge. This is nothing but our pure Self (*ātmā*). In *adhiyajña* therefore, the vital factor is the Self.

By these three, the divinity of man is declared by the Lord.

अन्तकाले च मामेव स्मरन्मुक्त्वा कलेवरम् ।
यः प्रयाति स मद्भावं याति नास्त्यत्र संशयः ॥५॥

antakāle ca mām eva smaran muktvā kalevaram |
yaḥ prayāti sa madbhāvaṁ yāti nāsty atra saṁśayaḥ ||5||

One who, leaving the body, goes forth remembering Me only at the time of his death also, he attains My being. There is no doubt in this.

The *Vedas* declare that the final thoughts of a dying man decide his future life.

Normally, all our life our actions pertain to our ego and our surroundings. Our mind is full of *vāsanās* (imprints) pertaining to our physical selves. This will be carried till our death and these thoughts order our future. If we are wicked, we take birth in the lower order of creation, i.e., worms, insects, reptiles, etc.

Or we will be born with animal tendencies and continue to destroy ourselves.

By thinking of the Lord at the time of death one attains liberation. This is a common understanding of all Hindus. Near every death-bed, usually the loved one of that person will be asking the dying person to recite *oṁ*, Rāma, Kṛṣṇa, Śiva, Nārāyaṇa, etc. This point is given by the Lord in detail in this verse.

The Lord says "*antakāle ca*" which means "at the time of death also". The word 'also' is important. To get the reward of liberation, one must be remembering the Lord at the time of death also. This means one should be remembering the Lord at other times of living.(Remember Him always, is the actual meaning hidden in this verse.)

We do not know when death or senility hits us. To try to remember the Lord suddenly at that time is not possible unless one has known Him before. One must have been practising divinity since an early age. *Sādhanā* (practice) must begin early in life when distractions are the least (i.e., childhood). It then becomes a second nature. Automatically it will be possible to remember Him at the time of death. Such a person, no doubt, will attain Godhood, The Lord states that, that state is what we know as *mokṣa*.

For those who repeat the name of the Lord at the time of death (because somebody asked them to do so) the benefit cannot be total liberation. They get blessed in proportion to their good act. They will have some benefits only from such acts.

यं यं वापि स्मरन्भावं त्यजत्यन्ते कलेवरम् ।
तं तमेवैति कौन्तेय सदा तद्भावभावितः ॥६॥

yaṁ-yaṁ vāpi smaran bhāvaṁ tyajaty ante kalevaram |
taṁ tam evaiti kaunteya sadā tad-bhāvabhāvitaḥ ||6||

O Kaunteya, whosoever leaves the body, thinking of whatsoever object, form or being at the end, to that only he goes, because of his constant thought of that.

The law which we all know is: "As you think so you become". In Sanskrit, it is *yadbhāvam tad bhavati*.

Our *saṁskāras* (tendencies) are our thoughts and contemplations in our life. What we think and contemplate frequently becomes our nature. This nature will remain at the time of death also. If we die with that nature, our future birth will be according to that nature only. In Sanskrit it is called *pūrva janma saṁskāras*. Our thoughts are created by us only. Hence it is a *Vedic* declaration that 'each man is totally responsible for his destiny'.

In contrast to egotistic nature, one can cultivate spiritual and moral habits and tendencies as early as possible in one's life. This will direct one to have new channels to spiritual progress. Such person's tendencies (*saṁskāras*) will be directed to divine aspirations. This is called *adhyātma-saṁskāras*. Automatically, at the time of death he will retain that *saṁskāra* which will get him *mokṣa*.

तस्मात्सर्वेषु कालेषु मामनुस्मर युध्य च ।
मय्यर्पितमनोबुद्धिर्मामेवैष्यस्यसंशयम् ॥७॥

tasmāt sarveṣu kāleṣu mām anusmara yudhya ca ।
mayy arpitamanobuddhir mām evaiṣyasy asaṁśayam ॥7॥

Therefore, remember Me at all times and fight with mind and intellect surrendered to Me. You shall attain Me alone, without doubt.

This is a confirmation of what has been said in the last few verses.

'You' here, can be Arjuna in the battlefield of Kurukṣetra or can be me or you, in the battle of life. Our daily battle in life is with the forces of different thoughts (good and bad) that bring in ripples of waves in the calm ocean of our mind. The mind is controlled by *buddhi* (intellect). The intellect is always in a state of agitation to decide on good and bad actions.

The Lord says, remembering Him at all times in one's life and not letting the mind and intellect be taken over by agitations from the outer world. "Keep your mind calm. Do not let the pluralistic world disturb you and, in return for that, you will attain Me", is the advice by the Lord. No doubt this statement is His promise.

The Lord uses the word *anusmara*. It means continuous thought of the Lord to be kept up. Hear Him always, think of Him always, meditate on Him always and you will not be frightened when death approaches you.

If one wants to make a journey on a train, he must have a valid ticket. It does not matter as to when the train comes. He should prepare himself so that he has enough money to buy the ticket. Similarly, one should have the ticket of thoughts of the Lord for his journey in life to attain liberation. To buy the ticket, he must have enough *sādhanā* of constant meditation on the Lord.

The Lord also says "remember Me always and fight". He does not say "remember Me" only. It is a very valid statement. "Do your duty, think of Me during your duty and dedicate the duty to me", is the Lord's advice to all mankind. This is the message by the Lord in his teaching of *Gītā* to us and we should remember this always.

An educated man will not forget his education. He applies it in his day-to-day life and achieves success in his field of activity. He does not just sit back and read books always. The memory of his studies will always be with him. This memory of his studies is his awareness of what he has studied.

Similarly, the true *sādhaka*, trying for spiritual progress from early life, will be able to retain the awareness of "God in him and God everywhere" and will be acting divinely all his life. He will achieve the success he worked hard for and gets liberated.

अभ्यासयोगयुक्तेन चेतसा नान्यगामिना ।
परमं पुरुषं दिव्यं याति पार्थानुचिन्तयन् ॥८॥

abhyāsayogayuktena cetasā nānyagāminā |
paramaṁ puruṣaṁ divyaṁ yāti pārthānucintayan ||8||

O Arjuna, with the mind not going towards other objects, harmonised in yoga *of practice, meditating constantly one reaches the supreme* puruṣa.

In this verse, the Lord has given three steps needed to reach Him. It is important to note that the Lord does not say 'after death'. It means that following the three steps, one will attain freedom even in this life.

(1) **Cetasā nānyagāminā:** Mind not going towards other objects. Concentration of the mind is essential as we have learnt it several times in the previous chapters. Without concentration, it is impossible to achieve success in any field of activity. The mind easily gets diverted towards objects of the outer world. It should be given a different object to meditate upon by repeating *OṀ* (*upāsanā*) or fixing the mind on an idol of God (*bhakti*) Think of *paramam puruṣam divyam* (supreme, divine *puruṣa*).

(2) **Abhyāsayogena**: By the *yoga* of constant practice, one will climb up the ladder to *mokṣa*. Practice is essential for success. Practice is nothing but repetition of some habit or other. Any practice, as long as it is divine in nature, should be repeated so that it becomes a habit (second nature). Initially, practice will be difficult but later on it will be easy. A student studying for exams, will find it hard to get up early to study. If he has not got up early in the earlier terms of study, he will find it hard in the last term before exams. Compared to him, a student who normally gets up early will have no such difficulty.

We have all developed several habits which are not contributory to progress towards spiritual liberation. Develop goodness and purity in our action and make a habit of it by practising it; this is what we have to understand here.

(3) **Anucintayan:** Thinking of the Lord continuously. This is also a habit one has to develop. It is not only a habit in action but the practice in thoughts is also essential. "As you think, so you become" is what we have learnt already. The flow of thought on the divine in our mind should be constant. Divinity gets filled in so fast that it will burst out and show itself out.

कविं पुराणमनुशासितारमणोरणीयांसमनुस्मरेद्यः ।
सर्वस्य धातारमचिन्त्यरूपमादित्यवर्णं तमसः परस्तात् ॥९॥

kaviṁ purāṇam anuśāsitāram
aṇor aṇīyāṁsam anusmared yaḥ ।
sarvasya dhātāram acintyarūpam
ādityavarṇaṁ tamasaḥ parastāt ॥9॥

प्रयाणकाले मनसाऽचलेन भक्त्या युक्तो योगबलेन चैव ।
भ्रुवोर्मध्ये प्राणमावेश्य सम्यक् स तं परं पुरुषमुपैति दिव्यम् ॥१०॥

prayāṇakāle manasā'calena
bhaktyā yukto yogabalena caiva ।
bhruvor madhye prāṇam āveśya samyak
sa taṁ paraṁ puruṣam upaiti divyam ॥10॥

Who, meditating upon the Omniscient, the Ancient, the ruler of the worlds, supporter of all, subtler than an atom, of inconceivable form, self-illumined like the sun and beyond darkness;

At the time of death, by the power of yoga, *fixing the* 'prāṇa' *between the eyebrows, he attains the supreme* Puruṣa.

In the last verse, we are asked to practise divinity. God, the supreme *Puruṣa*, the Self dwelling inside all of us, has no physical form. He is beyond mind and intellect. What one cannot see can only be described by its characteristics.

So, in this verse eight different attributes of the Lord are enumerated. The total of all eight attributes is the nearest one can go to explain the unknown.

(1) Kavi: *Kavi* is a poet. A poet is the one who knows the subject of his poem so well that he puts it in such beautiful words which make the poem great.

The Lord who is omniscient (knower of all) is therefore described as a poet. So, in this context *kavi* does not mean that the Lord has written a poem. It means that "He is all-knowing" (omniscient).

(2) Purāṇa: It means ancient. Our *Purāṇas* (mythology) are very ancient. God is more ancient than *Purāṇas*. He actually has no beginning. We cannot trace the Divine Lord to any particular date in history. The Eternal Truth, (primordial energy) has been the same before, the same now and will be the same in future.

(3) Anuśāsitā: Controller of all. He is not actually acting like a ruler. He, the Lord, is the presiding factor in all life's existence and hence He is the controller of all. If the energy of life is not there, we are considered dead. In that state none of our bodily organs can function any more. When the energy (*ātmā*/Soul) leaves, all other bodily organs cease to function and the person is considered to be dead. If He is not functioning, everything in the body dies. On the other hand, the Energy (*ātman*) will continue to be present even if one or more parts of the body are not functioning (e.g., paralysed arm, deafness, etc). The life continues. Hence the Lord is said to be the "controller of all".

Just like the gold in all golden ornaments, Self is there in all names and forms. (No gold ornament is ever available without the gold in it.)

(4) Aṇoraṇīyān: He is subtler than an atom. At one time we thought atom was the smallest particle. Now, with modern technology, we have managed to find still smaller particles. Particle physics deals with the smallest physically divisible particle which would still maintain its specific properties.

The Lord is so subtle that there is nothing subtler than Him. He is there in the smallest to the biggest of everything in the world because of His subtleness.

(5) Sarvasya dhātā: He is the nourisher, supporter of all. The constant factor behind all our modifications in various stages of our life is the 'Life-principle' (Self). The Self supports us at all times. Without the Self, there would not be any stages in our life. If we take the example of the cinema, we can understand it better. To see the film from beginning to end there should be a screen. Without it the film cannot be shown. The screen is the supporting, conscious principle in relation to the film.

Also, the crops we grow are essential to nourish us. The Lord is therefore the nourisher of all of us. The energy in the soil is essential for the growth of the crops. We put a small quantity of seeds, but we get plenty to eat in return.

(6) Acintyarūpa: Inconceivable form. He has no form and

hence we cannot perceive Him. We can see Him in those who show their divinity in their outward acts and we call such people saints, prophets, messiahs, etc. By total purification of the mind, (dropping of the ego), one can merge in Him.

(7) Ādityavarṇa: Luminous like the sun. The sun illuminates the whole world. Knowledge illuminates the mind. The person who knows all is knowledgeable. He shines brilliantly by his actions. This state of the Lord is beyond our comprehension because of our clinging to our ego (physical body). By transcending the mind and intellect, we can drop our connection with the world of names and forms.

(8) Tamasaḥ parastāt: He is beyond darkness (ignorance). *Māyā,* as we have discussed before, acts as a veil between the Self and the intellect. The Lord is beyond *māyā* and hence He is beyond ignorance.

By knowing these attributes, the *sādhaka* can practise meditation on the Lord in whichever path of *yoga* he finds easy. The tenth verse describes the technique of meditation at the time of death.

Prayāṇakālena: Literally, it means at the time of travel. Travel is a journey to another place. Journey to another place for permanent settlement is contemplated upon when one is not happy with the existing place. Some move on to find a better job, better education, etc. They do so, when they do not get what they want in the place where they are.

To find such a place, one enquires about the place before the journey, making sure that the new place can give what he is looking for. The traveller then gets prepared for the move and collects all necessary things for the journey.

Similarly, in life when we find unhappiness, difficulties, etc. we want to find happiness. The happiness we want should not bring us new sorrows. We, in other words, are travellers in search of permanent happiness.

The scriptures have given us the path to eternal bliss. This is not something one has to go to, after physical death. It is here, in this life only, that we get this eternal bliss. To prepare for the journey to the 'Land of Bliss', we must look at the land from all angles, we must believe in it and practise methods to purify our minds.

Leaving the body means, leaving the ego; provide ourselves with necessary things for travel means, providing ourselves with divine qualities. Destination means 'Land of Bliss'. For this travel, one should have *bhakti* and *yoga* (*dhyāna*). One should have love for the new land, and practise to get there straight without being distracted.

By *dhyāna-yoga* one can get the necessary concentration. Pure *dhyāna* is possible when one has complete *bhakti* (love) for the Self.

Yogabalena prāṇamāveśya bhruvormadhye: By the power of *yoga*, in the middle of the eyebrows, concentrate on the *prāṇa*. It is not physical strength. It is the mental strength one acquires by *bhakti* and *dhyāna* that is known as *yoga-balena.*

Prāṇa is the expression of the vitality of life through the organs of the body. Our *Vedic* seers believed that it is centred in the middle of the eyebrows. Hence they use the words "centred in the middle of the eyebrows".

Such a person, who will merge into Him, will attain the status of God, is the Lord's promise.

यदक्षरं वेदविदो वदन्ति विशन्ति यद्यतयो वीतरागाः ।
यदिच्छन्तो ब्रह्मचर्यं चरन्ति तत्ते पदं संग्रहेण प्रवक्ष्ये ॥११॥

yad akṣaraṁ vedavido vadanti
***viśanti yad yatayo vītarāgāḥ* ।**
yad icchanto brahmacaryaṁ caranti
***tat te padaṁ saṁgraheṇa pravakṣye* ॥11॥**

That which the knowers of Vedas *declare Imperishable, that into which the self-controlled and free from attachment enter, desiring which men practise the vow of celibacy, that goal will I declare to you in brief.*

Śrī Kṛṣṇa says that He would describe briefly about the Supreme. He says that the knowers of the *Veda*s declare the Supreme as imperishable.

Who are the knowers of the *Vedas*? What are the *Vedas*? *Vedas* are the ancient existing scriptural teachings of the Hindus. The great *ṛṣis* of the past compiled the *Vedas*. They actually did not give their authorship of the *Vedas*. They said that during some moments of inspiration, a divine force made them say these words. Collection of such teachings were made into the four great *Vedas*, *Ṛgveda, Yajurveda*, *Sāmaveda* and *Atharvaveda*.

The knowers of *Vedas* are our ancient ancestors. They were learned men who practised divinity in their actions. They are all Godly men. They declared through the *Vedas* that the Supreme is eternal with no past, present and future. He is imperishable.

The Lord then says that one can enter into the Imperishable. By this, one has to understand that it is like the rivers entering into the ocean, and losing their identity. As we have discussed in the earlier chapters, the rivers originate as droplets of rain from the clouds which collected water-vapours from the ocean. Drops from the ocean come back to enter the ocean. The ocean remains the same. The learned people aim to enter into the *Brahman*, the Imperishable.

He then gives three requisites to enter the Supreme:

(1) self-control;
(2) freedom from attachment;
(3) practising the vow of celibacy.

Yatayaḥ: Self-controlled ascetics. We have already gone into this in detail. Control of the mind which wanders to the outer world because of its connection with the sense-organs is a necessary pre-requisite for liberation. This can start only when one has belief in the existence of the Lord and wants to know the Lord.

Vītarāgāḥ: Free from attachment. We get attached to worldly objects. Why? Because of our desires to possess this and that object in the world. This, we have learnt in earlier chapters, will lead us in a downward path to our destruction though it now and then gives a temporary state of happiness. Freedom from *kāma* and *krodha* will help one to free himself from *lobha*, *moha*, *mada*, *mātsarya,* etc. This is achieved by purifying the mind of impure tendencies. Freedom from attachment should not be by forcibly restraining the desires. It is obtained by gradually developing a sense of detachment, by growing out of attachments.

Let us take an example. A child is attached to its mother. Initially, she will be with her mother always. Gradually she goes out to play with her friends and comes back frequently to make sure her mother is still there. Later on, she spends longer hours away from mother pursuing studies. She still comes back to her mother whenever she can. When she gets attached to another man and gets married, she leaves the house. She, in the course of later years, sees her mother occasionally. She has, in the course of years freed herself from attachment to her mother. She did not simply drop everything one day and run away.

By growing out of passionate attachment to finite objects, one can blossom his intellect. He makes use of his intellect to develop the sense of renunciation.

(3) Brahmacarya: Practising the vow of celibacy. Desires are the ones that toss our minds. The greater the desires, the greater will be the waves of agitations in our minds. The practice of self-control and purity can be achieved by learning to have as few desires as possible. This, they say, is by practising vow of celibacy which is termed as *brahmacarya*. This is freedom from sensuality at all three levels, i.e., thought, word and deed (intellectual, mental and physical).

सर्वद्वाराणि संयम्य मनो हृदि निरुध्य च ।
मूर्ध्न्याधायात्मनः प्राणमास्थितो योगधारणाम् ॥१२॥

sarvadvārāṇi saṁyamya mano hṛdi nirudhya ca |
mūrdhnyādhāyātmanaḥ prāṇam āsthito yogadhāraṇām ||12||

ओमित्येकाक्षरं ब्रह्म व्याहरन्मामनुस्मरन् ।
यः प्रयाति त्यजन्देहं स याति परमां गतिम् ॥१३॥

om ity ekākṣaraṁ brahma vyāharan mām anusmaran |
yaḥ prayāti tyajan dehaṁ sa yāti paramāṁ gatim ||13||

Who having restrained all the gates (of the senses), fixing the mind in the heart (ātmā), *holding the vital breath in the head, concentrating on* ātmā *by yogic practice;*

Repeating the one-syllabled OṀ—the symbol of Brahman—*remembers Me at the time of death, he attains the Supreme Goal.*

The practice of concentration on *Brahman* is repeated in the beginning and the result of the practice one achieves is given at the end of these two *śloka*s.

The gates to any town bring in visitors. The doors in the house let wind in. Our sense-organs are the first source of our contact with the outer world. Restraining the senses is necessary for meditation. The mind also can get into turmoil by inwardly dwelling on memories of the past; restraining the mind is still more important for meditation.

Giving the mind a new channel to divert its attention upon is the next step. This is by 'fixing the mind in the heart'. Heart here means 'Soul' (*ātmā*). Literally, we use the word heart to describe one's love. "I love you with all my heart" is a common saying. What does the heart do? It distributes the fresh blood to all organs of the body every second of its life, and receives very small amounts to itself. It gives out selfless love to all the organs of the body. The source of all love is the heart. Spiritually, the love emanating from us is from our soul. The soul is an ocean of love. "Fix your mind on your soul" is what is implied here.

Mūrdhni (*brahmarandhra*: in the head) *prāṇam ādāya* (holding vital breath in the head): Life expresses itself through outer actions by our bodily organs. Instead of expressing life outwardly, "concentrate your life energy on your mind, intellect", is the meaning. Save your energy, do not waste it on your outward actions. Use it to develop spiritual progress. Give your intellect the energy to take you up the ladder of maturity. It is vital in your progress. If you do not hold it there, you are wasting energy on worldly pleasures and you will not attain purity and you will suffer pains in the course of time. This method of practice is called *yoga-dhāraṇā*.

Think of the Lord continuously (*om ityekākṣaraṁ vyāharan*).

The word *OṀ* is used here for the first time. What is *OṀ*? Why is it so great? *OṀ* is a word. It is the first word used to express *Brahman* in all His manifestations. One has to have a word to express something in brief. The word should mean the thing in detail. The word 'book' means something which has several sheets bound together into one volume which may or may not have something written inside the pages. Simply using the word 'book' denotes the entire meaning.

Akṣara is a syllable. It also means that which is not perishable. The syllables and words we learn in childhood are not perishable. They remain as our mode of expression and communication for the rest of our lives (till our death). In relation to our life-span they remain imperishable.

Our *ṛṣis* denoted *Brahman* and all His features by the 'one unperishable' word *OṀ*. The word for meditation is *ekākṣara OṀ*. Remembering Him at the time of death has been described before. It means thinking and contemplating on Him from earlier days of one's life. It is not repeating the word *OṀ* but the concept behind the word that should be thought of constantly (i.e., divinity).

By constant chanting of the *mantra OṀ*, if one departs dropping his ego, he will attain the supreme goal, the Lord promises again.

अनन्यचेताः सततं यो मां स्मरति नित्यशः ।
तस्याहं सुलभः पार्थ नित्ययुक्तस्य योगिनः ॥१४॥

ananyacetāḥ satataṁ yo māṁ smarati nityaśaḥ |
tasyāhaṁ sulabhaḥ pārtha nityayuktasya yoginaḥ ||14||

I am easily attainable by one, O Arjuna, who thinks of Me with single-minded devotion continuously and ever.

nityayukta	: ever united with Me;
satatam	: ever;
smarati	: remembers;
ananyachetāḥ	: single-minded devotion.

It is not difficult to attain Me, the Lord says. Just be devoted to me, think of nothing else, do it continuously and ever. This is all you need to do, He says. Practising the habit of thinking of Him constantly will make one perfect, in the course of time. If one can take the word divinity to mean the Lord, this becomes easy to understand. "Be godly always in your actions and thoughts" is all you need to do. It does not cost you anything.

मामुपेत्य पुनर्जन्म दुःखालयमशाश्वतम् ।
नाप्नुवन्ति महात्मानः संसिद्धिं परमां गताः ॥१५॥

mām upetya punarjanma duḥkhālayam aśāśvatam ।
nāpnuvanti mahātmānaḥ saṁsiddhiṁ paramāṁ gatāḥ ॥15॥

Having attained Me, these great souls do not again take birth on earth which is the place of pain and is non-eternal. They have reached the highest perfection.

First of all, the Lord uses the word *mahātmā* (great souls) to denote those who have attained Godhood by *sādhanā* as described before. Why should one attain Godhood? What is its benefit? Godhood is a state of absolute bliss where there is no room for sorrow.

What is birth? It is being born with a physical body and get a name and form to it. Because of having been born, one has to die also after sometime. One also has to suffer agonies of life due to attachment to our body and the outer world of objects. So, re-birth is described as a place of pain. Birth is non-eternal. Continuing the theme of the last paragraph, birth has to have death. Birth of happiness of being born will also include sorrow due to death of happiness by physical death. In simple words, happiness ends in sorrow. As discussed before, we are constantly looking for happiness. The perfect, happy state is one where there is no sorrow to follow.

By dropping the ego, by uniting with God, one attains this state of perfect happiness. Happiness is only a state of experience. One can only experience it. It cannot be described physically.

So, a *mahātmā* is one who has rejected the false (ego) and united with the real (*ātmā*). He is holding on to eternal joy. In contrast, *alpātmās* (little souls) are those who hold on to ego which is non-eternal (temporary joys).

आब्रह्मभुवनाल्लोकाः पुनरावर्तिनोऽर्जुन ।
मामुपेत्य तु कौन्तेय पुनर्जन्म न विद्यते ॥१६॥

***ā brahmabhuvanāl lokāḥ punarāvartino'rjuna* I**
***mām upetya tu kaunteya punarjanma na vidyate* II16II**

O Kaunteya, all worlds including that of Brahmā are subject to re-birth. But he who reaches Me has no re-birth.

Hindus believe that there are worlds like heaven (*svarga-loka*), *Brahma-loka*, *Kailāsa*, *Vaikuṇṭha-loka,* etc. They describe the place to be the abode of one specific *devatā* or God who resides there with those that reach Him after death. They also say that those who reach such places enjoy happiness and peace.

Śrī Kṛṣṇa, while teaching *advaita* philosophy through *Gītā* gives a different meaning to this belief. He says such places are not permanent residences for one to reach after death. They are only temporary. After having performed a *yajña* to obtain a result from a particular *devatā,* the person would reach the abode of such a *devatā*. When he has enjoyed the benefits of his *yajña*, he will fall back into the world again.

One gets happiness in proportion to his meritorious action. During that state of happiness, he is living in his own world of happiness. After sometime he will again reawaken to his worldly existence. This is what is meant by going to all the *loka*s.

It is not really true that such *loka*s exist. *Loka*, from what we have understood already, is what we perceive from our sense-organs and our mind and intellect. Let us take an example. We all are used to the idea of holidays. Holiday-resorts are places to enjoy. We start saving to plan for holidays. The cost depends upon where and when and what type of holidays we decide. Special holidays cost more money. We fly or drive or sail to the holiday-resort and enjoy a life of near bliss. At the end of the period, when we have got what we paid for, we return to our usual day-to-day life. A five star international hotel could be compared to the highest *loka*.

The *lokas* are nothing but the idea of holidays. They are places of reward for good work. The only happiness which is permanent is in merging with one's Self and that is called *mokṣa* or liberation. This is *advaita* philosophy. You and God are not two entities. Ego merging with Self (shadow merging with you) is *mokṣa*. As there is no ego, there is no feeling of suffering of pain, sorrow, etc. This state of eternal bliss is above the best of all *lokas*, i.e., *Brahmaloka*.

सहस्रयुगपर्यन्तमहर्यद्ब्रह्मणो विदुः ।
रात्रिं युगसहस्रान्तां तेऽहोरात्रविदो जनाः ॥१७॥

sahasrayuga-paryantam ahar yad brahmaṇo viduḥ I
rātriṁ yugasahasrāntāṁ te'horātravido janāḥ II17II

Those people who know the length of a day of Brahmā which lasts a thousand yugas *and the night which lasts a thousand* yugas, *they know day and night.*

An estimate of the duration of length of time for the day and the night of Brahmā is given here. Those who know it, the Lord says, know that even Brahmā is limited in relation to the time-span.

The day of Brahmā is 1000 *mahāyugas* and his night is 1000 *mahāyugas*. One complete day of Brahmā is therefore 2000 *yugas*.

Kaliyuga	432000	years	
Dvāparayuga	864000	years	(2 times *Kaliyuga*)
Tretāyuga	1296000	years	(3 " ")
Kṛtayuga	1728000	years	(4 " ")
	4320000	years is one *mahāyuga*.	

1000 *mahāyugas* is one day for *Brahmā*.

This will look silly for sceptics. They laugh at the life-span of *Brahmā* given in such mathematical terms. By bringing the notion of day and night and years, the concept of time has been introduced.

What is time? Time is truly the measure of the interval between two experiences. We are aware that in situations where and when we are happy the time flies. (On holidays we feel it has finished quickly. "Have we really finished our fortnight in Disneyland", we ask ourselves.) Similarly, when we are not happy, time goes slowly. When we are staying in a hospital bed or performing an unpleasant task, time moves slowly. If we are asked to keep silence for five minutes, we feel it is like an hour.

In one single experience, there is no time at all. The single experience of absolute bliss on merging with the Self is therefore eternal. As long as there is no experience (no personal attachment to objects) one can stay in this state. During sound sleep, we have no experience of time at all. The more composed we are at any level of happiness, the more we are away from contact with thought of the outer world, the longer will be that state of happiness. There will not be any "time" at all once we merge with our Self.

Brahmā has a span of time as His day. That is the time when creation takes place. (Our minds are full of creative, active thoughts in the day time.) But He also has a night where there is no activity and the entire universe comes to a state of halt. (In deep sleep there are no creative agitations in our minds.) So, it is said, at cosmic level that the Creator Brahmā conceives the gross world only during His waking hours.

अव्यक्ताद्व्यक्तयः सर्वाः प्रभवन्त्यहरागमे ।
रात्र्यागमे प्रलीयन्ते तत्रैवाव्यक्तसंज्ञके ॥१८॥

avyaktād vyaktayaḥ sarvāḥ prabhavanty aharāgame I
rātryāgame pralīyante tatraivā vyaktasaṁjñake II18II

From the unmanifested all manifest beings proceed at the coming of the day. At the coming of the night, they dissolve in that only which is called unmanifested.

Aharāgame: Coming of the day.

भूतग्रामः स एवायं भूत्वा भूत्वा प्रलीयते ।
रात्र्यागमेऽवशः पार्थ प्रभवत्यहरागमे ॥१९॥

bhūtagrāmaḥ sa evāyaṁ bhūtvā bhūtvā pralīyate I
rātryāgame'vaśaḥ pārtha prabhavatyaharāgame II19II

O Pārtha, that multitude of beings keep coming forth again and again, and are dissolved helplessly at the coming forth of 'night' and they come forth again and again at the coming of the 'day'.

These two verses have a subtle meaning one has to understand. What is day? What is night? What is creation? What is *pralaya* or dissolution? The day is to be taken as 'birth' and night as 'death'. The day is 'creation' and night is *pralaya* (dissolution).

Creation is the production of something new. Philosophically, creation is the production from existing material of something new. The life is created out of five gross elements in existence. Once created, it gets a name and form. It also gets qualities of its own. That is what we are—creations by the God as individuals in the universe.

The names and forms are said to be in an unmanifest form (*avyakta*) in the elements of nature. When they get life and a form they become manifest (hence the words used at cremation —earth to earth). Taking it to one lower level of our day-to-day life, we can analyse this concept further.

Our today is what we thought of and acted yesterday. Our actions, thoughts, all leave an imprint of *vāsanā*s on our mind. The thought-impressions lie in unmanifest form at the beginning of the day and manifest themselves as the day blossoms. Our actions, good or bad, therefore depend upon our existing imprints. We automatically proceed to act in that channel of thoughts. As there are millions of imprints at any time, the strong and large number of similar thoughts will manifest into action first.

Let us now take up night of deep sleep. We do not have any physical activity at that time. Our minds still have the imprints. But they are unmanifest. In the unmanifest state there are no differences. In deep sleep a king and a beggar are the same. One cannot differentiate between the two. Philosophically, the two are in a state of *pralaya* or unmanifested thought-period.

As soon as the two wake up, they show their manifested thoughts in their actions. This is, philosophically, the state of 'creation'. We get enslaved by our own thoughts and act accordingly. We are born again and again and manifest our thoughts, in spite of ourselves (*avaśaḥ*). Can we not break this chain? Yes, we can. By using our intellect in the wakeful state—by using our *buddhi* and acting accordingly. *Niṣkāma karma* and *karma-phala-tyāga*, we have discussed before, are the way to act in order to get liberated.

The past always follows us till the light of knowledge is lit. On physical death, the subtle body with its impressions is carried by a force which manifests itself again (through the five gross elements) to express its thoughts of the past again and to fulfil the thoughts of the past.

परस्तस्मात्तु भावोऽन्योऽव्यक्तोऽव्यक्तात्सनातनः ।
यः स सर्वेषु भूतेषु नश्यत्सु न विनश्यति ॥२०॥

***paras tasmāt tu bhāvo'nyo'vyakto'vyaktāt sanātanaḥ* I**
***yaḥ sa sarveṣu bhūteṣu naśyatsu na vinaśyati* II20II**

But there exists higher than that unmanifested, another unmanifested, which is eternal, which is not destroyed even when all beings are destroyed.

This verse is a continuation of the theme of the two previous verses. The unmanifested thoughts (*vāsanās*) keep on manifesting to fulfil the thoughts entertained in the past. But there should be one factor on which all the unmanifested and the manifested are supported. And that factor is *Brahman*. The Creator and His creation are Absolute existence and relative existence respectively. The phenomenal universe has also its manifest state (perceived by the senses and intellect) and the unmanifest state. This manifest and unmanifest state of the universe and its beings come within relative existence. But there is an Absolute Existence which is eternal and unmanifest.

In some theatres, different shows are shown on any one day. One film may be sexy, one a cartoon, one a western and one religious. All films were unmanifest in the reels in the projector room. On projection, they become manifest. At the end of the cinema they are unmanifest again. We go and see the ever-changing cinemas that day. What was beyond the unmanifest cinemas which got manifested was the screen. Without the screen there would not be any cinemas. The screen is in front of us (the Self is in us) but we do not see it or it does not register itself or we do not take notice of it.

Our ignorance of the existence of the Self is *avidyā*. By opening our inner eye of knowledge, we can see it (realise it). As soon as the light of knowledge is lit, the ignorance is burnt away and we can merge into the Self (higher unmanifest) or Absolute Existence. This higher unmanifest is (1) Eternal (2) Supreme (3) Exists even when all beings perish.

अव्यक्तोऽक्षर इत्युक्तस्तमाहुः परमां गतिम् ।
यं प्राप्य न निवर्तन्ते तद्धाम परमं मम ॥२१॥

avyakto'kṣara ity uktas tam āhuḥ paramāṁ gatim I
yaṁ prāpya na nivartante tad dhāma paramaṁ mama ||21||

That which is called unmanifested and imperishable, that they say, is the highest goal. They who reach it return not, that is My highest abode.

We, the mortals, should be aiming for higher goals in life. We all get excited when we score a goal. What is a goal? It is a point scored against our opponent. We feel happy when we score against our opponents.

In life, the opponents are happiness and sorrow. Each goal scored is happiness against sorrow. What we do not realise is, the ball that was hit to score the goal bounces back and causes sorrow (hits a goal against us). We can never score only happiness in our lives. The only goal which does not bounce back to the goal-post of sorrow is the highest goal which is the abode of the Self. The Self does not let the ball bounce back and then one is said to be in a state of bliss because of the victory achieved.

Our *Vedas* describe this as *Paramātmā* (*Brahman*), who is unmanifest and imperishable. The symbol of *Brahman* is *OṀ* and *Vedic* seers advocate *upāsanā* (meditation) on *OṀ*.

पुरुषः स परः पार्थ भक्त्या लभ्यस्त्वनन्यया ।
यस्यान्तःस्थानि भूतानि येन सर्वमिदं ततम् ॥२२॥

puruṣaḥ sa paraḥ pārtha bhaktyā labhyas tv ananyayā |
yasyāntaḥsthāni bhūtāni yena sarvam idaṁ tatam ||22||

O Pārtha, that highest puruṣa *is attainable by unswerving devotion to Him alone, within whom all beings dwell and by whom all this is pervaded.*

Śrī Kṛṣṇa calls the eternal substratum, the one which is above the unmanifested *vāsanās*, as the highest *puruṣa*. Where does this *puruṣa* abide? He says that the *puruṣa* abides inside all of us, and also pervades the total universe. He is omniscient. How can one reach Him? How can one reach His abode? By total devotion (*ananya bhakti*) one can reach His abode.

If I want to leave my town and go and settle down in a city, I must do so only when I think I will be secure in the new place. I must develop a love for that place. The details of the place should be known to me. I should have read books on it and enquired from people who know about this place.

If I am not sure where I want to go, whether to the U.K. or Australia or America, etc., I will be tossing over restlessly in my bed and cannot make up my mind. I keep on changing my plans and will not reach anywhere to reside permanently. Similarly, I must learn to love God—this method is called *bhakti* or devotion. Devotion is total selfless identification with the object devoted to. (I must be devoted totally to go to the U.K. and to settle there permanently. I must have total love for the U.K.). I must dissociate myself from the outer world. I must drop my 'I'- and 'My'-ness.

Once I have totally identified myself with the Self, I will come out of the cycle of births and deaths. Our aim in life is to realise the truth that the Lord in us in *Parama Puruṣa*. At the same time we must be able to see this *Parama Puruṣa* all round us in all objects which have names and forms.

यत्र काले त्वनावृत्तिमावृत्तिं चैव योगिनः ।
प्रयाता यान्ति तं कालं वक्ष्यामि भरतर्षभ ॥२३॥

yatra kāle tv anāvṛttim āvṛttiṁ caiva yoginaḥ I
prayātā yānti taṁ kālaṁ vakṣyāmi bharatarṣabha II23II

O best of Bharatas, departing at what time yogīs *never return, and at what time* yogīs *return after their departure, those times I will tell you now.*

A *yogī*, in this context, is one who is trying to achieve unity with *Paramātmā*. He is a *sādhaka*. We know that it is easy to get the mind distracted in the path to get *mokṣa*. There are different types of *sādhaka*s who get different end-results.

(1) Those who strive sincerely but die before achieving the end-result.
(2) Those who achieve the end-result in this life (*jīvan-muktas*).
(3) Those who get distracted and lose track of the goal.
(4) We can add those how do not try at all. They are always enjoying the pleasures of the world and are ignorant of liberation.

Depending on these, there are two paths to pursue. One path leads the *sādhaka* upwards towards *mokṣa*. It is the path of 'no return'. The other path leads one back to the pluralistic world and that is the path of 'return'. Śrī Kṛṣṇa is going to tell his disciple as to when the *sādhaka*s go on the two different paths.

अग्निर्ज्योतिरहः शुक्लः षण्मासा उत्तरायणम् ।
तत्र प्रयाता गच्छन्ति ब्रह्म ब्रह्मविदो जनाः ॥२४॥

agnir jyotir ahaḥ śuklaḥ ṣaṇmāsā uttarāyaṇam I
tatra prayātā gacchanti brahma brahmavido janāḥ II24II

Fire, light, day-time, bright fortnight, six months of northern solstice—following this path, men who know Brahman *go to* Brahman.

In the Upaniṣads (*Praśnopaniṣad*), while describing the origin of life, it is said that Prajāpati, the creator, got the desire to create. He then manifested himself as energy (sun) and matter (moon). The *yogīs* who worship the sun are said to be those who will attain final liberation. Those who worship matter (moon) are those that are interested in worldly pleasures and end up by being born again. This is the *Upaniṣad*'s teaching. We have to understand the verse in this context.

What is 'sun'? He is light, ever shining and blesses all. The sun is therefore compared to knowledge. Those who worship knowledge will get liberation in course of time. The examples given here, if we look carefully, point to brighter things. *Agni,* light and day-time all refer to brightness.

In a month there are two cycles. The first fortnight ends in full moon and second fortnight ends in new moon. The full moon fortnight is the period of ascending brightness till the day of the full moon. This fortnight is called *śukla pakṣa* or bright fortnight. This is used to signify light again.

In a year the first six months, spring and summer, are brighter and the other six months, autumn and winter, are comparatively darker. The first six months of spring and summer are the northern solstice, commonly known as *uttarāyaṇa.*

Those who follow the path of light to reach knowledge will attain *brahmajñāna*. This will lead to liberation. It is not literally the fornight part of the month, day time of a full day or first six months of a year. It is only a philosophical statement indicating brightness which is only a symbol of knowledge. A *jñānī* attains *jñāna* is all its meaning.

धूमो रात्रिस्तथा कृष्णः षण्मासा दक्षिणायनम् ।
तत्र चान्द्रमसं ज्योतिर्योगी प्राप्य निवर्तते ॥२५॥

***dhūmo rātris tathā kṛṣṇaḥ ṣaṇmāsā dakṣiṇāyanam* I**
***tatra cāndramasaṁ jyotir yogī prāpya nivartate* II25II**

Smoke, night-time, the dark fortnight, also six months of the southern solstice, attaining by these to the lunar light, the yogī *returns.*

This is in contrast to the last verse. Moon, the matter-representation of Prajāpati in *Praśnopaniṣad* is compared to darkness. What is not true knowledge, in philosophical terms, is ignorance. If knowledge is "bright", ignorance is "dark". If sun is light, moon is dark. The moon represents the worldly life because it is matter (philosophically).

Smoke clouds the light of the fire and causes 'darkness'. Night-time is dark and the second half of the month leads to new moon (comparatively dark). Lastly, autumn and winter are dark seasons. These six months are called southern solstice or *dakṣiṇāyana.*

Those who follow the path away from knowledge, and go towards the path of ignorance, will therefore be satisfying the ego. They will do *karma*s to obtain the benefits promised in the *Veda*s and come back to this world or *saṁsāra* again.

In the *Upaniṣad*s, this path of return is called *pitṛyāna* (path leading to the world of ancestors). In *Mahābhārata,* we find Bhīṣma staying on the bed of arrows waiting for *uttarāyaṇa* so that he can go to the abode of knowledge. This has been understood wrongly.

Really speaking, Bhīṣma had known the wrong things he had done on account of the promise given to his father. He had promised that he would protect the throne of Hastināpura, and that he would not marry. Because of that, whatever mistakes Dhṛtarāṣṭra committed, he did not take retaliatory action. Even when Pāṇḍavas were deprived of the kingdom by the devious and dubious means followed by Duryodhana and even when Duḥśāsana disrobed Draupadī, he remained silent and unmoved. He even sided with Kauravas (unrighteous). He had one boon and it was that he could die anytime he wished. He used this boon to ask to be laid on the bed of arrows when he got wounded. He really wanted to pay the penalty for his mistakes and gave himself the punishment. He wanted the light of knowledge to dawn and repent for his mistakes.

One should not therefore take the literal meaning that those who die in the first six months attain *mokṣa* and those who die in *dakṣiṇāyana* do not attain *mokṣa.* A lot of great people who have died in *dakṣiṇāyana*, we are sure, will not fail to attain *mokṣa* because of dying at the 'wrong' time of the year.

शुक्लकृष्णे गती ह्येते जगतः शाश्वते मते ।
एकया यात्यनावृत्तिमन्ययावर्तते पुनः ॥२६॥

śuklakṛṣṇe gatī hy ete jagataḥ śāśvate mate |
ekayā yāty anāvṛttim anyayāvartate punaḥ ||26||

The paths of light and darkness are both thought to be eternal. By the one, man does not return, by the other, he returns again.

The Path of Light is the path of spiritualism. The Path of Darkness is the path of materialism. Saying that the paths are eternal means that the paths were there for our ancestors, the paths are there for us and the paths will be there for our future generations. Men of the past, present and future would have or will have the choice always to attain liberation or fall into *saṁsāra*. The whole world of objects is revolving around the two paths.

नैते सृती पार्थ जानन् योगी मुह्यति कश्चन ।
तस्मात्सर्वेषु कालेषु योगयुक्तो भवार्जुन ॥२७॥

naite sṛtī pārtha jānan yogī muhyati kaścana |
tasmāt sarveṣu kāleṣu yogayukto bhavārjuna ||27||

O Pārtha, knowing these two paths, no yogin *is deluded. Therefore at all time, be steadfast in* yoga.

This chapter is on imperishable *Brahman*. A *yogī* is one who is working to get united with *Brahman*. He knows that by attaining liberation, he would be united with *Brahman* and would be part of the imperishable.

In one sense, the Lord is asking us not to be deluded by the periods of time mentioned in these examples, but to realise the meaning behind the examples. "Do not take the literal meaning of the examples" is His behest.

In another sense, Śrī Kṛṣṇa is advising Arjuna to keep the thought of knowledge (truth) always as his goal and not let ignorance distract him even for a second. Be a steadfast *yoga-yukta*, the Lord says. "O Arjuna, while engaged in the activities of this world, constantly keep the awareness of the divine in you and act accordingly", is Kṛṣṇa's great message (for *karma-yogī* Arjuna). Identify yourself as part of *akṣara-parabrahma* is His plea to this disciple.

वेदेषु यज्ञेषु तपःसु चैव दानेषु यत्पुण्यफलं प्रदिष्टम् ।
अत्येति तत्सर्वमिदं विदित्वा योगी परं स्थानमुपैति चाद्यम् ॥२८॥

vedeṣu yajñeṣu tapaḥsu caiva
dāneṣu yat puṇyaphalaṁ pradiṣṭam I
atyeti tat sarvam idaṁ viditvā
yogī paraṁ sthānam upaiti cādyam II28II

Whatever fruit or merit is declared to arise from the study of the Vedas, *the performance of sacrifices, practise of austerities, and the offering of gifts, beyond all these goes the* yogī *who knows the imperishable* Brahman *and attains the supreme primeval state.*

Vedeṣu: By the study of the *Veda*s. The followers of *jñāna-mārga* are those who study the *Veda*s.

Yajñeṣu: The followers of *karma-yoga* are those who perform *yajña*s. The *yajña*s are performed to attain reward as mentioned in *karma-kāṇda*.

Tapaḥsu: Those who perform different austerities.

Dāneṣu: Those who give for charitable purposes what they have.

All these people, true, are *sādhaka*s on the spiritual path. They attain good results for their acts. They may not attain final liberation. *Māyā* is round the corner and can catch anyone unaware at any time. The *yogī* who knows the imperishable *Brahman* attains the supreme, divine state.

What does this "state" mean? "The one who knows" is a very important statement here. Real knowing means actually uniting in with the Lord. One can know something only when he understands it fully. By understanding fully, one will act according to what one understands. Understanding something and doing something else are contradictory terms. If you do not do as you understand, it means you have not understood it.

Understanding *Brahman* which is 'Pure Divinity' means acting in 'Total Pure Divinity'. In essence, one should be divine. "You will attain *mokṣa*" is the Lord's promise for those who know 'Him' fully.

इति श्रीमद्भगवद्गीतासूपनिषत्सु ब्रह्मविद्यायां योगशास्त्रे
श्रीकृष्णार्जुनसंवादे अक्षरपरब्रह्मयोगो नाम अष्टमोऽध्यायः ॥

Iti śrīmadbhagavadgītāsūpaniṣatsu brahma-vidyāyāṁ yogaśāstre śrīkṛṣṇārjuna-saṁvāde akṣara-parabrahma-yogo nāma aṣṭamo'dhyāyaḥ **II**

CHAPTER 9

RĀJAVIDYĀ-RĀJAGUHYA-YOGA

This chapter deals with the *yoga* of royal knowledge and royal secret. Rājā is a king. King is a supreme, powerful leader of his people who live in his kingdom.

In our body our Self is the ruler or the king. Knowledge of the ruler or Self is *rājavidyā.* It is not a secret in the real meaning of the term. It should be imparted to those who seek it. If a thing is there openly, everybody can get it easily. A thing that is obtained easily will not have the same value as something that is obtained by hard work. Hence this is a royal secret. But it is open to anybody who wants to find it. Scriptures show the way.

This chapter continues to dwell on the theme of *'tat'* or 'That' part of *tat tvam asi*. Another interpretation for this chapter is as follows: In ancient days, the people were ruled by kings and emperors. It was important that the king and his ministers should know the scriptures which teach moral laws. Only a properly trained person could become the king. As it was an inherited post, they were taught *Veda*s at an early age. They were taught to consider the welfare of their subjects as a divine act. So, it is called *rājavidyā, rājaguhya-yoga*. The kings possessed and practised this knowledge of *ātman*.

श्रीभगवानुवाच
इदं तु ते गुह्यतमं प्रवक्ष्याम्यनसूयवे ।
ज्ञानं विज्ञानसहितं यज्ज्ञात्वा मोक्ष्यसेऽशुभात् ।।१।।

śrī bhagavān uvāca
idaṁ tu te guhyatamaṁ pravakṣyāmy anasūyave **I**
jñānaṁ vijñānasahitaṁ yaj jñātvā mokṣyase'śubhāt **II1II**

The Lord said

To you, free from envy, I shall declare this profound secret knowledge combined with realisation, which having known, you shall be freed from all evil.

'Do not envy others, whatever may be the situation' is the Lord's command to mankind. Many wars have been fought because of envy.

Jñānaṁ vijñānasahitam: "Knowledge combined with realisation". Knowledge comes from reading and wisdom comes from realising what is read.

For example, many people in India have knowledge of Britain and America. They have read or heard about it. They can give you all the facts about these countries. But they would have no personal experience of these countries. Those who have gone to Britain and seen Buckingham Palace can describe it better.

There are many medical books in the shops. By reading them one does not become a doctor. One has to undergo hard training to become a doctor. The doctor who has personal experiences of some problems relating to the health of himself or his family is the wiser of the lot because he understands others with similar problems much better.

Finally, the Lord says, by having got the wisdom, you shall be freed from evil. Evil here, means the cycle of *saṁsāra* of births and deaths with associated problems of decay, disease etc.

राजविद्या राजगुह्यं पवित्रमिदमुत्तमम् ।
प्रत्यक्षावगमं धर्म्यं सुसुखं कर्तुमव्ययम् ॥२॥

rājavidyā rājaguhyaṁ pavitram idam uttamam |
pratyakṣāvagamaṁ dharmyaṁ susukhaṁ kartum avyayam ||2||

This is royal secret, royal knowledge, purifier, supreme, realisable by direct knowledge, according to dharma, *very easy to perform and imperishable.*

What is 'This' the Lord is talking about? It is "the knowledge of *ātmā*". It is *brahmajñāna.* The Lord enumerates the qualities of this knowledge.

Śrī Kṛṣṇa calls his teaching 'profoundest secret'. We do know that the subject under discussion is *ātma-jñāna* or 'Knowledge of *ātman*'. Why should it be a secret? It is not really a secret in the sense of something that others should not know. It is something that all should know. Unfortunately, all of us have different qualities. Because of some weak qualities that some people have, they do not really understand *ātmā*. Such people not only do not understand but even misrepresent it by giving wrong meaning to what is written or said. By doing so they will spread the word that the *Gītā* is not good. This would affect some other people as well who take these people's words as gospel truth, and stop looking at it themselves. If the secret is given to those with better qualities, they will make use of it to analyse themselves and better themselves. In return they will benefit others and keep the 'Light of the *Gītā*' shining.

The Lord then tells Arjuna that He will declare this secret to him. He would do so because Arjuna is free from envy. Among all bad qualities, envy is the worst. Arjuna's heart is pure; there is no trace of envy. We know that Arjuna with his brothers faced humiliation at the hands of Duryodhana. Duryodhana and his brothers insulted the Pāṇḍavas. Still, Arjuna was willing to give them the kingdom. He considers Duryodhana is ignorant. He is fighting him in the war but does not hate him.

Envy and jealousy are bad qualities. One must look upon all equally. "So and so is a rich man; he has so many material possessions; I should attain his status", should not be the feeling one should develop. Similarly, "so and so is clever. I am not so clever. I do not like him". Such feelings would disrupt the calmness of mind which is essential for Self-control. It is royal knowledge and royal secret. This has been discussed in the beginning of this chapter.

It is a purifier. It imparts purity to the *sādhaka*s. One will be free from all sins. By understanding the Self in oneself and in others, the person will be able to look at the world in a different angle, his actions will make the world a better place to live in peacefully. It is therefore supreme knowledge (*param*) also.

Pratyakṣāvagamam: It is to be realised by direct intuition. It can be comprehended. It is not difficult to realise the *ātmā*. One must have belief in it and scriptures and *guru*s will show him how easy it is for him to understand it. One can appreciate the mango fruit when one actually eats it. Any amount of description will not help.

It is according to *dharma* and pertaining to *dharma*. *Ātmā* is the conscious principle behind life's manifestation. The rest of our body is only made up of minerals which have no life without the *ātmā* inside. The knowledge is according to the scriptures. Śrī Kṛṣṇa is not teaching a new mode of religious order. He is re-iterating the philosophy of the *Veda*s.

Once an attempt is made to understand it and one has belief in it, it is not difficult to obtain the knowledge. One need not require any material wealth to buy it. It does not involve hard physical labour. It does not stop one from doing one's worldly duties. One can be a *saṁsārī*. In other words, it is simply an 'art of right action' in our daily actions. It does not stop us from our work. Hindus therefore say that the *Gītā* is nothing but 'a way of living' for the welfare of society, by purifying individuals in society.

Avyayam: This knowledge is imperishable. No one can take it away from us. We may lose anything else we possess but we cannot lose our wisdom.

अश्रद्दधानाः पुरुषा धर्मस्यास्य परंतप ।
अप्राप्य मां निवर्तन्ते मृत्युसंसारवर्त्मनि ॥३॥

***aśraddadhānāḥ puruṣā dharmasyāsya parantapa* I**
***aprāpya māṁ nivartante mṛtyusaṁsāravartmani* II3II**

O Parantapa, those without faith in this dharma, not attaining Me, return to the path of the world of death.

The Lord brings out two important facts in relation to *ātmajñāna*. First of all, he states that one must have faith in the subject. Faith is not mere blind faith. A person with blind faith cannot sustain his efforts towards achieving the object of his desire. Real faith comes with right intellectual comprehension.

The degree of success in life depends on the intensity of one's faith. Strong effort in concentration on what to achieve and strong effort to remove what obstructs the aim, depends on one's faith.

The explanation for drop-outs from colleges can be given on this principle. The student must have strong faith in the degree he wants to achieve. He must be prepared to sacrifice some personal pleasures in the process. If he gets distracted, he finds the effort too hard and drops out. He would repent his action sooner or later.

If one has no belief in *ātmā* and if one has no faith in scriptures then he is not going to achieve liberation. *Ātmajñāna* is the one that gives permanent bliss, all other knowledge brings temporary happiness. Those without faith in *ātmā*, will end up facing innumerable births and deaths.

मया ततमिदं सर्वं जगदव्यक्तमूर्तिना ।
मत्स्थानि सर्वभूतानि न चाहं तेष्ववस्थितः ॥४॥

***mayā tatam idaṁ sarvaṁ jagad avyaktamūrtinā* |**
***matsthāni sarvabhūtāni na cāhaṁ teṣv avasthitaḥ* ||4||**

By Me all this universe is pervaded in the unmanifested form. All beings are in Me and I do not abide in them.

Kṛṣṇa says that he is Omniscient. The entire universe is pervaded by Him. We are all inside Him and He is not in us. This would cause confusion to the ignorant who have not understood the teaching so far. It is true that the Lord said that there is *ātmā* inside each one of us. How can then one say 'He is not in us'?

The Lord has also said that the Lord inside us is the same Lord who is inside all of us. If the same is everywhere, where is the individual existence? This is *advaita* philosophy. As long as the feeling of duality exists (*dvaita*), one sees two entities. Once he realises the 'oneness', then He will not see anything different anywhere. He sees oneness in all. The divinity which has no physical form, which is only an essence has to be one single factor. It appears in many names and forms but is only one.

When we look inside a room with a lot of mirrors, we can see our reflections in all mirrors. Theoretically speaking, I am in each one of those reflections but it is the "same me" 'in all'. I am therefore pervading all my reflections. The Lord therefore says He pervades the universe in unmanifest form and all beings are in Him.

We should therefore have love and compassion for all. We should not hurt others. Hurting others will be like hurting oneself.

In my own body, my hand is me. Technically, I am in my hand also. That hand is mine and not anybody else's. I am pervading my whole body. 'Myness' is in all parts of the body. I am pervading them all. I show the same love to all parts of my body and tenderly care for them all. This comparison would make one understand the meaning in this verse.

न च मत्स्थानि भूतानि पश्य मे योगमैश्वरम् ।
भूतभृन्न च भूतस्थो ममात्मा भूतभावनः ॥५॥

na ca matsthāni bhūtāni paśya me yogam aiśvaram I
bhūtabhṛn na ca bhūtastho mamātmā bhūtabhāvanaḥ II5II

Nor all beings exist in Me. Behold My divine yoga. Supporting all beings, but not dwelling in them, I am the 'efficient cause' of all beings.

This is an apparent contradiction to the last verse. But to one who has understood it, it is no contradiction at all.

Being as what we are, is due to superimposition of ego on our Self with an apparent physical body with mind and intellect. There is no form and name if there is no life in us. If all of us drop our ego, there is only one thing left, that is, the 'life force' or 'energy' or in scriptural terms 'divinity'. Inside this 'divinity' there is nothing because there are no more physical entities of name and form.

This is again stressing *advaita* philosophy. This is the 'royal secret'. There is nothing but only *Parabrahma*, the Creator, who is playing a game to amuse Himself. The cosmic illusion is apparent.

The dreamer dreams that he is in a palace and enjoying its benefits. He is existing only in the body who is dreaming. The body is pervading the dreamer with its palace and all luxuries in it. The body is not in a dream. When awakened, the dream did not exist as far as the body is concerned. The awakened body will say there was no king and palace. This is because the illusion of the dream vanished once the person woke up. He is said to be a knowledgeable person as far as the dream is concerned.

यथाकाशस्थितो नित्यं वायुः सर्वत्रगो महान् ।
तथा सर्वाणि भूतानि मत्स्थानीत्युपधारय ॥६॥

***yathākāśasthito nityaṁ vāyuḥ sarvatrago mahān* I**
***tathā sarvāṇi bhūtāni matsthānīty upadhāraya* II6II**

As the mighty wind, moving everywhere, rests always in space (ākāśa) *even so, know you, all beings are in Me.*

This verse is a beautiful example which brings out the all-pervasive character of the Supreme. It is difficult (as we discussed before) to describe the Lord because He is subtler than the most subtle, and beyond comprehension at mental and intellectual levels.

The universe is subtle. It is also not really seen. We all understand:

(1) That the wind moves in space and space does not move. The space is occupying infinite area and wind occupies only a few miles of the surface of the space. Similarly, all of us are inside *Paramātmā*, He is occupying space infinitely bigger than the Universe.

Wind carries all types of smell but space does not get affected by it. Similarly, we all act differently, but it does not affect the Lord.

(2) *Ākāśa* is subtler than wind. The Lord is subtler than we are.

(3) Space pervades all. *Paramātmā* pervades all.

Still, space is not *Paramātmā*. We all respect and fear the powerful. Why not respect the Divine Lord and stop undivine acts?

Though we have very little strength or power in us, we act so proudly and proclaim our strength. Think of the Supreme, who is stronger than all of us. Let us not be proud of our temporary strength. Let us realise that the subtlest Lord is a witness to all our actions. Would one commit a crime in front of people he knows and respects? We try to hide our crimes in front of others, including our loved ones. Then why commit a sin when you know that the Lord is seeing it all?

सर्वभूतानि कौन्तेय प्रकृतिं यान्ति मामिकाम् ।
कल्पक्षये पुनस्तानि कल्पादौ विसृजाम्यहम् ॥७॥

sarvabhūtāni kaunteya prakṛtiṁ yānti māmikām |
kalpakṣaye punas tāni kalpādau visṛjāmy aham ||7||

O Kaunteya, all beings go into My prakṛti *at the end of a* kalpa. *I bring them forth again at the beginning of a* kalpa.

A *kalpa* is the time from creation of the universe to the total dissolution of the universe. We poor mortals are not aware of its span and also not aware of how many times it has repeated itself.

All creation is brought to life at the beginning which is called *sṛṣti*. When the creation is withdrawn, it is called *pralaya*. The period of existence is *sthiti*. Creation, existence, dissolution is one circle (*sṛṣṭi*, *sthiti*, *laya*).

All this is happening because the Supreme had a desire to project Himself out and play. He produced the total body-mind-intellect equipment which is His nature, called *prakṛti*. He projects out again and again through His *prakṛti*.

This is better understood on looking at a child playing on her own in her room. She is, at the time of play, living in an imaginary world. She comes out of imaginary play when she wants to, and starts play when she wants to. It is her decision only. The imaginary world is a puppet in her hands.

The child decides that part of her room is a castle. She imagines she is wearing royal clothes and has servants attending to her needs and at her command. She does not take notice of the real world during such periods. Whatever material she has in her room gets imaginary names and forms during playtime. Suddenly when she has had enough, the imaginary world goes inside her and materials with names and forms become simple materials again.

She repeats it as often as she wishes and changes the imaginary scenes at her own free will. She created the world and caused its dissolution. Nothing happened to her in the process. She remained as a witness to the entire scene.

प्रकृतिं स्वामवष्टभ्य विसृजामि पुनः पुनः ।
भूतग्राममिमं कृत्स्नमवशं प्रकृतेर्वशात् ॥८॥

prakṛtiṁ svām avaṣṭabhya visṛjāmi punaḥ punaḥ |
bhūtagrāmam imaṁ kṛtsnam avaśaṁ prakṛter vaśāt ||8||

Animating My prakṛti, *I again and again send forth all this multitude of beings who are helpless by the force of nature.*

This is in continuation of the theme of the last verse. The Supreme is responsible for constant recurrence of creation and dissolution. It is His nature or *prakṛti* which binds us all with its *māyā*. Except the rare liberated souls all others are bound by *māyā*.

The Lord says that the beings are helpless by the force of nature. Our *vāsanā*s (thought imprints) dictate our actions. As we discussed before, the king and beggar in a hall were no different during sleep. They automatically show their attitudes as soon as they wake up. We are also bound by our *vāsanā*s.

The only way we have to come out of it is to purify our minds. *Niṣkāma karma* and *karma-phala-tyāga* will liberate us. All the rest will fall into the repetitive cycle of *saṁsāra*.

न च मां तानि कर्माणि निबध्नन्ति धनञ्जय ।
उदासीनवदासीनमसक्तं तेषु कर्मसु ॥९॥

na ca māṁ tāni karmāṇi nibadhnanti dhanañjaya |
udāsīnavadāsīnam asaktaṁ teṣu karmasu ||9||

O Dhanañjaya, nor do those actions bind Me, who remain indifferent and unconcerned to those actions.

The Lord is not attached to His actions in creating the imaginary world, and He remains indifferent to the actions. The child imagining the world she created, does not get attached to her world and is indifferent. She imagines the whole scene, she imagines the words spoken by the characters created etc. but she as the child is only a witness. The sun bestows light equally everywhere. Our actions in sunlight vary from good to bad. They do not affect the sun. The scenes on a cinema screen do not leave any imprint on the screen but without the screen the film cannot be shown. Similarly, all our egocentric thoughts leave *vāsanā*-imprint on our mind. Thoughts without egotistic feelings do not leave imprints. This is because, egotistic thoughts want a result and our mind keeps those thoughts till the desire is fulfilled by proper action.

The Lord's creation of the universe is just His līlā. He is not directly attached to anybody. He is letting His creatures decide their own future. As long as we have *vāsanās* to burn, the Lord dynamises the subtle body and gives it a channel to burn itself out. But what the physical body that ensues from the subtle body does, is up to the individual body.

मयाध्यक्षेण प्रकृतिः सूयते सचराचरम् ।
हेतुनानेन कौन्तेय जगद्विपरिवर्तते ॥१०॥

***mayādhyakṣeṇa prakṛtiḥ sūyate sacarācaram* I**
***hetunānena kaunteya jagad viparivartate* II10II**

O Kaunteya, by Me as a supervisor, prakṛti *produces the moving and unmoving. Because of this, the world revolves.*

sūyate: produced
viparivartate: revolves

This verse brings out the relationships between the Self (*Puruṣa*) and *prakṛti* (nature).

Whatever is unmanifested (due to *vāsanās*) in nature gets its life (manifested) by the mere presence of the Self. As long as the *vāsanās* remain, the person is thrown into the cycle of *saṁsāra*. After the death of the physical body the subtle body with its *vāsanās* gets its new life by the power of the Self. The universe revolves around this principle. The Lord only acts as a spark to kindle the light of life and gives the life the force to express itself in its varied manifested forms. The Lord acts only as a supervisor who is personally not affected but is essential to activise the engine of life. A number of examples will illustrate this point.

(1) A magnet is essential for an inert needle to move near its vicinity. The movement produced has no effect on the magnet but the magnet must be present.

(2) The mere presence of the sun in day-light makes people get up and get on with their daily activities. The activities are different and plenty but the sun is not affected. Day-light has to be there for people to get on with their work.

Similarly, the *ātman* (Lord) by His presence, illumines the gross and subtle body and helps them to manifest their unmanifested *vāsanās*.

अवजानन्ति मां मूढा मानुषीं तनुमाश्रितम् ।
परं भावमजानन्तो मम भूतमहेश्वरम् ॥११॥

***avajānanti māṁ mūḍhā mānuṣīṁ tanum āśritam* I**
***paraṁ bhāvam ajānanto mama bhūta-maheśvaram* II11II**

Fools disregard Me, dwelling in human body, not knowing My form as the Lord of all beings.

The Lord uses the word fools to mean the ignorant. The majority of us are ignorant. We are ignorant of the presence of the Lord in all beings. They also do not realise the importance of the Lord who is in the control of the entire universe. He is the one and only controller of the entire universe.

We have two types of fools. The first type are the ones who do not recognise divinity in others. The Lord who is in me is also in all. They perform sinful acts on others and in return have to pay the penalty but do not realise so. Love for all is the Lord's message to us, the humans, who are supposed to have *buddhi*. Religion, caste, status of the person should not dictate one's relation to others. All are the same.

The second type of fools are those who think they are powerful because they are wealthy or strong physically. They do not think there is anybody who is stronger. Power makes them get a sense of superiority. They do not realise the presence of the most powerful *Puruṣa* (the Lord) without whom nobody would exist.

This verse also brings out the notion that the person who is giving this great secret is the Lord himself. He is not just Kṛṣṇa, an ordinary human being. That Śrī Kṛṣṇa was an incarnation of God was realised only by very few people at the time. Bhīṣma knew Kṛṣṇa was the Lord Himself. Dhṛtarāṣṭra even when given a chance to see the universal form (*viśvarūpa*) of the Lord did not understand it. Himself and his sons disregarded His divine nature.

मोघाशा मोघकर्माणो मोघज्ञाना विचेतसः ।
राक्षसीमासुरीं चैव प्रकृतिं मोहिनीं श्रिताः ॥१२॥

***moghāśā moghakarmāṇo moghajñānā vicetasaḥ* I**
***rākṣasīm āsurīṁ caiva prakṛtiṁ mohinīṁ śritāḥ* II12II**

Of vain hopes, vain actions, vain knowledge and senseless, they verily are possessed of the deluding nature of the rākṣasa*s and* asura*s.*

mogha: vain
śrītāḥ: possessed of
vicetasaḥ: devoid of understanding
rākṣasāḥ: devilish
asura: undivine

We are all a combination of three *guṇas*, *sāttvika, rājasika* and *tāmasika,* (these will be discussed later). Any one of the *guṇa*s dominates at any one time. *Sattva-guṇa* brings forth divine actions and *tamo-guṇa* brings forth undivine actions. *Rajo-guṇa* is in between the two. The *guṇa* that dominates the majority of our actions is expressed as what we are by nature. In this verse, the Lord is explaining about persons who express a majority of undivine actions.

How do they do it? Actions as we know are due to our thought-imprints (*vāsanās*). We are what we think of. The thoughts are due to desires.

Tāmasika people, deluded by the power of *māyā*, are ignorant. They do not have the intellectual capacity to realise the foolishness of their desires. They live in foolish hopes and desires (wanting to express their sensual nature of *kāma*). Automatically, their actions become foolish and egocentric. Their mind runs after sensual pleasures and disregards the intellect. They develop a great sense of 'I'-ness in all their actions. So, they are of vain understanding. Because of this, they are termed as 'senseless' by the Lord. All their actions are senseless, demoniacal and monstrous. They are *rākṣasa*s and *asura*s. Their nature is that of devilish and undivine creatures.

महात्मानस्तु मां पार्थ दैवीं प्रकृतिमाश्रिताः ।
भजन्त्यनन्यमनसो ज्ञात्वा भूतादिमव्ययम् ॥१३॥

***mahātmānas tu māṁ pārtha daivīṁ prakṛtim āśritāḥ* I**
***bhajanty ananyamanaso jñātvā bhūtādim avyayam* II13II**

O Pārtha, the mahātmās*, possessing My divine nature, worship Me, with a single mind, knowing Me to be the origin of all beings and imperishable.*

*Mahātmā*s are men of wisdom. They have understood the divine nature of the Lord and have taken refuge in the Lord. They are great souls. There are not many great souls in the world. There are plenty of little souls (*alpātmās*).

The nature of these *mahātmā*s is divine. They have predominance of *sattva-guṇa*. They realise the presence of divinity in all and worship the Lord as such. Their actions are always for the welfare of all. They understand that the Lord is the final cause for everything (*bhūtādi*) and is imperishable (eternal). Because they understand it, they have single-minded devotion to the Lord (*ananyamanasa*). Their mind does not run after sense-pleasures.

सततं कीर्तयन्तो मां यतन्तश्च दृढव्रताः ।
नमस्यन्तश्च मां भक्त्या नित्ययुक्ता उपासते ॥१४॥

***satatam kīrtayanto mām yatantaś ca dṛḍhavratāḥ* I**
***namasyantaś ca mām bhaktyā nityayuktā upāsate* II14II**

Always glorifying Me, striving firm in vows, prostrating before Me with devotion, always steadfast, they worship Me.

In this verse are given the manner of worship undertaken by *mahātmās*. It is to be taken as an example to follow by spiritual *sādhakas*.

(1) **Satatam kīrtayantaḥ:** Always glorifying. *Kīrtana* is not just singing of prayers (*bhajanas*) to the accompaniment of musical instruments. It is an act of the mind. It means expressing divinity constantly. Undivine thougths should not enter the mind. The mind should have a sign, 'house-full' of devotion. Entry only for divine thoughts. No entry for others. This is expressed in the form of welfare acts to the society, imparting one's knowledge to those who seek it and performing selfless acts in day-to-day life.

(2) **Yatantaśca:** Striving. **Bhaktyā:** With devotion. One should strive constantly to express devotion in their acts. Constantly and with conscious effort one should root out undivine thoughts. There is no use performing divine acts (going to temple, giving alms) in the day and doing undivine acts at other times (activities in an egotistic manner, work for personal benefit with no regard to others, working against the spirit of scriptural teachings, etc). Self-perfection needs constant effort.

(3) **Dṛḍhavrataḥ:** Firm in vows. Towards self-perfection one should learn to reject strong temptations. Sense-objects bring in temporary pleasures and act as temptations for the weak personality. Vows to undertake an act towards purification (like fasting, silence, etc.) must be firm and resolute. Once a vow is taken, it must not be broken. That must become a habit. Obstacles that come in the path of fulfilling the vows should be overcome with determination.

(4) **Namasyantaśca:** Prostrating. An act of prostration involves physically bowing down flatly on at the revered feet of God or a revered person. It is a physical expression. The real meaning is : "Drop your ego. Forget your total physical self. Respect the divinity in front of you". One's position in society, (king, minister, rich man, etc.) has no relation to the position of the person we prostrate to. One bows to the knowledge or Truth in front of him.

Upāsanā is meditation. *Nitya-yukta* means always attached. "With the above qualifications, meditate always and be attached to the Lord always", is the Lord's behest to mankind. All great souls have done similar acts of *upāsanā* and we *alpātmā*s should do the same if we have to uplift ourselves.

ज्ञानयज्ञेन चाप्यन्ये यजन्तो मामुपासते ।
एकत्वेन पृथक्त्वेन बहुधा विश्वतोमुखम् ॥१५॥

***jñāna-yajñena cāpy anye yajanto mām upāsate* I**
***ekatvena pṛthaktvena bahudhā viśvatomukham* II15II**

Others also, sacrificing with the yajña *of knowledge worship Me as one, as distinct, and as manifold, in all forms with faces everywhere.*

Different people worship the Lord in different ways. Some worship Him as the Omnipresent (God existing everywhere). Some worship Him as God with a distinct name. Others do so recognising Him as God with a multitude of names and forms.

A *jñānī* or man of wisdom is one who understands the different people who worship Him in different ways. He also knows and has realised the Lord in himself. He has realised the same Lord in all forms of life in this world. He has realised *tat tvam asi*. *Jñāna-yajña* is an attempt by the *jñānī* to see the one conscious principle, the Self everywhere and keep that thought consistently. He acts accordingly.

If one goes into a sweet stall, one will find various kinds of sweets. One common ingredient is the 'sweetness' and hence the name of the stall is 'sweet stall'. Amounts of sugar may vary, the different sweets may vary in names and forms. That person is wise who knows that sweetness is common to all. Similarly the wise man is one who sees divinity in all.

Viśvatomukham: If the Self is everywhere, instead of seeing different faces around, the *jñānī* sees with his eye of knowledge the Lord in every form. Hence the word *viśvatomukham* (universal form facing everywhere). Wherever he sees, he sees *Paramātmā* only.

अहं क्रतुरहं यज्ञः स्वधाहमहमौषधम् ।
मन्त्रोऽहमहमेवाज्यमहमग्निरहं हुतम् ॥१६॥

ahaṁ kratur ahaṁ yajñaḥ svadhāham aham auṣadham |
mantro'hamaham evājyam aham agnir ahaṁ hutam ||16||

I am the kratu, *sacrifice I am, I am the offering to the* pitṛs, *I am the medicinal herbs, I am the* mantra, *I am also the clarified butter, I am the fire and the offering.*

kratu: A kind of *Vedic* sacrifice.
svadhā: Offering to *pitṛs* (ancestors).
ājyam: *Ghī*
hutam: Offering.

In the next four verses, the Lord enumerates the different forms of *yajña*s and declares that 'He' is the principle behind it. In the olden days, ritualistic acts were performed as a form of worship of the Lord. There are a number of *Vedic* ritualistic acts and all of them together are known as *kratu*. The presiding deity in all *kratu*s is the Lord.

Some forms of rituals involve invoking the ancestors and offering some food to them. The food offered is the Lord. Other acts involve having a sacrificial fire and pouring clarified butter, rice and foodgrains, while chanting *mantra*s. The fire, butter, food offered and *mantra*s are also the Lord.

Herbs for preparing medicines were used by ancient Hindus before the advent of the Western system of medicine. It was called the Āyurvedic system. Diseases affected mankind from the time man was born and treating them is very important.

Medicinal plants therefore get a special mention by the Lord in His enumeration of universal form.

पिताहमस्य जगतो माता धाता पितामहः ।
वेद्यं पवित्रमोङ्कार ऋक्साम यजुरेव च ॥१७॥

pitāham asya jagato mātā dhātā pitāmahaḥ ।
vedyaṁ pavitram oṁkāra ṛk sāma yajureva ca ॥17॥

I am the Father of this world, the Mother, the Dispenser, the Grandfather. I am the 'One' to be known, the Purifier and the syllable OṀ. *And also the* Ṛgveda, Sāmaveda *and* Yajurveda.

dhātā: Dispenser (of fruits of action), the giver.

As the entire creation is done by the *Paramātmā*, He becomes our Father, Mother and Grandfather. In this verse *pitāmahaḥ* may be interpreted as Grand-Father or as Grandsire 'Brahmā'. Parents are the ones who sustain their children; the Lord is the sustainer of all.

He is the One to be known. We can know a lot of things in this world, but it is still not complete knowledge in its true sense. The Self is "That, having known which, everything else becomes known". Once the Self is known, the person is said to have attained "perfection of knowledge".

The *Vedic* seers are the authors of all the *Veda*s. *Veda*s are the ancient religious scriptures which explain all about the *Paramātmā* (life principle). Our seers have symbolised the Creator (Brahmā) and the created universe in one word, *OṀ*. *OṀ* represents the infinite *Brahman* and the finite world. The theme of the three *Veda*s is *OṀ* (*Brahman* is the ultimate goal to be reached by studying the *Veda*s). The Lord is therefore *OṀ* and all the *Veda*s declare so.

गतिर्भर्ता प्रभुः साक्षी निवासः शरणं सुहृत् ।
प्रभवः प्रलयः स्थानं निधानं बीजमव्ययम् ॥१८॥

gatir bhartā prabhuḥ sākṣī nivāsaḥ śaraṇaṁ suhṛt ।
prabhavaḥ pralayaḥ sthānaṁ nidhānaṁ bījam avyayam ॥18॥

> *I am the goal* (gatiḥ), *supporter, the witness; the abode* (nivāsa) *the shelter* (śaraṇam), *the friend* (suḥrt). *I am also origin, the foundation and dissolution* (prabhavaḥ, sthānam, pralayaḥ). *I am the treasure house (nidhānam) the seed and Imperishable.*

All spiritual *sādhaka*s have one common goal, and that goal is the Lord Himself. One can approach the goal in different ways but the goal is one and the same for all paths.

He is the bhartā: He supports all and hence He is *jagat-bhartā*. In Telugu language, *bhartā* means a husband. A husband supports his wife and children. God becomes *bhartā* to all His creation. He is the Lord and is the witness in all of us. A witness is one who sees an event taking place of its own accord in his presence. The witness is neutral and has seen things as they happen. The Self inside us is a *sākṣī* to all our actions. We are therefore answerable to all the minor and major crimes we commit. When we do a wrong act, we try to make sure nobody sees what we do. Unfortunately, we forget that there is an eternal witness to our acts, and that witness is "our conscience" known as the Lord.

I am the abode: The Self is the *nivāsa* for *Paramātmā*. Individually speaking, His address is therefore 'Self'. 'Self' addressed envelope is all one needs to write a letter to the Lord. Address your problems to 'yourself'. (You can solve them right and nobody else.)

Similarly, the Lord is the abode of the whole world. He is the world. And we, false egos, move in Him. Our universal address is *Paramātmā*.

I am the refuge (śaraṇam): In troubles, we want to take shelter from the troubles. During heavy rains one takes shelter under a tree or in a house with a roof. Our worldly troubles bring unhappiness. When we realise that the troubles are experienced by the physical body and we are not the real body, then the troubles do not appear as troubles any more. Realise that you are the 'Self' and not the physical body. This is what is meant by "I am the shelter" (*advaita* philosophy).

For the dualists who consider the Lord as a separate entity, the Lord is still the shelter. They get peace of mind on approaching the Lord for shelter. The true devotee is one who goes to the Lord who blesses Him with a calm, quiet mind. The devotee requests His help in controlling the agitations of his mind.

Of course the Lord is the best friend one can have. A friend is one who gives support and good impartial advice. Our conscience is our friend. It will clearly tell us what is right and what is wrong.

He is *bīja* and *avyaya*. He is the imperishable seed for all. Seeds normally perish when they germinate, but the seed, normaly, the Lord, where we germinated from, does not perish. Our ancestral origin is our *gotra*. Really speaking our true origin or *gotra* is *Paramātmā*.

He created the world, He is sustaining it and He will cause its *pralaya* at His own will.

तपाम्यहमहं वर्षं निगृह्णाम्युत्सृजामि च ।
अमृतं चैव मृत्युश्च सदसच्चाहमर्जुन ॥१९॥

tapāmy aham ahaṁ varṣaṁ nigṛhṇāmy utsṛjāmi ca |
amṛtaṁ caiva mṛtyuśca sad asac cāham arjuna ||19||

O Arjuna, I give heat, I withhold and send forth rain. I am immortality, death, existence and non-existence.

tapāmi: Heat, I cause.
utsṛjāmi: Send forth,
nigṛhṇāmi: Withhold.

The sun is the source of all heat in this world. The Lord is the source of this light and heat. The sun causes absorption of water, formation of clouds and releases it in the form of rain. The Lord is therefore the one who withholds or sends forth rain.

I am immortality and death. Death is change from one form to another. Self is deathless, immortal and illumines the life (living) or withdraws from life (death). It remains the same immortal Self and changes (death) take place only to the physical body (baby-child-teenager-adult-old age-death-birth). I am the existence and non-existence (*sat* and *asat*). He is *Brahman,* the existence (*sat*) and He is the finite world or ego (*asat*).

त्रैविद्या मां सोमपाः पूतपापा यज्ञैरिष्ट्वा स्वर्गतिं प्रार्थयन्ते ।
ते पुण्यमासाद्य सुरेन्द्रलोकमश्नन्ति दिव्यान्दिवि
देवभोगान् ॥२०॥

traividyā māṁ somapāḥ pūtapāpā
***yajñair iṣṭvā svargatiṁ prārthayante* |**
te puṇyam āsādya surendralokam
***aśnanti divyān divi devabhogān* ||20||**

The knowers of the three Vedas, *the drinkers of* soma, *purified of sins, worshipping Me by sacrifices, pray for the stay to heaven. They, having attained the world of Indra, enjoy the heavenly pleasures of the* devas.

One group of people who have read the three *Veda*s are those who want to fulfil some desire or the other. In the process of achieving the desire, they lose track and do not reach *Vedānta. Vedānta* means end of the *Veda*s. The end-result of knowing the *Veda*s properly is to understand *Brahman* and get *brahmajñāna.* Once *brahma-jñāna* is achieved, one attains *mokṣa* or total liberation from the cycle of *saṁsāra.*

Unfortunately, those who perform rituals as per *Vedic* procedure to fulfil a desire, will not attain *brahma-jñāna.* They, on the other hand, do get a reward for their hard work, "the heaven". They reach the world of Indra (king of *deva*s) and enjoy heavenly pleasures.

The *Vedic* rituals include performance of *yajña*s (sacrifices). At the end of each *yajña*, they drink the juice of *soma. Soma* is an intoxicating drink made from the milky juice of a creeper-plant.

Drinkers of *soma* are purified of sins. Drinking *soma* means, the *yajña* has been performed as per rituals and completed. Because of that, their sins are destroyed.

As we have read before, the performers of *yajña* worship the

Brahman. So, in return for the work (*karma-yajña*) performed properly (though for fulfilment of a desire) the Lord blesses them with due reward. The performer of the *karma* (*yajña*) gets his due reward, namely, the fulfilment of his desires.

ते तं भुक्त्वा स्वर्गलोकं विशालं क्षीणे पुण्ये मर्त्यलोकं
विशन्ति ।
एवं त्रयीधर्ममनुप्रपन्ना गतागतं कामकामा लभन्ते ॥२१॥

te taṁ bhuktvā svargalokaṁ viśālaṁ
***kṣīṇe puṇye martyalokaṁ viśanti* |**
evaṁ trayīdharmam anuprapannā
***gatāgataṁ kāmakāmā labhante* ||21||**

They, having enjoyed the vast world of heaven, enter the world of mortals when their merits are exhausted. Thus, those who desire enjoyments, abiding by the law of the Vedas, *have to attain the state of going and returning endlessly.*

Such people (as those described in verse 20) stay in heaven until the merit of their work according to *Veda*s (scriptures) is exhausted. When the merits are exhausted they are born again into the ever-revolving cycle of *saṁsāra*.

Because of desire-prompted activites, even though the activities are according to scriptures, one cannot attain *brahma-jñāna*. From this we have to understand that the world we are in is *karma-bhūmi*. As we are humans with *buddhi*, this is *jñāna-bhūmi* also for us. We have been given the weapon by the Lord to cut the link in the chain of *saṁsāra*. It is up to us to use our *buddhi* and attain the highest *jñāna*.

One can also look at it carefully and understand that actually there is no real heaven as such. Heaven is a state of the mind, achieved by fulfilling a desire-prompted action. Because it is prompted by desire, that state of mind will not last for ever. The mind runs after further desires and gets agitated. It loses its tranquil state. To reach the state of tranquillity, one does not need tranquillizers. One should develop *dvandvātīta* state of mind.

अनन्याश्चिन्तयन्तो मां ये जनाः पर्युपासते ।
तेषां नित्याभियुक्तानां योगक्षेमं वहाम्यहम् ॥२२॥

***ananyāś cintayanto māṁ ye janāḥ paryupāsate* I**
***teṣāṁ nityābhiyuktānāṁ yogakṣemaṁ vahāmy aham* II22II**

Of those men who worship Me alone, thinking of no other, ever united with Me, I secure for them what they do not possess and preserve what they possess.

It is one of the most important verses in the entire discourse appropriately named The *Bhagavadgītā*. Most scholars consider this verse to be right in the middle of the discourse. It is the 360th verse out of 701 verses in the *Gītā*.

Kṛṣṇa promises to look after the welfare of those who possess the following three virtues:

(a) those who worship Him alone;
(b) those who think of Him alone;
(c) those who are always united with the Lord.

Ananyāścintayanto mām: "Without any other thoughts, thinking of Me". As we know, our mind is an ocean of thoughts. They are waves that agitate the ocean (mind). Thoughts are responsible for our actions. The stronger the thought, the actions will be that much more powerful and determined. Because of our ever-changing thoughts, the actions in general become less efficient. We have experienced it in our own lives several times. What we determine to do today, is not as strong as it was yesterday. Something new takes over and our previous determination gets weaker. On the other hand, if we think of only one thing and nothing else, that thought becomes a determined action. Thinking of the Lord alone, makes our actions divine and worshipping Him alone brings forth strong divine actions from us.

Ye janāḥ paryupāsate: Those men who worship continuously. *Upāsanā* means worship. It is a *Vedic* word. It is a method to invoke the deity. *Veda*s are in three parts. The first part is *karma-kāṇḍa*, the second part is *upāsanā-kāṇḍa* and the third part is *jñāna-kāṇḍa*. *Karma-kāṇḍa* deals with rituals to fulfil the desires. Majority of the people who read the *Vedas*, get more interested in *karma-kāṇḍa,* as it describes various rewards for various actions. *Karma-kāṇḍa* is only a primary course in the process of graduation to spiritual progress. *Karma* is easy to perform and one finds immediate results which please.

One should aim to go to secondary education which is *upāsanā*. *Upāsanā* is a form of worship by meditation. Constantly and lovingly thinking of *Paramātmā* and showing *Paramātmā* in actions is *upāsanā. Japa* is thinking and *tapas* is acting. *Japa* and *tapa* on the Lord constantly is *upāsanā.*

In the *Vedic* period there were no personalised Gods like Viṣṇu, Rāma, Kṛṣṇa, etc. It was simply *Brahman* represented as *OṀ*.

In *Purāṇic* periods, to make worship easier, gods with names and forms were created out of the concept of *Brahman*. Worship of God with names and forms was much easier. That form of worship of gods with name and form is known as *bhakti*.

Ever united with me (nityābhiyuktānām): As discussed in verse 9 the thoughts have to be concentrated on Him alone. By self-control, one can concentrate on the Lord and hold back the impulses from the sense-organs which disturb the single-pointedness in thought. Keep the thought of the divine in mind always and always act divine by self-control, is what is meant by *nityābhiyuktānām*.

For such people, the Lord promises to look after their welfare. He uses the word *yogakṣema*, which is a very beautiful and meaningful word. *Yoga*, as we know, is the union of *jīva* with *ātmā. Yoga* in ordinary terms would mean "securing a thing which is not already possessed". Scripturally (we who do not understand the presence of the *ātmā* in us and act egotistically). *Yoga* means to possess *ātmā*. As *ātmā* is divine, possessing divinity is *yoga*.

Kṣema means looking after what we possess. In day-to-day life we are engaged in a constant battle of *yogakṣema*. We want to achieve various things at various times and we struggle to look after what we achieve. What fools we are that we fail to realise that not even one object we achieve, will stay permanently with us. There is no such thing as permanent happiness in getting any object. It is bound to end in sorrow sooner or later.

There is only one thing on achieving which we get permanent bliss. That is divinity. 'Achieve total divinity and I will promise to keep it safe for you', is the Lord's promise. Let us all be sincere and truthful. Let our devotion to the Lord be honest and straightforward and constant. Let us have faith in Him, and the Lord will see to it that we do not suffer the sorrow and pains of worldly life (*saṁsāra*).

येऽप्यन्यदेवता भक्ता यजन्ते श्रद्धयाऽन्विताः ।
तेऽपि मामेव कौन्तेय यजन्त्यविधिपूर्वकम् ॥२३॥

***ye'py anyadevatā bhaktā yajante śraddhayā'nvitāḥ* |**
***te'pi mām eva kaunteya yajanty avidhipūrvakam* ||23||**

O Arjuna, even those devotees who endowed with faith worship other gods, worship Me alone, by the wrong method.

Faith in any field of activity will bring results in due course. Faith in worship also brings its due results. Worship nowadays seems to be under different names and forms of God. Śrī Kṛṣṇa, by saying "Those who worship other gods, worship Me alone", is telling all mankind that there is only one God, whatever may be His name and form. He is indirectly advocating people not to be fanatical because of their faith in one form of God.

The Lord also says that the fruits of merit of worship are different in different forms of worship. Different gods may be approached by various devotees aspiring after different fruits, like health, wealth, prosperity, etc. As the approach is only for 'a reward', the method is wrong.

Total liberation of *mukti* is by total faith in the Supreme Lord. All other forms of worship are wrong methods to follow for liberation. If you want liberation, worship Him alone constantly with faith. If we are worshipping to gain something, we will get it if we worship faithfully. But achieving something we desire is not liberation. We will end up again in the cycle of *saṁsāra*.

अहं हि सर्वयज्ञानां भोक्ता च प्रभुरेव च ।
न तु मामभिजानन्ति तत्त्वेनातश्च्यवन्ति ते ॥२४॥

***ahaṁ hi sarva-yajñānāṁ bhoktā ca prabhur eva ca* |**
***na tu mām abhijānanti tattvenātaś cyavanti te* ||24||**

I alone am the enjoyer in, and the Lord of, all sacrifices. But they do not know Me in essence and hence they fall.

cyavanti: Fall

The Lord is the one Total Reality in this universe and everything else is untrue. The Lord is present everywhere, He is Omniscient. Whatever *yajña*s one may perform, in reality it is presided over by the Lord as He is in all. Whatever we offer in *yajña*s is to Him, the Lord alone.

Unfortunately, those ignorant men who do not realise it, and think they are invoking a particular deity, will get only the result of what they think. As their thinking is for the fulfilment of a particular wish, they end up by not attaining liberation. They enjoy temporary benefit and fall down into the cycle of *saṁsāra*.

We all fall down (*cyavanti*) from a higher plane because of our ignorance. We are in a relatively higher plane in the order of evolution. We have got intellect to direct us in the right path. As we do not use it, 'we fall'. The one who does not fall is *acyuta*. The Lord is Acyuta. We can achieve that state by the right method described in *Veda*s, i.e., by Truth, which in essence is reality of the presence of the Lord in all names and forms.

यान्ति देवव्रता देवान्पितॄन्यान्ति पितृव्रताः ।
भूतानि यान्ति भूतेज्या यान्ति मद्याजिनोऽपि माम् ॥२५॥

***yānti devavratā devān pitṝn yānti pitṛvratāḥ* |**
***bhūtāni yānti bhūtejyā yānti madyājino'pi mām* ||25||**

The worshippers of the devas *go to the* devas. *The worshippers of the ancestors go to the ancestors. Worshippers of* bhūtas *go to the* bhūtas. *And the worshippers of Me go to Me.*

The Lord is not giving us any new theory. He is stating the simple law "As you think, so you become". Our object of worship will determine the goal we achieve. *Deva*, *pitṛ* and *bhūta*s are different channels on which one tends to worship.

*Deva*s, as we know, are presiding deities of our sense-organs and mind. We experience the outer world through our sense-organs and mind. Worshipping *deva*s means, trying to achieve the external world of joys and successes with total faith and constant efforts. We will get worldly rewards in proportion to our efforts. So worshippers of *deva*s go to *deva*s.

*Pitṛ*s are our ancestors. There are those who worship their ancestors. They think of their ancestors and they try to follow their footsteps or try to fulfil their desire. They think that if they fulfil their desire, they will be happy. They tend to live the life of ancestors and hope to keep up the good name of their family. Their actions are therefore limited to their thoughts. If their actions are with total faith, they will achieve the desired result. Of course it will not be total liberation. An illustration on this channel is as follows:

Mr. X wanted to see his son get a degree and become an engineer. Unfortunately, he died before he could see his son become an engineer. The rest of his family members then concentrated on getting his son to go to the university and achieve the qualification. They feel happy the day the son becomes an engineer.

The worshippers of *bhūta*s go to the *bhūta*s. The study of objective sciences about nature is the study of *bhūta*s. All scientific studies in the field of physics, chemistry, biology, history, etc. are examples of the same. In other words, such people are termed scientists, historians, etc. Those who diligently apply their efforts in such fields will also get proper rewards. Scientific discoveries, inventions, finding out about new undiscovered parts of the world are all possible by those who put in consistent application in their efforts.

All these do not achieve freedom from the cycle of *saṁsāra*. Only by worshipping the *Paramātmā* consistenly, can one achieve the "state of Godhood". Be "*ātmavrata*" (worshippers of *ātmā*) is the Lord's advice to those in search of liberation.

पत्रं पुष्पं फलं तोयं यो मे भक्त्या प्रयच्छति ।
तदहं भक्त्युपहृतमश्नामि प्रयतात्मनः ॥२६॥

patraṁ puṣpaṁ phalaṁ toyaṁ yo me bhaktyā prayacchati I
tad ahaṁ bhakty upahṛtam aśnāmi prayatātmanaḥ II26II

Whoever offers Me with devotion, a leaf, a fruit, a flower or water that I accept, offered by the pure-minded with devotion.

This is a poetically beautiful verse and its meaning is also beautiful. All religions in the world advocate offerings of some sort or other to the deity. The Lord lovingly says that He is not very particular about what one offers. He only puts two conditions for accepting the offerings.

(1) It must be offered with a pure mind.
(2) It must be with sincere devotion.

The entire world is the Lord's. So, what you take to Him is already His. In a manner of speaking, it is like stealing something and presenting a part of it back to the person one stole from.

By advocating offering of simple things, like leaf, flower, water or fruit, the Lord is indirectly saying, "I do not care for your wealth or position. All are equal to Me. If you show devotion and if you have a pure mind I will accept what you offer." One cannot expect God's favour by offering riches to Him. It does not mean that one should keep all his wealth with himself. The spirit of *dāna* (charity) of all forms of wealth must be practised. Devotion to the Lord should be shown by actions to help the living who need help and approaching the Lord at the altar with simple offerings. Committing a sin, and taking an offering to the temple does not receive the Lord's grace. Pure mind means a mind without sins. Sins are those acts prohibited by the *śāstra*s. Act according to the *śāstra*s, work for the welfare of all you can and go to the temple with leaf, flower, water or fruit and the Lord will bless you.

I would like to add the meaning to this verse as given by Śrī Hari Har Ji Maharaj in his discourse at the 10th International Gītā Conference in the U.K. (August '94).

The Lord uses singular words for *patram, puṣpam, phalam* and not plural. The Lord also does not give names of any particular leaf, flower or fruit. Why?

Knowing us as most of us really are, the Lord knows that if He named any fruit or flower or leaf, automatically the business mentality in us would make that items scarce and the vendors demand more money for such an item to be taken to the Lord. Suppose the Lord had said He liked bananas, the price of bananas would go up; people would hoard bananas. Because the Lord said that He likes bananas, the sincere devotees would go and buy bananas whatever their price!

Patram: It means a leaf. What is the significance here? Botanists can, with the help of a leaf know all its genetics and hereditary characteristics of the plant. They can give family history of the plant with the help of one leaf. The Lord, even with offering of one leaf, will be able to judge us. He will know our sincerity and *bhakti* in Him.

Puṣpam: It means a flower. Why flower? In Hindu *śāstra*s, each part of the body and every sense-organ and organ of action is compared to a flower. The heart also is compared to a flower. They say lotus-eyed God, God with lotus-like hand, God with lotus-like feet, God with lotus-like face. If, we have to offer the flower of our sense-organs or organ of action to the God, that part must understand that our actions with our organs of actions and sense-organs must be pure and divine.

The best flower to offer to the Lord would be the flower of the heart (*hṛtkamala*). The flower from our intellectual garden will be the best flower to offer to the Lord.

Phalam: We can offer any fruit to the God. The best fruit to offer is *karma-phala-tyāga*. By not looking for fruits of action, we will not accumulate new *vāsanā*s and we will attain *mokṣa* quickly.

यत्करोषि यदश्नासि यज्जुहोषि ददासि यत् ।
यत्तपस्यसि कौन्तेय तत्कुरुष्व मदर्पणम् ॥२७॥

***yat karoṣi yad aśnāsi yaj juhoṣi dadāsi yat* I**
***yat tapasyasi kaunteya tat kuruṣva mad arpaṇam* II27II**

Whatever you do, whatever you eat, whatever you offer in sacrifice, whatever you give as charity, whatever you practise as austerity, O Kaunteya, do it as an offering to Me.

aśnāsi: You eat,
juhoṣi: offer in sacrifice,
dadāsi: offer as gifts.

We all have to do some work or other to exist. The *Gītā,* in principle, is teaching one to develop the right mental attitude. Mere physical acts sometimes are an act of showmanship. Offering to the God is a method of unconsciously remembering the Lord always. Once we develop an attitude of *kṛṣṇārpaṇam astu* (Lord, I offer it to you) in all our actions, that attitude becomes a habit. This is a very simple method of purifying one's mind and which pleases the Lord immensely.

Whatever we eat comes from Him and offering it to Him should be a form of gratitude. We should give some of our food that we eat daily to a deserving person or animal or bird before we eat.

What we have earned (money, knowledge) is from the grace of God. We should partake that with fellow living creatures. We should give *dāna* (charity) to deserving people. It should not be from a superior to inferior feeling. It should be the other way round. We should feel and see the God in the person we are giving any offering.

When we perform any *yajña* to fulfil a desire, we offer something in the fire of *yajña.* That something should not be in an attitude of bribing the giver to give us what we desire. Even when we perform austerities to purify ourselves, we should not develop egotistic feelings. We should not be proud that we are superior to others because of our austerities. The act of *tapas* should be in a spirit of humbleness.

Constantly remembering the Lord in all our daily acts, is the only way we can give respect to the 'life in us'. What we give to life, life gives it back to us.

> शुभाशुभफलैरेवं मोक्ष्यसे कर्मबन्धनैः ।
> संन्यासयोगयुक्तात्मा विमुक्तो मामुपैष्यसि ॥२८॥
>
> ***śubhāśubhaphalair evaṁ mokṣyase karma-bandhanaiḥ*** **|**
> ***saṁnyāsa-yoga-yuktātmā vimukto mām upaiṣyasi*** **||28||**
>
> *Thus you shall be liberated from the bonds of actions yielding good and evil fruits. With steadfast mind in the* yoga *of renunciation, you shall come to Me, by being liberated from* karma.

By following the principle of surrender to the Lord in the spirit of *kṛṣṇārpaṇam astu*, as described in the previous verses, we will be liberated from bonds even of pure actions. We have learnt about *vāsanā*s before. *Vāsanā*s are thought-imprints of our desires. The initial stages of *sādhanā* (towards burning of *vāsanā*s) involve dropping of all actions yielding bad results. Avoiding sinful acts, rising from *tamas* to *rajas* and *rajas* to *sattva* helps us to purify our minds.

In the later stages of *sādhanā,* we should lift ourselves from *sattva* to pure *sattva* (*śuddha sattva*). We should drop even those actions that yield good results. This would mean dropping our ego totally from our actions. We should not be looking for any fruits of actions. This would help by not adding any new *vāsanā*s to our minds.

The Lord is clearly advocating, in this verse, a life of action with a sense of renunciation of the fruits of action. *Saṁnyāsa* is really *karma-phala-tyāga*. This leads us to *mokṣa* which is nothing but freedom from bondage. Bondage comes from acts done with a sense of personal doership with desire for fruits of action. This *saṁnyāsa* should be with a steadfast mind. The ocean of mind should be so calm that no ripples should form from thoughts arising from the outer world. Impulses from outside should not disturb the single-pointed concentration which is the only way to purify our minds of all *vāsanās* (*vāsanā-kṣaya* and *manonāśa*).

समोऽहं सर्वभूतेषु न मे द्वेष्योऽस्ति न प्रियः ।
ये भजन्ति तु मां भक्त्या मयि ते तेषु चाप्यहम् ॥२९॥

***samo'haṁ sarvabhūteṣu na me dveṣyo'sti na priyaḥ* I**
***ye bhajanti tu māṁ bhaktyā mayi te teṣu cāpy aham* II29II**

The same am I to all beings. There is none hateful or dear to Me. Those who worship Me with devotion, are in me and I am also in them.

In simple words, the summary here is, "we get what we deserve from our actions". There is no favouritism shown by the Lord to anybody in this world. 'Those who worship Him' means, those who realise the existence of the life-principle behind their existence. They do not have any sense of attachment to the physical body. In such people, the Lord is inside them and they are in the Lord. Their actions being divine, they become divine in due course. It becomes one single, united, divine principle. As it becomes one unit, it does not matter whether you say they are in God or that God is in them.

We always complain that God has not been kind to us when things go wrong. But when something good happens to us, we do not thank God. We think that we are responsible to ourselves for our actions totally. We reap what we sow.

The Self is the same to all beings. But we, the physical bodies (ego), are not the same to the Self. We, the ego, show different attitudes to different people (who have Self in them also). We hate some, we envy some, we love some and we are indifferent to many, yet we complain about the Lord!

The Lord is near to us and it is up to us to go near Him by our actions. On a cold day, the more we sit near the fire-place, the warmer we feel. The fire has no affinity for anybody. It is the same to all. By our divine actions, we go near Him. By sinful acts we are distancing ourselves from Him. Scripturally, those who go near the fire-place are blessed by the fire but even those who do not go near the fire-place are not cursed by it.

We have the power to lift ourselves up from this world of *saṁsāra.* We can remain in it and get carried away in its whirlpool or we can swim out of the whirlpool with our own strength inside us.

अपि चेत्सुदुराचारो भजते मामनन्यभाक् ।
साधुरेव स मन्तव्यः सम्यग्व्यवसितो हि सः ॥३०॥

api cet sudurācāro bhajate mām ananyabhāk ।
sādhur eva sa mantavyaḥ samyag vyavasito hi saḥ ॥30॥

Even if the most sinful worships Me, with undivided heart, he too should be regarded as righteous, for he has rightly resolved.

"The most sinful person worships Me with undivided heart." What does it mean? It means that the person has come to realise that there is something more powerful than his personal ego. Knowledge has dawned on him that there is Self inside him and around him. Only then can he be expected to worship Him with undivided heart.

The Lord is asking us not to judge a sinner by his past actions. It is the present we are looking at, which is the foundation for tomorrow. Forget about the past. The moment a ray light has entered a cave, that cave is not dark anymore. One can walk inside it with open eyes.

Vedic literature does not condemn the sinner but only the sin. Our actions are due to thoughts in our mind. By giving a jail sentence, one's mind does not get pure. We have no power to purify anyone's mind. That person has to purify his mind himself. Scriptures and teachers lead the way to help him. If he asks for help sincerely, he should get it. If one can change the texture of thoughts flowing through one's mind, the texture of his behaviour could also be changed.

The day the sinner decides to worship the Lord, the day he realises that there is nobody other than the God to help him, that day he is said to have become righteous. The label on him has to be changed from 'sinner' to 'worshipper'. He has to be judged as a 'righteous person'.

There are two points to learn in this verse. The first point is for those surrounding the sinner. We should not condemn the sinner. If possible, we should try to show the sinner the right path by our actions. If he comes for help, we should not withhold helping him; the spark of light in a sinner can become a flame of knowledge with our help.

The second point is for the sinner. The sinner should not dwell on his past actions. He should constantly think of God and accept whatever punishment he gets as God's grace on him. He should look upon his sufferings (from the day the knowledge dawned on him) as God's kindness to him to help burn his *vāsanās*. "I have now paid the price for my sin", should be his attitude and he should not deviate from his new path.

क्षिप्रं भवति धर्मात्मा शश्वच्छान्तिं निगच्छति ।
कौन्तेय प्रतिजानीहि न मे भक्तः प्रणश्यति ॥३१॥

kṣipraṁ bhavati dharmātmā śaśvacchāntiṁ nigacchati |
kaunteya pratijānīhi na me bhaktaḥ praṇaśyati ||31||

Soon he becomes righteous and attains eternal peace. O Kaunteya, know for certain, My devotee is never destroyed.

The term 'he' here means the sinner of the past. As soon as he realises the Lord and constantly keeps that thought in his mind, his actions become righteous (divine). Divine actions, as we have learnt before, purify our mind and purity leads to perfect bliss. This is the place of 'eternal peace'. This place is not in a faraway land. It is in one's own heart.

We have to reach a right decision, accept it and act accordingly in any field of action. The same applies to spiritual progress. Once we believe in God, accept Him as our saviour and confirm it by our actions (divine), then we would be considered as righteous. The Lord calls such people *dharmātmā*.

Dharmātmā is Lord's devotee. The Lord promises that His devotee never perishes. A true devotee is one who has true love for God. True love is one's total indentification with his loved one. By dropping one's ego, one would no more suffer any pains or sorrows in this world. He would attain total liberation.

मां हि पार्थ व्यपाश्रित्य येऽपि स्युः पापयोनयः ।
स्त्रियो वैश्यास्तथा शूद्रास्तेऽपि यान्ति परां गतिम् ॥३२॥

***mām hi pārtha vyapāśritya ye'pi syuḥ pāpayonayaḥ* I**
***striyo vaiśyās tathā śūdrās te'pi yānti parām gatim* II32II**

For taking refuge in Me, O Arjuna, even those of sinful birth as well as women, vaiśyas and śūdras also attain the supreme goal.

This *śloka* has to be understood properly. Lord Kṛṣṇa in chapter 4, verse 13, has said "*cāturvarṇyam mayā sṛṣṭaṁ guṇa-karma-vibhāgaśaḥ*" (The four castes are created by Me according to the *guṇa*s and actions).

From our mythological studies we get an impression that women had an inferior role in those days. Women were asked to be subservient to men. This was partly because the olden days were days when kings ruled and tried to expand their kingdom. There were many wars. Men physically being strong were warriors. Also, as men were killed in battle, there was need for larger families. They needed to produce more children. Hence women's role was brought down to the level of looking after the household. They were not entitled to education. (Sītā was sent to the forest by Rāma. Draupadī was insulted in the royal assembly.)

Śrī Kṛṣṇa made a bold attempt to condemn such acts. At the same time, the education which was mainly moral and scriptural teaching was reserved for kṣatriyas and brāhmaṇas. Kṛṣṇa simplifying the *Vedic* teaching (which was misunderstood), condemned such partiality in respect of women and men of lower caste. He declared that the path to *brahma-jñāna* is open to all. The only criterion was "purity of thought" and not "purity as birthright".

Any person, despite his status on account of sex or birth can attain *mokṣa* by attaining knowledge. The Lord is equal in compassion for such people, the Lord has also stated that it is the *guṇa*s and actions that make us what we are. We have all the three *guṇa*s in us. The predominant *guṇa*s is expressed as what we are. As *guṇa*s are due to our *vāsanā*s, our *vāsanā*s are due to our thoughts, we can change our caste ourselves. 'We are born into it' means, we are born with our existing *vāsanā*s. It is not a birthright as is misinterpreted even now. We all have a divine right to change our *vāsanā*s and we have an equal right to attain Godhood.

Society has also developed a system of marking people not only by sex but also by their actions. We tend to consider some qualities as feminine and some as masculine. We use the phrase 'don't act like a woman', several times. In general, women tend to be soft, loving and affectionate. Men tend to be firm and resolute and strong. The Lord may be saying that do not be feminine in actions which bind you to this world. 'Act with detachment' like a firm man may also be his advice.

Similarly vaiśyas as traders look out for profit in their actions. In other words they look for 'fruits of action'. 'Do not look for fruits of action' may also be His request.

Śūdras are those with slothful, lazy actions. Any of the above category of people can also enquire into the 'Truth' and attain *brahma-jñāna*. This is another interpretation to this verse.

किं पुनर्ब्राह्मणाः पुण्या भक्ता राजर्षयस्तथा ।
अनित्यमसुखं लोकमिमं प्राप्य भजस्व माम् ॥३३॥

kiṁ punar brāhmaṇāḥ puṇyā bhaktā rājarṣayas tathā |
anityam asukhaṁ lokam imaṁ prāpya bhajasva mām ||33||

How much more (easily) then the holy brāhmaṇas and the royal saints attain the goal. Having entered this world (which is) impermanent and unhappy, do worship Me devoutly.

Having described the lower qualities, now the Lord is looking at high quality of birth. It means that quality of *vāsanā*s which endow one with predominant *sāttvic guṇa*. Qualities of *puṇya* (holy), *bhakti* (devotion), self-control, knowledge (*jñāna*) are high qualities. Saintly kings (*rājarṣi*) will have all such qualities.

It is easy for those people to attain Godhood. Such type of men and women are still in this present world. All have to realise the truth that this world is impermanent and unhappy. The world of names and forms is not permanent; birth and death is a continuous cycle. Our world is a world of birth and deaths, of happiness and sorrow. As happiness always ends in sorrow, it is *asukham* (unhappy). So all the various types of people should do one thing only to achieve Godhood, that is, "Worship the Lord devoutly".

मन्मना भव मद्भक्तो मद्याजी मां नमस्कुरु ।
मामेवैष्यसि युक्त्वैवमात्मानं मत्परायणः ॥३४॥

***manmanā bhava madbhakto madyājī māṁ namaskuru* I**
***mām evaiṣyasi yuktvaivam ātmānaṁ matparāyaṇaḥ* II34II**

Fix your mind on Me, be devoted to Me, sacrifice to Me, bow down to Me. Having thus united youself with Me, taking Me as the supreme goal, you shall come to Me.

This verse again repeats the theme "As you think, so you become". 'Me' here represents *Brahman*, the 'Ultimate knowledge'. Fix your thought on knowledge that you are the Self and not the body, that the whole world is '*Brahman*' though with superimposition of name and form. Fix your thought on divine qualities (*manmanā*).

Madbhakta: Be devoted to Me. Be a true devotee and identify totally with the Lord.

Madyājī: 'Sacrifice to Me'; let all our actions be with the sense of *kṛṣṇārpaṇamastu.*

Māṁ namaskuru: Bow down to knowledge. There is nothing superior to 'real knowledge'. The highest knowledge is knowledge of *Brahman.* By thought and action, be divine.

If we take a single-pointed path to attain Godhood and staunchly believe that the Lord is the supreme goal, then the Lord promises that we will attain liberation. It means uniting with the Self within and becoming one with the Self. It involves dropping the outer coat of ego. We will then realise by experience the '*tat*' aspect of *tat tvam asi*. This knowledge of all knowledges is a supreme secret and supreme knowledge. It is a realisation which, once achieved, will not desert us.

इति श्रीमद्भगवद्गीतासूपनिषत्सु ब्रह्मविद्यायां योगशास्त्रे
श्रीकृष्णार्जुनसंवादे राजविद्याराजगुह्ययोगो नाम नवमोऽध्यायः ॥

***iti śrīmadbhagavadgītāsūpaniṣatsu brahmavidyāyāṁ yogaśāstre śrīkṛṣṇārjuna-saṁvāde rājavidyā-rājaguhya-yogo nāma navamo'dhyāyaḥ* ॥**

CHAPTER 10

VIBHŪTI-YOGA

Vibhūti means glory. This chapter deals with the glory of the Lord. By understanding His glory or His greatness in all things and situations, at all levels of one's perception, one could be able to tune himself to recognise Him everywhere.

This chapter is a prelude to the next chapter entitled *viśvarūpa-darśana-yoga.* Before showing His disciple the universal form, the *guru* is preparing him for such a splendid and magnificent vision. He would like to give His disciple examples of manifold life in the universe and tell him that He, the Supreme, is in those forms.

Śrī Kṛṣṇa has described His power and pervasiveness in the universe. He tells Arjuna that He is the essence of all beings. He is the abiding spirit in all and without that animating spirit there is no existence of that being.

Śrī Kṛṣṇa has described His power and pervasiveness in the universe. He tells Arjuna that He is the essence of all beings. He is the abiding spirit in all and without that animating spirit there is no existence of any being.

श्रीभगवानुवाच
भूय एव महाबाहो शृणु मे परमं वचः ।
यत्तेऽहं प्रीयमाणाय वक्ष्यामि हितकाम्यया ॥१॥

śrī bhagavān uvāca
***bhūya eva mahābāho śṛṇu me paramaṁ vacaḥ* I**
***yat te'haṁ prīyamāṇāya vakṣyāmi hitakāmyayā* II1II**

The Lord said

Once again, O mighty armed Arjuna, listen to My supreme words, As you find delight in My words, I, wishing your welfare, will declare unto you all about it.

This stanza brings out the relationship and attitude between a teacher and a sincere student. Arjuna was in a state of total despair in the beginning. He had studied the *Veda*s before but evidently had not understood them really. Chapter after chapter, *śloka* after *śloka*, listening to his master, the student's mind and intellect are opening up. Any student, when he understands what is being taught, will get a sense of happiness in himself. The real teacher, just by looking at his student's face and by listening to the type of questions his student asks, will get stimulated to teach more and more. He would not wait for another occasion to continue his teaching.

Śrī Kṛṣṇa was very pleased with Arjuna. Arjuna's face showed intense happiness on hearing the Lord. Arjuna's doubts were clearing fast. The Lord therefore says, "Again listen to My words". He repeats His universality so that on hearing the truth again and again, Arjuna will find it easy to meditate on it. Śrī Kṛṣṇa says "I will declare it to you, wishing your welfare". He wishes to do good to His student. He wishes the spiritual welfare and not material welfare of the student. It shows the compassion the Lord has on Arjuna and through the medium of Arjuna on all sincere spiritual seekers.

न मे विदुः सुरगणाः प्रभवं न महर्षयः ।
अहमादिर्हि देवानां महर्षीणां च सर्वशः ॥२॥

***na me viduḥ suragaṇāḥ prabhavaṁ na maharṣayaḥ* |**
***aham ādir hi devānāṁ maharṣīṇāṁ ca sarvaśaḥ* ||2||**

Neither the hosts of devas, *nor the great* ṛṣis *know My origin. I am in every way, the source of all the* devas *and* ṛṣis.

*Deva*s and *ṛṣi*s are the most ancient beings that existed, according to Hinduism. The Lord says even they came after Him and they came from Him. Even those great ancestors were also unaware of the origin of the Lord.

No one can measure the infinite. Our mind and intellect cannot grasp the infinite form of the Lord. The Lord has repeatedly said that one has to merge and become one with the Supreme. "Knowing is by becoming one", He has said before. Therefore, the *deva*s and *ṛṣi*s who knew Him have become one with Him.

यो मामजमनादिं च वेत्ति लोकमहेश्वरम् ।
असंमूढः स मर्त्येषु सर्वपापैः प्रमुच्यते ॥३॥

yo mām ajam anādiṁ ca vetti lokamaheśvaram I
asaṁmūḍhaḥ sa martyeṣu sarvapāpaiḥ pramucyate II3II

He who knows Me as birthless, without beginning, the Lord of all the worlds, he among mortals is freed from all sins.

martyeṣu: Among men.
pramucyate: is freed.

The Lord is:

(1) birthless,
(2) eternal, and
(3) Lord of all the worlds.

These three attributes are repeated again to stress their importance. All except *Paramātmā* have a beginning and an end. The Lord is *aja* (unborn) and *anādi* (no beginning). The Lord of all the worlds means the Lord of all worlds of perception, viz., what we perceive through our sense-organs and mind. The Intellect cannot exist without the power of conscience; and conscience is the presiding chief of existence of the total universe.

One should know Him with the above three attributes, not mere knowledge, but a true spiritual apprehension. This is possible when the person constantly meditates on the Truth and lives in Truth through his actions and thoughts.

Such a person who has purified his mind is called sinless. He has burnt all his *vāsanā*s and has not accumulated new *vāsanā*s. Whatever sin he has committed, he has accepted his punishment in his present life and he lives a pure life from the time of realisation. Such a person of true realisation, who is freed from all sins, becomes himself the 'Lord of the worlds'.

बुद्धिर्ज्ञानमसंमोहः क्षमा सत्यं दमः शमः ।
सुखं दुःखं भवोऽभावो भयं चाभयमेव च ॥४॥
***buddhir jñānam asaṁmohaḥ kṣamā satyaṁ damaḥ śamaḥ* I**
***sukhaṁ duḥkhaṁ bhavo'bhāvo bhayaṁ cābhayam eva ca* II4II**

अहिंसा समता तुष्टिस्तपो दानं यशोऽयशः ।
भवन्ति भावा भूतानां मत्त एव पृथग्विधाः ॥५॥
***ahiṁsā samatā tuṣṭistapo dānaṁ yaśo'yaśaḥ* I**
***bhavanti bhāvā bhūtānāṁ matta eva pṛthagvidhāḥ* II5II**

Intellect, wisdom, non-delusion, forgiveness, truthfulness, self-restraint, calmness, happiness, pain, birth or death, fear and fearlessness; non-injury, equanimity, contentment, austerity, charity, fame, ill-fame—these different kinds of qualities of beings arise from Me alone.

The two stanzas together enumerate different dispositions of living beings. The Lord says they arise from Him according to their respective *karma.*

As we have discussed before, the Self projects out as the ego with mind-intellect and sense-organs. We are all born from the Lord, we accept. Similarly, we have to accept that our qualities are born from the Lord. It does not mean that the good and bad qualities are distributed by the Lord. He is not partial to anybody. We develop the qualities that are inherent in our *vāsanās* and we manifest those qualities. As is the mind, so is the man. The Lord is the witness to all our actions.

महर्षयः सप्त पूर्वे चत्वारो मनवस्तथा ।
मद्भावा मानसा जाता येषां लोक इमाः प्रजाः ॥६॥
***maharṣayaḥ sapta pūrve catvāro manavas tathā* I**
***madbhāvā mānasā jātā yeṣāṁ loka imāḥ prajāḥ* II6II**

The seven great ṛṣis *and the four ancient Manus possessed powers like Me and were born of My nature from My mind—and from them have come forth all these creatures in the world.*

In Hinduism, we believe that the four ancient *devarṣis*, the seven *ṛṣis* and fourteen Manus are the original ancestors of this world. All of them were the greatest *jñānīs* and possessed all qualities of *jīvanmuktas*. Hence the Lord uses the word *madbhāva*'. They were born out of divine will of the Lord (*mānasā jatā*). From these great ancestors, all the creatures in the world are born. Knowing our greatest heritage and such hoary ancestry, everyone of us should feel heartened. We have genetically inherited their wisdom also and we should make use of it and uplift ourselves up.

The four *devarṣis* are—Sanaka, Sanandana, Sanatkumāra and Sanatsujāta. They are considered as our *gurus*. They taught us the path of withdrawal from worldly life. The path is known as *nivṛtti-mārga*. The four are considered as eternal boys.

The Manus formulated the laws of behaviour for all. These laws cover family, community and national life. They gave the rules for righteous conduct for everyone. This path is called *pravṛtti-mārga*. *Pravṛtti* is forward progress. We have been shown the path towards progress and survival of the universe. If we uphold the laws (*dharma*) as given to us by them, the whole world would be an ideal place to live in. Unfortunately our moral values are declining fast at individual level as well as at the level of our community. All the sufferings we see around us are a result of our moral decline.

The seven great *ṛṣis* are Bhṛgu, Marīci, Atri, Pulaha, Pulastya, Kratu and Aṅgirasa.

एतां विभूतिं योगं च मम यो वेत्ति तत्त्वतः ।
सोऽविकम्पेन योगेन युज्यते नात्र संशयः ॥७॥

etāṁ vibhūtiṁ yogaṁ ca mama yo vetti tattvataḥ I
so'vikampena yogena yujyate nātra saṁśayaḥ II7II

He, who knows in essence, the manifold manifestations of Mine, and the yogic power of Mine, harmonised with unfaltering yoga (so'vikampena), *unites with Me. There is no doubt about this.*

We should all remember that we are His manifestations. We must realise His presence everywhere, and in everything both small and big. There is no power in anybody without His presence inside. In this context the word *vibhūti* represents manifestations of the Lord and "*yoga*" represents His power. This must be known and realised through the subjective experience of *ahaṁ brahmāsmi* and *tat tvam asi*' (*tattvataḥ*).

Not only should we know His *vibhūti* and *yoga*, but also we should fix our mind on it firmly. We should not let the impulses from the outer world disturb us. The term used here is *avikampena yogena* which means 'unshakable *yoga*'. Our beliefs and actions should be so firm that our minds should not have agitations at all. The only flow into our minds should be that of 'The Lord'. All the individual sparks of the flame of knowledge in us should be on the *Vibhūti Yoga* of the Lord both internally and externally. We must be able to see the Lord and His manifestations and power. Our faith must be unshakable. All the power we exhibit and see is only His. Without His presence there will be no power anywhere.

अहं सर्वस्य प्रभवो मत्तः सर्वं प्रवर्तते ।
इति मत्वा भजन्ते मां बुधा भावसमन्विताः ॥८॥

ahaṁ sarvasya prabhavo mattaḥ sarvaṁ pravartate |
iti matvā bhajante māṁ budhā bhāvasamanvitāḥ ||8||

I am the source of all. From Me, everything evolves, thus understanding, the wise worship Me with pure devotion.

What is worship? It is adoration of something superior, something special. This adoration is expressed as devotion to the Lord. True love or devotion involves total identification with the beloved. Experiencing the Lord inside us and identifying ourselves with Him totally is true devotion. One should drop one's 'I' and 'My'-ness totally. 'It is all God's', should be the attitude. The thought on the Lord with total devotion is *bhāvasamanvitaḥ*. Just repeating and meditating (*japa* and *dhyāna*) on the Lord's name and form are not true worship. One should have faith in the Lord to keep up the concentrated continuous effort.

Such faith is possible only when we know that the Lord is the original cause for all and the power behind all. One should know and realise the Lord's *vibhūti-yoga.* It should be unshakable determination (*avikampena yogena*). Once we understand His creative power and manifestations, we can develop the proper thought-process to worship Him. To experience the *bhāva* (thought), devotion is essential. To develop devotion, true understanding is essential. So, knowing the Lord's *vibhuti-yoga* helps us to unite with the Lord.

मच्चित्ता मद्गतप्राणा बोधयन्तः परस्परम् ।
कथयन्तश्च मां नित्यं तुष्यन्ति च रमन्ति च ॥९॥

***maccittā madgataprāṇā bodhayantaḥ parasparam* I**
***kathayantaś ca māṁ nityaṁ tuṣyanti ca ramanti ca* II9II**

With their intellect wholly absorbed in Me, with their life absorbed in Me, enlightening one another and always speaking of Me, they are satisfied and delighted.

This verse enumerates how the true devotee, mentioned in the last verse, worships the Lord.

Maccittā: His intellect is totally absorbed in the Lord. His intellect which is his *buddhi* (discriminating capacity) knows that the entire manifestation is the Lord and the power is the Lord. Total devotion is possible for him, because he has developed a single-pointed concentration upon the Supreme. He has constant awareness of the Self in him and around him, and is also aware of the power of the Self.

Madgata-prāṇāḥ: The five senses send impulses from the outer world of the brain which reacts to them. A true devotee develops a discriminative knowledge when exposed to the impulses. He takes the impulses that are pure and rejects all other impulses. He does not run away from the outer world. His mind discriminates easily the impulses that are not godly. He carries on living without getting attached to the world of objects. He does his duty with a sense of *kṛṣṇārpaṇamastu.*

Bodayantaḥ parasparam: Mutually discussing with one another. When a group of people sit together, they usually talk about a subject that is dear to them all. They understand the subject-matter better by mutual discussion. They confirm their values, they express their doubts, try to clear them and receive inspiration. When they go away they tend to work on that subject with more determination. This, we know, is the result of attending conferences and seminars on different subjects.

Socially also, one finds that similar-minded people when they meet, talk on a subject endlessly as long as the subject is of some interest to them. Similarly, a true devotee mixes only with devotees. He finds more satisfaction from such company. He expresses his views and sees the reaction in others. He listens to others and analyses himself. At the end, his faith in God is intensified.

Kathayantaśca mām nityam: Speaking of Me always. A true devotee remembers the Lord always. "Speaking of Me" is only an expression, it is not just simple speaking. All his actions constitute speaking (an honest person does what he speaks). He shows his divinity in all his actions.

Tuṣyanti ramanti: He feels satisfied and delighted. By expressing the above-mentioned qualities, the true devotee is constantly satisfied and delighted. He has no cause to moan or groan. It shows itself in his facial expression. Constant smiles express his contentment.

तेषां सततयुक्तानां भजतां प्रीतिपूर्वकम् ।
ददामि बुद्धियोगं तं येन मामुपयान्ति ते ॥१०॥

***teṣāṁ satata-yuktānāṁ bhajatāṁ prītipūrvakam* I**
***dadāmi buddhi-yogaṁ taṁ yena mām upayānti te* II10II**

To these, ever steadfast in worshipping Me with love, I give 'Buddhi-Yoga' *by which they come to Me.*

The Lord is continuing the theme of devotees. He explains that two requisites are necessary for a true devotee:

(1) ever steadfast in the lord,

(2) worshipping with love.

Steadfastness is achieved when the mind does not think of anything else but the Lord. This is possible by seeing and feeling God everywhere. This is possible by understanding His *vibhuti-yoga*. By understanding the Lord's universal manifestation and power, one can achieve the steadfastness needed. It should be 'for ever', the Lord stresses (*satata*).

Worshipping with love brings more faith in one's path to progress. Remembering that our sufferings in this life are our own doing and by suffering we are actually paying for our mistakes of the past, we should really be thankful to Him. We should say, "Thank you Lord, you have punished me for my crime". Our love for God must enhance after each and every pain we suffer; of course, we must thank Him also for the pleasures we get. This increases our love for Him. To such a devotee, the Lord promises *buddhi-yoga*.

What is *buddhi-yoga*? Buddhi is discriminative knowledge, the ability to distinguish between right and wrong, true and false, real and unreal. To realise that God is real and the universe is false, to realise that the Self is real and the ego is unreal, is *buddhi*. Once this *buddhi* becomes a permanent feature, i.e., when one unites with this feeling, it becomes *buddhi-yoga* (one has attained *buddhi*). 'I' and 'My'-ness are gone for ever and *aham̐ brahmāsmi, sarvam khalvidam brahma* takes over the true devotee.

How does one attain *buddhi-yoga*?

(1) By continuing the worship of the Lord in the image of the devotee's choice.
(2) Continuing true love on that form.
(3) Saturating the mind with thoughts and feelings of the Lord.
(4) Dropping the egoistic feeling.

By these methods, the Lord will be pleased and He bestows *buddhi-yoga*. It does not mean a sudden appearance of God in front of the devotee who promises *mokṣa*. It is a process of gradual integration with the Lord and disintegration of the ego.

Bhakti leads to *jñāna* and *jñāna* leads of liberation. By *bhakti* in God with form, *jñāna* of Lord without form is achieved (*sākāra* to *nirākāra*). By *bhakti* in God with attributes, *jñāna* about God without attributes is achieved (*saguṇa* to *nirguṇa*).

We should not indulge in a tug of war as to which path is superior, A true devotee is a *jñānī* and a true *jñānī* is a *bhakta*. Ādi Śaṅkarācārya is an exceptional example of a *jñānī* and *bhakta*. All his songs glorify the Lord. At the same time his teachings show the *so'ham*, and *aham brahmāsmi* aspect in him.

Finally, this gift we get from the Lord is something we cannot buy anywhere. We have to achieve this state which is gifted to us by the Lord at His free will.

तेषामेवानुकम्पार्थमहमज्ञानजं तमः ।
नाशयाम्यात्मभावस्थो ज्ञानदीपेन भास्वता ॥११॥

teṣām evānukampārtham aham ajñānajaṁ tamaḥ I
nāśayāmy ātmabhāvastho jñānadīpena bhāsvatā II11II

Out of compassion for them I, dwelling in their heart, destroy the darkness born of ignorance by the luminous light of knowledge.

Bhāsvatā: Luminous. For the true devotees as described before, the Lord says He is ever merciful and he will destroy the darkness born of ignorance and reveal Himself. The Lord (the Self, the knowledge) is inside all of us. If it is not apparent in all of us, This is because of *māyā* which acts as ignorance.

There are a number of things in the world around us. They are not seen all at the same time, by us. This is because the object has not got favourable condition to be seen by us. For example, if we stay in bed with the windows closed and curtains drawn, we will not be letting any light in. We switch the lights off before going to bed. Under such circumstances, we are said to be living in darkness. If it is night time, we can light a lamp or switch the lights on. In the day-time we can open the curtains and the windows. The sunlight will came through. In both situations, we are then said to be living in light. The light was there, but we had not made attempts to put it on. All articles in the room were there in their own places, yet we could not see them because of darkness. If we are looking for some book in that darkness, not having switched on the lights, we fail to see the book.

Similarly, the Self which is in us is self-luminous. But the three *guṇa*s draw a veil in front of it and it does not shine through. It is like a self-luminous radium watch hidden underneath the papers in a dark room. When the papers are removed, the watch is seen immediately.

For a true devotee, the Lord bestows *buddhi-yoga*. By attaining the knowledge, he reaches the Lord. He becomes one with the Lord. The Lord (divinity) shines through such a devotee.

This is the basis of the olden temples in India. We have in those temples, an inner *sanctum sanctorum* which has got the idol of God. We usually keep that place totally dark. In that room, there will be lamps with wicks in. The inner room with the idol of God inside is shut at night. It will be totally dark. The devotees stand in darkness outside this room and wait for the priest to go in, light the wicks in the lamp. He will then offer prayers and moves a plate with a burning wick all around the idol in a circular manner three times (*āratī*). The lit lamps and the *āratī* plate will illumine the God's idol for the devotees to see. The God in the temple, who was in darkness, was made to shine in His full glory with the light of the lamps.

Similarly, our body is a temple. The inner sanctum has the Self in it. Our three *guṇa*s (*māyā*) make it invisible to the outer world and also to us. *Tamo-guṇa*'s veil is like a dense fog where one cannot even see ten yards ahead. *Rajo-guṇa*'s veil is a little thinner (with visibility of 100 yards). *Sattva-guṇa*'s veil is very thin (like thin layer of mist in air). By acquiring knowledge, this veil is removed and Divinity shines through such a person. The Lord promises *buddhi-yoga* for such a devotee. This is a technique for Self-development and Self-realisation.

अर्जुन उवाच

परं ब्रह्म परं धाम पवित्रं परमं भवान् ।
पुरुषं शाश्वतं दिव्यमादिदेवमजं विभुम् ॥१२॥

arjuna uvāca
paraṁ brahma paraṁ dhāma pavitraṁ paramaṁ bhavān I
puruṣaṁ śāśvataṁ divyam ādidevam ajaṁ vibhum II12II

आहुस्त्वामृषयः सर्वे देवर्षिर्नारदस्तथा ।
असितो देवलो व्यासः स्वयं चैव ब्रवीषि मे ॥१३॥

āhus tvām ṛṣayaḥ sarve devarṣir nāradas tathā I
asito devalo vyāsaḥ svayaṁ caiva bravīṣi me II13II

Arjuna said

"You are the supreme Brahman, *the Supreme abode, the Supreme purifier, eternal, divine* puruṣa, *the God of all gods, unborn and omnipresent. Thus all the* ṛṣis *have declared thee, so also* devarṣi *Nārada, Asita, Devala and Vyāsa. And now the same you, yourself say that (to Me).*

dhāma: Abode.
dibhum: Omnipresent.
āhuḥ: Declared.
bravīṣi: Say.

It is evident from these two verses, that the Vedic teaching Arjuna had in his younger days was good. He was taught that *Brahman* is supreme, purifier of all sins, eternal, self-luminous *puruṣa*—the first *deva*, birthless and all-pervading. His abode was the greatest place. He had learnt that *Brahman* with these attributes was formless. It was given as a description of the indescribable eternal truth. He was told that his ancestors like Nārada, Asita, Devala, Vyāsa had also agreed with that view of the Lord.

Kṛṣṇa, as known to Arjuna, was the son of Devakī, the cowherd boy. He was Arjuna's friend. He cannot comprehend the idea that Kṛṣṇa, his friend, is *Brahman*. He had knowledge of *Brahman* from his teachers but no experience yet of *Brahman*. He cannot see *Brahman* in Kṛṣṇa.

Asita: (1) A priest who was present during Pāṇḍavas' time. He is said to have been one of the *purohit*s in *rājasūya yajña*.

(2) He is also an ancient sage.

Nārada: Mythical seer. He is a sage who can freely wander at will in all the three worlds. He can enter any kingdom at His will. He is known as *kalahapriya* i.e., the one who likes quarrels. He brings about fights between two people. But the end-result of the quarrel is always for the welfare of mankind.

सर्वमेतदृतं मन्ये यन्मां वदसि केशव ।
न हि ते भगवन्व्यक्तिं विदुर्देवा न दानवाः ॥१४॥

***sarvam etad ṛtaṁ manye yan māṁ vadasi keśava* I**
***na hi te bhagavan vyaktiṁ vidur devā na dānavāḥ* II14II**

O Keśava, I believe all this that you say to me is true. Verily, O Lord, neither the devas *nor the* dānavas *know your manifestation indeed.*

Ṛtam: Truth.
Keśava: Another name of Kṛṣṇa. It means remover of sorrows. It also means long-haired. Kṛṣṇa got this name after killing the demon Keśī.

Arjuna in the first half of the verse, admits that he believes that what Kṛṣṇa has said is true. He has faith in Kṛṣṇa's words and teachings.

"*Devas* and *dānavas* do not know You and Your manifestation (and glory)". *Devas* are celestial powers. They are deification of natural phenomenon. They are regarded as auspicious and as the higher intellectual comprehension of the Lord. *Dānavas* are the sons of Danu, one of the daughters of Diti. Danu is the wife of Kaśyapa Muni. They challenge the authority of *devas* in heaven and lead an undivine life.

Subjectively, *devas* are the nobler qualities in us, and *dānavas* are the undivine, negative qualities in us. Even the good in us cannot embrace the Truth in reality. Both good and bad in us do not comprehend the true omnipresent nature of the Lord.

स्वयमेवात्मनात्मानं वेत्थ त्वं पुरुषोत्तम ।
भूतभावन भूतेश देवदेव जगत्पते ॥१५॥

***svayam evātmanā'tmānaṁ vettha tvaṁ puruṣottama* I**
***bhūtabhāvana bhūteśa devadeva jagatpate* II15II**

O Purṣottama, You yourself know yourself by yourself. O source of all beings, God of all gods, ruler of the world.

We have discussed several times about our capacity to comprehend the Self in us. The Self is not an object or a subject. We cannot see it with our sense-organs and mind-intellect. We can only realise it by study of the *śāstra*s, teaching by *guru*s and by practical knowledge. We have to get absorbed into the Self and that is the only way to know the Self. Hence Arjuna uses the phrase "You yourself know yourself by yourself". **You yourself:** You, the person; **yourself by yourself:** Your ego by the Self. Through the *ātman* in you (Self) you understand the false nature of yourself (ego.) The *ātman* is your inner Self, it is the awareness, knowledge in all of us.

Arjuna has now understood the subject-matter *ātmā* taught by Kṛṣṇa. He has realised that his friend is none other than *Brahman* who is the eternal father, Supreme God and the ruler of the world. He addresses Kṛṣṇa as Puruṣottama. *Puruṣa* is the knowledge (Self or *ātmā*) inside all of us. *Puruṣa* vitalises the elements of *prakṛti* and manifests Himself as life in all of us. Śrī Kṛṣṇa the supreme knowledge is the best of all *puruṣa*s. Hence the title "Puruṣottama".

वक्तुमर्हस्यशेषेण दिव्या ह्यात्मविभूतयः ।
याभिर्विभूतिभिर्लोकानिमांस्त्वं व्याप्य तिष्ठसि ॥१६॥

***vaktum arhasy aśeṣeṇa divyā hy ātmavibhūtayaḥ* I**
***yābhir vibhūtibhir lokān imāṁs tvaṁ vyāpya tiṣṭhasi* II16II**

So, you should indeed tell Me without reserve of your divine glories, by which glories you exist, pervading all these worlds.

tiṣṭhasi: Exist.
atmavibhūtayaḥ: Thy glories.
arhasi: Competent.

Arjuna requests Kṛṣṇa to tell him all about His divine manifestations and glories. He wants to know what is the fundamental principle behind the variety of names and forms in the entire universe. He is greatly impressed by knowing the true identity of his friend. He now would like to know in what form He could see his friend in others.

कथं विद्यामहं योगिंस्त्वां सदा परिचिन्तयन् ।
केषु केषु च भावेषु चिन्त्योऽसि भगवन्मया ॥१७॥

***kathaṁ vidyām ahaṁ yogiṁs tvāṁ sadā paricintayan* I**
***keṣu keṣu ca bhāveṣu cintyo'si bhagavan mayā* II17II**

O yogī, *how shall I ever know you? By meditation? In what various aspects are you to be thought of by me, O my Lord?*

Yoga, as we have discussed before, is union of the ego with the soul. The person who has achieved it is a *yogī*. Lord Kṛṣṇa is *yogeśvara*. We, if and when we become *yogī*s, would really merge inside the *yogī* Kṛṣṇa. Arjuna has realised the *yogī* Kṛṣṇa who has shown His identity in His actions. He is the greatest *karma-yogī*.

What Arjuna is asking now, is nothing but what every spiritual seeker wants to know. How shall we meditate on the Lord? In what forms and features would he be recognised by us? It is not easy for an ordinary man to realise the subtle *ātmā* which is totally different from the gross body. In our day-to-day life, facing its problems, how can we remember Him and how should we know Him in what we see in and around us?

विस्तरेणात्मनो योगं विभूतिं च जनार्दन ।
भूयः कथय तृप्तिर्हि शृण्वतो नास्ति मेऽमृतम् ॥१८॥

***vistareṇātmano yogaṁ vibhūtiṁ ca janārdana* I**
***bhūyaḥ kathaya tṛptir hi śṛṇvato nāsti me'mṛtam* II18II**

O Janārdana, tell me again in detail of your yogic power and glory, for I do not feel satisfied by hearing your nectar-like speech.

One of the important characters in the science of self-development is brought out in this verse. That character is: "Desire to know more". In Sanskrit it is called *jijñāsā* (curiosity to listen). There is so much to know about the Lord of all gods. As He is covering the whole universe, it will never be possible to describe wholly His glory and manifestations.

Tṛpti is satisfaction. When we eat food we get satisfied and we enjoy what we have eaten. After sometime, we cannot eat anymore. When we go to a cinema, we get immersed in the life depicted in the pictures. We always want to know "what next"? We can never fully know the minute-to-minute action of individual characters in the picture. If it is a really an interesting film, we would like to sit and see more of it.

Similarly, when the greatest teacher on earth is enunciating the philosophy of life, the true listener will never find satisfaction. He wants more and more of the teachings. The teachings are supposed to give us 'immortality' or nectar or *amṛtam*. *Amṛtam* is the beverage of immortality in *Vedic* and Hindu mythology. The *deva*s were given the beverage to attain immortality.

Here Arjuna considers the teaching by His teacher as 'Nectar'. He therefore asks Him to give him more and more of it.

श्रीभगवानुवाच

हन्त ते कथयिष्यामि दिव्या ह्यात्मविभूतयः ।
प्राधान्यतः कुरुश्रेष्ठ नास्त्यन्तो विस्तरस्य मे ॥१९॥

śrī bhagavān uvāca

hanta te kathayiṣyāmi divyā hy ātmavibhūtayaḥ |
prādhānyataḥ kuruśreṣṭha nāsty anto vistarasya me ||19||

The Lord said

O Arjuna, now I will declare to you My divine glories according to their prominence, for there is no end to the details of My divine glory.

Śrī Kṛṣṇa in the next several verses in this chapter enumerates His presence in all His manifestations and the glory in those manifestations. He says that His glory is infinite and so it is impossible to enumerate in detail all His glories. He would try to declare the most excellent ones in which one could discover the Lord's presence. The examples He will choose will be carefully selected ones where one can see divinity most clearly.

अहमात्मा गुडाकेश सर्वभूताशयस्थितः ।
अहमादिश्च मध्यं च भूतानामन्त एव च ॥२०॥

***aham ātmā guḍākeśa sarvabhūtāśayasthitaḥ* |**
***aham ādiśca madhyaṁ ca bhūtānām anta eva ca* ||20||**

O Guḍākeśa, I am the Self seated in the hearts of all beings. I am the origin, middle and end of all beings.

Guḍākeśa: One who has conquered sleep. Sleep is a *tāmasika* quality. One who has conquered *tamas* is Guḍākeśa.

In the description of His glory and manifestations, in the first verse, the Lord starts with a definitive summarised statement. He says that He is the *ātmā* seated in the hearts of all beings. There is no creature, great or small, that exists without the Self inside and that Self is no other than the Lord Himself.

Śrī Kṛṣṇa, by using the phrase 'Guḍākeśa', is asking all of us to know this truth. There is nothing that can exist without the Self and ego is nothing but projection of the Self via mind-intellect. We should come out of the ignorance (*tamas*) and see the God inside all and develop universal love. We should show that in our actions.

The Lord says He is the origin, middle and end of all beings. Individually speaking, it means that the Self being there inside us from our birth, will remain so in all stages of our life till our death. It will still be there after death. Depending on the *vāsanās* left behind, it will either merge with *Paramātmā* or find its way into forming another living creature. The Self is therefore birthless and deathless and our physical body is an outer suit for the Self.

Universally speaking, the Lord was present in the past, He is present now and He will be present in the future. He is the eternal substratum for the universe.

आदित्यानामहं विष्णुर्ज्योतिषां रविरंशुमान् ।
मरीचिर्मरुतामस्मि नक्षत्राणामहं शशी ॥२१॥

ādityānām ahaṁ viṣṇur jyotiṣāṁ ravir aṁśumān I
marīcir marutām asmi nakṣatrāṇām ahaṁ śaśī II21II

Among the Ādityas, I am Viṣṇu, among the luminaries I am the radiant sun. Among the Maruts I am Marīci. Among the stars, I am the Moon.

Ādityas are sons of *Aditi*, who is the goddess of space. She is the daughter of Dakṣa. Ādityas personify the various aspects of nature. The number of Ādityas vary from 5 to 12 in various traditional beliefs. In the *Brāhmaṇa* portion of the *Veda*s, Ādityas are said to be 12, representing the 12 months of the year.

They are: (1) Dhātā, (2) Mitra, (3) Aryamā, (4) Śakra, (5) Varuṇa, (6) Aṁśu, (7) Bhaga, (8) Vivasvān, (9) Pūṣā, (10) Savitā, (11) Tvaṣṭā, (12) Viṣṇu.

In *Viṣṇu Purāṇa*, Viṣṇu is considered to be the most powerful of the Ādityas. There is no mention of Viṣṇu, as the God, in the early *Vedic* period. His name comes in the later parts of *Vedic* literature. Among the luminaries, He is the most powerful radiant sun. We know that the sun is the source of all energy.

Maruts are considered storm-gods and friends of Indra. They represent the presiding deity of storms, wind and breeze. Their origin and number varies in different literatures. Some consider them as sons of Rudra and Pṛṣṇi. Others consider them as sons of Marutvatī, wife of Dharma. Some others say they are the offspring of Diti and Kaśyapa. (Indra is said to have cut Diti's womb into many pieces. Diti requested him to make them into a troop (*gaṇa*) of gods. They are therefore known as Marutgaṇas). Their numbers vary from 7-49. Here are seven:

(1) Āvaha, (2) Pravaha, (3) Nivaha, (4) Parāvaha, (5) Udvaha, (6) Saṁvaha, (7) Parivaha (Marīci).

Among the Maruts, Marīci is the chief. Marīci means a ray of light (of the sun or moon). It is the name given to Prajāpati, son of Brahmā.

Among the stars, He is the moon.

वेदानां सामवेदोऽस्मि देवानामस्मि वासवः ।
इन्द्रियाणां मनश्चास्मि भूतानामस्मि चेतना ॥२२॥

vedānāṁ sāmavedo'smi devānām asmi vāsavaḥ |
indriyāṇāṁ manaś cāsmi bhūtānām asmi cetanā ||22||

Among the Vedas, *I am* Sāmaveda. *Among the Gods, I am Indra. Among the senses, I am the mind and I am the intelligence among living beings.*

There are four *Veda*s, *Ṛk, Yajus, Sāma* and *Ātharvaṇa. Sāmaveda* is nothing but the essence of *Ṛgveda.* It is composed of sacred songs, which consist of hymns from *Ṛgveda* so arranged as to suit music. They are chanted by the priests in Soma sacrifices. *Gāyatrī mantra* is from *Sāmaveda.* The essential element is melody. They consist of three or four musical intervals which are the earliest examples of Indian musical scale. *Sāmaveda* is considered the best of the four, because of the beautiful melody of its hymns. (Śrī Kṛṣṇa is the most melodious player of flute music, which enchanted one and all. He is the infinite Lord tuned to music.

Among the Gods in heaven, He is Vāsava, Vāsava is Indra. Indra is the chief god of heaven.

Our sense-organs send in their impulses to the mind which analyses the impulses and sends messages through to the organs of action. The mind is the central station for the senses. Without the mind, the sense-organs will not perform their duty and organs of action will not act properly. Hence, the Self is like the mind, king of all sense-organs; and so Indra, King of Gods, at subjective level is the mind.

Among all the living creatures, we humans are considered the best. This is because we have the power of discrimination called intelligence (*buddhi*). The power (or gift) of *cetanā* (life-intelligence or consciousness) makes us the best amongst all forms of life on this earth.

रुद्राणां शंकरश्चास्मि वित्तेशो यक्षरक्षसाम् ।
वसूनां पावकश्चास्मि मेरुः शिखरिणामहम् ॥२३॥

rudrāṇāṁ śaṁkaraś cāsmi vitteśo yakṣarakṣasām |
vasūnāṁ pāvakaś cāsmi meruḥ śikhariṇām aham ||23||

Among the Rudras, I am Śaṅkara. Among Yakṣas and Rākṣasas I am Kubera. Among Vasus, I am fire and among mountains I am Meru.

vitteśa: Kubera, Lord of wealth.
pāvakaḥ: Agni (fire).

Rudra is considered as the deity of destruction. Brahmā was disrupted during meditation on the creative process. His anger at being disturbed, burst forth from His forehead as Rudra. During *yajña*s, no oblations are made to Rudra.

Destruction is a necessary precedent to subsequent creation. If there was no destruction, life would have been hell for all. The dead make way for the living.

Seven to eleven *rudra*s are mentioned in the scriptures and among them Śaṅkara is the chief. (Hara, Bahurūpa, Tryambaka, Aparājita, Vṛṣākapi, Śambhu, Kapardī, Raivata, Mṛgavyādha, Śarva and Kapālī.)

*Yakṣa*s are considered as godlings. They are said to live in fields, forests and jungles. *Rākṣasa*s are demons including *bhūta*s and other (malevolent) spirits. They are said to wander about in the night and can assume any form. They are the offspring of Khasā, one of Dakṣa's daughters. Others attribute their origin to Pulastya. Among the *yakṣa*s and *rākṣasa*s, the best is Kubera. Kubera is also known as *rākṣasendra* (Lord of *rākṣasas*). He is the divine treasurer. He is described as an ugly creature having a pot belly, fat and short, with a small head and eight protruding teeth. (One can interpret this to mean that our ancient *ṛṣis* detested material wealth so much, that they depicted Kubera as an ugly creature).

Vasus are *Vedic* deities presiding over the seasons. They are called Viśvedevas and Agni is the chief among them. The *Ṛgvedic* hymns ask Viśvedevas to protect us from all distress.

There are eight *Vasus*. In *Mahābhārata*, Ādiparva, it is said that *Vasus* disturbed *ṛṣi* Vasiṣṭha during his meditation. He cursed them to be born on earth. On pleading guilty and requesting pardon, they were born to river Gaṅgā and king Śāntanu. River Gaṅgā promised to kill the Vasus at birth so that they will not live on earth for long. Gaṅgā consented to marry Śāntanu on condition that he should not question her on whatever she did with their children. The day he questioned her, she would leave him. The first seven children (Vasus) born to them were drowned by her in the river Gaṅgā. Śāntanu stops her from drowning the eighth one. He is Bhīṣma, the famous grandsire of Kauravas, Bhiṣma vows that he will never marry.

Meru is a mythological golden mountain, believed to be the centre of the universe. According to Hindu cosmography, on top of it lives the divine Lord and below it are seven islands that constitute the world. Among the moutains, Meru is considered the best.

पुरोधसां च मुख्यं मां विद्धि पार्थ बृहस्पतिम् ।
सेनानीनामहं स्कन्दः सरसामस्मि सागरः ॥२४॥

***purodhasāṁ ca mukhyaṁ māṁ viddhi pārtha bṛhaspatim* I**
***senānīnām ahaṁ skandaḥ sarasām asmi sāgaraḥ* II24II**

O Arjuna, among the household priests, know Me as the chief Bṛhaspati. Among the generals, I am Skanda. Among the bodies of water, I am the ocean.

Bṛhaspati is the Lord of prayers. He represents moral ideals. He is supposed to make sure that the benefits of the ritualistic sacrifice go to the right person. As householders are the ones who perform sacrifices, Bṛhaspati is considered as the chief among priests. Bṛhaspati is also considered as the planet Jupiter, the Lord of all planets.

Among generals, I am Skanda. Skanda is Lord Subrahmaṇya, the son of Lord Śiva. He is given the role as the general for the army of the Gods.

Among the lakes and rivers, the best is the ocean. Even though there is no direct relationship, if there were no oceans, rivers would dry up in the course of time.

महर्षीणां भृगुरहं गिरामस्म्येकमक्षरम् ।
यज्ञानां जपयज्ञोऽस्मि स्थावराणां हिमालयः ॥२५॥

***maharṣīṇāṁ bhṛgur ahaṁ girām asmy ekam akṣaram* I**
***yajñānāṁ japayajño'smi sthāvarāṇāṁ himālayaḥ* II25II**

Among the great ṛṣis, *I am Bhṛgu. Among words, I am the one syllable. Among sacrifices, I am the sacrifice of silent repetition. Among immovable objects, I am the Himalayas.*

girām: Among words.

Among *saptarṣis,* the chief is considered to be Bhṛgu. He is the fire-spirit. By His magical power the altar fire was kindled. He is recognised as the son of Manu, who himself was Brahmā's son born from his mind. (Mānasaputra). Bhṛgu recites *Mānava Dharmaśāstra* which is the sacred text of *dharma* (righteousness).

Among words, I am the one syllable. That syllable is *Oṁ. Oṁ* is the *Vedic* representation of the infinite *Brahman* and the finite world. Just as we use a word like apple to mean the fruit apple, we eat, *Oṁ* is one word to mean *Brahman.* It is the most sacred of all *mantras*. Meditating on this *mantra*, one attains *mokṣa* (liberation). *Oṁ* is meditated upon on its own, in which case, it becomes a *mantra. Oṁ* is also prefixed to the various names and forms of divinity. By doing so, it means that *Oṁ* was before that divinity and given its due respect by prefixing it, e.g., *Oṁ namaḥ Śivāya.*

Among sacrifices, I am *japa-yajña. Japa* is a technique by which the performer of *japa* (meditation) maintains a constant stream of the same divine thought in his mind. It is a process for purification of the mind. Unbroken remembrance of the Self in thoughts and action is *japa*, which will confer *mokṣa* in due course.

The Himalayas among mountains is the best. The atmosphere near mountains is so peaceful and serene. Among such beautiful moutains, the Himalaya mountain is considered the best. Our ancient *ṛṣis* went to the Himalayas to meditate on the Lord. They found it a very calm place to contemplate on the Lord and realise Him.

अश्वत्थः सर्ववृक्षाणां देवर्षीणां च नारदः ।
गन्धर्वाणां चित्ररथः सिद्धानां कपिलो मुनिः ॥२६॥

***aṣvatthaḥ sarvavṛkṣāṇāṁ devarṣiṇāṁ ca nāradaḥ* I**
***gandharvāṇāṁ citrarathaḥ siddhānāṁ kapilo muniḥ* II26II**

Among all trees, I am Aśvattha. Among the divine ṛṣis, I am Nārada, among gandharvas, I am Citraratha, among siddhas, I am sage Kapila.

Aśvattha tree is Ficus Religiosa, commonly known as *pīpal* tree. It is sacred to Hindus and is worshipped by many. It lasts for centuries and hence among trees, it can be considered eternal. It is described in detail in chapter 15 verse 1.

Among the heavenly seers, I am Nārada (verse 13, chapter 10). Among *gandharvas*, I am Citraratha. *Gandharvas* are said to be mythological musicians. They entertain gods of heaven. They sing sweetly on the moutains. The art of music is sometimes called *Gāndharva Vidyā*. Citraratha is the best king among *gandharvas* and *apsarās* (heavenly maidens who dance for the gods). The four white horses which carried Arjuna on the battlefield of Kurukṣetra, were a gift to Arjuna from Citraratha. They were supernatural and could travel anywhere in the three worlds.

Among *siddhas*, I am Kapila Muni. The followers of the spiritual path are called *sādhakas*. Those who achieve the goal are called *siddhas*. The goal to achieve is *sādhya*. A *siddha* is a 'perfected one' in spiritual progress. *Siddhas* attain liberation while living and hence are also called *jīvanmuktas*. *Siddhas* continue to give moral and spiritual guidance to the aspirants and are considered as teachers.

Kapila is the author of *Sāṁkhya* philosophy. He is considered as the son of Brahmā. According to the legends, he burnt 60,000 sons of king Sagara, by his fierce glance. Later on, to get them to heaven, king Bhagīratha performed penance. He managed to bring the sacred river Ganges to earth. Goddess Ganges ran over the ashes of Sagara's sons and they achieved liberation by getting their sins destroyed. Ganges is the most sacred of the rivers in India. Kapila's name is attributed to the city of Kapilavastu, the birthplace of Buddha. Kapila is also a *muni*. *Muni* means one who has learnt 'the art of reflection'. He is a great thinker among thinkers. Kapila is the best, the Lord says.

उच्चैःश्रवसमश्वानां विद्धि माममृतोद्भवम् ।
ऐरावतं गजेन्द्राणां नराणां च नराधिपम् ॥२७॥

***uccaiḥśravasam aśvānāṁ viddhi mām amṛtodbhavam* I**
***airāvataṁ gajendrāṇāṁ narāṇāṁ ca narādhipam* II27II**

Among horses, know Me as Uccaiḥśravas, born of nectar; among elephants, as Airāvata, and among men as the King.

Churning of the Ocean

This is a very famous ancient Indian *Purāṇic* story. It is said that both *devas* and *dānavas* together churned the Milky Ocean to get nectar which would confer immortality. In the process several great things came out of the ocean. *Devas* and *dānavas* shared those between them.

Churning is an act by which one agitates a liquid violently to separate the constituents of the liquid. Curds are churned to extract butter from it. *Purāṇas* say that the great mountain Mandara was used as a rod to churn the ocean. The serpent Vāsuki was used as a rope to rotate the mountain.

Mountain Mandara being very heavy would have submerged in the ocean. *Devas* and *dānavas* prayed to Lord Viṣṇu and begged his help in overcoming the problem. Lord Viṣṇu blessed them and took the form of a turtle (*kūrma avatāra*, 2nd incarnation of Lord Viṣṇu). The turtle bore the weight of the mountain and kept it afloat so that the ocean could be churned.

There is a philosophical interpretation to this story. The Milky Ocean can be compared to *saṁsāra*. *Devas* and *dānavas* can be compared to good and bad people. The turtle is of course Lord Viṣṇu.

Saṁsāra means endless births and deaths, pleasures and pains in worldly life. As long as one is looking for pleasures in this world, one would be immersed in the ocean of *saṁsāra*. One would have to undergo various modifications including births and deaths in the process of enjoying the pleasures. The pleasures, as we know, do end up in pains. There is only one pleasure which does not end in pain. That pleasure is when one experiences *ātma-jñāna* and realises his real identity and lives in that state. That state is pure bliss (*ānanda*) and is commonly known as *mokṣa*. *Mokṣa* is said to be the state of immortality where there are no pleasures and pains of any kind.

One would get drowned in the ocean of *saṁsāra*. Our life is a mountain of experiences which would get us drowned in *saṁsāra*. To get out of this we need the help and blessings of the Lord. When we churn our ocean of experiences, we get both good and bad. We get poisonous experiences as well as those that give us happiness.

What did Lord Viṣṇu do in this story? He took the form of a tortoise. The tortoise is an animal which can withdraw its limbs and head into its shell on contact with external objects. The shell then protects it against possible dangers. It then rests satisfied with the self-provided security.

The Lord has given us an example of how to live in this life. If we can withdraw our senses from sense-objects, our wisdom is said to be firm (*sthithaprajña* character, Chapter 2, verse 58). We should train our minds to turn towards the *ātmā* inside us. If we can withstand with equanimity both pleasures and pains in this life, if we can withdraw our senses from sense-objects and concentrate on the divine, we will in course of time attain *mokṣa*.

This story is a comparison of the eternal progress of good and bad people churning the ocean of life to get happiness through wealth, learning and prosperity. One can get permanent happiness only by following the spiritual path and obtaining spiritual knowledge.

आयुधानामहं वज्रं धेनूनामस्मि कामधुक् ।
प्रजनश्चास्मि कन्दर्पः सर्पाणामस्मि वासुकिः ॥२८॥

āyudhānām aham vajram dhenūnām asmi kāmadhuk |
prajanaś cāsmi kandarpaḥ sarpāṇām asmi vāsukiḥ ||28||

Among weapons, I am the thunderbolt, among cows Kāmadhenu, among the progenitors I am Kandarpa and among serpents, I am Vāsuki.

Vajra is the magical weapon of Indra, which could never be shattered. The sage Dadhīci offered his rib-bone for the construction of this weapon, to kill a demon who was fighting the *devas*.

Kāmadhenu: It was another product to come out of the churning of the Milky Ocean. It is a white cow from which one can milk all one's desires. It is called the "cow of plenty". Its other names are Surabhi, Savala. Kāmadhenu's son is Bhṛṅgī, Lord Śiva's bull.

Of all the causes of offspring, I am Kandarpa, the Lord says. Kandarpa is popularly known as Manmatha (cupid) who is considered as the god of love. Manmatha once disturbed Lord Śiva in His meditation, Śiva got angry and burnt him to ashes. Later on, at the request of his wife, He restored him to life but made him live as a blind man. Hence the common saying that 'love is blind'.

Vāsuki: It is the legendary serpent which adorns Lord Śiva's ring finger. He is considered the king of serpents. He volunteered to be the churning rope to turn the mountain Mandara. Vāsuki is a *sarpa*, which means a single-hooded serpent. He is the serpent son of Kadru who is the daughter of Dakṣa.

अनन्तश्चास्मि नागानां वरुणो यादसामहम् ।
पितॄणामर्यमा चास्मि यमः संयमतामहम् ॥२९॥

anantaś cāsmi nāgānām varuṇo yādasām aham |
pitṝṇām aryamā cāsmi yamaḥ saṁyamatām aham ||29||

I am Ananta among nāgas. *I am Varuṇa among water-deities. Of the* pitṛs *I am Aryamā, of the controllers I am Yama (the Lord of death).*

Nāgas are many-hooded serpents. Among them the chief is Ananta, a thousand-headed Śeṣa-nāga. He forms the bed on which Lord Viṣṇu reclines in His *yoga* sleep.

Yādasas are water-deities. In the Vedic period, the elemental forces were deified. Varuṇa is said to be responsible for the rains. Whenever there is drought, *Varuṇa-yāga* is performed to please Varuṇa.

In Hinduism there is a belief that the departed souls live together in a world of their own. It is called *pitṛloka*. People who die holding on to one or the other desire, enter the world of matter (moon). They return to earth after some time to fulfil their desires. Aryamā is the chief of *pitṛloka*. He is one of the sons of Aditi.

Yama is considered as the Lord of death, who rules the world of death (*yama-loka*). Death as a phenomenon has an important role in maintaining equilibrium in the world. The law of physics states that 'no two things can ever remain at one and the same period of time occupying one and the same place'. The principle of death is a prerequisite for the principle of creation. In Hinduism therefore, death is also worshipped in a form. Yama, the ruler of the world of death, dictates as to when a person is to die. That person is first taken to yama-*loka* where he is rightly judged for his actions of the past. Depending on the judgement, the person is sent to heaven for enjoying benefits of good deeds or to hell to suffer punishment for sins committed.

प्रह्लादश्चास्मि दैत्यानां कालः कलयतामहम् ।
मृगाणां च मृगेन्द्रोऽहं वैनतेयश्च पक्षिणाम् ॥३०॥

prahlādaś cāsmi daityānāṁ kālaḥ kalayatām aham |
mṛgāṇāṁ ca mṛgendro'haṁ vainateyaśca pakṣiṇām ||30||

Among the daityas, *I am Prahlāda. Among reckoners, I am time. Among beasts, I am lion. And among birds, I am Garuḍa, son of Vinatā.*

Prahlāda is a very famous boy, a devotee of Lord Viṣṇu in Hindu mythology. His father was Hiraṇyakaśipu, a *daitya* or demon who hated the very name of Viṣṇu. Hiraṇyakaśipu tortured his son in several ways to dissuade him from praising Viṣṇu. Finally he challenges his son to show Viṣṇu inside a pillar. Lord Viṣṇu, in the incarnation of Lord Narasiṁha (man-lion) comes out of the pillar and kills Hiraṇyakaśipu.

Time, according to Hindu philosophy, is eternal. It is only the individual minds that reckon it as past, present and future. When happy, one feels that time was spent too quickly. When unhappy, the same time drags on very slowly. Hence time and Prahlāda are given as further examples of Lord's existence in the universe.

The lion is considered to be the king of beasts, because of its majesty and splendour. Garuḍa is the white-necked eagle on which flies Lord Viṣṇu. He is the son of Vinatā, who is wife of Kaśyapa. Vinatā is the sister of Kadru. Kadru is considered to be the mother of snakes. Both were wives of Kaśyapa. There was a quarrel between the two sisters which ended in Kadru enslaving her sister Vinatā. Hence it is said that Garuḍa became the enemy of all snakes.

By giving examples of animals and birds, the Lord is trying to show His manifestations in all living creatures, in birds of the air and beasts of the earth.

पवनः पवतामस्मि रामः शस्त्रभृतामहम् ।
झषाणां मकरश्चास्मि स्रोतसामस्मि जाह्नवी ॥३१॥

pavanaḥ pavatām asmi rāmaḥ śastrabhṛtām aham |
jhaṣāṇāṁ makaraś cāsmi srotasām asmi jāhnavī ||31||

Among purifiers, I am the wind. Among warriors, I am Rāma. Among fish, I am makara *and among rivers, I am the Ganges.*

jhaṣāṇām: Among fish.
makara: Shark.
srotasām: Among rivers

Fresh wind blows away the smells and germs in the air and hence wind is considered as a purifier. Rāma is considered to be the incarnation of Viṣṇu (before Kṛṣṇa). He is depicted as an ideal ruler, ideal son, ideal husband, ideal brother and ideal father. His weapon is the bow (*kodaṇḍa*) and He killed, among many demons, the ten-headed Rāvaṇa.

The Lord says He is the shark among fish and the Ganges (Jāhnavī) among rivers. The shark among the fish species is dangerous and strong. *Makara* is a mythological shark, vehicle of Varuṇa (God of rain). It is also a fertility symbol and it appears on the banner of Kāma (God of love). It is depicted as an auspicious sign on the hand of Lord Viṣṇu.

The river Ganges is the most sacred of the rivers in India. It is considered as a purifier of all sins. According to the legend, when the Ganges came down to earth (following Bhagīratha's efforts), she flowed so strongly and powerfully, that it was causing damage to property and life. The sage Jahnu drank it all. Later, on request, he pardoned her and Ganges poured out of his ears.

This story can be interpreted symbolically. The Ganges represents spiritual culture and knowledge of the Hindus. The *ṛṣi* Jahnu, drank all the waters of the Ganges, because he had a thirst for knowledge. Knowledge then came out from him, for all to hear. (The *Vedic* term *śruti* means the sacred knowledge (*Veda*s) heard by our ancient *ṛṣi*s and transmitted verbally to their disciples to listen and learn).

सर्गाणामादिरन्तश्च मध्यं चैवाहमर्जुन ।
अध्यात्मविद्या विद्यानां वादः प्रवदतामहम् ।।३२।।

sargāṇām ādir antaś ca madhyaṁ caivāham arjuna |
adhyātmavidyā vidyānāṁ vādaḥ pravadatām aham ||32||

Among all creations, I am the beginning, middle and end, O Arjuna. Among sciences, I am the science of self-knowledge and among arguments, I am the logic.

sargāṇām: Among creations.
adhyātma-vidyā: Self-knowledge.
pravadatām: Various forms of arguments.
vādaḥ: Logical argument.

By saying that He is the beginning, middle and end of all creatures, the Lord is asserting that He is the fundamental essence in all. Without Him, there would be no life. Without 'life', no creation is possible.

There are a number of sciences in the world. They are all related to material things. They have done wonders for the progress of the world but not brought peace to the world. The moral values are declining and we are all becoming more and more selfish and materialistic. By learning the spiritual knowledge one can find peace in oneself and uplift moral standards. Hence, Self-knowledge is the best.

There are three kinds of arguments: (1) *vāda,* (2) *jalpa,* (3) *vitaṇḍā*. *Vāda* is reasoning, free from malice and hatred. It is aimed at reaching the 'Truth'. There are no intentions to harm others in *vāda*. This is supposed to be the technique used by lawyers in a court of law. *Jalpa* is a kind of argument for the purpose of establishing one's own importance and belittling others. *Vitaṇḍā* is another kind of argument aimed at destroying other's views by any means (fair or foul). It is used to condemn others. *Jalpa* and *vitaṇḍā* may help to weaken the opposition but they would not help one to arrive at the truth. Logical reasoning is a glory come from God.

अक्षराणामकारोऽस्मि द्वन्द्वः सामासिकस्य च ।
अहमेवाक्षयः कालो धाताहं विश्वतोमुखः ॥३३॥

***akṣarāṇām akāro'smi dvandvaḥ sāmāsikasya ca* |**
***aham evā'kṣayaḥ kālo dhātāhaṁ viśvatomukhaḥ* ||33||**

Among letters I am the letter 'A'. I am the dual among compounds. I am verily the everlasting time. I am the dispenser having faces in all directions.

sāmāsikasya: Among all compounds.
dhātā: Dispenser.

Kṣara means the one that perishes. *Akṣara* is one that does not perish. The alphabet one learns as a child, will last till death (or insanity) or unconsciousness overtakes one and hence alphabets are *akṣara*. Out of these, the letter '*A*' is the first of the alphabets and a 'vowel' also. Importance is therefore given to the letter '*A*'. In Sanskrit, the letter '*A*' is used more often to add to letters or words and actually it makes it sweeter to listen to, for this reason.

A compound is a substance made up of two or more products. By saying 'dual among compounds', we have to think in terms of philosophy of the Hindu religion. We are made up of the soul and the body. They appear as one, but they are 'dual'. The soul cannot manifest without the body and the body cannot be alive without the energy of the soul.

The Lord is the eternal time. This idea has been brought out in verse 30 of this chapter. There, the Lord says He is the reckoner of time. The time divided into past, present and future, was its theme. In this context, by saying He is "reckoner of time", he means "Time is etrnal" and "the Lord is eternal".

The Lord is the dispenser of fruits of action. Once we do a certain work, it brings its own results in course of time, depending on how we did the work. We sow the seeds and as long as the conditions of sowing and maintaining it are fulfilled. One will get the crops. Similarly, if we do sinful acts, we will get punished for such acts in course of time. 'He' is the dispenser of 'fruits of action'. When we do good deeds, we must also develop the sense of not attaching 'I'-ness to it. We should not claim that the result is on account of our 'self-effort'. We must develop the attitude that "the result is the blessing of the Lord", and thank him for the results. We should also thank Him for our 'hard times' in life. (He has given us punishment for our sins of the past and so helped us to burn the *vāsanā* imprint).

He has faces in all directions: As He is inside all of us, He is witness to all our actions. Hence He is said to have faces in all sides. Another way of looking at it is also possible. As 'He' is in eveybody, 'He has faces everywhere'. If one can see the 'soul' in others and not the physical body of *nāma* and *rūpa*, one can easily realise "His face" everywhere.

All our physical, mental and intellectual comprehensions are possible only because of the presence of "The soul" in us. We can, therefore, say that the Lord is *viśvatomukhaḥ* (face everywhere; in all our actions at three levels of perception).

> मृत्युः सर्वहरश्चाहं उद्भवश्च भविष्यताम् ।
> कीर्तिः श्रीर्वाक्च नारीणां स्मृतिर्मेधा धृतिः क्षमा ॥३४॥
> ***mṛtyuḥ sarvaharaś cāhaṁ udbhavaś ca bhaviṣyatām* I**
> ***kīrtiḥ śrīr vāk ca nārīṇāṁ smṛtir medhā dhṛtiḥ kṣamā* II34II**
>
> *And I am the all-devouring death, the birth of those who are to be born. Among feminine qualities, I am fame, prosperity, speech, memory, intelligence, firmness and forgiveness.*

Death and birth are the alternate processes of manifestation of the universe. One cannot be without the other. Even at the time of *pralaya* (total destruction) there is new creation. Destruction is really a modification of an existing object. Philosophically, death and birth can be attributed to a particular state of existence. For example, childhood-stage will lead to the teenage-stage. Technically speaking childhood has died and the teenager is born. The soul of the dead childhood and the soul of the born teenager is the same.

Seven virtues which are considered as feminine qualities are enumerated here. The Lord says that they are ''divine qualties''. He is the principle behind these seven qualities. Wherever one finds these virtues, be it in men or women, one is asked to consider them as 'divinie quality'.

The Lord accords an exalted position to women. Women were considered as weak and due respect was not given to them. Lord Rāma sent His wife Sītā to the forest, on the words of suspicion expressed by one of his subjects. Draupadī was insulted in royal court in the presence of all elders. Draupadī was offered as a stake in the game of dice by her husband Yudhiṣṭhira. Kṛṣṇa condemns such acts on women and asks men to show due respect to them.

Mythologically, there is a story behind the seven virtues. Prasūti (daughter of Manu) married Dakṣa Kīrti Devī, Medhā Devī, Dhṛti

Devī, Smṛti Devi, Kṣamā Devī are five of his twenty-four daughters. Śrī Devī is the daughter of Bhṛgu and Vāgdevī is the wife of Brahmā. These seven constitute the seven virtues respectively.

बृहत्साम तथा साम्नां गायत्री छन्दसामहम् ।
मासानां मार्गशीर्षोऽहं ऋतूनां कुसुमाकरः ॥३५॥

bṛhatsāma tathā sāmnāṁ gāyatrī chandasām aham I
māsānāṁ mārgaśīrṣo'haṁ ṛtūnāṁ kusumākaraḥ II35II

Among hymns, I am Bṛhat-Sāma. *Among metres, I am* Gāyatrī. *Among months, I am* Mārgaśīrṣa. *Among seasons, I am the flowery spring.*

In verse 22 of this chapter, the Lord has already said that He is *Sāmaveda* among the *Veda*s. Among all the hymns in *Sāmaveda, Bṛhatī* is the most difficult and complicated. The hymns sung in this metre are *Bṛhat-Sāma*.

Gāyatrī is the name of a *Vedic* metre, consisting of 24 syllables, divided into 3 lines of 8 syllables each. It is considered as the most divine and extremely powerful metre. There are a number of hymns composed in this metre, the most sacred being the one addressed to the Sun-God (Savitā). The prayer's meaning is this: "We meditate on the excellent light of the divine Sun, may He illuminate our minds.'' This *mantra* is chanted by the 'twice-born' (those who have undergone *upanayana* ceremony, have been offered the sacred thread by the *guru* who repeats the prayer three times in the ears) during their morning and evening devotions. This *mantra* is also repeated while pouring *ghī* into the sacrificial fire in *havana* and *yajña*.

The month of Mārgaśīrṣa corresponds to December-January in the English calendar. For Indians, the winter months are a welcome break after a really hot summer and a wet monsoon. New harvests are obtained in this season.

Among seasons, Spring is the best. It is beautiful with new blossoms and flowers. There is a sweet fragrance in the air.

द्यूतं छलयतामस्मि तेजस्तेजस्विनामहम् ।
जयोऽस्मि व्यवसायोऽस्मि सत्त्वं सत्त्ववतामहम् ॥३६॥

***dyūtaṁ chalayatām asmi tejas tejasvinām aham* I**
***jayo'smi vyavasāyo'smi sattvaṁ sattvavatām aham* II36II**

I am the gambling of the fraudulent. I am the splendour of the splendid. I am victory, I am determination (vyavasāyo'smi). *I am the goodness in the good.*

By saying that He is the 'gambling of the fraudulent', Śrī Kṛṣṇa is not supporting the gambling spirit. He is the same in all, good and bad, He is the principle behind the act. It is a game. A game has to be taken in its true spirit and should not be carried too far (out of proportion). Śrī Kṛṣṇa is indirectly reminding one of the consequences of misusing the spirit of the game of dice by Arjuna's elder brother. He is giving us the message, "Do not gamble away what you have".

Splendour, victory, determination are all to be considered as His manifestation. One's splendour should not be taken as due to one's self-effort, but due to God's grace. Similarly, victory should be attributed to God's help. One should not become proud of his splendour or victory.

Determination will lead one to victory, it is a divine character. It should be used in divine spirit for divine purposes. It should not be used to perform 'sinful acts'.

He is the good in the goodness, Among *guṇas*, *sattva-guṇa* is the best, it is nearer to the Soul.

वृष्णीनां वासुदेवोऽस्मि पाण्डवानां धनंजयः ।
मुनीनामप्यहं व्यासः कवीनामुशना कविः ॥३७॥

***vṛṣṇīnāṁ vāsudevo'smi pāṇḍavānāṁ danañjayaḥ* I**
***munīnām apy ahaṁ vyāsaḥ kavīnām uśanā kaviḥ* II37II**

Among the Vṛṣṇīs, I am Vāsudeva, among Pāṇḍavas, I am Arjuna, among the munis, *I am Vyāsa and among the poets, I am Uśanā, the seer.*

Vṛṣṇīs are Yādavas, descendants of Vasni, son of Bhīma Sātvata. Their kingdom was in north-western India. Vasudeva, father of Kṛṣṇa and Balarāma was the great, great grandson of Vṛṣṇī. Śrī Kṛṣṇa is called Vāsudeva also.

Arjuna's other name is Dhanañjaya, which means a winner of wealth. He achieved this title after victory in *Rājasūya-yajña*. We can add to it the achievement of being the first one to listen to the wealth of the great *Gītā* from Lord Kṛṣṇa.

Vyāsa: It is a general name for 'compiler' of literary compositions. In *Vedic* times, the literature was in *mantra* form and not so interesting. In *Purāṇic* times, eminent *ṛṣi*s compiled the *Veda*s and they all are given the title of 'Vyāsa'.

Among Vyāsas, the prominent one is Kṛṣṇa Dvaipāyana, composer of the *Mahābhārata*, of which the *Gītā* is an integral part. It is believed that he got Lord Gaṇeśa to write the script while he narrated it. Grammatically, Vyāsa means "one who elaborates every point of discussion".

Uśanā is considered as a famous *Vedic ṛṣi*, closely associated with Agni. He composed hymns for the 'Fire ritual' *Uśanā* is also the name of a priest of Yayāti (ruler of *daitya*s). He became the *guru* of Kaca, (son of Bṛhaspati). Kaca wanted to become the pupil of Śukra to obtain *'Sañjīvanī Vidyā'* (secret of immortality).

Kavi was a title given to *ṛṣi*s who first gave us the *Vedic mantra*s. They did not accept the authorship of those *mantra*s. They said that the *mantra*s came to them at moments of inspiration which was not explainable. They attributed them to divine power.

दण्डो दमयतामस्मि नीतिरस्मि जिगीषताम् ।
मौनं चैवास्मि गुह्यानां ज्ञानं ज्ञानवतामहम् ॥३८॥

***daṇḍo damayatām asmi nītir asmi jigīṣatām* I**
***maunaṁ caivāsmi guhyānāṁ jñānaṁ jñānavatām aham* II38II**

Of the punishers, I am 'Punishment'. Of the seekers of victory, I am 'Statesmanship'. Of the secrets, I am 'Silence'. And I am 'The Knowledge' of the knowers.

damayatām: Of punishers.
jigīṣatām: Seekers of victory.

The act of punishing the culprits who break the governing laws of any community is called punishment. In any society, this power is given to certain people. Judges award punishment to the people who commit any crime. The policemen arrest suspected criminals. Spiritually speaking, we suffer for our own sins. Punishment for our sins is dictated by our own 'Self'.

Without 'statesmanship' there is really no victory at all. After any wars, there is usually a compromise to rule by the victors. Even though the victors rule, there is usually statesmanship in the agreement which is needed for the welfare of the people against whom the victory is achieved. One cannot punish the entire community after a war.

Silence is the best form of secret. Secret in any other form can be unearthed at any time. If it is in one's own brain, nobody else can find it out. Secret is also nourished by silence. During deep silence-state (meditation) one can meditate on the 'Soul within'. This knowledge of the Self is also a secret and is understood better by silent contemplation. Silence in word and thought are essential to attain Self-control.

The knowledge in the *jñānī* is the expression of divine glory in that person. It is not the physical body (ego-*jīva*) but really the 'Soul within' who is the real person.

यच्चापि सर्वभूतानां बीजं तदहमर्जुन ।
न तदस्ति विना यत्स्यान्मया भूतं चराचरम् ॥३९॥

yac cāpi sarvabhūtānāṁ bījaṁ tad aham arjuna I
na tad asti vinā yat syān mayā bhūtaṁ carācaram II39II

O Arjuna, whatsoever is the seed of all beings, that also am I. There is no being moving or non-moving that can exist without Me.

Two meanings can be given to the word 'seed' in this verse. The first meaning is 'seed is the source-plant' and similarly 'the Lord is the source of all beings'. Knowing this, we should realise that the Lord is in us, around us and everywhere. Seed is also a dormant condition of the plant. It has all the potential but is not manifest. Under favourable circumstances it will become manifest and start growing. In our day-to-day life, when we are sleeping, our personality is in à dormant state (seed) and on waking up, our activities begin. The state when the whole universe is in a sleeping state is called 'the state of *pralaya*' (Hiraṇyagarbha). This is a condition of dormant primordial energy which, after some time, under favourable conditions, expresses itself as the manifold activities in the universe. The state of dormancy (Hiraṇyagarbha) is 'the seed' of the whole universe. By saying so, the Lord is identifying Himself with the total causation of the universe.

The comparison to seed is not total. A normal seed destroys itself and becomes the plant. But the seed (Lord) of the universe, does not get destroyed. The 'energy' remains to sustain the life. The Lord remains to sustain the universe.The soul remains after the physical death of the body.

There is nothing moving or unmoving that exists without the Lord. It is like saying "no type of pot can exist without mud", "no waves, big or small, can exist without the ocean".

नान्तोऽस्ति मम दिव्यानां विभूतीनां परन्तप ।
एष तूद्देशतः प्रोक्तो विभूतेर्विस्तरो मया ॥४०॥

nānto'sti mama divyānāṁ vibhūtīnāṁ parantapa |
eṣa tūddeśataḥ prokto vibhūter vistaro mayā ||40||

O Arjuna, there is no end to My divine glories. This indeed is brief statement by Me of the particulars of My glories.

So far, Śrī Kṛṣṇa has given fiftyfour examples of His manifestations. The world has millions and millions of beings and it is impossible to show the total manifestations. To prove the existence of electricity one can give examples of a few appliances. One need not show all appliances and different varieties of the same appliances. One need not drive all cars to realise the power behind them. One can stand over a motorway bridge and see the various vehicles moving and realise the energy that makes them move. The Lord is not seen by anybody. But one can understand Him (see with internal eyes) by the examples given so far.

यद्यद्विभूतिमत्सत्त्वं श्रीमदूर्जितमेव वा ।
तत्तदेवावगच्छ त्वं मम तेजोंऽशसंभवम् ॥४१॥

yad yad vibhūtimat sattvaṁ śrīmad ūrjitam eva vā |
tat tad evāvagaccha tvaṁ mama tejo'ṁśasaṁbhavam ||41||

O Arjuna, whatever that is glorious, prosperous and powerful in any being, know that to be only a fragment of My splendour.

ūrjitam: Powerful.
avagaccha: Know.

To put it another way, whatever makes a person feel justly proud in any field of activity (e.g., study, wealth, power, beauty etc.), that has to be attributed to the power and grace of the Lord. We should not be unjustly proud of anything. We should be humble and consider that what makes us proud is only God's blessing. We must not keep up the egoistic attitude in what we possess. Similarly, what others have that makes them great in any field of life is also God's manifestation only. We must see the Lord in that manifestation.

By looking at the infinite in finite, by seeing the soul in *jīva* in all manifestations in this universe, one should gradually drop the ego. This will lead to the union with *Paramātmā*.

अथवा बहुनैतेन किं ज्ञातेन तवार्जुन ।
विष्टभ्याहमिदं कृत्स्नं एकांशेन स्थितो जगत् ॥४२॥

athavā bahunaitena kiṁ jñātena tavārjuna |
viṣṭabhyāham idaṁ kṛtsnaṁ ekāṁśena sthito jagat ||42||

O Arjuna, but of what avail to you is the knowledge of all these details? I exist, supporting this whole universe with one fragment of Myself.

kṛtsnam: All.
viṣṭabhya: Pervading.

Śrī Kṛṣṇa ends this chapter by telling His student that it is impossible to describe the infinite. The infinite cannot be perceived by our intellect, mind and sense-organs. The examples given so far are only a tiny part of the Lord's glory. Even this *jagat* (universe) which is ever-changing, is itself only a fragment of the Lord. We, having heard this, should now think, "What am I after all in the presence of the Lord?" We should become humble and praise His glory in all His manifestations. We should feel the Lord's presence in us and show it in our daily actions and thoughts (i.e., show our divinity). We should also see the Lord in all around us and show our respect to them. We are all part of the 'Great One', we are nothing but 'One'. This is *advaita* phiosophy.

इति श्रीमद्भगवद्गीतासूपनिषत्सु ब्रह्मविद्यायां योगशास्त्रे
श्रीकृष्णार्जुनसंवादे विभूतियोगो नाम दशमोऽध्यायः ॥

iti śrīmadbhagavadgītāsūpaniṣatsu brahmavidyāyāṁ yogaśāstre śrīkṛṣṇārjuna-saṁvāde vibhūti-yogo nāma daśamo'dhyāyaḥ ||